Nonprofit and Civil Society

An International Multidisciplinary Series

Series Editors

Paul Dekker
Institute for Social Research, The Hague, The Netherlands

Lehn Benjamin
Indiana University – Purdue University Indianapolis, Indianapolis, IN, USA

More information about this series at http://www.springer.com/series/6339

Lonneke Roza • Steffen Bethmann • Lucas Meijs
Georg von Schnurbein
Editors

Handbook on Corporate Foundations

Corporate and Civil Society Perspectives

Editors
Lonneke Roza
Rotterdam School of Management (RSM)
Erasmus University Rotterdam
Rotterdam, Zuid-Holland, The Netherlands

Lucas Meijs
Rotterdam School of Management (RSM)
Erasmus University Rotterdam
Rotterdam, Zuid-Holland, The Netherlands

Steffen Bethmann
Center for Philanthropy Studies (CEPS)
University of Basel
Basel, Basel Stadt, Switzerland

Georg von Schnurbein
Center for Philanthropy Studies (CEPS)
University of Basel
Basel, Basel Stadt, Switzerland

ISSN 1568-2579
Nonprofit and Civil Society Studies
ISBN 978-3-030-25761-3   ISBN 978-3-030-25759-0   (eBook)
https://doi.org/10.1007/978-3-030-25759-0

© Springer Nature Switzerland AG 2020, Corrected Publication 2020
This work is subject to copyright. All rights are reserved by the Publisher, whether the whole or part of the material is concerned, specifically the rights of translation, reprinting, reuse of illustrations, recitation, broadcasting, reproduction on microfilms or in any other physical way, and transmission or information storage and retrieval, electronic adaptation, computer software, or by similar or dissimilar methodology now known or hereafter developed.
The use of general descriptive names, registered names, trademarks, service marks, etc. in this publication does not imply, even in the absence of a specific statement, that such names are exempt from the relevant protective laws and regulations and therefore free for general use.
The publisher, the authors, and the editors are safe to assume that the advice and information in this book are believed to be true and accurate at the date of publication. Neither the publisher nor the authors or the editors give a warranty, express or implied, with respect to the material contained herein or for any errors or omissions that may have been made. The publisher remains neutral with regard to jurisdictional claims in published maps and institutional affiliations.

This Springer imprint is published by the registered company Springer Nature Switzerland AG
The registered company address is: Gewerbestrasse 11, 6330 Cham, Switzerland

Contents

1 **Introduction**... 1
   Lonneke Roza, Steffen Bethmann, Lucas Meijs,
   and Georg von Schnurbein

Part I Governance and Management

2 **Challenges in Corporate Foundation Governance**............... 17
   David Renz, Lonneke Roza, and Frans-Joseph Simons

3 **Strategic in What Sense? Corporate Foundation Models
   in Terms of Their Institutional Independence
   and Closeness to Core Business**............................... 39
   Steffen Bethmann and Georg von Schnurbein

4 **Families, Firms, and Philanthropy: Shareholder
   Foundation Responses to Competing Goals**...................... 63
   Joel Bothello, Arthur Gautier, and Anne-Claire Pache

Part II Corporate Foundations in Various Institutional Contexts

5 **Corporate Foundations in Europe**............................. 85
   Theresa Gehringer and Georg von Schnurbein

6 **Corporate Foundations in the United States**.................. 107
   Joannie Tremblay-Boire

7 **Do Chinese Corporate Foundations Enhance Civil Society?**..... 125
   Lijun He and Qun Wang

8 **Corporate Foundations in Russia: Overview of the Sector**..... 149
   Irina Krasnopolskaya

9 **Corporate Foundations in Latin America**...................... 167
   Marta Rey-Garcia, Michael D. Layton, and Javier Martin-Cavanna

Part III Stakeholder Perspectives on Corporate Foundations

10 **Outsourcing of Corporate Giving: What Corporations Can('t) Gain When Using a Collective Corporate Foundation to Shape Corporate Philanthropy**.................... 193
Stephanie Maas

11 **The Social Impact of Corporate Citizenship Programs on Their Beneficiaries and Society at Large: A Case Study**................ 215
Marjelle Vermeulen and Karen Maas

12 **"Capturing People's Hearts, Hands, and Wallets": Corporate Foundations as a Vehicle for Promoting Volunteering**............. 235
Debbie Haski-Leventhal

13 **Revisiting the Political Nature of Corporate Philanthropic Foundations: The Case of Sweden**............................ 253
Johan Hvenmark and Johan von Essen

14 **Nonprofit Organizations' Views on Corporate Foundations**....... 271
Sterre Swen, Lonneke Roza, Lucas Meijs, and Alexander Maas

15 **Discussion and Conclusion**.................................. 287
Lonneke Roza, Steffen Bethmann, Lucas Meijs, and Georg von Schnurbein

Correction to: Handbook on Corporate Foundations: Corporate and Civil Society Perspectives......................... C1

The original version of this book was revised. The correction is available at
https://doi.org/10.1007/978-3-030-25759-0_16

Contributors

Steffen Bethmann Center for Philanthropy Studies (CEPS), University of Basel, Basel, Switzerland

Joel Bothello The John Molson School of Business, Concordia University, Montréal, QC, Canada

Johan von Essen Ersta Sköndal Bräcke University College, Stockholm, Sweden

Arthur Gautier ESSEC Business School, Cergy-Pontoise, France

Theresa Gehringer Center for Philanthropy Studies (CESP), University of Basel, Basel, Switzerland

Debbie Haski-Leventhal Macquarie University, Sydney, NSW, Australia

Lijun He Center of Corporate Social Responsibility Development Center, Shenzhen, China

Institute of Public Service, Seattle University, Seattle, WA, USA

Johan Hvenmark Ersta Sköndal Bräcke University College, Stockholm, Sweden

Irina Krasnopolskaya National Research University Higher School of Economics, The Centre for Civic Initiatives Assessment, Moscow, Russia

Michael D. Layton Inter-American Foundation, Washington, DC, USA

Alexander Maas University for Humanistics, Utrecht, The Netherlands

Karen Maas Impact Centre Erasmus (ICE), Erasmus University Rotterdam, Rotterdam, The Netherlands

Stephanie Maas Rotterdam School of Management (RSM), Erasmus University Rotterdam, Rotterdam, The Netherlands

Javier Martin-Cavanna Fundacion Compromiso y Transparencia, Madrid, Spain

Lucas Meijs Rotterdam School of Management (RSM), Erasmus University Rotterdam, Rotterdam, The Netherlands

Anne-Claire Pache ESSEC Business School, Cergy-Pontoise, France

David Renz Midwest Center for Nonprofit Leadership, Henry W. Bloch School of Management, University of Missouri-Kansas City, Kansas City, MO, USA

Marta Rey-Garcia University of A Coruña, A Coruña, Spain

Lonneke Roza Rotterdam School of Management (RSM), Erasmus University Rotterdam, Rotterdam, The Netherlands

Georg von Schnurbein Center for Philanthropy Studies (CEPS), University of Basel, Basel, Switzerland

Frans-Joseph Simons Rotterdam School of Management (RSM), Erasmus University Rotterdam, Rotterdam, The Netherlands

Sterre Swen Rotterdam School of Management (RSM), Erasmus University Rotterdam, Rotterdam, The Netherlands

Joannie Tremblay-Boire University of Maryland, College Park, MD, USA

Marjelle Vermeulen Impact Centre Erasmus (ICE), Erasmus University Rotterdam, Rotterdam, The Netherlands

Qun Wang Indiana University, Bloomington, IN, USA

List of Figures

Fig. 2.1	Key challenges and tensions to be balanced in corporate foundation governance....................................	29
Fig. 3.1	Visualization of independence ratings for two different foundations. The lines represent two different foundations.......	50
Fig. 3.2	Foundations' clusters.....................................	51
Fig. 3.3	Types of corporate foundations	54
Fig. 7.1	Geographic distribution of Chinese corporate foundations.......	136
Fig. 8.1	Foundations' budgets for the focused activities, *Industrial* vs. *Mass market*, mln USD∗	155
Fig. 8.2	Main areas, which are supported by corporate foundations ($n = 16$, 2016) (Boldureva 2016)..........................	158
Fig. 10.1	The make-or-buy decision of corporate philanthropy	206
Fig. 11.1	ToC behind Social Innovation Relay	220

List of Tables

Table 3.1	Determinants of the structural relationship between foundation and corporation	48
Table 3.2	Sample description	50
Table 4.1	Logic prescriptions on three salient dimensions for shareholder foundations	70
Table 4.2	Selected foundations studied in Denmark	71
Table 4.3	Selected foundations studied in Germany	71
Table 4.4	Selected foundations studied in France	72
Table 4.5	Organizational responses to logic prescriptions in Denmark	75
Table 4.6	Organizational responses to logic prescriptions in Germany	76
Table 4.7	Organizational responses to logic prescriptions in France	78
Table 5.1	Comparison of key variables over time	89
Table 5.2	Comparison of public-benefit and corporate foundations	92
Table 5.3	Models of non-profit sector regimes (Anheier and Salamon 1998)	98
Table 5.4	Categorization of Vodafone foundations in European countries	99
Table 7.1	Role of nonprofit organizations in contribution to civil society	133
Table 7.2	Measures of civil society with a focus on service and social capital dimension	134
Table 7.3	Full-time employees, tax-benefit type(s), evaluation grades, and volunteers of Chinese corporate foundation vs. all foundations	139
Table 7.4	Financial sustainability of Chinese corporate foundations	141
Table 9.1	Main civil society infrastructures leading institutionalization of corporate foundations in the region (author's elaboration)	168

Table 9.2	Key data sources used to approach corporate foundations (CFs) (author's elaboration)	175
Table 9.3	Age (year of creation) of corporate foundations in the region	176
Table 9.4	Model of activity and sources of income of Brazilian corporate foundations	179
Table 9.5	Largest endowed foundations in Brazil	180
Table 9.6	Model of activity of Mexican corporate foundations	182
Table 9.7	Model of activity, sources of income, and areas of activity of Colombian corporate foundations	185
Table 10.1	Illustrative comments supporting case findings	200
Table 11.1	Variables that influence entrepreneurial behavior and entrepreneurial intention	222
Table 11.2	KAP approach for the research questions	223
Table 11.3	Number of responses	224
Table 11.4	Mean and significance level for hypothesis 1	225
Table 11.5	Mean and significance level for hypothesis 2	226
Table 11.6	Mean and significance level for hypothesis 3	227
Table 11.7	Mean and significance level for hypothesis 4	228
Table 15.1	Similarities and differences among the institutional context throughout world regions	291

Chapter 1
Introduction

Lonneke Roza, Steffen Bethmann, Lucas Meijs, and Georg von Schnurbein

Abstract In the introduction, we set the context of this book on corporate foundations by discussing perspectives on corporate philanthropy and subsequently define how we view corporate foundations. Furthermore, we further elaborate on the role of understanding hybridity, and we outline the structure of the book.

Keywords Corporate foundations · Comparative · Hybridity · Definitions

The academic interest in charitable foundations recently gained more attention in literature, albeit reactive following a global rise of philanthropy and the strong growth of foundations in many countries (Leat 2016; Anheier 2018). However, the idea of leveraging corporate resources to form a charitable foundation (i.e., a corporate foundation) has been contested until today and only recently, corporate philanthropy became more visible (Harrow 2013). Corporate philanthropy—in line with the general definition of philanthropy—includes voluntary financial contributions, in-kind donations and donating time (i.e., corporate volunteering and corporate giving) to social and charitable causes (Gautier and Pache 2015; Liket and Simaens 2015; Porter and Kramer 2006). While some companies organize their corporate philanthropy in-house, others set up a corporate foundation to formalize their corporate philanthropy with a long-term commitment.

The editors would like to thank Frans-Joseph Simons for his valuable support throughout this project.

L. Roza (✉) · L. Meijs
Rotterdam School of Management (RSM), Erasmus University Rotterdam, Rotterdam, The Netherlands
e-mail: lroza@rsm.nl

S. Bethmann · G. von Schnurbein
Center for Philanthropy Studies (CEPS), University of Basel, Basel, Switzerland

From the broader perspective of corporate philanthropy, both from business and nonprofit literature, one can find arguments for and against corporate involvement in philanthropic action. In business literature, it is questioned if managers should direct money to societal causes and, in doing so, limit shareholder profits (Friedman 1970). To counter this, scholars have built the business case of corporate philanthropy (for an overview, see Liket and Simaens 2015). An alternative perspective argues that companies should act as corporate citizens, which stems more from a moral appeal (Gadberg and Fombrun 2006). In the nonprofit literature, some dispute the influence of companies in the nonprofit sector (Nickel and Eikenberry 2009), whereas others put the emphasis on the valuable contributions companies can add to social projects in both financial resources and nonfinancial resources such as volunteers or other resources of the company (Roza et al. 2017).

Even though we are building a better understanding of corporate philanthropy, we so far have neglected the role of corporate foundations as an intermediary organization that facilitates corporate giving in this emerging field. In the universe of nonprofit organizations, the galaxy of charitable foundations is not in the core of both practical appearance and scientific analysis. However, in the galaxy of charitable foundations, corporate foundations are a constellation even at the outer limits. Henceforth, the available literature on this type of foundation is extremely limited, while this form of institutional philanthropy is increasingly applied in practice. Consequently, corporate foundations are considered complex phenomena where many stakeholders are involved which are less explicit in traditional foundations, such as corporate employees, corporate leadership and shareholders (Renz et al. Chap. 2). Hence, corporate foundations have a unique relationship with a market actor: the founding company.

Indeed, corporate foundations are often linked to the founding company through their name, funding, trustees, administration, and potential employee involvement (Westhues and Einwiller 2006). As these foundations are growing in number (Herlin and Pedersen 2013), size, and importance (Rey-García et al. 2012), they are becoming increasingly visible in the philanthropic sector. Corporate foundations are specific in many ways. They are positioned between the business sector and the civil society and have commonalities with both sectors. In contrast to grant-making foundations, they usually have no endowment, but receive annual contributions by one dominant donor: the parent company (Petrovits 2006). The founder is a legal entity that can pursue constant influence on all areas of the corporate foundation: governance, asset management, grant-giving, communication, who to employ and so forth (Bethman and von Schnurbein, Chap. 3). At the same time, corporate foundations oftentimes are structured in a framework of foundations, albeit heavily influenced by the legal and fiscal arrangements, and traditions in (corporate) philanthropy in their context. Due to these contextual factors, the commonalities of corporate foundations on a global level are limited. As such, a thorough debate on the role of corporate foundations as a form of institutionalized philanthropy and its working is needed.

To better understand corporate philanthropy in all its aspects, we need to study through which paths corporate philanthropic efforts are being channeled, including that of corporate foundations. This discussion needs to deal with very basic questions while using current theoretical perspectives to better understand this construct including: What is the role of corporate foundations in our society, and in different societal contexts? What are governance structures and how are these affected by the parent company and the hybrid nature of corporate foundations? How are stakeholders involved and how are they affected? And, how do nonprofit organizations as the ultimate beneficiary of corporate foundations make sense of their collaborations with corporate foundations? These and other questions will be addressed in the following chapters.

In the next sections, we set the context of this book on corporate foundations by discussing perspectives on corporate philanthropy and subsequently corporate foundations, the conceptual framework in the light of hybridity, and the outline of the book.

1.1 The Corporate Philanthropy Context

1.1.1 Philanthropy as a Result of Economic Activities

The history of philanthropy is closely connected with economic action. Generally, philanthropy is based on values and an expression of pity and interest in other people not closely connected to the benevolent (Payton and Moody 2008). Next to this value-driven perspective, philanthropy entails a transaction of resources without a valuable return. Hence, economic success and abundance are preconditions for a significant role of philanthropy beyond pure altruism (Adloff 2010). Many well-known philanthropists were successful businessmen prior to their social engagement. Especially in the nineteenth century in the United States, industrialization created a new category of individuals that accumulated great wealth. Meyer Guggenheim or Andrew Carnegie developed within a lifetime from poor immigrants to the wealthiest persons of their time. Others, such as John D. Rockefeller or W. K. Kellogg, came from the middle class and some such as John P. Morgan already grew up well situated. In Europe, Joseph Rowntree, Maurice de Hirsch, or Robert Bosch were also successful businessmen who dedicated large parts of their fortune to social causes (von Schnurbein 2015). However, all these men have in common that their philanthropic actions, were an individual action clearly separated from their companies. In fact, donations by companies were banned by law in the United States until the 1950s (Sharfman 1994). With the development of corporate philanthropy, it became institutionalized. Ever since, the debate turns around the question of whose benefit corporate philanthropy is—the company, the society, or both (Aakhus and Bzdak 2012)?

1.1.2 Various Perspectives on Corporate Philanthropy

The primary aim and ultimate right to exist for companies is to make profits (Friedman 1970). In that sense, corporate philanthropy has to adhere a clear business case that leads to a better performance. As philanthropy is about giving without a direct commercial benefit, the search for a business case is not self-evident (Campbell and Slack 2007). Nevertheless, literature and practice search for a business explanation of the existence of corporate philanthropy.

The theoretical debate on the question if companies should be involved in philanthropic causes is dominated by two diverging perspectives. The first, critical, perspective is based on agency theory. It follows the assumption that philanthropy never can be decided by an institution, but only by individuals. Hence, Friedman (1970) argued that corporate philanthropy reduces the profits for the shareholders and is conducted by the managers based on their own priorities. Other researcher backed this perspective, emphasizing that the reputational enhancement a manager might gain from philanthropic activities of the company is more important than the public purpose (Buchholtz et al. 1999; Galaskiewicz 1997; Werbel and Carter 2002).

The second, supporting, perspective emphasizes the positive influence of corporate philanthropy on firm performance. Although studies are inconclusive on the potential of corporate philanthropy to increase the company's profits (Gautier and Pache 2015), it can have a positive influence through goodwill, the positive image, and an improved reputation (e.g. Liket and Simaens, 2015). These effects influence various stakeholder groups, for example, investors, employees, suppliers, or customers (Choi and Wang 2007). Operationalized as corporate social performance (CSP), several studies have measured a positive relationship with corporate financial performance (Orlitzky et al. 2003; Margolis et al. 2007). Other researchers emphasize the value of CSP to enhance strategic reassessment and process improvement (Ribstein 2005) or they attribute an insurance aspect to CSP due to good reputation (Fombrun et al. 2000; Klein and Davar 2003; Peloza 2005). In an assessment of the literature on the relationship of CSP and corporate financial performance, Wood (2010) criticizes the schismatic diverge into believers and unbelievers of the relationship, which still exists today.

From a more conceptual point of view, corporate philanthropy is mostly dealt with as part of corporate social responsibility (Burlingame and Young 1996; von Schnurbein et al. 2016). In its seminal work on the corporate social responsibility (CSR) pyramid, Carroll (1979) put philanthropic responsibility on top of economic, legal, and ethical responsibilities of the firm. Economic responsibilities refer to the firm's role in society, and thus the business as a producer of goods and services. The legal responsibilities refer to the compliance with laws and regulations at all levels. Carroll's description of ethical responsibilities was, in this model, already quite clear: He states that, after the fulfilment of the economic and legal responsibilities, "there are additional behaviors and activities that are not necessarily codified into law but nevertheless are expected of business by society's members" (Carroll 1979: 500). However, he gave no clear-cut definition of discretionary responsibilities (later on classified as 'philanthropic'). He rather stated that these 'expectations' actually could not be classified as responsibilities, since the decision to pursue them or not is "at a business's discretion" (Carroll 1979: 500). While economic and legal responsibilities are categorized as required, ethical responsibility is expected, and philanthropy is desired (Carroll and Shabana 2010). It seems that throughout the growing debate on CSR, corporate philanthropy always played a minor role of interest (von Schnurbein et al. 2016). In recent years, the notion of strategic corporate philanthropy has overcome this ignorance (Gautier and Pache 2015). Especially, the shared value approach has changed the perception of corporate philanthropy. Shared value follows the performance-enhancement paradigm and states that businesses can do both: Doing well by doing good (Karnani 2011). Porter and Kramer (2002) develop a system based on the value chain approach that should lead to a competitive advantage through corporate philanthropy. Their major statement is that companies have to focus on the core business in philanthropy as well in order to use their best competencies for social purposes. However, Aakhus and Bzdak (2012) argue that the shared value approach ranks business interests over social interests and, thus, is limited in solving social problems.

In civil society and philanthropy literature, the relationship between businesses, state institutions, and nonprofits is of major interest as it affects the independence and catalytic strength of the nonprofits (Nickel and Eikenberry 2009). Fundamentally, the question is posed, for what purpose a for-profit company engages in charitable activities? Gan (2006) argues that corporate philanthropy is after all a compromise between firm goals and public purpose. As Harrow (2013: 236) follows, "[t]his approach then offers the setting of organization, policy and even values compromises as the stage upon which corporate philanthropy activities are played out." Many studies contest corporate philanthropy as a problem-solving concept for public purposes, highlighting the inherent trade-offs (Tesler and Malone 2008). For instance, Al-Tabbaa et al. (2013) argue that nonprofits have to become more proactive in cross-sector collaborations in order to increase the scale and sustainability of the corporate donations. At the same time, the marketization of philanthropy is questioned, because it reduces the transformative power of philanthropy (Nickel and Eikenberry 2009). In addition, nonprofit representatives tend to overestimate the return of corporate partners (Cho and Kelly 2013), leading to a mismatch between expectations and reality. It might be that corporate philanthropy is made bigger than it actually is. This might be due to the fact that corporate giving is perceived in a similar vein as giving by foundations—as core activity. Rather, corporate giving is actually at the periphery for corporates. More trade-offs seem to come into play when including nonfinancial resources in corporate philanthropy (Haski-Leventhal, Chap. 12). Analyzing corporate volunteering, Roza et al. (2017) highlight the challenges nonprofit organizations face when dealing with corporate philanthropy actions. In addition, beneficiaries' interests get too little consideration in corporate volunteering settings (Samuel et al. 2016).

The above shows that the purpose and justification of corporate philanthropy are not straightforward. From both the business and the civil society perspectives, corporate philanthropy is applauded and contested—albeit for different reasons. For instance, some scholars doubt that corporations can do good by themselves. For them, the managers do good with the money of the shareholders without having their permission. From a civil society perspective, corporate philanthropy entails an inherent goal conflict between business aims and public benefit (Hvenmark & von Essen, Chap. 13). However, the proponents of strategic philanthropy emphasize the win–win situation if businesses give access to their knowledge and resources for public purposes by developing their core business. In the same light, civil society researchers see the advantage for nonprofits to benefit from the collaboration with the more business-like corporate foundations. Thus, we have to ask if corporate philanthropy is in fact a hybrid organization, combining the best from business and civil society logic, or if it is closer to a boundary spanner, offering joint activities between business and civil society. And, to what extend do corporate foundations play a role in this?

1.2 Defining a Corporate Foundation

Defining a charitable foundation is no easy task as there exist many different understandings and traditions (Anheier and Daly 2006). Generally, the literature differentiates various types of foundations: private independent foundations, corporate and company-sponsored foundations, shareholder foundations, community foundations, public foundations, and operating foundations (Frumkin 2006, Toepler 1999). The complexity of delineating corporate foundations from other foundations is illustrated by a few large foundations in Germany: First, Volkswagen Foundation. Although the name suggests a typical corporate foundation, it is seen as a state-sponsored foundation, as the endowment of the foundation was funded by the privatization of state-owned stocks (Toepler 1999). The Robert Bosch Foundation is a shareholder foundation with charitable activities. And, the "Gemeinnützige Hertie-Stiftung" [Charitable Hertie Foundation] was once a shareholding foundation of the Hertie department stores without voting rights or any influence on the management. Today, the Hertie department stores do not exist anymore and the Charitable Hertie Foundation is an independent foundation (despite its company name).

While various interpretations exist of what a corporate foundation may be, we define a corporate foundation as an independent legal entity for a public benefit purpose without any direct commercial benefits that is set up, funded, and controlled by a for-profit entity. We hold three criteria as essential for corporate foundations. First, a corporate foundation is a separate legal entity. In some countries, a foundation is a specific legal form; in others, the identification depends on the taxation of activities. Despite the legal differences, a corporate foundation has to be legally distinct from the parent company. This ensures also that the establishment of a corporate foundation is a voluntary act and not bound to any public regulation. Second, a corporate foundation aims for a public benefit purpose. In the periphery of an enterprise, different types of foundations may exist, for example, pension funds, stakeholder foundation, private purpose trusts, and so on. For a corporate foundation, it is essential that its purpose is for the good of the greater public. There might be some alignment with the core business of the parent company, but the foundation's activities should not lead to a direct commercial benefit of the company. Again, there may be differences in what is legally defined as public benefit purpose, based on national law. But this criterion enables us to draw a clear line on the reason for existence of a corporate foundation. Hence, a corporate foundation exists primarily out of an understanding of corporate responsibility and incorporates a genuine interest in the greater society that goes beyond profit. Here, it is differentiated from an internal philanthropic department by the idea of being a separate legal entity. It is also different from a sponsoring department as the company's goals are not leading anymore but the goals and mission of this separate entity (e.g. the philanthropic mission) are leading in their decision-making processes. In terms of operations, a corporate foundation might execute its mission either through grant-making, venture philanthropy, or operating own projects. As we learned in the development of this book, different traditions and norms have an influence. For example, in Latin America, corporate foundations are more operative (Rey-Garcia et al., Chap. 9). In Europe, there are corporate foundations using venture philanthropy principles, while in the US, the typical corporate foundation is grant-making (Tremblay-Boire, Chap. 6).

Third, a corporate foundation is set up, funded, and, to a large extent if not totally, controlled by a for-profit entity. This maybe the most important difference to other types of foundations, as Anheier (2001) and others emphasize the independence of foundations as a selective criterion. We expect corporate foundations to have an ongoing relationship with their parent company. As we focus on the foundation as an object of interest, we do not make any differentiation concerning the for-profit entity. The ongoing relationship between a foundation and its parent company is bound on the two legal entities and not on individuals (as in the case of family foundations). For instance, if the company gets sold, the foundation is part of the bargain. As corporate foundations usually are funded by annual donations and not an initial large endowment, the company continuously preserves a dominant influence on the foundation. As a consequence, the companies' management has a major influence on the foundation. So coming back to the above examples: The Volkswagen Foundation never was a corporate foundation and the Hertie Stiftung ceased to be one when the company went out of business. Even though both have historical links with corporations, they cannot be considered to be corporate foundations today.

Additionally, we delineate a corporate foundation from an individual or family foundation set up by the company owner from his own wealth and from a so-called "shareholder foundation". In both cases, the control over the foundations is not limited to the company, other interest groups (especially owners) may execute an influence on the foundation. However, we will address the specific type of "shareholder foundation"—holding a significant number of the shares of a company—in this volume separately as these foundations often support public purposes although they are not obliged to (Bothello et al., Chap. 4).

By applying a broad definition and a set of criteria, we offer the contributors to this volume enough room for differentiation and specific variations that they study. As such, each chapter will clarify what are the extensions or restrictions of this definition in the specific context and institutional setting.

1.3 Hybridity at Its Core

We approach the mere existence of corporate foundations[1] as hybrid entities in which institutional logics coexist (see for a review on institutional logics Lounsbury and Boxenbaum 2013). Initially developed for analyzing the behavior of individuals, institutional logics are defined as "the socially constructed, historical patterns of material practices, assumptions, values, beliefs, and rules by which individuals produce and reproduce their material subsistence, organize time and space, and provide meaning to their social reality" (Thornton and Ocasio 1999: 804). Translated to the study of organizations, institutional logics serve for a better understanding on competing models and hybrid manifestations dealing with conflating institutional sectors and increasing means of organizations, such as bureaucracy or regulation. For instance, DiMaggio and Powell (1991) emphasize processes of imitation and alignment in organizational fields as a result of coercion, insecurity, and norms. Community, market, or state can be key institutional orders that define the self-concept of organizations (Thornton et al. 2012).

In literature, the combination of at least two different institutional logics is referred to as hybridity (Billis 2010). In search for solutions to the increased complexity of social problems, balancing different norms and needs through hybrid structures offers several advantages. Hybrid structures facilitate the inclusion of constituents from different sectors—state, market, individuals, or nonprofits (Evers 2005). Additionally, hybridity promises to combine advantages of different logics to a better result, for instance, the mix of market and social aims in impact investing (Emerson 2003). Finally, research on hybridity offers better understanding of mission alignment. Several studies have emphasized the existence of combined or rivaling aims within nonprofit organizations (Minkoff 2002; Joldersma and Winter 2002; Skelcher and Smith 2014). In respect to philanthropy, Salamon (2014) highlights the new frontiers of philanthropy as more diverse, more entrepreneurial, more global, and more collaborative. As a consequence, philanthropic action has to take into consideration expectations of other actors more broadly. Smith (2016) gives an oversight on the variety of new instruments for philanthropy following the trend of hybridity. Especially in the US and the UK—but also in other countries—donor-advised funds (DAFs) are used as an alternative to establish a private foundation. The advantage of a DAF over a foundation for the donor is that it leaves more flexibility in terms of grant distribution, reporting obligations, and public information (Harrow et al. 2016). Another recent trend is that philanthropic action is closer connected to financial investing including concepts such as venture capital, impact investing, and blended finance structures. The overarching idea is to create leverage through multiple uses of the resources available for charity (Salamon 2014). With the announcement of the Chan Zuckerberg Initiative, this development even went beyond the traditional borders of legal charitable status, as Mark Zuckerberg tunnels his philanthropic engagement through a limited liability company (LLC). In con-

---

[1] As a preliminary remark we assume that corporate foundations are there for a good reason. Thus, we do not aim to question their existence, rather we aim to explain their functioning.

trast to a private foundation, an LLC offers the donor more control at the cost of fewer tax advantages (Worth 2018).

For Smith (2016), corporate foundations are a very typical hybrid structure because 'these foundations often need to manage different logics such as a market logic tied to the strategic direction of the company and the needs of the community or citizenry, broadly defined' (p. 328). In the realm of this book, we investigate the shifts or conflicts between these two logics, address contestations and integrate different perspectives on corporate foundations.

Corporate foundations operate between business interests and societal purpose. As a consequence, the modes of operation can be very different, depending on the dominant logic and the primary orientation of action. Motivation for creation of corporate foundations is based on both business and civil society logic. The dominant logic defines the self-concept of the corporate foundation as either part of the company or part of the civil society. Which one dominates depends on legal requirements, organizational factors of parent companies, structure of ownership, and so forth. Subsequently, the corporate foundation might also shift from a more businesslike approach to a civil society approach. Reasons for a shift may be changes in the company's business model, new regulations, or a new field of activity of the corporate foundation. One can also think of potential conflicts between the two logics. Business and social aims are not always aligned and—depending on the power distribution on the foundation's board—program decisions may follow either business or social purposes, first. The classic 'What is good for the business is good for society' is not satisfying anymore (Aakhus and Bzdak 2012), nor it is vice versa. At the same time, companies are more urged to taking their philanthropic activities to general accepted topics and fields. In the following chapters, the influence of institutional logics on corporate foundations will be analyzed based on geographical differences, patterns of governance and management, as well as different stakeholder perspectives.

1.4 Outline of the Book

The primary aim of this volume is to deliver a holistic analysis of the current state-of-the-art on corporate foundations. For that reason, we include different perspectives on and use a hybrid concept of corporate foundations.

First, we further explore the different logics that explain the existence and utility of corporate foundations. Corporate foundations are complex organizations as they are the proverbial example of a cross-sector hybrid organization that includes competing and complicating logics from both market and civil society (Billis 2010). They have the legal form of a civil society organization, but oftentimes include the logic of a for-profit organization due to their closeness to their founder (Bethmann and von Schnurbein 2015). As a consequence, corporate foundations can be seen as complex governance structures in which corporate and public benefit logics are combined. There are four chapters covering governance of corporate foundations:

The first chapter explains the governance challenges of corporate foundations, the second one relates to the (in)dependence of corporate foundations, the third looks at the benefits and challenges of choosing the governance structure of a collective corporate foundation, and the fourth one looks at various logics in play when choosing a particular governance structure, that is, a shareholder foundation.

Second, we address different levels of understanding: regional or country level, institutional context, and organizational level. We cover five regions or countries to give an overview of the global state of corporate foundations. While the United States and Europe share a longer tradition and a broader application of corporate foundations, they are rather new to Latin America, Russia, and China. The institutional context serves as a starting point to discuss different logics and perceptions of corporate foundations. Additionally, we analyze the corporate foundation at the organizational level. Looking further into the organizational processes of corporate foundations, we analyze governance, operations, and impact as major aspects of organizational performance. More precisely, we look at components of corporate foundations, divided into board, staff, operations, funding, and communication.

Third, we analyze the connection between the corporate foundation and its stakeholders. We discuss which role corporate foundations may play in stimulating (corporate) volunteering and social capital, what impact corporate foundations may have on beneficiaries, the role of corporate foundations as political actors in a welfare state and finally how nonprofits make sense of their collaboration with companies.

Thus, this book explores the corporate foundations in the galaxy of institutionalized philanthropy. It contributes to the current body of literature by describing, analyzing, and exploring various potentially unique aspects of corporate foundations, such as the role in the philanthropic sector, governance, the complex relationship with the company, and as a means for collective action.

References

Aakhus, M., & Bzdak, M. (2012). Revisiting the role of "shared value" in the business-society relationship. *Business & Professional Ethics Journal, 31*(2), 231–246.

Adloff, F. (2010). *Philanthropisches Handeln. Eine historische Soziologie des Stiftens in Deutschland und den USA*. Frankfurt/New York: Campus.

AL-Tabbaa, O., Leach, D., & March, J. (2013). Nonprofit-business collaboration as a strategic option for the nonprofit sector. *International Journal of Voluntary and Nonprofit Organizations*. 1–22.

Anheier, H. K. (2001). Foundations in Europe: A comparative perspective. In A. Schlueter, V. Then, & P. Walkenhorst (Eds.), *Foundation handbook Europe* (pp. 35–82). London: Directory of Social Change.

Anheier, H. K. (2018). Philanthropic foundations in cross-national perspective: A comparative approach. *American Behavioral Scientist, 62*(12), 1591–1602.

Anheier, H. K., & Daly, S. (2006). *The politics of foundations: A comparative analysis*. London: Routledge.

Bethmann, S., & von Schnurbein, G. (2015). Effective Governance of Corporate Foundations. *CEPS Working Paper Series* No. 8. Basel: CEPS.

Billis, D. (Ed.). (2010). *Hybrid organizations and the third sector: Challenges for practice, theory, and policy*. New York: Palgrave Macmillan.

Buchholtz, A. K., Amason, A. C., & Rutherford, M. A. (1999). Beyond resources: The mediating effect of top management discretion and values on corporate philanthropy. *Business and Society, 38*(2), 167–187.

Burlingame, D., & Young, D. R. (Eds.). (1996). *Corporate philanthropy at the crossroads*. Bloomington/Indianapolis: Indiana University Press.

Campbell, D., & Slack, R. (2007). The strategic use of corporate philanthropy: Building societies and demutualisation defences. *Business Ethics: A European Review, 16*(4), 326–343.

Carroll, A. B. (1979). A three-dimensional conceptual model of corporate performance. *Academy of Management Review, 4*(4), 497–505.

Carroll, A. B., & Shabana, K. M. (2010). The business case for corporate social responsibility: A review of concepts, research and practice. *International Journal of Management Reviews, 12*(1), 85–105.

Cho, M., & Kelly, K.S. (2013) Corporate Donor–Charitable Organization Partners. *Nonprofit and Voluntary Sector Quarterly, 43*(4), 693–715.

Choi, J., & Wang, H. (2007). The promise of a managerial values approach to corporate philanthropy. *Journal of Business Ethics, 75*(4), 345–359.

DiMaggio, P. J., & Powell, W. W. (1991). Introduction. In W. W. Powell & P. J. DiMaggio (Eds.), *The new institutionalism in organizational analysis* (pp. 1–38). Chicago: University of Chicago Press.

Emerson, J. (2003). Where the money meets mission: Breaking down the firewall between foundation investments and programming. *Stanford Social Innovation Review (Summer), 1*, 38–47.

Evers, A. (2005). Mixed welfare systems and hybrid organizations: Changes in the governance and provision of social services. *International Journal of Public Administration, 28*(9/10), 737–748.

Fombrun, C., Gardberg, N. A., & Barnett, M. L. (2000). Opportunity platforms and safety nets: Corporate citizenship and reputational risk. *Business and Society Review, 105*, 85–106.

Friedman, M. (1970). *The social responsibility of business is to increase its profits*. The New York Times Magazine, 13 September SM17.

Frumkin, P. (2006). *Strategic giving. The art and science of philanthropy*. Chicago: University of Chicago Press.

Gadberg, N., & Fombrun, C. (2006). Corporate citizenship: Creating intangible assets across institutional environments. *Academy of Management Review, 31*(2), 329–346.

Galaskiewicz, J. (1997). An urban grants economy revisited: Corporate charitable contributions in the twin cities, 1979–81, 1987–89. *Administrative Science Quarterly, 42*(3), 445–471.

Gan, A. (2006). The impact of public scrutiny on corporate philanthropy. *Journal of Business Ethics, 69*(3), 217–236.

Gautier, A., & Pache, A. C. (2015). Research on corporate philanthropy: A review and assessment. *Journal of Business Ethics, 126*(3), 343–369.

Harrow, J. (2013). Contested perspectives on corporate philanthropy. In K. Haynes, A. Murray, & J. Dillard (Eds.), *Corporate social responsibility: A research handbook* (pp. 234–254). London: Routledge.

Harrow, J., Jung, T., & Phillips, S. D. (2016). Community foundations: Agility in the duality of foundation and community. In T. Jung, S. D. Phillips, & J. Harrow (Eds.), *The Routledge companion to philanthropy* (pp. 308–321). New York: Routledge.

Herlin, H., & Pedersen, J. T. (2013). Corporate foundations: Catalysts of NGO-business partnerships? *Journal of Corporate Citizenship, 2013*(50), 58–90.

Joldersma, C., & Winter, V. (2002). Strategic management in hybrid organizations. *Public Management Review, 4*(1), 83–100.

Karnani, A. (2011). Doing well by doing good: The grand illusion. *California Management Review, 53*(2), 69–86.

Klein, J., & Davar, N. (2003). Corporate social responsibility and consumers' attributions and brand evaluations in a product-harm crisis. *International Journal of Research in Marketing, 21*, 203–217.

Leat, D. (2016). *Philanthropic foundations. Philanthropic foundations, public good and public policy.* London: Palgrave Macmillan.

Liket, K., & Simaens, A. (2015). Battling the devolution in the research on corporate philanthropy. *Journal of Business Ethics, 126*(2), 285–308.

Lounsbury, M., & Boxenbaum, E. (Eds.). (2013). *Institutional logics in action, research in the sociology of organizations* (Vol. 39).

Margolis, J., Elfenbein H., & Walsh J. (2007). *Does it pay to be good? A meta-analysis and redirection of research on the relationship between corporate social and financial performance.* Harvard University, Working Paper.

Minkoff, D. (2002). The emergence of hybrid organizational forms: Combining identity-based service provision and political action. *Nonprofit and Voluntary Sector Quarterly, 31*, 377–401.

Nickel, P., & Eikenberry, A. (2009). A critique of the discourse of marketized philanthropy. *American Behavioral Scientist, 52*(7), 974–989.

Orlitzky, M., Schmidt, F. L., & Rynes, S. L. (2003). Corporate social and financial performance: A meta-analysis. *Organization Studies, 24*, 403–441.

Payton, R., & Moody, M. (2008). *Understanding philanthropy. Its meaning and mission.* Bloomington/Indianapolis: Indiana University Press.

Peloza J. (2005). Corporate social responsibility as reputation insurance. *Paper presented at the 2nd annual corporate social performance conference.* Berkeley: Haas School of Business, University of California.

Petrovits, C. (2006). Corporate-sponsored foundations and earnings management. *Journal of Accounting and Economics, 41*(3), 335–362.

Porter, M. E., & Kramer, M. R. (2002). The competitive advantage of corporate philanthropy. *Harvard Business Review, 80*(12), 56–68.

Porter, M. E., & Kramer, M. R. (2006). Strategy and society: The link between competitive advantage and corporate social responsibility. *Harvard Business Review, 84*, 78–92.

Rey-García, M., Martín, C. J., Álvarez, G., & Luis, I. (2012). Assessing and advancing foundation transparency: Corporate foundations as a case study. *The Foundation Review, 4*(3), 77–89.

Ribstein, L. E. (2005). Accountability and responsibility in corporate governance. *Law and Economic Working Paper*, University of Illinois Collage of Law, Paper no. 34.

Roza, L., Shachar, I., Meijs, L.C.P.M., & Hustinx, L. (2017). The nonprofit case for corporate volunteering: a multi-level perspective. *The Service Industries Journal, 37*(11–12), 746–765.

Salamon, L. (2014). *Leverage for good: An introduction to the new frontiers of philanthropy and social investment.* New York: Oxford University Press.

Samuel, O., Roza, L., & Meijs, L. C. P. M. (2016). Exploring partnerships from the perspective of HSO beneficiaries: The case of corporate volunteering. *Human Service Organizations: Management, Leadership & Governance, 40*, 220–237.

Sharfman, M. (1994). Changing institutional rules: The evolution of corporate philanthropy 1883–1953. *Business & Society, 33*(3), 236–269.

Skelcher, C., & Smith, S. R. (2014). Theorizing hybridity: Institutional logics, complex organizations, and actor identities: The case of nonprofits. *Public Administration, 93*(2), 433–448.

Smith, S. R. (2016). Hybridity and philanthropy. In T. Jung, S. D. Phillips, & J. Harrow (Eds.), *The Routledge companion to philanthropy* (pp. 322–333). New York: Routledge.

Tesler, L.E., & Malone, R.E. (2008). Ethical Conduct in public and private arenas corporate philanthropy, lobbying and public health policy. *American Journal of Public Health, 98*(12), 2123-2133.

Thornton, P.H., & Ocasio, W. (1999). Institutional logics and the historical contingency of power in organizations: Executive succession in the higher education publishing industry.*American Journal of Sociology, 105*, 801–844.

Thornton, P. H., Ocasio, W., & Lounsbury, M. (2012). *The institutional logics perspective: A new approach to culture, structure and process.* Oxford: Oxford University Press.

Toepler, S. (1999). On the problem of defining foundations in a comparative perspective. *Nonprofit Management & Leadership, 10*(2), 215–225.

Von Schnurbein, G. (2015). Der Stifter als Unternehmer: Parallelen und Unterschiede der Philanthropie im 19. und 21. Jahrhundert. In S. Von Reden (Ed.), *Stiftungen zwischen Politik und Wirtschaft: Geschichte und Gegenwart im Dialog*, Beiheft Nr. 66 der Historischen Zeitschrift, 2015, 237–260.

Von Schnurbein, G., Seele, P., & Lock, I. (2016). Rethinking the nexus of CSR and corporate philanthropy. *Social Responsibility Journal, 12*(2), 280–294.

Werbel, J., & Carter, S. (2002). The CEO's influence on corporate foundation giving. *Journal of Business Ethics, 40*(1), 47–60.

Westhues, M., & Einwiller, S. (2006). Corporate foundations: Their role for corporate social responsibility. *Corporate Reputation Review, 9*(2), 144–153.

Worth, M. J. (2018). *Nonprofit management: Principles and practices* (5th ed.). Los Angeles: Sage.

Lonneke Roza is an adjunct assistant professor at Rotterdam School of Management, Erasmus University. Her research focuses on (microfoundations of) Corporate Philanthropy/Corporate Citizenship. Her work is published in, among others, the *Journal of Business Ethics*, *Nonprofit and Voluntary Sector Quarterly*, and *Voluntas*.

Steffen Bethmann (PhD, University Heidelberg) is a Research Fellow at the Center for Philanthropy Studies of the University of Basel. He is also an organizational consultant and Associated Researcher at the Centro de Filantropía y Inversiones Sociales of the University Adolfo Ibañez in Santiago Chile. His area of expertise is especially in strategies and governance of foundations, as well as in the field of social innovation.

Lucas Meijs is Professor of Strategic Philanthropy and Volunteering at Rotterdam School of Management, Erasmus University Rotterdam. His current research focuses on strategic philanthropy, volunteer/nonprofit management, corporate community involvement, and involved learning. He served two terms as the first non-American Co-Editor-in-Chief of *Nonprofit and Voluntary Action Quarterly* and was a member of the Raad voor Maatschappelijke Ontwikkeling—the official policy advisory body for the Dutch government and parliament.

Georg von Schnurbein is Associate Professor for Foundation Management at the Faculty of Business and Economics and Founding Director of the Center for Philanthropy Studies (CEPS) at the University of Basel. He serves in several functions on boards in the field of international research on philanthropy and has co-authored the latest edition of the *Swiss Foundation Code* and published in several impact journals such as *Nonprofit & Voluntary Sector Quarterly* and *European Management Journal*. His research interest is in nonprofit governance, financial health of nonprofits, and impact measurement.

Part I
Governance and Management

Chapter 2
Challenges in Corporate Foundation Governance

David Renz, Lonneke Roza, and Frans-Joseph Simons

Abstract This chapter focuses on the challenges experienced by those who govern corporate foundations. Based on three key theoretical perspectives (agency theory, resource dependency theory, and institutional theory) and insights drawn from interviews and informal conversations with leaders and decision-makers in more than a dozen corporate foundations in the United States and the Netherlands, we offer a theory-based framework in which the most common governance conditions and dynamics are identified. The framework defines three questions posing key challenges, based on 11 correlated tensions in hybrid organizations: (1) Why do corporate foundations exist and to what end? (2) Who really governs a corporate foundation and with what orientation? (3) To whom are corporate foundations accountable and for what? The chapter demonstrates that, although corporate foundations are subject to multiple and divergent logics posing tensions and challenges, the dynamics experienced vary by the type of corporation and are not always considered as problematic, relative to the way they are experienced as problematic by other types of hybrids (e.g., social entrepreneurs). Notwithstanding that there is always a tango between the corporate foundation and both community and corporate stakeholders.

Keywords Corporate foundations · Governance · Comparative · Challenges · Hybrid organizations

---

D. Renz (✉)
Midwest Center for Nonprofit Leadership, Henry W. Bloch School of Management, University of Missouri-Kansas City, Kansas City, MO, USA
e-mail: renzd@umkc.edu

L. Roza · F.-J. Simons
Rotterdam School of Management (RSM), Erasmus University Rotterdam, Rotterdam, The Netherlands

2.1 Introduction

Corporate foundations exist and function at the very intersection of the nonprofit and for-profit worlds and, therefore, their governance must navigate the complexities posed by this intersection. Corporate Foundations are an eminent example of hybrid organizations that exemplify the blurring of sector boundaries (e.g., Billis 2010; Weisbrod 1998), since these types of foundations straddle the boundaries of and tend to exhibit certain characteristics of both commercial and philanthropic organizations. Their founding is grounded in the domain of business and commerce, with all of this sector's expectations for private benefit and private wealth creation, yet their explicit mission and practices are (by the laws of most nations) mandated to deliver social benefits that will serve the interests and needs of communities and civil society.

Corporate foundation governance is especially interesting to study as it epitomizes the complexity and conflicts of an organization that exhibits the characteristics and conditions of a hybrid. While there is some debate in the literature on what constitutes a hybrid organization, we adopt the perspective shared by most scholars and practitioners that "hybrid organizations contain mixed sectoral, legal, structural, and/or mission-related elements" (Smith 2010: 220). Corporate foundations usually articulate missions of social benefit and impact, yet they also exhibit characteristics identified with commercial or for-profit business practices and interests. This necessarily includes the implications of single-funder or single-donor resource dependence, as a business allocates certain of its resources (financial and nonfinancial resources) to a corporate foundation—as its agent—and this usually is linked to both corporate and philanthropic strategy (Kania et al. 2014; Gautier et al. 2013). Many facets of their design and operation must blend to reflect the imperatives of different sectors, with a commensurate mix of seemingly inconsistent expectations and logics, and all the aspects that need consideration from those who govern corporate foundations.

Therefore, this chapter focuses on the challenges experienced by those who govern corporate foundations—including those who serve as members of the foundation's governing board as well as top foundation executives. It is our aim to contribute both theoretically and practically by explaining the context and articulating the challenges for the governance of corporate foundations, linking to the governance literature of for-profits, nonprofits, and hybrid organizations, and sharing preliminary insights from an ongoing study.

This chapter discusses the challenges of corporate foundations that typically become manifest as corporate foundation leaders engage in the actual process of governing their foundations. To gain more insight into how governance theory would apply to corporate foundations, we had informal conversations and conducted formal semi-structured interviews with more than a dozen US and Dutch corporate foundations on the board composition, relationship with the founding firm, relationship between corporate foundation executives and their boards and decision-making processes. Drawing on insights obtained through these observations and interviews, we first identify the most common conditions and dynamics experienced by these leaders as they engage in the process of governance, and consider how and why these dynamics pose significant challenges. In the subsequent section, we explore the implications of these insights from the perspectives of three key theories (agency theory, resource dependence theory, and institutional theory) to offer a more nuanced understanding of the dynamics associated with the governance of these hybrid organizations. Based on both governance dynamics and theoretical insights, we present a basic framework to classify the tensions experienced by those who govern corporate foundations. We conclude the chapter with suggestions for future research that can help inform theory and practice with regard to the effective governance of these unique types of hybrid organizations.

2.2 Who Are Involved in Corporate Foundations' Governance?

As governance is a broad umbrella term, it is important that we articulate our definition of governance. We build on the definition advanced by Cornforth (2014: 5): Governance comprises "the systems and processes concerned with ensuring the overall direction, control and accountability of an organization." As such, the work of governance includes setting strategic direction and goals, making policy and strategy decisions, overseeing and monitoring organizational performance, and ensuring overall accountability (Renz 2004). We also consider it essential to highlight the distinction between "board" and "governance," although they typically overlap. Governance is a function, whereas a board is a structure (Renz and Andersson 2014). In this chapter, we discuss both boards and executives as we examine the challenges of foundation governance.

Understanding who are key stakeholders of corporate foundations is fundamental to understanding these organizations' governance, as all organizations exist and operate within a web of stakeholders. Central to the existence and identity of any corporate foundation is the related company. The corporate foundation is a separate legal entity, yet its existence is caused by and its work is to varying degrees controlled by the corporate entity. While it exists for the benefit of the greater society and its work is separate from generating direct commercial benefit to the corporation, the foundation's existence also grows out of (and often is a manifestation of) a corporation's orientation toward its corporate responsibility and/or its philanthropy.

This orientation will vary with regard to many factors, including its industry, how it was founded, its history, age, and size (Kotler and Lee 2005). Its perspective will serve as the grounding for the corporation's views on the work of its corporate foundation and how it is to link with what corporate leaders consider to be an appropriate and desirable relationship with its various stakeholders and constituents. As Zadek (2004) explains, a corporation's motivation for and orientation toward its engagement with society may be as narrow as acting in compliance with demands of legal authorities or as broad as being a proactive civic leader in the community. A dominant but contested view on corporate philanthropy is strategic corporate philanthropy and shared value creation as argued by Porter and Kramer (2006). They encourage corporations to pursue a more self-centered "strategic orientation" toward philanthropy, wherein the corporation pursues strategies that achieve mutually beneficial outcomes for both the company and society. However, this orientation assumes that corporate interests do not collide with societal interest, as well as ignores the wider role that companies (may want to) play in the development of society because it uses the single lens of instrumentality toward corporate philanthropy (Crane et al. 2014).

Despite this academic debate on strategic corporate philanthropy, we also observe corporate leaders using their philanthropic orientation (either instrumental or more morally inclined) as the basis for determining the corporate foundation's mission. The board members of the parent corporation may include major stockholders or their representatives. However, they are also likely to include people with a closer connection to the corporation—especially likely, the highest ranking of the corporation's top executives. These parent corporation board member characteristics typically have a significant bearing on their expectations of the corporate foundation and what it will achieve (see Marquis and Lee 2013).

In addition, Masulis and Reza (2015) found that the choice and level of corporate giving in corporations that have relatively weak corporate governance was highly associated with the CEO's personal preferences and ties to charities—not to some grand level of corporate philosophy or strategy. Marquis and Lee (2013: 487) report that this relatively high level of senior management influence exists even in cases wherein the corporations have relatively large separate corporate foundations (i.e., large with regard to size of the foundation's assets and, notably, the number of staff employed by the foundation itself, separate from the corporation). Therefore, at a fundamental level, the main orientation of corporate leadership (corporate, shared value, or truly societal) is very likely to have significant impact on the governance of the corporate foundation.

While overtly linked to the parent corporation, the foundation—which is at the core of what we seek to understand—also has its own story on its founding and mission. The origin of a corporate foundation oftentimes influences the policy, the connectedness with the founding company, and/or the decision-making processes on the means that are allocated for public benefit. For instance, the Dutch Rabobank, a cooperative bank first founded by Dutch farmers and horticulturists in the late nineteenth century, founded the Rabobank Foundation in 1972. Nowadays the bank has broadened its scope significantly to consumers and other business sectors. But the foundation is still very active in supporting agricultural businesses, albeit now in developing countries. Moreover, the foundation uses an impact investment approach to achieve its social mission, which is very much related to the bank's business methods.

By definition, the governing board of the corporate foundation is a central actor in the foundation's governance. There is no comprehensive research on which to make a determination but, based on our observations of US and Dutch corporate foundations, it appears most common that senior executives of the corporation (and especially the CEO) are likely to occupy an important (sometimes even the majority or all) seat(s) on the corporate foundation's governing board. In some countries, like the Netherlands, law does not allow founders to have a majority in the corporate foundation board (voting power) if these foundations have public benefit status (including tax exempt status). Despite being the minority in those cases, company representatives are strongly accounted for in decision-making processes in boards of corporate foundations. Some even choose not to have an official public benefit status, because the company wants to retain the control over the foundation. From a risk-management perspective, it is not surprising that many companies feel they must safeguard themselves against threats to their reputation. This could be an concern if the board were being governed truly independently.

Another important actor to consider in the governance process is the foundation's executive leadership. It may be comprised of one or more people and be solely employed for and engaged in the work of the foundation, or actually be employed by the corporation and their time assigned or "donated" to the foundation. It is obvious that there will be a significant blurring of identity and allegiance if the foundation's top executive is a direct employee of the corporation. Indeed, in many corporate foundations in the US and the Netherlands, employees are not at all under the control of the foundation or its board. Instead, the people doing the work in the foundation are in fact employees of the parent corporation, which establishes their terms of employment and standards for performance. At its most extreme, this kind of role combination or allocation structure will ensure that the governance and strategic direction of the foundation will be well synchronized with (if not entirely dominated by) the agenda of the corporation. Even if the corporation has some interest in separating its governance and strategic direction from that of the foundation, it is inevitable that there will be some tendency on the part of the foundation chief executive to link the foundation's interests with those of the corporation. And in many cases, this role alignment will be an explicit tactic intended to assure that the work of the foundation does not stray too far from the interests of the corporation. At the same time, corporate foundations' leadership is also influenced by its directors' social embeddedness. Several researchers report evidence that the degree to which the members of a corporate foundation board are embedded in networks and relationships with external actors (i.e., those who are outside the corporation and the foundation) will have significant influence on their philanthropic practices and preferences (e.g., Useem 1984; Galaskiewicz 1997).

The list of actors that could influence the governance process of a corporate foundation does not end with the corporation, its executive leadership, and boards. The community—including state authorities, specialized organizations like trade unions, nonprofits, and civil society—is an important stakeholder in regard to which corporations are supposed to perform responsibly (Pesqueux and Damak-Ayadi 2005). Fairly little has been written on the role of community as a stakeholder, and systematic ambiguity in the notion of "community" has recently begun to be explored (Freeman et al. 2001; Phillips et al. 2003). What we observe is a shift from relationships geared toward a single (close) community toward more complex relationships with a multitude of communities that can be both close and more distant (Waddock and Boyle 1995). This complexity of what constitutes the community to corporate foundations may well be influenced by a multiplicity of stakeholder groups.

2.3 Theoretical Perspectives and the Challenges of Hybridity in Governance

There has been little scholarly writing to date on corporate foundation governance, and what has been written tends to be quite basic, anecdotal, and a-theoretical. And yet, our understanding of and appreciation for the challenges of corporate foundation governance improves substantially when we employ relevant theories to inform our understanding of the realities of corporate foundation governance. For this chapter, we draw on three of the most commonly employed organizational theoretical perspectives to inform our analysis: agency (or principal–agent) theory, resource dependence theory, and institutional theory. It is useful to employ these multiple perspectives for this chapter as governance is complex and often paradoxical. Therefore, reliance upon any single theory will be too one-dimensional and narrow to effectively explain the phenomenon (see also Cornforth 2014), as will become apparent in the next sections of this chapter.

2.3.1 *Institutional Theory*

The central premise of (neo-) institutional theory is that organizations are shaped by their institutional environment as they seek legitimacy vis-à-vis external constituencies, which improves their chance of success and survival (DiMaggio and Powell 1991; Meyer and Rowan 1977). To increase the likelihood they will be perceived as legitimate, organizations adopt and employ the values, norms, beliefs, practices, and expectations that are consistent with those of their operating environments. Institutional theory provides an essential perspective to complement those of agency and resource dependence theories and enriches our understanding of one specific set of corporate foundation governance challenges.

Integral to institutional theory is the central orientation in this chapter—the multiple and divergent orientations to logics and heuristics (i.e., the processes used by people, professions, and organizations to make decisions and do their work) of corporate foundations. As noted earlier, due to their hybrid nature, corporate foundations generally are characterized by working under conditions in which they must recognize and address multiple and often divergent logics as they seek to achieve legitimacy and accomplish their work. Here, it is imperative that a corporate foundation retains its legitimacy and acceptance with each of two quite different domains—the commercial or business domain, and the public benefit or community domain. The commercial or business domain expectations for the foundation tend to focus on business-like practice and performance that will enhance corporate standing and legitimacy. Indeed, the existence of a corporate foundation itself usually is a parent corporation strategy designed to enhance the corporation's legitimacy in and with a community. In one of the Dutch cases studied, the corporate foundation board and director developed several performance frameworks based on decision models used in their business to support their decision-making processes. Alternatively, the public benefit or community domain has its own expectations that it imposes as it judges the legitimacy of the corporate foundation—to deliver social value and benefit to the community.

Interestingly, there are two primary dimensions to the public benefit domain, because corporate foundations need to sustain their legitimacy with communities within which they operate and to which they make grants, but they also need to have legitimacy with their professional peers—those who are members of the philanthropic foundation community. In fact, an important way corporate foundations gain and sustain legitimacy is to adhere to and perpetuate the norms, values, and characteristics of philanthropic foundation "good governance" and "best practices" as prescribed in the professional literature of the field. These expectations can be very different from those of the business domain (Jaquette 2013). For instance, corporate foundations may adhere to reporting standards that are developed in the field of philanthropy rather than adhering to corporate reporting. Similarly, wherein typical business environments it is expected to employ economic reasoning (e.g., what is the business case, how can my company and shareholders gain from this), in a philanthropic environment it is expected to think not in terms of self-interest but in terms of public interest.

Further, corporate foundations' philosophical orientations and cultures typically are drawn directly from and express the motivations and values of their founding or "parent" for-profit organizations, even as they find it necessary to execute at least some aspects of their operations from the orientation and perspective of the nonprofit and (especially) philanthropic foundation world. As organizations, this complicated mix impacts their approach to strategy, planning, budgeting, performance evaluation, and more (Bromley and Meyer 2014; Ebrahim 2003; Hwang and Powell 2009). To the extent that the sets of logics guiding an organization's actions are inconsistent and competing, the result will be reflected in internal and external tensions and accommodations. This poses special challenges to those who engage in governance (Thornton and Ocasio 1999). Thus, the divergent and sometimes mutually exclusive interests and expectations of these different sectors often create some of the most significant challenges for those governing corporate foundations (as well as those who are foundation executives) since corporate foundations need to retain at least a moderate degree of legitimacy with each.

Abzug and Galaskiewicz (2001) found institutional theory especially useful in understanding (nonprofit) board composition because one can expect "that environmental pressures for legitimacy would be met organizationally through the recruitment of trustees with the proper educational, professional, and managerial credentials to signal compliance with the institutional order" (p. 53). We have seen this in the case of corporate foundation boards, in the Netherlands and in the US. In one of our Dutch foundation cases, a community representative holds a seat on the board. In another Dutch case—a foundation of a family owned corporation—board's membership actually is comprised of a number of family members. These family members serve as gatekeepers for family values in their work as board members. Both corporate foundations also appointed executives of the parent corporation to their boards to encourage the foundation to employ business practices. Adding such board members enables the foundation to gain access to specific competencies, one foundation explains, but perhaps more important, it also enables their foundation to demonstrate that they are "business-like." This, in turn, is believed to signal greater adherence to professionalism, efficiency, and a competitive posture (this also has been documented in US studies by Abzug and Galaskiewicz 2001; Young 2002; Dart 2004).

2.3.2 Agency Theory

The most commonly employed theory to both explain and drive (in a legal prescriptive sense) the work of governing boards, especially in the business and accounting world, is agency theory (Huse 2009). Since this theory is the basis for the most prevalent explanations for how governing boards and executives should and do relate to each other in any organization, it is highly relevant to corporate foundations too. The theory posits an "agency problem" because principals (those who provide the resources) and agents (those to whom responsibility is delegated to decide how to use those resources) often have different and even misaligned interests. Under such conditions, the agents can be inclined to act in their own interests rather than those of the principals unless specific incentives and controls are put in place (Eisenhardt 1989). We see the tension between principals and agents demonstrated in several ways in corporate foundation governance.

To start with, in corporate foundations it is not necessarily obvious who is the principal and who is the agent. Corporate foundations have no clearly defined owner (in the sense of equity) and, as we have discussed, they must answer to multiple stakeholders (e.g., Anheier 2005). Many assume that boards are the principals and they hire executive directors to manage the organization. But that may be overly simplistic, as different stakeholders may view quite differently the question about who is the principal and who is the agent. This can vary depending on which logics and perspectives are employed.

Indeed, corporate foundations are likely to be accountable to a variety of "principal" stakeholders (e.g., Freeman 1984), such as funders, founders, corporation boards, directors, and ultimately the beneficiaries of the corporate foundation. Thus, corporate foundations must combine and reconcile potentially divergent and competing stakeholder interests. Furthermore, corporate foundations are confronted with the often-diverging interests of the beneficiaries that are the focus of their social mission. This is not a straightforward principal–agent setting in which the problem for principals or owners, as assumed to be represented by governing boards, is to ensure that managers carry out their interests (Dalton et al. 2007; Jensen and Meckling 1976). Instead, it is a context in which the multiple principal stakeholders may have different objectives, and some can enforce their interests and others cannot. Thus, a key task of governance here is the proper alignment and prioritization of diverse and sometimes conflicting interests. Central to this is the question of whose interests are deemed (by governance decision-makers) to be most important and/or relevant. The dual objectives of the corporate foundation and its founding company are not necessarily aligned and may even be contradictory, and this may create a risk to the mission of the foundation.

Indeed, the typical corporate foundation mission states that the benefit of its work is to accrue to the community or some segment of it. Yet it usually is a parent corporation's resources being deployed in the work of the corporate foundation, and the foundation and its board are viewed as the agents for the parent corporation. So the agency obligation can be to the parent corporation. This usually is accomplished by having top executives of the parent corporation serve on the foundation board as agents for the corporation. However, these executives (exhibiting the classic agency problem) often have limited incentives to maximize the interests of the corporation's owners at the expense of their own. Further, we have found it is common that these same top corporate executives constitute the majority of the membership of the foundation board, and the executive director of the corporate foundation then becomes their agent in the operations of the foundation.

Recent studies suggest that sometimes it is more accurate to recognize that there may be multiple agency relationships because there legitimately are two or more principals. This further complicates the process of understanding principal–agent relationships, yet it better explains the reality of hybrid organizations (e.g., Child and Rodrigues 2003). This is likely the most accurate way to understand the behaviors of community representatives on corporate foundation boards; they recognize they are agents for both community and parent corporation. However, in some instances, both the external board members and the parent corporation executives on the foundation board all perceive themselves to be agents of the parent corporation first, and the community interests come second in their deliberations. In fact, in our US and Dutch cases, we find external representatives on foundation boards often perceive their responsibility to be to the parent corporation even though they try to help the foundation act in mutually beneficial ways. Thus, while each stakeholder group theoretically wants the foundation to prioritize its interests highly, we observe that it is relatively common that even community stakeholders accept that the corporation's interests are to be pre-eminent in the foundation's decision-making. This is true in spite of the broad legal constraints that control for inappropriate self-dealing and private enrichment on the part of corporate and foundation personnel. This is usually not a point of contention in countries where the law grants a foundation board substantial latitude to decide where to expend resources. Of course, this is subject to the general confines of charity law in that country.

Some scholars have utilized the agency perspective to focus on an organization's obligation to honor its mission or purpose. Since boards are legally responsible for ensuring the organization pursues its mission, boards play a central role in ensuring loyalty and accountability to all stakeholders' interests and expectations relevant to mission (e.g., Miller-Millesen 2003). But a complication exists when the governing board membership is dominated by only one stakeholder, the corporation. This is typical in many of our Dutch and US corporate foundation cases, since their boards are composed predominantly of representatives of the company. It also can occur when there are equal numbers of community board members and corporate board members on the board. The community board members may not have full voting power, decreasing their formal influence in decision-making. This way, the theoretical obligation to the community may actually be under pressure under these conditions.

2.3.3 Resource Dependence Theory

The third theoretical lens is resource dependence theory. It posits that organizations are dependent on actors in the environment for resources essential to their survival and, therefore, they will engage in behaviors that will help reduce uncertainty and manage this dependence (Pfeffer and Salancik 1978). Similar to family foundations (with living founders), corporate foundations typically have only the single corporate funder on which they are entirely or almost-entirely dependent for their resources. The resource dependence perspective leads us to examine the characteristics of the flow of resources to the foundation, and the characteristics of these sources, including how dependent the foundation is on individual actors and units within the parent corporation and how these corporate actors exercise power or influence in their relationship with the foundation. This may even be reflected in the formal or structural alignment of the foundation with the corporation, such as when the foundation reports to the corporate public affairs department, or the marketing department, or the CEO's office.

Resource dependence theory suggests that there will be a greater bias on the part of decision-makers toward the needs and interests of the corporate funder (unless they overtly conflict with law) because corporate foundations are heavily reliant on the corporation for resources that are critical to their work and, thus, for their very existence. In the both the US and the Netherlands, such corporate resources usually include the funds needed for grants to the community, the time of corporate personnel, and the corporate employees who volunteer at projects of nonprofit partners of the corporate foundation. In many corporate foundations, foundation staff are actually employees of the corporation, even though their time may be dedicated up to 100 percent to the work of the foundation. Obviously, however, in the case of a corporate foundation that has a substantial endowment that it controls independent of the parent corporation, the nature of the dependence on the corporation is likely to be substantially less.

Thus, corporate foundations can experience extreme resource dependence for their functioning. They run the risk that if the foundation pursues philanthropic activities or practices that are inconsistent with the expectations of the parent corporation or its key executives, the flow of resources will stop. In certain US cases, corporate foundations actually have been eliminated as a result of the corporate parent CEO's displeasure with the foundation's actions. It is therefore imperative for the foundation and those who govern it to have the knowledge and relationships necessary to know what will and will not be acceptable practice, and to understand the criteria being employed by the parent corporation decision-maker(s) as they assess the value and appropriateness of the foundation's performance. In the US cases we have examined, these decisions have been made by the corporate CEO and a few select others in top management. Interestingly, it is not unusual that many of these same executives also serve on the foundation board and set goals and oversee foundation performance. As such, there is a substantial blurring and even conflicts of interest as these executives play both their corporate and foundation leadership roles.

This implies another challenge for corporate foundation governance: mission drift. This is a condition in which an organization loses sight of its mission (Jones 2007) as it pursues its efforts to remain in favor of the corporation's key decision-makers. This is not unique to corporate foundations, yet it is an issue for them. They logically can be at risk of giving priority to the interests of their corporate parent over those of their community stakeholders, even if social impact is overtly stated (as it usually is) in their legally defined mission. As a result, the foundation may well fail to achieve its mission of delivering social value to its beneficiaries and this may threaten its societal and legal legitimacy.

While agency theory suggests members are appointed to board seats to ensure accountability to the principal actors and their interests, resource dependence theory suggests that members are appointed to the board because they can help the foundation relate to, understand, and influence the perspectives of those in the external environment who are likely to have an important impact on the flow of resources to the foundation. For corporate foundations, these external resources may be social and political rather than financial. Thus, these foundation boards will recruit community members who understand and can attend to the interests and expectations of community or civil society leaders and organizations (such as nonprofit and/or governmental entities, including regulators) as they work to sustain and enhance the foundation's credibility, legitimacy, and trust with them. With family business corporate foundations, the resource dependence of the foundation usually also is influenced by the relationship with the family, as well as the company. This often is reflected by one or more family members holding seats on the foundation's board as well.

2.4 Key Challenges and Tensions for Those Who Govern Corporate Foundations

Our understanding of the complex environment—including multiple stakeholder interests—in which corporate foundations function, leads us to articulate the actual governance challenges of these organizations. Here, we identify and discuss three primary challenges and the associated tensions experienced by those who govern a typical corporate foundation. Many of the most common challenges and issues experienced by those governing a corporate foundation are fundamentally related to the question of how best to address the hybridity paradox. Based on the theoretical perspectives we describe above, Fig. 2.1 illustrates the basic framework we have developed to categorize the nature of the tensions experienced by those who govern corporate foundations.

This figure articulates the challenges corporate foundations experience by identifying the nature of the tension and then illustrating the continuum by stating the two extreme orientations associated with each. The imperative for those who govern the corporate foundation is to determine the most appropriate posture or degree of balance along each continuum given their own situation. The challenge lies in the fact that there can be some merit to each orientation, as well as problems and consequences associated with each. Thus, these are competing tensions that fundamentally exemplify the challenge of corporate foundation governance. The nature of such governance decisionmaking is messy because these are not tensions that can be resolved. Rather, they must be strategically assessed and balanced. The central tensions highlighted in Fig. 2.1 relate to three fundamental questions that frame the key challenges confronting those who govern corporate foundations:

- Why do corporate foundations exist and to what end?
- Who really governs a corporate foundation and with what orientation?
- To whom are corporate foundations accountable and for what?

2.4.1 Why Do Corporate Foundations Exist and to What End?

There typically are multiple competing perspectives among those who are founders and key stakeholders of the corporate foundation but, of course, some are in charge and others are merely functionaries who are to execute the choices of those in charge. In practice, most corporate foundations know they legally cannot exist for private corporate benefit, and yet essentially all were created by and operate because, at some time in the development of the parent corporation, certain key actors wanted to have a foundation that would serve some purpose that would offer value to the parent corporation. Indeed, a fundamental challenge for those who govern the corporate foundation is confusion about purpose.

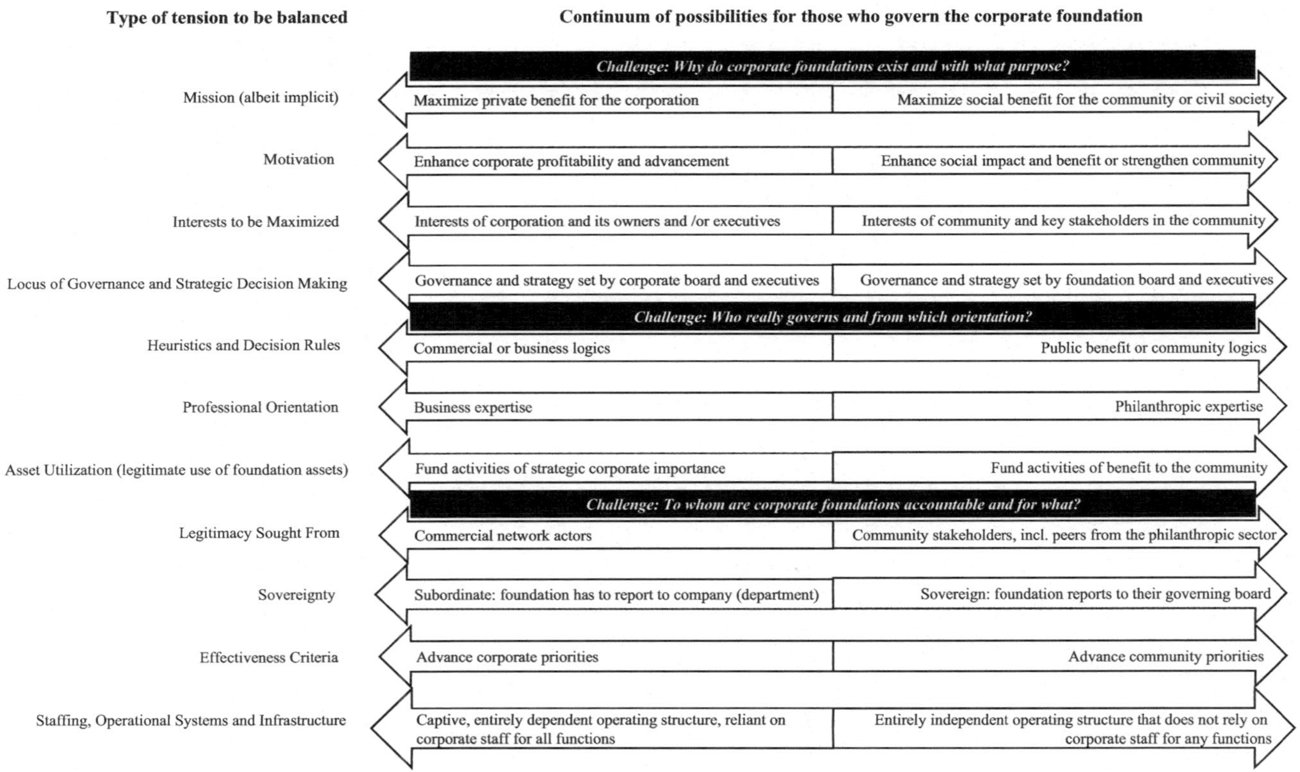

Type of tension to be balanced	Continuum of possibilities for those who govern the corporate foundation	
	Challenge: Why do corporate foundations exist and with what purpose?	
Mission (albeit implicit)	Maximize private benefit for the corporation	Maximize social benefit for the community or civil society
Motivation	Enhance corporate profitability and advancement	Enhance social impact and benefit or strengthen community
Interests to be Maximized	Interests of corporation and its owners and /or executives	Interests of community and key stakeholders in the community
Locus of Governance and Strategic Decision Making	Governance and strategy set by corporate board and executives	Governance and strategy set by foundation board and executives
	Challenge: Who really governs and from which orientation?	
Heuristics and Decision Rules	Commercial or business logics	Public benefit or community logics
Professional Orientation	Business expertise	Philanthropic expertise
Asset Utilization (legitimate use of foundation assets)	Fund activities of strategic corporate importance	Fund activities of benefit to the community
	Challenge: To whom are corporate foundations accountable and for what?	
Legitimacy Sought From	Commercial network actors	Community stakeholders, incl. peers from the philanthropic sector
Sovereignty	Subordinate: foundation has to report to company (department)	Sovereign: foundation reports to their governing board
Effectiveness Criteria	Advance corporate priorities	Advance community priorities
Staffing, Operational Systems and Infrastructure	Captive, entirely dependent operating structure, reliant on corporate staff for all functions	Entirely independent operating structure that does not rely on corporate staff for any functions

Fig. 2.1 Key challenges and tensions to be balanced in corporate foundation governance

The formal purpose of the foundation, as articulated in articles of incorporation, bylaws, and policies, usually reflects the hybrid nature of the foundation as has been described throughout this chapter. And yet, the design on paper must be operationalized by the governing board of the foundation, and oftentimes many of the people serving on the foundation's governing board also hold corporate positions with the duty of serving the parent corporation (or at least feel they need to represent the company's interest, too). Their personal performance criteria and advancement are rooted in the business logics and expectations of the corporation yet, for this peripheral assignment, they find themselves confronted with the obligation to consider other logics and expectations. Many are puzzled and go back and forth; some start from the perspective of being just an alter ego of the corporation with its priorities and goals, while others start from the perspective of the corporate foundation being an entity in its own right, with a distinct philanthropic or social benefit mission, vision, strategic priorities, and goals.

Thus, there is a continuous motivational tension within and among individuals (both board members and foundation executives): to what extent should they benefit the corporation and enhance advancement and profit, directly or indirectly? Or should they leverage corporate resources to achieve social impact and benefit or strengthen the community? Those involved in governing corporate foundations typically are not merely one or the other. They question themselves and each other on the alternatives and the appropriate balance that the corporate foundation is to achieve among these oftentimes competing motives. Questions related to the interests that need to be maximized form the existential challenge of foundation purpose: do we focus on corporate interests—and with them the interests of its owners and executives—or do we strive to maximize community interests and those of its key stakeholders? Confronted with the hybrid purpose, some executives on foundation boards broaden their horizons and incorporate alternate logics, and some merely retrench to the familiar business logics and the performance criteria that align with them.

To further complicate the work of governance, expectations often change or erode over time, leaving those who govern subsequent generations of the foundation with declining clarity about the purpose and focus of the foundation. In one of our cases, we observed a corporate foundation that exemplified the best of hybrid practice, with a governance process that thoughtfully embraced the hybridity built into their design. Its board was a champion for the social benefit mission of the foundation and was intentional and deliberate about striking a strategic balance in their governance and grant-making activities. They recruited and appointed a few highly influential community leaders with expertise in the issue areas they sought to address in their grant-making to serve on their board, they commissioned and used professional assessments of community conditions and needs, and their board meetings were filled with thoughtful debate about how best to achieve the blended value the foundation was designed to deliver. However, after several years of success, this foundation made a radical shift and reduced external involvement in governance and assumed a posture of maximizing corporate benefit. A single but fundamental change had occurred: a new corporate CEO took office with a radically different perspective on corporate responsibility and, especially, the purpose of a corporate foundation. He almost closed the foundation, although he ultimately backed away from that option due to community pressure. But even though the foundation's articles of incorporation and its mission statement did not change, the strategic direction and operation of the foundation did. This example also highlights the challenge articulated in the next section: Who really governs and with what orientation?

2.4.2 Who Really Governs and with What Orientation?

At the beginning of the chapter, we explained that governance provides for the overall direction, control, and accountability of an organization (Cornforth 2014). It turns out that a fundamental challenge of corporate foundation governance is rooted in the question of who really does this work or is accountable for this work. In the case of many corporate foundations, both the legal and normative expectations would suggest that governance authority lies with the governing board of the corporate foundation. Yet that is not necessarily the case.

Again, it is imperative to underscore that the official reality as formalized in the foundation's incorporation papers, bylaws, and policies is not necessarily how governance actually works. Indeed, based on our case analyses, who is actually in charge varies from foundation to foundation. Those involved in the governance process often must sort out how much sovereignty and independence the corporate foundation is to have relative to the parent corporation. As explained in Chap. 3 from Bethmann and von Schnurbein, corporate foundations have a certain degree of (in) dependence in identity and operation. And, to the extent that the foundation is not very independent, they must clarify how much latitude they have to govern and what are the parameters within which they must govern. Agency theory would suggest it is imperative to clarify whose interests are they to honor.

In addition, we observe two interlinked tensions. The first is that of the professional orientation of the foundation and the question whether this leans more toward business expertise or toward philanthropic expertise. In some corporate foundations, the executives and employees have a experience in the philanthropic sector, perhaps including other corporate foundations. Foundation size seems to be relevant in this respect. In many larger corporate foundations there seems to be a perceived need to have people on board who are experts on the social mission of the corporate foundation. In smaller corporate foundations, this need for expertise seems to be outsourced to the nonprofit partners with whom the corporate foundation collaborates.

The second tension concerns the legitimate use of the foundation's assets: Are the foundation's funding activities aimed at enhancing the corporation's strategic position in its environment or are they aimed at creating benefit for community? In some cases, executives of corporate foundations lament what they perceive as inappropriate intervention in the foundation's grant-making process by the corporation CEO, when that CEO directs (mandates) that a certain grant be made by the foundation. Foundation boards in these cases are relatively irrelevant, and the top corporate foundation executive is relegated to simply executing the CEO's wishes. In truth, it has been observed that many top corporate foundation executives who work in such environments take care to remain in close contact with the corporate CEO and never pursue foundation action unless it has been cleared with the CEO. In doing so, they are subverting the authority of the governing board, but often the members of such boards recognize the pragmatic value of doing this and accept it as "the way we do things around here."

These dynamics are not likely to be challenged by the foundation's governing board, in many cases because the majority of the board is comprised of senior corporate executives who serve at the pleasure of the CEO. This dynamic usually will not change even when the board has some noncorporate executive members, because they hold a minority of the seats and have too little power to resist even when they consider an action ill-advised. Indeed, it is not uncommon for a parent corporation's top executives (and especially their CEOs) to use the foundation as a vehicle for their own personal philanthropic interests and motives (Masulis and Reza 2015). Here, the balance of power and governance authority lies explicitly in the hierarchical business logics of the corporation.

2.4.3 To Whom Are Corporate Foundations Accountable and for What?

The third fundamental challenge we identify for corporate foundation governance is to whom corporate foundations are accountable and for what. Corporate foundations typically have at least two sets of stakeholders to whom they are accountable and with whom they must maintain their legitimacy: the corporate network actors and the community stakeholders. These stakeholders have relatively divergent interests and needs that they expect the foundation to address. The challenge is to be accountable as the foundation lives the existential paradox posed by the hybrid expectations and competing logics that guide and inform its work. It refers to organizational effectiveness of a corporate foundation, the criteria by which it is judged, and who has the power and authority to make such judgments. The foundation constantly needs to balance between advancing corporate and community priorities at the same time. Even though this might be clear for the corporate foundation itself, it might not be clear to those to whom they are accountable. As such, trying to achieve an appropriate balance of corporate benefit and community benefit and then account for it poses a pivotal challenge.

When logics are inconsistent and out of alignment, the result is likely to be reflected in internal and external tensions and accommodations (Thornton and Ocasio 1999). In particular, it is likely to cause cognitive dissonance for the people involved in its work. As Bryson et al. have observed, the existence of competing logics creates challenges because "actions, processes, norms and structures that are seen as legitimate from the vantage point of one institutional logic may be seen as less legitimate or even illegitimate from the perspective of another logic" (2006: 50). For example, as we described earlier, the staffing, operational systems, and infrastructure of corporate foundations and their governing boards in the US and many other nations are comprised largely of personnel from the parent corporation. These executives and staff experience cognitive dissonance as they go about their work because their decisions and practices are supposed to be grounded in and guided by the conflicting expectations and competing logics of two fundamentally different worlds. Here, it remains unclear how the multiple accountabilities are addressed.

It is typical for many corporate foundations to operate as though they are divisions or subordinate entities of their parent corporations. This subordinate nature or lack of sovereignty is reinforced when a foundation uses the parent corporation's infrastructure and administrative systems for most of its operations, and foundation governance and management personnel are accountable (at least loosely) to one or more executives in the parent's corporate hierarchy. Under these conditions, it is not uncommon for those who serve in board and executive roles to report to and be held formally accountable for their foundation work via the performance management system of the parent corporation's human resources function. The challenge posed by such an arrangement is that the foundation board typically has no overt input into the performance management system for the people who actually implement the work of the foundation. Their challenge is to govern the foundation well and demonstrate and document accountability for it using the business-oriented infrastructure of the parent corporation, with all of its assumptions about the values, principles, and priorities that are most important—even though applied to the hybrid dimensions of the foundation. It is only in the cases of the largest of corporate foundations—the ones that have separate funding streams (e.g., endowments) that enable them to operate substantially independently of the parent corporation—that these tensions are less likely to be a challenged.

2.5 Conclusion and the Road Ahead

The work of governance includes setting strategic direction and goals, making policy and strategy decisions, overseeing and monitoring organizational performance, and ensuring overall accountability (Renz 2004). In this chapter, we demonstrated that this work is uniquely complex for corporate foundations. Corporate foundations have to deal with multiple and oftentimes divergent logics which poses tensions and governance challenges. Based on theory and our observations from the field, we identified 11 tensions and three main governance challenges, namely why do corporate foundations exist and to what end, who really governs a corporate foundation and with what orientation and to whom are corporate foundations accountable and for what. These governance challenges are experienced in various degrees and dealt with in many different ways by those who govern corporate foundations.

It is our observation that these governance dynamics vary by the type of corporation. For example, as we have seen in our cases, it is very likely that the leadership and governance of a foundation of a family-founded/family-owned corporation will be influenced or even dominated by the members of the founding family, even after family members move out of top corporate executive roles. Among the factors that will influence this are the degree to which the family continues to hold equity in the corporation and what is the founder(s) wish with regard to ongoing family involvement. They may have little influence in the direction of the corporation and still retain significant influence in the course of the foundation. Similar founder influence often seems to exist for the founding entrepreneur(s) of a younger corporation, even as it grows to the size and scope that its stock is traded publicly (Schervish 2014).

We observe in both our US and Dutch corporate foundation cases that corporate foundations actually experience tensions based on their hybrid nature, as discussed in this chapter. Yet, for many, those tensions are less problematic for corporate foundations than for other types of hybrids, perhaps because the history and professional orientation of their dominant leadership (both board and executive) are fully rooted in the for-profit culture of the parent corporation. Thus, many unapologetically express and employ business logics in their approaches to governance. The setting where we observe this may differ is foundations of family-owned corporations, where we find the founding logics are more fully linked to the culture of the founding family as well as the business. There may be a form of dissonance in this that may confuse or even alienate external stakeholders (i.e., those in the community, such as grant recipients) who try to reconcile foundation behavior with the stakeholders' expectations that the foundation will behave more like a philanthropy. This is something further to study. However, we have observed in the US, foundations are able to operate with this "business-first" orientation because there remains a widespread perception (i.e., a key logic from which to assess foundation performance and legitimacy) among those citizens and even nonprofit leaders in the wider community that corporate foundation money remains practically (even though not legally) the donor's money to do with as they wish. That is to a lesser extent the case in the Dutch context, although there too corporate foundations always take into account some business relevance.

From a practical point of view, we observe that those who successfully lead and govern corporate foundations develop the capacity to "read between the lines" when it comes to understanding and addressing the actual expectations for both the foundation's and their own performance. As foundation executives, a significant challenge is to perform well and secure appropriate performance rewards by corporate standards while doing the foundation's work well. Successful corporate foundation leaders (at both board and executive levels) become adept at exercising the political competencies that enable them to discern the expectations of the parent corporation and its relevant executives, especially with regard to the level and nature of authority that they are expected or allowed to exercise and how that authority will differ by type of decision. And in spite of the success of such leaders' experience, essentially all corporate foundation leaders find themselves confronted with the challenge of changing expectations posed by leadership succession.

As our information is based only on a convenient sample of cases, it would be beneficial to have an outlook how this research agenda could move forward. As we see corporate foundations operate around the globe in various patterns (see the regional chapters in this volume), we suggest that we need studies taking into account the institutional environment. For instance, to what degree do the dynamics and challenges articulated in this chapter exist across the world, in various civil society regimes and/or philanthropic traditions? As we only used examples from the US and the Netherlands, we have yet to determine if the conditions and challenges articulated herein exist for most corporate foundations or if our cases are outliers. For instance, how do these dynamics vary as a function of laws and national legal regimes, as well as by different cultures? Another starting point for future research could well proceed from an organizational level of analysis. For instance, how—if at all—do these dynamics vary by corporate type (especially for family-founded firms, new-generation entrepreneurs, global multinationals, etc.)? By size? And finally, are patterns of foundation dominance or independence different in different industries, such as high-tech or agri-business?

References

Abzug, R., & Galaskiewicz, J. (2001). Nonprofit boards: Crucibles of expertise or symbols of local identities? *Nonprofit and Voluntary Sector Quarterly, 30*(1), 51–73.

Anheier, H. K. (2005). *Nonprofit organizations: Theory, management, policy.* London: Routledge.

Billis, D. (Ed.). (2010). *Hybrid organizations and the third sector: Challenges for practice, theory and policy.* Basingstoke: Palgrave Macmillan.

Bromley, P., & Meyer, J. W. (2014). "They are all organizations" the cultural roots of blurring between the nonprofit, business, and government sectors. *Administration and Society, 49*(7), 939–966.

Child, J., & Rodrigues, S. B. (2003). Corporate governance and new organizational forms: Issues of double and multiple agency. *Journal of Management and Governance, 7*(4), 337–360.

Cornforth, C. (2014). Nonprofit governance research: The need for innovative perspectives and approaches. In Cornforth, C., & Brown, W. A. (Eds.). *Nonprofit Governance: Innovative Perspectives and Approaches.* New York: Routledge.

Crane, A., Palazzo, G., Spence, L. J., & Matten, D. (2014). Contesting the value of "creating shared value". *California Management Review, 56*(2), 130–153.

Dalton, D. R., Hitt, M. A., Certo, S. T., & Dalton, C. M. (2007). 1 The fundamental agency problem and its mitigation: Independence, equity, and the market for corporate control. *The Academy of Management Annals, 1*(1), 1–64.

Dart, R. (2004). The legitimacy of social enterprise. *Nonprofit Management & Leadership, 14*(4), 411–424.

DiMaggio, P., & Powell, W. W. (1991). Introduction. In *The new institutionalism in organizational analysis* (Vol. 17, pp. 1–38). Chicago: University of Chicago Press.

Ebrahim, A. (2003). Accountability in practice: Mechanisms for NGOs. *World Development, 31*(5), 813–829.

Eisenhardt, K. M. (1989). Agency theory: An assessment and review. *Academy of Management Review, 14*(1), 57–74.

Freeman, R. E. (1984). *Strategic management: A stakeholder approach*. Boston: Cambridge university press.

Freeman, R. E., Dunham, L., & Liedtka, J. (2001). *The soft underbelly of stakeholder theory: Towards understanding community*. Darden School Working Paper.

Galaskiewicz, J. (1997). An urban grants economy revisited: Corporate charitable contributions in the Twin Cities, 1979–81, 1987–89. *Administrative Science Quarterly, 42*, 445–471.

Gautier, A., Pache, A. C., & Chowdhury, I. (2013). Nonprofit roles in for-profit firms: The institutionalization of corporate philanthropy in France. In *Academy of management proceedings* (Vol. 2013, No. 1, p. 17464). Briarcliff Manor, NY: Academy of Management.

Huse, M. (2009). *The value creating board: Corporate governance and organizational behaviour*. New York: Routledge.

Hwang, H., & Powell, W. W. (2009). The rationalization of charity: The influences of professionalism in the nonprofit sector. *Administrative Science Quarterly, 54*(2), 268–298.

Jaquette, O. (2013). Why do colleges become universities? Mission drift and the enrollment economy. *Research in Higher Education, 54*(5), 514–543.

Jensen, M. C., & Meckling, W. H. (1976). Theory of the firm: Managerial behavior, agency costs and ownership structure. *Journal of Financial Economics, 3*(4), 305–360.

Jones, M. B. (2007). The multiple sources of mission drift. *Nonprofit and Voluntary Sector Quarterly, 36*(2), 299–307.

Kania, J., Kramer, M., & Russell, P. (2014). Strategic philanthropy for a complex world. *Stanford Social Innovation Review, 12*(3), 26–33.

Kotler, P., & Lee, N. (2005). *Corporate social responsibility: Doing the Most good for your company and your cause*. Hoboken: John Wiley & Sons.

Marquis, C., & Lee, M. (2013). Who is governing whom? Executives, governance, and the structure of generosity in large US firms. *Strategic Management Journal, 34*(4), 483–497.

Masulis, R. W., & Reza, S. W. (2015). Agency problems of corporate philanthropy. *The Review of Financial Studies, 28*(2), 592–636.

Meyer, J. W., & Rowan, B. (1977). Institutionalized organizations: Formal structure as myth and ceremony. *American Journal of Sociology, 83*(2), 340–363.

Miller-Millesen, J. L. (2003). Understanding the behavior of nonprofit boards of directors: A theory-based approach. *Nonprofit and Voluntary Sector Quarterly, 32*(4), 521–547.

Pesqueux, Y., & Damak-Ayadi, S. (2005). Stakeholder theory in perspective. *Corporate Governance: The International Journal of Business in Society, 5*(2), 5–21.

Pfeffer, J., & Salancik, G. R. (1978). *The external control of organizations. A resource dependence perspective*. New York: Harper & Row.

Phillips, R., Freeman, R. E., & Wicks, A. C. (2003). What stakeholder theory is not. *Business Ethics Quarterly, 13*(4), 479–502.

Porter, M. E., & Kramer, M. R. (2006). Strategy and society. *Harvard Business Review, 84*, 78–92.

Smith, S. R. (2010). Hybridization and nonprofit organizations: The governance challenge. *Policy and Society, 29*(3), 219–229.

Renz, D., & Andersson, F. (2014). Nonprofit governance: A review of the field. In C. Cornforth & W. A. Brown (Eds.), *Nonprofit governance, innovative perspectives and approaches* (pp. 17–46). London: Routledge.

Renz, D. O. (2004). Governance of nonprofits. In D. Burlingame (Ed.), *Philanthropy in the U.S: An encyclopedia*. Santa Barbara: ABC-CLIO.

Schervish, P. (2014). High-tech donors and their impact philanthropy: The conventional, novel and strategic traits of agent-animated wealth and philanthropy. In *Handbook of research on entrepreneurs' engagement in philanthropy* (pp. 148–182). Cheltenham: Edward Elgar Publishing.

Thornton, P. H., & Ocasio, W. (1999). Institutional logics and the historical contingency of power in organizations: Executive succession in the higher education publishing industry, 1958–1990. *American Journal of Sociology, 105*(3), 801–843.

Useem, M. (1984). *The inner circle: Large corporations and the rise of business politics in the U.S. and U.K.* New York: Oxford University Press.

Waddock, S. A., & Boyle, M. E. (1995). The dynamic of change in corporate community relations. *California Management Review, 37*(4), 125–140.

Weisbrod, B. A. (1998). The nonprofit mission and its financing: Growing links between nonprofits and the rest of the economy. In *To profit or not to profit: The commercial transformation of the nonprofit sector* (pp. 1–22). Cambridge/New York: Cambridge University Press.

Young, D. R. (2002). The influence of business on nonprofit organizations and the complexity of nonprofit accountability: Looking inside as well as outside. *The American Review of Public Administration, 32*(1), 3–19.

Zadek, S. (2004). The path to corporate responsibility. *Harvard Business Review, 82*(12), 125–133.

David Renz is Professor of Nonprofit Leadership and Management and the Director of the Midwest Center for Nonprofit Leadership at the Henry W. Bloch School of Management at the University of Missouri-Kansas City. He has published in various journals including *Nonprofit and Voluntary Sector Quarterly* and *The American Review of Public Administration* and is the editor of *The Jossey-Bass Handbook of Nonprofit Leadership and Management*.

Lonneke Roza is Adjunct Assistant Professor at Rotterdam School of Management, Erasmus University. Her research focuses on (microfoundations of) Corporate Philanthropy/Corporate Citizenship. Her work is published in, among others, *Journal of Business Ethics*, *Nonprofit and Voluntary Sector Quarterly*, and *Voluntas*.

Frans-Joseph Simons is a Researcher at the Rotterdam School of Management, Erasmus University. After completing his Master's in Social History, he completed his Master's in Business Administration cum laude and won a research prize with his thesis. His special research interests are voice, power structures, leadership, and learning organizations within the context of nonprofit organizations, corporate philanthropy, and corporate citizenship.

Chapter 3
Strategic in What Sense? Corporate Foundation Models in Terms of Their Institutional Independence and Closeness to Core Business

Steffen Bethmann and Georg von Schnurbein

Abstract With the growing number of corporate foundations and their increasing visibility as philanthropic actors, interests are raised regarding the way these corporate foundations function as well as about the nature of their relationship with the founding company. The foundation literature generally assumes that a foundation's ability to create social impact and innovation rests to a large part on their independence from external control. However, corporate foundations are dependent to varying degrees on the support of their founding company. Therefore, apparent tensions between corporate control and the freedom a foundation needs to maximize its impact exist. In this chapter, we look at the special relationship between the two entities. Based on an exploratory study, we build ideal types of foundations in relation to their institutional independence. We then test and refine these through data gathered at the first European meeting of corporate foundations. The findings allow us to distill pull and push factors that lead to a stronger alignment of corporate goals and foundation activities. The ideal types show that full independence is not necessarily the best option, as corporate foundations can benefit greatly from corporate resources in achieving their social mission.

Keywords Corporate foundations · Mixed methods · Typology · (In)dependence · Strategy

3.1 Introduction

An increasing number of corporations have set up their own foundation in recent years (Eckhardt et al. 2017; Rey-García et al. 2012; Pedrini and Minciullo 2011). With the growing number of corporate foundations and their increasing visibility as philanthropic actors, interest has risen in the way these corporate foundations

S. Bethmann (✉) · G. von Schnurbein
Center for Philanthropy Studies (CEPS), University of Basel, Basel, Switzerland

function, as well as about the nature of their relationship with the founding company. Recent approaches on corporate philanthropy emphasize that the highest impact can be achieved when there is a strong alignment between the core business area and the objectives of philanthropic programs (Porter and Kramer 2002; Foster et al. 2009). The assumption is that philanthropy is strategic when it brings benefits to the firm as well as to society (Thorne McAlister and Ferrel 2002). To ensure this, the corporate foundations must be under considerable control of the company to align its activities with the firms' mission, goals, and objectives.

However, corporate foundations have their own legal organization form. To qualify for tax exemption and to be classified as charitable, corporate foundations must show that they are exclusively focused on furthering their social purpose. The foundation literature generally assumes that a foundation's ability to create social impact and innovation rests to a large part on its independence from external control (Frumkin 2006; Anheier and Leat 2006; Fleishman 2007; Kania et al. 2014). Therefore, there are apparent tensions between the corporate control and the freedom a foundation needs to maximize its impact.

But how do these tensions play out in practice? How is the relationship between the corporation and the foundations structured? How does the corporate foundation benefit from its links to the company?

Little is known about the actual challenges and opportunities that stem from the structural linkages of the two entities. Corporate foundations are black boxes. If they appear in research, most articles deal with them exclusively from the perspective of the company. The main themes evolve around the question how the foundation can add to corporate goals, making the business case for corporate philanthropy (Carroll and Shabana 2010). There are hardly any studies that take the view of the corporate foundations in determining the challenges and opportunities of this dual relationship. This has led to a biased view on corporate foundations.

In this chapter, we strive to correct this one-sided view on corporate foundations by elaborating the perspective of the foundation. We do so through an iterative research approach. First, we identify the structural determents of the relationships by reviewing the main literature on corporate foundations. As the body of knowledge is rather limited, we draw on practice-driven governance codes and corporate philanthropy literature. Second, we use the findings from the literature as guidance for exploratory case studies. Third, we refine and extend the findings from the cases, using data collected at a workshop with 35 corporate foundations. In both steps, interviews with executive directors are our most important data sources.

Our final findings allow us to describe four ideal typical corporate foundation models in accordance to the relative degree of independence of the foundation, and its alignment with the core business objective of the corporation. We call these Instrumental, Reputational, Complementary, and Purpose Driven. The characteristics of each model are explained. Overall, we conclude that corporate foundations are at their best when they have considerable freedom in choosing and executing their own programs, while having access to corporate resources. A corporate foundation acts strategically when the corporation empowers it to effectively achieve its mission.

3.2 The Case for Alignment

In a famous quote, Waldemar Nielsen (1972, p. 3) describes foundations as "strange and improbable animals in the jungle of democracy and capitalism, virtually denying basic premises: as aristocratic institutions, they live on the privileges and indulgence of an egalitarian society; they are aggregations of private wealth which, contrary to the proclaimed instincts of Economic Man, have been conveyed to public purposes."

In his quote Nielsen had the great philanthropic foundations in the United States in mind. However, corporate foundations might be even stranger creatures than their independent cousins. Corporate foundations are special animals in the breed of foundations. They are established by a profit-seeking corporate entity as a nonprofit organization, pursuing social causes. As such, they diminish the private profits of company owners. As separate legal entities, corporate foundations are tax exempt when exclusively concentrating on a philanthropic mission. They may fulfill their purpose through grant-making activities or by running their own programs or a mix of both (Frumkin 2006; Leat 2016). By their nature, corporate foundations are rarely independent from the corporation. A strong relationship is usually forged through the flow of capital and by having corporate directors as members of the foundation board. Therefore, corporate foundations show a complex connection to the corporation often resulting in a subordinate dependence on the firm (Rey-García et al. 2012).

Literature names several reasons why a corporate foundation is established. These include ethical motives and the willingness to contribute to society (Liket and Simaens 2015). The managers or owners of a company may feel an intrinsic responsibility or obligation to support local communities, protect the environment, or fund cultural institutions (Sanchez 2000). Corporate foundations in this sense are an expression of the corporate citizenship commitment of the company (Westhues and Einwiller 2006). The activities of the foundation may follow the moral values or aesthetic pleasure of the decision-makers within the corporation (File and Prince 1998) or the desire to meet perceived community needs (Kasper and Fulton 2006). Generally, CEOs influence the giving patterns of corporations in direction of their own personal interest (Werbel and Carter 2002). However, corporate philanthropy is also influenced by industry characteristics (Brammer and Millington 2005). The timing of the establishment often relates to a special occasion, such as a company going public, the sale of a business unit, a company anniversary, or the retirement of a long-time director. Social expectations about corporate behavior are also a strong deciding factor (Carroll 1991). Contrary to donations and sponsorship, establishing a foundation signals a long-term commitment of the corporations to its philanthropic goals.

On the other side of the spectrum of altruism, are profit-seeking motives (Lantos 2001; Gautier and Pache 2015; von Schnurbein et al. 2016). Based on a well-known critique by Friedman (1970), public corporations should not engage in philanthropy. The social responsibility of business is to make profits. Shareholders may individually decide about their own philanthropic activities from the dividends they receive, but it is not within the right of corporate management to do so. Hence, if a corporation decides to engage in philanthropy then it must have tangible benefits for company profit (Porter and Kramer 2002). Corporate foundations in that view are tools to increase company success.

For a long time, corporate foundations were somewhat detached from the main business areas of the funding firm. A bank would establish a foundation related to the arts, or an industrial corporation a foundation for supporting children in need (Smith 1994). The business area and the foundation activities hardly overlapped. The foundation programs might have had positive reputational spillovers for the firm, but they were not directly motivated by the aim to increase company profits (Westhues and Einwiller 2006).

In the last years, a dominant narrative has developed that argues that corporate philanthropy can only be considered strategic if it brings benefits to the company and society alike. This view takes a midpoint between altruism and profit-seeking. It is based on the belief that social and economic aims do not need to contradict each other. One of the main proponents of this view are Porter and Kramer (2002) who argue that corporate philanthropy can especially add to the success of the firm when it is directed at the context in which the company operates. Corporate philanthropy should, for example, support educational programs increasing the number of sophisticated customers, helping the socio-economic development of geographical areas, to build new market opportunities or increase the general business climate through donations related to industry topics. By following this approach, corporations gain competitive advantage over other companies through the means of philanthropy. Saiia et al. (2003) make a similar claim, arguing that a company can increase its position, and ultimately its bottom line, when its philanthropic programs are closely related to the well-being of the community it operates in. In their view, corporations can contribute to the community in a more meaningful way when "charity begins at home" (p. 170). Strategic philanthropy in this view is seeking to achieve organizational and social benefits alike (Thorne McAlister and Ferrel 2002).

There are also strong voices that argue that corporate philanthropy should be in close connection to the core business area of the firm (Smith 1994; Porter and Kramer 2002; Bruch and Walter 2005). In these cases, companies can use their own knowledge to solve social problems. The businesses' core resources and skills are seen as valuable assets for philanthropic goals. In this view, corporate philanthropy is most effective when companies stick to what they know best (Westhues and Einwiller 2006). It is even argued that contrary to altruistic giving charitable organizations, profits from such an approach are more likely to rely on steady income (Campbell and Slack 2008). At the same time, the corporation benefits on different levels. The corporate foundations programs can be used to strengthen business competences, to enter new markets, or for finding new business models (Smith 1994). In this case, corporate managers see the foundation as an opportunity to support strategic objectives of the firm. Synergies are sought that support the operations of the company and the foundation alike (Urriolagoitia and Vernis 2012). The corporate foundation may also serve as an antenna, gathering insights about social expectations from various stakeholders (Westhues and Einwiller 2006). In this line of argument, corporate philanthropy is strategic when it has a strong market and competence orientation (Bruch and Walter 2005). The foundation should be managed with the same rigor as the corporation, setting goals and basing their granting decisions on hard data. There is a strong belief that philanthropy would be more effective if it followed management techniques from capitalistic firms (Bishop and Green 2008).

In sum, the literature mentions many good reasons for investing in corporate philanthropy. In addition, other reasons include higher employee satisfaction and retention, increased customer loyalty as well as better chances of community or government cooperation (Smith 1994; Gadberg and Fombrun 2006). From a corporate perspective, a foundation can bring many benefits to the corporation if managed properly. But to achieve this, the foundation must be under considerable control so the corporation can be sure that it acts in its interest (Fama and Jensen 1983). If it is to be a part of corporate strategy, the corporation must be able to direct and influence the management of the corporate foundation. Corporate foundations are hybrid in nature. They face the challenge of reconciling market and civil society (Billis 2010; Smith 2016). On the one hand, their purpose should focus on solving societal challenges; on the other hand, there is a strong narrative that proclaims the utility of corporate foundation in achieving market-oriented goals.

3.3 The Case for Independence from a Foundation Perspective

The huge bulk of the literature on corporate philanthropy is written from the perspective of the corporation. There are hardly any studies or articles that take the side of the corporate foundation or even refer to the foundation literature. Despite the fact that tight control of the corporate foundation is necessary to exploit business advantages, the foundation literature mainly argues that foundations are especially suited to create social impact due to their independence (Frumkin 2006; Anheier and Leat 2006; Kania et al. 2014). The absence of external stakeholders on the board allows foundations to run ahead of public opinion, take up controversial topics, and speak their mind freely. Foundations can take risks that other organizations cannot. They may support causes with little chances of success. Failure of their partners to achieve the intended social impact has little negative consequences for the foundation itself. Foundations count as one of the most independent institutions in democracies (Anheier and Leat 2006; Fleishman 2007). Only bound by their deed, foundations have maximum freedom to plan and execute their activities. They do not depend on public majorities as politicians. Contrary to public administrations who are bound by official norms on how to spend public funds, foundation can choose their program freely and strategically fund projects. Following a civil society logic, foundations should not seek profits, and hence are more trusted than companies by other actors in the nonprofit sector and governmental offices alike. They can take an important bounding position, build cross-sector coalitions, comment on public policy, or issue official statements without being suspected to follow a hidden agenda (Kramer et al. 2006; von Schnurbein 2009; Hammack and Anheier 2013). From this position foundations have a special ability and even responsibility to create social impact (Porter and Kramer 1999). The notion of independence is the underlying reason for many success stories of foundations in addressing the most pressing social challenges of our times.

Following this observation, there is an apparent tension between the necessity of the corporation to control its foundation to reap business benefits, and the need for independence of the corporate foundation to strive for impact maximization. However, that does not mean that the foundation cannot benefit from close ties to its funding entity. The corporation can actively support the foundation with more than just financial resources. These include management knowledge, infrastructure, staff support, technological expertise, networks, or services from units such as legal, IT, human resources, or marketing (Frooman 1999). From a foundation perspective, the corporation may be a source of resources multiple times more powerful and abundant than its own.

A profound discussion of the dual relationship between the corporation and the foundation is missing in the academic literature so far. None of the studies mentioned address the question of independence explicitly. This might be due to the dominance of the business perspective within the corporate philanthropy literature. However, there is a body of literature that shows strong concerns for the independence of corporate foundations. These are governance codes and recommendations developed by national association of foundations or governmental authorities.

In Germany, the Federal Association of Foundations has published Principles of Good Governance of Corporate Foundations (BDS 2010). A more comprehensive *Good Practice Guide* is provided by the Association of Charitable Foundations (ACF 2016) in the UK. Also, from the UK is the Guide for Corporate Foundation from the Charity Commission (2010). The Polish Donors Forum developed Standards for Corporate Foundations (Ćwik-Obrębowska et al. 2015). The principles of the Swiss Foundation Code (SFC) for all types of grant-making foundations are applicable to corporate foundations (Sprecher et al. 2015). All codes give guidance for setting up and running well-managed corporate foundations. They emphasize that foundation governance systems should strengthen the foundation's independence to fulfill its purpose most effectively. Thus, in this view independence is a prerequisite for the effectiveness of corporate foundations. The Charity Commission even sees independence as the most crucial factor for the foundation to be tax exempt. Any attempts by the corporation to influence that foundation's decision-making can lead to the derecognition of this status (CC 2010).

3.4 The Structural Relationship Between the Foundation and the Corporation

Besides providing norms for rational corporate foundation behavior, the codes shed light on the main structural linkages between the foundation and the corporation. In the following, we discuss the main themes of this relationship based on the core organizational structure of foundations and the different roles foundations may play as discussed above. The following variables determine the degree of independence or integration of the foundation with the corporation.

3.4.1 Board of Directors

The strongest structural link between the foundation and the corporation is established through the board of directors (Westhues and Einwiller 2006). The board is the foundation's ultimate decision-making body (Bethmann et al. 2014). It is legally responsible for the actions taken by the foundation. It oversees the activities and approves the strategy of the foundation.

It is very common in corporate foundations that boards are comprised of members of the corporation. Instances where the entire board is appointed without any company engagement are extremely rare (ACF 2016). Most often, the CEO of the company is also the chair of the foundation board (Marquis and Lee 2013). In some cases, the director of the trustee board may hold this position. In effect, this means that the corporation practically governs the foundation. Out of this constellation, possible tension can arise. Corporate directors or employees on the foundation board may run into conflicts of interest and loyalty (CC 2010). The governance codes stress that independence means that the foundation board members always exercise their responsibility in the best interest of the foundation. Corporate foundations will not engage in controversial topics to avoid negative spillovers to the company reputation.

The codes propose inviting external experts to the board or even allowing external organizations to appoint members, to increase the independence and competence of the foundation board. Having experts with specific knowledge in the foundations' fields of activities increases the public reputation as well as the potential for sophisticated impact strategies (Anheier and Leat 2006). However, corporate foundations may also profit from the strategic knowledge of corporate directors. In general, the selection of board members should be based primarily on their ability to support the mission of the foundation (Sprecher et al. 2015). If the foundation itself can pick external board members, its degree of independence is high.

3.4.2 Staff

The same can also be said about foundation staff. Knowledge of the foundation field of activities is crucial (Brest and Harvey 2008). The degree of independence increases if the staff is not on the payroll of the corporation, selected by and exclusively working for the foundation and when its reporting line is within the foundation. Often corporate foundations may be able to draw in corporate employees to volunteer in the execution of the foundation programs (Haski-Leventhal et al. 2017). Most often, foundation staff is marginal compared in numbers of the corporation. Corporate foundations act most efficiently when staff members are subject matter experts and knowledgeable about foundation and nonprofit management. Foundations can act more independently when they are able to recruit their own staff. The codes argue that it is important that the position of the CEO is filled with a strong personality that steers the foundation with an entrepreneurial spirit. The CEO should not report to any person within the corporation but solely to the foundation board (BDS 2010). A foundation has a higher potential for social impact when it can choose its employees freely.

3.4.3 Operations

The alignment of the foundation's operation with the core business area is one of the main issues discussed within the literature. While the proponents of strategic corporate philanthropy argue for close alignment (dependency) of foundations' operations with the core business purpose, the codes and business ethicist provide a more critical view on this aspect (CC 2010; Morvaridi 2012). As the foundations must exclusively pursue charitable purposes for the public benefit, strong ties with the core business may tilt the foundation too closely to serving business purposes. There are also reputational risks for the foundations and the corporation alike, if the public perceives the foundation as supporting corporate aims rather than concentrating on its charitable mission (Westhues and Einwiller 2006; CC 2010; ACF 2016). If the deed of the foundation is formulated too narrowly then it has little space to maneuver. Within the deed, the selection of the foundation activities is ideally based on need assessment and an analysis of where the foundation can have the biggest impact in relation to its resources (Ćwik-Obrębowska et al. 2015; Sprecher et al. 2015). The more operations of the foundation overlap with the corporate business, the lower is the independence of the foundation. In some cases, there might be strong ties between the CSR department and the corporate foundation. This can lead to productive synergies. However, the corporate foundation should not be the extended arm of the CSR department but maintain its own identity (ACF 2016). The Charity Commission even demands that the corporate foundation not participate in a company's corporate social responsibility policy (CC 2010).

3.4.4 Funding

Usually the only income of the foundation comes from the parent company and its subsidiaries. Corporate foundations that have an endowment high enough to finance their own overhead and program costs are extremely rare (Petrovits 2006).[1] In general, the funding company has the responsibility to provide sufficient means so that the foundational goals can be achieved (Ćwik-Obrębowska et al. 2015). Arrangements vary from fixed annual budgets to floating budgets that are tied to company success, a percentage of annual pretax profits. In some countries, it is forbidden that foundations hold shares of their founding company. Contract periods may also vary. Some corporations decide annually on the foundation budget while others offer long-term contracts. Corporations may use funding as a mean of control and only provide earmarked project funds instead of general operating support. Foundation managers most likely will seek long-term unconditional funding to have planning certainty.

3.4.5 In-Kind Contribution

In addition to financial means, corporations can provide in-kind services for the foundation (Saiia et al. 2003). This may include assistance from the legal department, IT services, or the human resources department. These services can be very costly if purchased on the market. However, if the foundation solely relies on the company's will to provide these services and does not allocate sufficient funds to manage contracts on its own, the degree of dependence is stronger than when the foundation can choose its own providers (BDS 2010).

3.4.6 Visibility

From a corporate perspective, strong visibility of the foundation in the public may bring image spillovers that lead to a higher corporate reputation (Westhues and Einwiller 2006). In most cases, the logo and public appearance share some resemblance with the corporate design. The codes, however, demand that the public can clearly differentiate between the two entities (BDS 2010; ACF 2016). Complete independence would mean having distinct logos, whereas high dependence means that there are only minimal changes made. The same applies to the general design of foundations' communication means, such as the webpage, magazines, or any

---

[1] Some foundations from banks are set up as philanthropic service providers for their customers. Overhead is paid by the bank but the money for programs comes from bank clients. This special case is not considered here.

other print material. Another indicator of dependence is whether the foundation is described in a subsection of the corporation, instead of publishing its own annual reports. It also makes a difference if the foundation does have its own physical space or if it is merely an office within the corporation—or even situated within the PR department. In most cases though, corporate foundations hare hosted on company premises (Rey-García et al. 2012).

3.5 An Iterative Research Approach

As shown, the dual relationship between the corporation and the corporate foundation can take various forms. The main variables that determine the relationship are summarized in Table 3.1. Whereas corporation might tend to seek close control over the foundation, the foundation itself may strive for a high degree of independence.

But how do these tensions play out in practice? The upper assumptions are based on a review of the corporate philanthropy literature, the foundation literature, and governance codes, as well as the few empirical studies that exist about corporate foundations. However, none of the empirical studies addresses the question of independence explicitly nor do they take the perspective of the corporate foundation. The literature is biased toward a corporate perspective about the utility of the foundation for the company.

We lack knowledge about the structural relationship of the foundations and their founding companies. As seen above, foundations may benefit from corporate resources but also be exploited by them for reputational reasons. A strong degree of dependence expressed through board control, strict and short-term financing agreements, and strong influence of the CSR department may leave the foundation with little room to maneuver, prohibiting it to play out its supposed advantage of being one of the freest institutions in democracies. From a civic perspective, we may assume that a high degree of independence is what foundations' executives would seek, giving the foundation a strong mandate to concentrate on its mission. From a more market-based perspective though, it would make sense for corporate directors to align the foundation activities. The mission is relevant but mostly when the programs bring benefits to the company. A strong control may be achieved through

Table 3.1 Determinants of the structural relationship between foundation and corporation

Board	Composition, selection, expertise
Staff	Payroll, reporting line, recruitment
Operations	Relation to core business, project selection, connection to CSR
Funding	Main source of income, funding based on corporate profits, length of commitment
Communication/ visibility	Brand similarity, own webpage, location of offices
In-kind	Provision of services

control of the foundation's board by company directors, and as consequence having direct a reporting line of the foundation's executive director to the corporate board. Strict funding agreements may be a tool to ensure the foundation is following the company's interest. How these relationships play out in practice though has yet to be researched. There are hardly any empirical studies about corporate foundations in general, and even less on the governance relationship of the two entities. Theoretical perspectives are also absent, as shown by Renz & Roza in Chap. 2.

In areas of knowledge that lack sound empirical studies as well as strong body of theory, exploratory research approaches are most appropriate (Gerring 2009). A well-established research designed to generate new knowledge are case studies (Eisenhardt and Graebner 2007). Through a combination of different methods and data sources, case studies allow deeper understanding of organizational relations. By triangulating multiple data collection methods, strong constructs and hypotheses can be developed (Eisenhardt 1989). Following these claims, we followed an iterative research approach to shed light on the complex connection between the foundation and the corporation.

In a first step, we conducted eight in-depth case studies. The results were consequently used to develop a set of assumptions that were further tested and refined in the second round of data collection, with 35 corporate foundations using a combination of surveys, interviews, as well as formal and informal discussions of knowledge exchange of corporate foundations in Europe. We followed a sequential selection technique of cases, aiming for variety on the variables identified. Also, we concentrated on Swiss and German foundations, due to reasons of data accessibility and case comparability. In both countries, corporate foundations act under comparably similar legal backgrounds. We also added one foundation from the UK, in order to gain more insights on how stricter regulation may affect corporate foundation activities. In terms of budget, we only looked at foundations that spent more than one million USD per year. Table 3.2 shows the core program areas of the foundations, their annual budget, as well as the core business area of the corporation.

First, we collected all publicly available information (websites, annual reports, program descriptions, media releases, etc.). Then we asked the foundations to send to us a range of documents that were specific to our research interest, such as statutes and internal policies. As a final step, we scheduled interviews with the executive directors of the foundations. The interviews were semi-structured, following 45 questions based on the structural variables identified above.

Our preliminary findings confirmed that foundations with closer alignment to the core business had a more formal, structured, and dependent relationship with the corporation. However, agreements varied considerably on the different variables. We therefore started coding each variable in terms of their degree of dependence. To do so, we used a scale of four categories: D2, very dependent (corporation has full control and decision-making power); D1, relatively dependent (corporation has high influence); I1, relatively independent (corporation has some influence, but foundation is in strong position); I2, very independent (foundation holds most decision-making power, can act independently). To compare cases, we developed visual representations as shown in Fig. 3.1.

Table 3.2 Sample description

Foundation	Foundation program areas	Annual budget in USD	Business area
A	Education (youth, culture)	3.5 million	Bank
B	Reducing the risk of disaster; preparedness, prevention, and prediction	1.6 million	Tobacco
C	Vocational training (within company)	1.4 million	Automobiles
D	To create decent affordable housing for people in need	2.7 million	Mortgage bank
E	Nutrition research	~2 million	Food
F	Smallholder farming, increasing productivity, and developing markets	14.3 million	Seeds/agriculture
G	Sustainable development, education and integration, and health. Post-disaster relief	6.9 million	Commodities
H	Education, integration, and social mobility	5.7 million	Communication technology

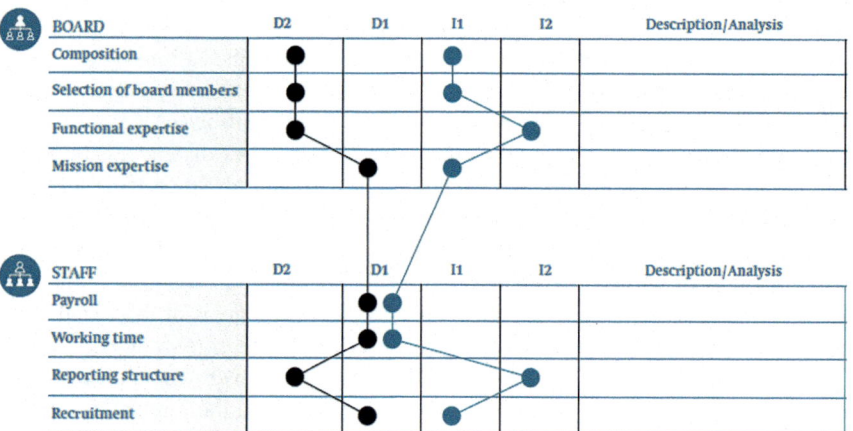

Fig. 3.1 Visualization of independence ratings for two different foundations. The lines represent two different foundations

The visual representation and qualitative data constituted the basis for cross-case comparison. As a result, we could identify four similar clusters according to the relative degree of independence of the foundation (high/low) and the alignment of the foundations' actives with the core business of the corporation (high/low). We formulated some initial descriptions and labels for the clusters. As the results rested only on eight, albeit very strong cases, we searched for opportunities to strengthen the validity of our exploratory research. Such an opportunity arose when one of the authors was invited by a colleague to jointly conduct a workshop at the first

3 Strategic in What Sense? Corporate Foundation Models in Terms of Their…

Knowledge Exchange of Corporate Foundations in Europe.[2] The meeting was organized by the Donors and Foundations Networks in Europe (DAFNE) and the Centre Français des Fonds et Fondations (CFF), and held at the INSEAD business school in Fountainbleau in December 2016. The meeting presented an optimal opportunity for further data collection. During the knowledge exchange, single sessions were organized around the topics of governance, mission alignment, and strategies of corporate foundations. There was a strong overlap with our research questions and the content of the knowledge exchange that allowed the author to gather additional data through participant observation, front- and backstage discussion, as well as private conversations. In the workshop, we used a template similar to the line chart above, explained to participants how to rate each dimension and asked them to assess their own situation on each variable. We could gather 35 valid data sets. Thirty-one of the respondents held the position of the foundation's director, four indicated that they were project managers. The sample was heterogeneous in terms of the country of origin (7 France, 1 Germany, 1 Hungary, 1 Italy, 1 Northern Ireland, 7 Poland, 4 Portugal, 3 Spain, 5 Switzerland, 4 UK, and 1 anonymous). As final task, we asked respondents to position the foundation in the grid we developed from our first research. We also added five cases from the first study (three foundations from the first study were also participants of the exchange). The graphical result of this survey is shown in Fig. 3.2.

A post-evaluation of the data revealed a small and insignificant bias toward the right two quadrants. Some foundation rated themselves more independent in the drawing, as their answers in the survey would have indicated. We adjusted the cases where we found an apparent mismatch. A little less than half of the foundations had no relations with the core business areas. Some chose to position themselves in the

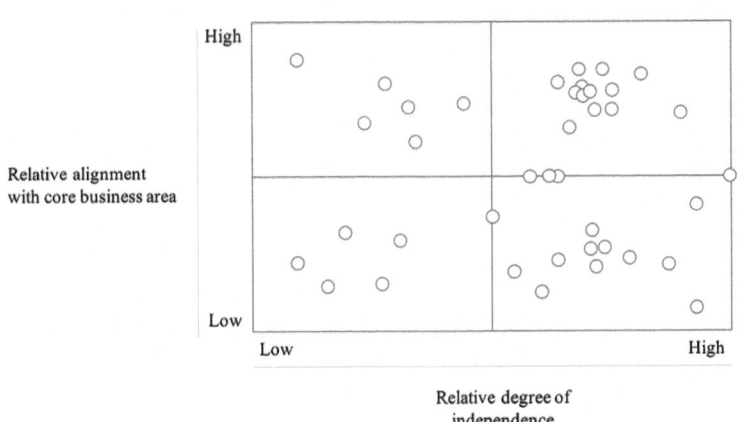

Fig. 3.2 Foundations' clusters

---

[2] The workshop was delivered by the Steffen Bethmann and Lonneke Roza.

middle due to alignment of one funding area with core business area, but no alignment of other program areas.

As the chart shows within each cluster, apparent differences exist. This is the consequence of the heterogeneity of corporate foundations. In most cases the relationship between the two entities has grown over the years without any profound discussion about best governance practices. They could be best described as rag rugs that developed over time. However, the clusters also shared enough commonalities to enhance our initial model descriptions. Before we present these, we provide some observations about the complex relationship that became apparent at the knowledge exchange.

3.6 Findings

Generally, the level of dependency is a major concern of foundation managers. This became very clear during our data collection and discussions with foundation CEOs. As corporate foundations are highly dependent on corporate resources (no foundation had endowments higher than two-year operating expenses), the relationship with the corporation determines the foundation's ability to act. Also, a strong trend could be observed: foundations were shifting toward stronger alignment with the core business of the corporation. We encountered different pull and push factors for this development.

3.6.1 Pull and Push

If the corporation is actively seeking to gain more control of the foundation, we speak of pull factors. Within the group of our respondents, the main reasons for pull factors were economic stressful times for corporations, the change of the company CEO, institutional pressures, as well as foundation success.

The first reason seems the most obvious. Whenever the business was going less well than expected, foundation CEOs felt increased pressure to make the business case for the foundation. They actively had to show that the foundation adds value to the corporation. Funding decisions in the foundation board were evaluated through a business lens by corporate foundation board members. However, two foundation directors also reported situations where no funding cuts for the foundation were made, even when the corporation had to lay off workers. They associated this with strong altruistic values of the CEOs, who genuinely believed in the foundation programs, even when they were not aligned with business objectives.

The second pull factor is related to the activism of new corporate CEOs when they arrive at the top of the corporation. One foundation director who held his position for more than 20 years had experienced five changes at the top of the corporation. With each change, the foundation was integrated more strongly. The reverse process was not reported. It is unlikely that a foundation is granted more independence once the degree of integration is high.

Third, foundation mangers agreed that institutional pressures for stronger integration were high. This was associated with the dominant approach to corporate philanthropy as perceived by corporate managers, as rational behavior leading to normative isomorphism (DiMaggio and Powell 1983). The foundations managers felt that there is a pressure within the business community to follow corporate philanthropy models, which are labeled as strategic as discussed above.

The last factor might be the most surprising one. In two cases, the foundation had run very successful programs that were publicly recognized. The foundations were originally established without any strategic goals from the corporation, but were merely something "that almost every company that went public was doing," as a foundation manager put it. The increasing success led to increasing interest by the corporation. Consequently, the corporation asked the foundation CEO to develop equally strong programs that were in line with the business objectives of the corporation. The foundation in that case fell victim to its own success, losing some of the flexibility it had before.

Additional to these four pull factors, we also encountered push factors where the foundation managers were seeking a closer integration of the foundation. These included staff remunerations, access to company resources, and a need for recognition.

The first factor came out in more informal discussions about which payroll the foundation staff should be on. While the codes clearly argue for a separation of corporate and foundation employees, we found that foundation's CEOs did not feel the same for a simple reason. The salaries and social benefits that corporations offer to executive employees are much higher than in the third sector, in general. One CEO spoke of chocolate jobs being able to do well but being paid like a corporate manager. Thus, entangling the relationship with the corporation was not the priority of some foundation managers.

The second factor had to do with efforts for achieving better access to company resources to enhance program quality. In one specific case, a foundation established by a bank was deliberately trying to build synergies with the corporation. While the bank had a presence on almost every high street, the foundation concentrates on the most vulnerable of society, supporting people in the back street. The foundation was looking for ways these two missions could interact better. The foundation managers therefore tried to build up programs with bank employees, for example, in financial literacy programs. These efforts were also based on the desire to get more recognition for the foundation work. In a sense, some foundation CEOs wanted to feel more strongly valued by the corporation. A need for recognition was felt.

Additional to these pull and push factors, we also made some more general observations. Some foundations' directors explained that it is most difficult to work with middle managers with strong career ambitions. In these cases, the corporate managers would push for stronger alignment. In contrast, senior corporate CEOs or trustees would be more supportive, asking younger proponents of alignment "to relax and not to put a business perspective on everything in life." In some cases, corporate representative on the foundation board "would take off their suits when coming to the foundation, taking a break from harsh corporate live," as a foundation director told us. Instead of numbers, they rather liked to see reports of what good the foundation has done; the highlight being when the foundation CEO brought into the meeting some Saint Bernard rescue dogs from a nonprofit the foundation was funding under their disaster relief program.

Some tensions were mentioned when the company had its own CSR department. Two major issues emerged. First, as CSR is more integrated within the company whenever joint activities were planned, the CSR departments opted toward PR relevant projects. Second, there were some conflicts of ownerships about projects. In some instances, CSR departments and the foundation were literally fighting about project ownership when it was an attractive partner for the foundation and the CSR department alike.

3.6.2 The Four Models

Building on these observations and in-depth analysis of our data we could substantially improve the initial description of the four clusters as shown in Fig. 3.2. In the following, we present these in ideal-typical manner, exaggerating certain characteristics to increase conceptual clarity (Weber 2002). Ideal types often do not exist in their purity. As indicated in the visual chart the boundaries between the quadrants are not clear. However, by providing these types, it is possible to describe four general philanthropy models for corporate foundations, based on their independence and closeness to core business as indicated in Fig. 3.3.

Instrumental Philanthropy

We speak of Instrumental Philanthropy when the relation to the core business of the corporation is high and the foundation's independence is low. The philanthropy style resembles much of the models of shared value put forward by Porter and Kramer (2002) or Saiia et al. (2003). The foundation activities are closely

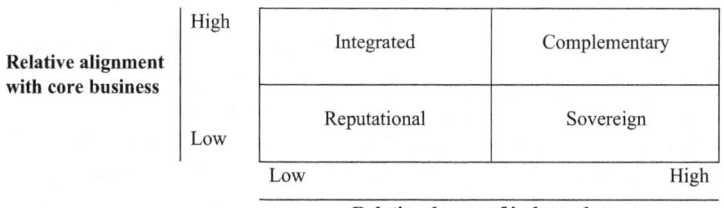

Fig. 3.3 Types of corporate foundations

aligned with the core business area. Philanthropic programs may be specifically used to prepare or develop new markets. The foundations therefore share many structural links with the corporation. Even though there might be external board members as experts invited to the board, the strategic direction is driven by the corporation CEO setting goals for the foundation. Board members are strategically chosen by the corporation. Their task is to find synergies between corporate activities and foundation programs, as well as to signal legitimacy to the public. The model is instrumental in the sense that the foundation has little maneuver to operate outside the boundaries the corporation sets. Despite being a proper legal entity, the foundation is closely linked to the corporation. Often there is an exchange of employees between the corporation and the foundation. External recruiting is not the rule. The foundation is hosted on company premises and there is a strong knowledge exchange among the two entities. Funding depends on the perceived benefit the foundation brings to the corporation. One example of such an approach is a foundation of a mortgage. The foundation advocates for housing loans for low income families and organizes financial literary programs. Another example is a foundation that supports small precommercial farmers in developing countries to increase the productivity of their land. The corporation is a producer of pesticide and genetic seeds for larger and medium farmers. In both cases the foundations' work supports the development of new potential markets and bringing value to underprivileged people as well.

Complementary Philanthropy

When the alignment with the core business is high and the degree of independence from the corporation is high, we speak of Complementary Philanthropy. This model allows the foundation to create its own programs in the area in which the corporation is active, without having to seek potential benefits for the corporation. Positive spillovers may still occur but predominately as side effect of the philanthropy program. Foundations under this model concentrate on social impact rather than thinking of how to create benefits for the corporation. In many aspects, the model is similar to the one above; however, the decisive difference is that strategy development is driven by the foundation executives, focusing on how they can leverage company resources to increase social impact. Funding agreements between the corporation and foundations tend to be long term and rather built on trust in programs than on instrumental objectives. The board may have invited external experts in its rows. Under this model one often can find sophisticated corporate volunteering programs that leverage employee skills for the public good. One example is the foundation of a consultancy firm that gives grants to social entrepreneurs, as well as offering pro bono strategy consultation to small nonprofits. Another example is the foundation of a European drinking water supplier that supports programs for safe and clean water in remote and underdeveloped regions of the world.

Reputational Philanthropy

When there is low or no alignment with the business activities of the corporation and a low degree of independence, we call this Reputational Philanthropy. The interest of the parent company lies predominantly in the communicative opportunities that are created by the foundation's work. It allows the corporation to clearly show its dedication and support toward certain causes. Consequently, the selected causes are usually not controversial and suitable for public relations. The foundation's board is predominantly constituted by corporate managers who frequently appear at foundation-sponsored events. Funding is predominantly tied to corporate success. The foundation is hosted on company premises and has strong relation to the PR department of the firm. The public appearance and corporate design of both institutions are very similar. Sometimes public figures from the arts, sports, academia, or even politicians are part of a sounding board or act as ambassador for the foundation. One example is a foundation established by a bank or insurance supporting the arts. This model is also found when there is a strong CEO in the company that uses the foundation to address his or her own philanthropic interests.

Purpose-Driven Philanthropy

The fourth model is defined by its high independence from the founding company and a low or no relation to the core business of the corporation. We call this model Purpose-Driven Philanthropy as it has the highest potential to fully concentrate on the fulfillment of the foundation objective, as laid down in the deed. In this pattern, the board is primarily staffed with experts. The corporate members of the board ensure that enough resources are available and they support the foundation strategy, independent of its benefit for the corporation. The public is aware of the relation between the foundation and the parent company but perceives the foundation as an independent entity. Staff members are recruited externally. They are most often on the payroll of the foundation and do not report to anybody in the corporation. Funds are not earmarked based on long-term contracts and are independent of company profits. One example is a foundation from a telecommunications company that supports projects in gender equality and children rights. The foundation organizes conferences in symbolic venues with participation of politicians and is perceived to be an important think tank on modernization gaps in society.

3.7 Discussion

The four types show different philanthropy models for corporate foundations based on the closeness of the foundation program areas with the core business area of the corporation, and relative degree of independence of the foundation. These models add to other attempts to structure different management styles of corporate foundations (Bruch and Walter 2005; Urriolagoitia and Vernis 2012; Boesso et al. 2015). They enhance our limited understanding of the complex relationship between the foundation and the corporation. In contrast to other models, the focus is on the unique characteristics of foundations as proper institutions.

Each of the models has its own advantages and disadvantages. None is necessarily better than the other. They have to be seen in the context in which they operate. In one case, dependence might be an asset if it means strong support from the company, in another it might restrict the foundation to choose a more effective path due to corporate restrictions. Also, not each model is applicable for each corporate foundation. Consider one of our cases, a corporate foundation established and financed by a multinational tobacco vendor. An instrumental approach aiming at higher tobacco sales would certainly be questioned in the public. However, when there is little alignment with the business, the foundation might also run into difficulties. The International Red Cross had rejected funds from the same foundation even though they were dedicated to a disaster relief program, as the money from the foundations originates from company funds generated by tobacco sales.

According to the dominate view in the business literature, the instrumental model is the gold standard of corporate philanthropy. If executed with care, it does have high potential to create social and economic value at the same time. However, this model might also raise ethical questions and even lead to legal problems if the programs are too clearly aligned with the business purpose (Aakhus and Bzdak 2012). Risks include reputational damage and losing the tax-exempt status. The reputational model does not run into these risks. However, it seems unnecessary to establish a proper institution for this cause when the same can be better achieved through corporate sponsoring programs. Also, the high dependency on the likes and dislikes of the board chair suggests risks of random philanthropic behavior. One of our favorite stories being the case of "in-flight magazine philanthropy." It was the running joke in one foundation that the corporate CEO, albeit foundation board chair, got his philanthropy ideas from reading airline magazines on long business trips. These ideas would range from saving the dolphins in the Amazon River to bringing the latest African art to be displayed in museums in Zurich.

From a foundation perspective, the complementary and purpose-driven models seem most desirable. A relatively high degree of independence matched with access to corporate expertise and resources seem to build on the core strength of foundations, while adding to potential power of corporations to play an important role in tackling today's pressing challenges. We therefore argue against the position that corporate philanthropy is only strategic when it is closely connected to corporate goals (Porter and Kramer 2002; Saiia et al. 2003). In our view, corporate foundations behave strategically when they have the ability and empowerment to fully concentrate on fulfilling their mission. Of course, by their very nature they must take corporate interests into account; however, mission accomplishment comes first.

With the models presented, we have shown different ways to structure the relationship between the company and the foundation. What we have not touched upon is linking the results with organizational theory. In line with the suggestions of Renz & Roza in Chap. 2, we also see special merit in linking further research with resource dependency theory, neo-institutionalism, and agency theory. Given our findings, we especially see potential in using a resource-based approach, as the corporate foundations are most likely to behave in a way that allows it to secure future funding and access to other company resources. Also, our models may serve as potential departing point of new empirical research. Interesting research questions include: How did purpose-driven foundations resist strong push and pull factors? What processes do corporate foundations follow when planning their strategies? What are the main influencing factors? Are there industry-specific factors that promote one of the models above another? Are instrumental foundations more effective than the other types in creating social impact? How do foundations strategize to get more company resources and remain independent at the same time?

3.8 Conclusion

Corporate foundations are indeed strange animals. Because of their very nature they are subject to different system logics and highly hybrid in nature. On the one hand, it is their duty to focus on effectively fulfilling their philanthropic mission. On the other hand, they are subject to market pressures as it is the duty of their "owners" to focus on profit generation. So far, the literature has followed an implicit view that what is best for business is best for the foundation. Our models question this assumption by taking the view of the corporate foundation. Even if there are strong pull and push factors that lead to less independence and stronger integration of the foundation into the corporation, it should not be forgotten that corporate foundations are first and foremost created to serve a social purpose. They are at their best when they receive the best support possible from the corporation to implement their mission. A company that empowers, rather than restricts the foundations, acts strategically in terms of its philanthropy.

References

Aakhus, M., & Bzdak, M. (2012). Revisiting the role of "shared value" in the business-society relationship. *Business & Professional Ethics Journal, 31*(2), 231–246.
ACF, Association of Charitable Foundations. (2016). *Good practice guide*. London: Association of Charitable Foundations.
Anheier, H. K., & Leat, D. (2006). *Creative philanthropy*. New York: Routledge.
BDS, Bundesverband Deutscher Stiftungen. (2010). *Grundsätze guter Stiftungspraxis*. Berlin: Bundesverband Deutscher Stiftungen.
Bethmann, S., von Schnurbein, G., & Studer, S. (2014). Governance systems of grant-making foundations. *Voluntary Sector Review, 5*(1), 75–95.
Billis, D. (Ed.). (2010). *Hybrid organizations and the third sector: Challenges for practice, theory, and policy*. New York: Palgrave Macmillan.
Bishop, M., & Green, M. (2008). *Philantrocapitalism. How the rich can save the world*. London: Bloomsbury Press.

Boesso, G., Cerbioni, F., Menini, A., & Parbonetti, A. (2015). Philanthropy by decree. *Nonprofit Management & Leadership, 25*(3), 197–213.

Brammer, S., & Millington, A. (2005). Corporate reputation and philanthropy: An empirical analysis. *Journal of Business Ethics, 61*(1), 29–44.

Brest, P., & Harvey, H. (2008). *Money well spent. A strategic plan for smart philanthropy.* New York: Bloomberg Press.

Bruch, H., & Walter, F. (2005). The keys to rethinking corporate philanthropy. *MIT Sloan Management Review, 47*(1), 49–55.

Campbell, D., & Slack, R. (2008). Corporate "philanthropy strategy" and "strategic philanthropy": Some insights from voluntary disclosures in annual reports. *Business & Society, 47*(2), 187–212.

Carroll, A. B. (1991). The pyramid of corporate social responsibility: Toward the moral management of organizational stakeholders. *Business Horizons, 34*(4), 39–48.

Carroll, A. B., & Shabana, K. M. (2010). The business case for corporate social responsibility: A review of concepts, research and practice. *International Journal of Management Reviews, 12*(1), 85–105.

CC, Charity Commission. (2010). *Guide for corporate foundations.* London: Charity Commission.

Ćwik-Obrębowska, N., Pękacka, M., & Tomaszewska, A. (2015). *Standards for corporate foundations.* Warsaw: Polish Donors Forum.

DiMaggio, P. J., & Powell, W. W. (1983). The Iron cage revisited: Institutional isomorphism and collective rationality in organizational fields. *American Sociological Review, 48*(2), 147–160.

Eckhardt, B., Jakob, D., & von Schnurbein, G. (2017). *Der Schweizer Stiftungsreport 2016*, CEPS Forschung und Praxis, Bd. 11,. Basel: CEPS.

Eisenhardt, K. M. (1989). Building theories from case study research. *The Academy of Management Review, 14*(4), 532–550.

Eisenhardt, K.M., Graebner, M.E. (2007): Theory Building From Cases: Opportunities and Challenges. In: The Academy of Management Journal, 50(1), S. 25–32.

Fama, E., & Jensen, M. (1983). Separation of ownership and control. *Journal of Law and Economics, 26*(2), 301–325.

File, K. M., & Prince, R. A. (1998). Cause related marketing and corporate philanthropy in the privately held enterprise. *Journal of Business Ethics, 17*(14), 1529–1539.

Fleishman, J. L. (2007). *The foundation. A great American secret.* New York: Public Affairs.

Foster, M. K., Meinhard, A. G., Berger, I. E., & Krpan, P. (2009). Corporate philanthropy in the Canadian context. *Nonprofit and Voluntary Sector Quarterly, 38*(3), 441–466.

Friedman, M. (1970). *The social responsibility of business is to increase its profits.* The New York Times Magazine, 13 September SM17.

Frooman, J. (1999). Stakeholder influence strategies. *Academy of Management Review, 24*(2), 191–205.

Frumkin, P. (2006). *Strategic giving.* Chicago: The University of Chicago Press.

Gadberg, N., & Fombrun, C. (2006). Corporate citizenship: Creating intangible assets across institutional environments. *Academy of Management Review, 31*(2), 329–346.

Gautier, A., & Pache, A. C. (2015). Research on corporate philanthropy: A review and assessment. *Journal of Business Ethics, 126*(3), 343–369.

Gerring, J. (2009): Case study research. Principles and practices. Cambridge, Mass.: Cambridge University. Press.

Hammack, D. C., & Anheier, H. K. (2013). *A versatile American institution: The changing ideals and realities of philanthropic foundations.* Washington, DC: Brookings Institution Press.

Haski-Leventhal, D., Roza, L., & Meijs, L. C. (2017). Congruence in corporate social responsibility: Connecting the identity and behavior of employers and employees. *Journal of Business Ethics, 143*(1), 35–51.

Kania, J., Kramer, M., & Russel, P. (2014). Strategic philanthropy for a complex world. *Stanford Social Innovation Review, 19*(2), 26–37.

Kasper, G., & Fulton, K. (2006). *The future of corporate philanthropy: A framework for understanding your options*. Cambridge: Monitor Institute.

Kramer, M., Pfitzer, M., & Jestin, K. (2006). Uncommon partners: The power of foundation and corporation collaboration. *Working paper no 21 of the Corporate Social Responsibility Initiative*. Cambridge, MA: John F. Kennedy School of Government, Harvard University.

Lantos, G. P. (2001). The boundaries of strategic corporate social responsibility. *Journal of Consumer Marketing, 18*(7), 595–632.

Leat, D. (2016). Philanthropic foundations. In *Philanthropic foundations, public good and public policy*. London: Palgrave Macmillan.

Liket, K., & Simaens, A. (2015). Battling the devolution in the research on corporate philanthropy. *Journal of Business Ethics, 126*(2), 285–308.

Marquis, C., & Lee, M. (2013). Who is governing whom? Executives, governance, and the structure of generosity in large U.S. firms. *Strategic Management Journal, 34*(4), 483–497.

Morvaridi, B. (2012). Capitalist philanthropy and hegemonic partnerships. *Third World Quarterly, 33*(7), 1191–1210.

Nielsen, W. A. (1972). *The big foundations*. New York: Columbia University Press.

Pedrini, M., & Minciullo, M. (2011). Italian corporate foundations and the challenge of multiple stakeholder interests. *Nonprofit Management & Leadership, 22*(2), 173–197.

Petrovits, C. (2006). Corporate-sponsored foundations and earnings management. *Journal of Accounting and Economics, 41*(3), 335–362.

Porter, M. E., & Kramer, M. R. (1999). Philanthropy's new agenda: Creating value. *Harvard Business Review, 77*, 121–130.

Porter, M. E., & Kramer, M. R. (2002). The competitive advantage of corporate philanthropy. *Harvard Business Review, 80*, 57–68.

Rey-García, M., Martín, C. J., Álvarez, G., & Luis, I. (2012). Assessing and advancing foundation transparency: Corporate foundations as a case study. *The Foundation Review, 4*(3), 77–89.

Saiia, D. H., Carroll, A. B., & Buchholtz, A. K. (2003). Philanthropy as strategy: When corporate charity 'begins at home'. *Business and Society, 42*(2), 169–201.

Sanchez, C. M. (2000). Motives for corporate philanthropy in El Salvador: Altruism and political legitimacy. *Journal of Business Ethics, 27*(4), 363–375.

Smith, C. (1994). The new corporate philanthropy. *Harvard Business Review, 72*(3), 105–114.

Smith, S. R. (2016). Hybridity and philanthropy. In T. Jung, S. D. Phillips, & J. Harrow (Eds.), *The Routledge companion to philanthropy* (pp. 322–333). New York: Routledge.

Sprecher, T., Egger, P., & von Schnurbein, G. (2015). *Swiss Foundation Code 2015. Grundsätze und Empfehlungen für Förderstiftungen*. Foundation Governance, Band 11. Basel: Helbing & Lichtenhahn.

Thorne McAlister, D., & Ferell, L. (2002). The role of strategic philanthropy in marketing strategy. *European Journal of Marketing, 36*(5/6), 689–705.

Urriolagoitia, L., & Vernis, A. (2012). May the economic downturn affect corporate philanthropy? Exploring the contribution trends in Spanish and U.S. companies. *Nonprofit and Voluntary Sector Quarterly, 41*(5), 759–782.

von Schnurbein, G. (2009). Foundations as honest brokers between market, state, and nonprofits through building social capital. *European Management Journal, 28*(6), 413–420.

von Schnurbein, G., Seele, P., & Lock, I. (2016). Rethinking the nexus of CSR and corporate philanthropy. *Social Responsibility Journal, 12*(2), 280–294.

Werbel, J. D., & Carter, S. M. (2002). The CEO's influence on corporate foundation giving. *Journal of Business Ethics, 40*(1), 47–60.

Westhues, M., & Einwiller, S. (2006). Corporate foundations: Their role for corporate social responsibility. *Corporate Reputation Review, 9*(2), 144–153.

Weber, M. (2002). Wirtschaft und gesellschaft: Grundriss der verstehenden Soziologie. Mohr Siebeck.

Steffen Bethmann (Ph.D., University of Heidelberg) is a Research Fellow at the Center for Philanthropy Studies of the University of Basel. He is also an organizational consultant and associated researcher at the Centro de Filantropía y Inversiones Sociales of the University Adolfo Ibañez in Santiago, Chile. His area of expertise is especially in strategies and governance of foundations as well as in the field of social innovation.

Georg von Schnurbein is associate professor for foundation management at the Faculty of Business and Economics and founding director of the Center for Philanthropy Studies (CEPS) at the University of Basel. He serves in several functions in boards in the field of international research on philanthropy and has co-authored the latest edition of the *Swiss Foundation Code* and published in several impact journals such as *Nonprofit & Voluntary Sector Quarterly* and *European Management Journal*. His research interest is on nonprofit governance, financial health of nonprofits, and impact measurement.

Chapter 4
Families, Firms, and Philanthropy: Shareholder Foundation Responses to Competing Goals

Joel Bothello, Arthur Gautier, and Anne-Claire Pache

Abstract In this chapter, we examine an alternate model of corporate foundation that inverts the control and equity relationship between firm and foundation. While other scholars have called them "industrial foundations" or "foundation-owned companies," we label this model the "shareholder foundation" because the founder of the company typically donates all his shares to a newly formed philanthropic foundation, making it full or majority owner of the company. The peculiar features of shareholder foundations give rise to a different set of governance challenges compared with conventional corporate foundations. While there are no a priori trade-offs between the pursuit of profit and public good with this model, it faces institutional complexity as its leaders deal with competing expectations and claims from firm representatives, family members, and philanthropy recipients. Using an inductive case comparison approach of nine shareholder foundations across three countries (Denmark, Germany, and France), we bring to the foreground the impact of the national institutional environment on foundation governance, linking it to the types of decisions that managers will make when facing situations with competing objectives.

Keywords Institutional complexity · Hybrid organizations · Corporate Governance · Shareholder foundations

---

J. Bothello (✉)
The John Molson School of Business, Concordia University, Montréal, QC, Canada
e-mail: joel.bothello@concordia.ca

A. Gautier · A.-C. Pache
ESSEC Business School, Cergy-Pontoise, France

© Springer Nature Switzerland AG 2020
L. Roza et al. (eds.), *Handbook on Corporate Foundations*, Nonprofit and Civil Society Studies, https://doi.org/10.1007/978-3-030-25759-0_4

4.1 Introduction

Corporate-related foundations account for a significant proportion of philanthropic activity and are growing in importance across the world: In the United States alone, these entities account for 3 percent of the foundation population but disburse 9 percent of all grants (Foundation Center 2014). In the UK, 126 corporate foundations are responsible for 18 percent of all corporate giving (The Guardian 2007); in continental Europe, French corporations are overcoming a historical separation between for-profit and welfare activities and establishing foundations at an accelerated pace to match their German counterparts (Bundesverband Deutscher Stiftungen 2016; ADMICAL 2016). As a result of their growth and outsized influence – and catalyzed by the broader development of corporate philanthropy, corporate social responsibility (CSR), and corporate sustainability practices (Matten and Moon 2008; Westhues and Einwiller 2006; Dyllick and Hockerts 2002) – corporate-related foundations have become a major topic of interest in recent years (Porter and Kramer 2002; Gautier and Pache 2015).

Research in this domain has nonetheless remained sparse and been limited by a specific definition of corporate-related foundations. Previous studies have generally conceived of these organizations as distinct, tax-exempt entities that are subsumed under a broader corporate philanthropy initiative; they are created by corporate actors to more systematically serve a particular public-benefit purpose than through alternative means such as one-time donations (Westhues and Einwiller 2006; Werbel and Carter 2002). Within this conceptualization, the corporate foundation figures as a fixed – albeit controlled – component of the overarching philanthropy agenda of a for-profit organization. In corporate governance work, the foundation acts as an agent for the interests – whether altruistic or not – of the principals (i.e., shareholders) with managers operating as intermediaries (Jensen and Meckling 1976; Werbel and Carter 2002). However, because of these parameters set by previous studies, we know little about alternative forms of corporate-related foundations that deviate from this relatively narrow definition.

In this chapter, we attend to this dearth of research by examining an alternate model of corporate foundation that inverts the control and equity relationship between firm and foundation. We label this model the "shareholder foundation" (Prophil 2015). Mainly a Germanic and Scandinavian phenomenon – although growing in other European countries – shareholder foundations are formed when the founder of a family business decides to establish a foundation to which he can subsequently and irreversibly donate his shares, either during his lifetime or posthumously. The newly formed organization is not only completely independent but also typically exercises a majority or full ownership of shares and voting rights in the focal firm, either directly or through a holding entity (Thomsen and Rose 2004; Thomsen 1999; Kronke 1988). The foundation disburses dividends toward a philanthropic cause, in accordance with the personal wishes of the founder, as outlined in a fixed charter. Family members (or those with affective ties to the founder) are generally involved either as participants on governance boards or as minority recipients of income, representing legacy, and heritage interests. Accordingly, in a reversal of typical corporate philanthropy arrangements, the firm is the agent that acts in the interests of the foundation.

The peculiar features of shareholder foundations give rise to a different set of governance challenges compared with conventional corporate foundations, and as such, the model opens new areas of inquiry. Firstly, the shareholder foundation side-steps the contentious issue of motive in contemporary corporate philanthropy research, specifically regarding whether corporate giving is instrumentally practiced to maximize shareholder wealth (i.e., through reputation and legitimacy benefits, which over time may materialize into increased profits) or whether it is genuinely driven by social need (Porter and Kramer 2002; Gautier and Pache 2015; Friedman 2007). Given that the shareholder foundation holds ownership rights over the firm rather than the reverse, wealth maximization within this model is aligned over the long term with service for the public good; even family involvement diminishes over time (Prophil 2015). In other words, the conventional trade-off assumed in mixing for-profit and charitable activities is mitigated, as higher returns provided to shareholder(s) directly improve the foundations ability to pursue its social mission through operation of philanthropic activities and grant disbursement.

However, compared with standard corporate foundations, shareholder foundations are apt to face situations of increased governance complexity stemming from their ownership status. Given that these organizations primarily interact with three sets of stakeholders (family members, business representatives, and philanthropy recipients), shareholder foundations operate in an environment of "institutional complexity," where they must handle multiple competing – and sometimes conflicting – claims on organizational rents and resources by different audiences (Friedland and Alford 1991; Thornton and Ocasio 1999, 2008). Unique challenges thus arise that are unlikely to emerge in standard corporate foundations: regarding decisions of profit allocation by a held firm, for example, how do shareholder foundations balance pressures to plough earnings back into the firm, issue dividends to serve the social mission or disburse profits to family members? In other words, how do they balance the welfare of the firm with the interests of philanthropy recipients and heritage maintenance?

In this chapter, we highlight how shareholder foundations handle the complexity stemming from multiple competing claims. In doing so, we build our arguments upon research into organizations facing similar issues, known as hybrid organizations (Pache and Santos 2010; Battilana and Dorado 2010). These organizations comprise social enterprises or family firms that, like shareholder foundations, manage multiple sets of goals and attend to multiple groups of stakeholders (Billis 2010). In this domain, researchers have highlighted how competing claims are based on prevailing regulatory and normative pressures in the institutional environment (Scott 2014) and explored how hybrid organizations structure their governance to best adapt to audience expectations (Pache and Santos 2010, 2013). We situate our chapter in this stream, indicating that factors from the institutional environment will influence the manner in which shareholder foundations respond to competing claims from different sets of stakeholders.

Specifically, we demonstrate that in shareholder foundations, responses are either constrained or incentivized by the national institutional framework. Using an inductive case comparison approach of nine shareholder foundations across three countries (Denmark, Germany, and France), we find that even in a national context where this new hybrid form is emergent (France), there is a high degree of homogeneity across foundations in terms of responses to institutional complexity. In those countries where the shareholder form is well established and taken-for-granted, there is counterintuitively a high degree of dissimilarity among the sample of firms. We account for this disparity by linking the patterns of response to the influence of the regulative institutions present in each country.

Our study contains not only theoretical significance but also practical implications. Specifically, we bring to the foreground the impact of the institutional environment on foundation governance, linking it to the types of decisions that managers will make when facing situations with competing objectives. In our examination, we outline how foundation managers converge on a pattern of decision-making that is derived less from established norms or governance "best practices," but more so from pressures and opportunities in the regulatory environment. In doing so, we highlight in particular the importance of the legal, political, and, to a certain extent, cultural influences that not only constrain but also enable decision-making for foundation managers.

4.2 Shareholder Foundations: An Overview

The model of shareholder foundations – also anachronistically referred to as "industrial foundations" in corporate governance literature (Thomsen 2006, 2012; Sinani et al. 2008) – is mainly a Germanic and Scandinavian phenomenon. In contrast to the dispersed model of shareholder ownership in Anglo-Saxon countries, this type of corporate governance is characterized by a concentration of firm ownership, with a single nonprofit entity (i.e., the foundation) holding all, a majority, or a blocking minority of equity shares. The foundation may also hold similar proportions of voting rights of the focal firm. Often, but not always, the founder's family retains a minority of shares or voting rights. The foundation disburses the dividends that it receives as a shareholder toward one or more philanthropic causes, in accordance with a charter created by the founder. In this sense, a shareholder foundation features a uniquely amalgamated structure: A not-for-profit organization owning a for-profit firm within a family influence.

In the vast majority of cases, this form of corporate governance is initiated when an entrepreneur makes the decision to bequeath ownership of his company to a newly created, eponymous foundation, in order to ensure the long-term stability of both corporate and philanthropic activities. In many cases, the founder does not have – or lacks confidence in – any apparent heirs; in others, he may wish to avoid inheritance taxes that may dilute ownership over time. However, in all cases, the establishment of a foundation and the endowment with company shares are an irreversible act: The newly formed organization is thus not only a completely independent entity but also permanently exercises significant influence (if not full control) over the focal firm through the holding of voting rights (Thomsen and Rose 2004; Thomsen 1999; Kronke 1988).

Although firms owned by shareholder foundations are present in Germanic countries, they are most prominent in Denmark, accounting for one-sixth of the market capitalization on the Copenhagen Stock Exchange. However, they are conspicuously absent from Anglo-Saxon nations, owing either to legal constraints or cultural illegitimacy: in the United States, for example, legislation dating back to 1969 has constrained the amount of voting stock that a foundation can own in a firm (Thomsen 2006; Hansmann and Thomsen 2013).[1] In the United Kingdom, the model of foundation governance is considered taboo following a series of high-profile governance failures by trusts and foundations in the 1980s (e.g. the Wellcome Trust, the Nuffield Foundation, and the Barings Foundation). Despite this scarcity in the Anglo-Saxon world, firms owned by foundations in continental Europe are observed as performing just as well financially as firms with dispersed ownership – and, indeed, are noted as having more stable long-term performance owing to their ownership structure (Thomsen 1999; Thomsen and Rose 2004). In addition, they provide considerable charitable donations to (mainly national) art, education, and social welfare projects, with an additional and peculiar emphasis on pharmaceutical research and development. Philanthropy causes are generally oriented toward "infrastructure building" which entails support of education, healthcare, and economic development. However, shareholder foundations have also been the subject of criticism by economists, who argue that these entities limit the possibility of market control, effectively immobilizing capital that could be allocated more efficiently elsewhere as Thomsen and Rose (2004, p.346) note, "the 'dead hand' (founder's will) [may be] less fortunate than the 'invisible hand' of the market."

Thus far, three broad motivations have been associated with the usage of shareholder foundations as compared to other forms. The first relates to the idea of "patient capital," where foundation ownership ensures a stable and predictable pattern of governance decisions for the firm, including expectations of long- rather than short-term returns. The second motivation is philanthropic, as shareholder foundations are typically found in countries where firms are perceived to have a social contract with their community and society (Matten and Moon 2008). As such, shareholder foundations are seen as vehicles for "idealized business management [and] custodians for the public interest" (Thomsen and Rose 2004). The last motivation pertains to asset protection, as well as personal and national legacy: The establishment of a foundation is a means to avoid onerous inheritance taxes levied upon succession; this, by extension, prevents diffusion of ownership over time. More importantly, it preserves the legacy of the founder as a philanthropist. In a related vein, such ownership maintains the national status of the firm, preventing acquisition by foreign entities and retaining employment in the region or country.

---

[1] This regulation stems from a concern of foundations being used as tax shelters for firms and their owners, within a broader context of political attack on foundations (Zunz 2012).

Despite their prevalence in many nations outside Anglo-Saxon countries, research on shareholder foundations has been thus far been strikingly scarce. The major exceptions are in historical German and Scandinavian legal literatures (e.g., Kronke 1988) and in contemporary corporate governance research, the latter of which compares the financial outcomes of foundation-owned firms to that of the more common dispersed-ownership corporation (Hansmann and Thomsen 2013; Thomsen 2006; Thomsen and Rose 2004). In this area, research involves investigating whether foundation managers are more incentivized to focus on performance vis-à-vis those under profit-seeking owners (Hansmann and Thomsen 2013). However, the characteristics of foundation governance and structures – outside of their implications for financial performance – have thus far been sparsely explored.

As a result of their unique structure – specifically, the confluence of founder/family heritage, philanthropic mission, and commercial viability – shareholder foundations face inherent conflicts in pursuing their goals. For example, given the dual purpose of ensuring firm longevity as well as philanthropy, how do foundation managers make the trade-off between retaining earnings and disbursing philanthropic funds? How do they ensure philanthropy is not restricted to the "pet cause" of the family and indeed reflects the well-being of society? In addition, given that the third motivation of establishing a foundation is to maintain the founder's vision over time (embodied through the charter), what is the impact of founder and family legacy upon the firm structure and functions? We aim to unpack how the governance of shareholder foundations is structured in order to attend to these three highly different goals. In doing so, we use a theoretical framing of "institutional logics."

4.3 Organizational Responses to Institutional Complexity

Institutions are comprised of socially constructed sets of rules, norms, and expectations that not only create meaning for individuals and prescriptions toward particular goals but also designate the means to achieve them (Friedland and Alford 1991). They provide interpretations for individuals to function in the social world; those institutions that provide compatible prescriptions aggregate into resilient and stable institutional orders that provide a coherent "logic" for individual sense-making (Friedland and Alford 1991; Thornton and Ocasio 2008). For organizations, such institutional orders also prescribe collectively valued outcomes for organizational actors to pursue, as well as the appropriate structures and practices to achieve them. Organizations that comply with prescriptions of logics are seen as legitimate by referent audiences and are thus able to gain resources from the external environment (Lounsbury and Glynn 2001; Suchman 1995).

Yet in many arenas, a multiplicity of institutional orders exert their influence over the behavior and sense-making of individuals and organizations, leading to a situation of "institutional complexity" (Scott 2014; Greenwood et al. 2011). Here, the prescriptions of institutional orders oftentimes prove to be incompatible with one another, leading to competition among logics (Reay and Hinings 2009; Reay 2005;

Pache and Santos 2013). Many types of organization experience this tension: hospitals, universities, publishing houses, or churches (Reay and Hinings 2009; cf. Kodeih and Greenwood 2013; Thornton and Ocasio 1999). The competition between logics also leads to a variety of responses on the part of organizational actors, from acquiescence and compromise to defiance and manipulation (Pache and Santos 2010). In this manner, the literature on institutional complexity opens a window to explore how actors express agency in reacting to competing institutional demands.

Despite the presence of institutional complexity in various types of organizations, the competition among logics becomes manifest most acutely in hybrid organizations (Battilana and Dorado 2010; Pache and Santos 2013). Unlike the other types of organization listed above, hybrids are those that *consciously* incorporate elements from different institutional logics, with the express purpose of pursuing multiple goals (Battilana and Dorado 2010). Such organizations are thus inherently arenas of contradiction, where the multiple competing and conflicting institutional demands become apparent in various facets, whether relating to governance, operational activities or human resource practices. Existing research in this area has mainly focused on social enterprises, investigating the organizational activities, structures, and processes by which these hybrids respond to the dual prescriptions derived from business and philanthropy logics (Battilana and Lee 2014; Battilana and Dorado 2010; Pache and Santos 2013; Jay 2013). Within this field, the existing work on responses to hybridity has been largely confined to exploring the dynamics between two competing sets of institutional demands and, furthermore, has been limited to explanations at the individual or organizational level, with little examination of the macro-level influences on organizational responses (Greenwood et al. 2011; Pache and Santos 2013).

In their review of institutional complexity, Greenwood et al. (2011) outline that we lack an understanding of how structures of authority influence the discretion of organizations to respond to institutional complexity. In order to systematically compare fields, the authors call for "more substantive and dynamic accounts of their institutional infrastructures … with a view to understanding how differences between them affect the organizational experience of complexity" (Greenwood et al. 2011, p.339). However, this call assumes that such enforcement mechanisms are transnational in character; while this may hold true for normative authorities like professional associations or certification agencies, structures of coercive authority are much more likely to be located at the national level. This distinction is important as coercive authority differs according to country rather than field. Thus, any comprehensive explanation of varying responses to complexity would need to account for idiosyncratic arrangement of domestic institutions – particularly the regulative institutions that produce coercive pressures on organizations (Scott 2014).

In this chapter, we use institutional complexity to account for how resource allocations are patterned in shareholder foundations and identify how domestic institutions influence these patterns. Using a cross-national case comparison of shareholder foundations in Denmark, Germany, and France, we examine how these organizations respond to the competing demands imposed upon them by business, philanthropic, and legacy logics. In accounting for response similarities within – and differences across – countries, we demonstrate that institutional arrangements at the national level play a role by either constraining or incentivizing hybrid organizations to adopt a particular pattern of responses. More specifically, we examine whether these institutions allow for variation in the management of different logics within hybrid organizations or whether they converge toward a homogeneous arrangement.

4.4 Methodology

Our methodology for this project is a comparative case study of nine foundations (see Tables 4.2, 4.3, and 4.4) spread across three countries. Data collection involved two stages: The first was an exploratory study, where the aim was to identify the main decision-making areas or structural features of these organizations where competition between logic prescriptions would become manifest. To this end, we used existing reports and academic studies conducted on foundations (Herrmann and Franke 2002; Kronke 1988; Prophil 2015; Thomsen 2006, 2012), in addition to press articles on the topic.

In doing so, we uncovered three main dimensions of shareholder foundations where the tensions between the three logics would become salient. Table 4.1 outlines the different prescriptions of the family, philanthropic, and business logics according to three dimensions of board composition, profit allocation, and donation targets. In order to compare the influence of the three logics, we used different measures for each dimension: For board composition, we elected to evaluate the presence of a legacy logic through the percentage of board members with affective ties to the founder (family members or close friends), the philanthropic logic through percentage of civil society/state representatives (given their role in advising the board about philanthropy/ensuring fulfilment of "public utility"), and the business logic through percentage of firm representatives. Board members could have multiple "labels" applied to them, for example, in a situation where a family member also served as a firm executive. Profit allocation was the second dimension where the logics of legacy, philanthropy, and business would compete; we thus opted to

Table 4.1 Logic prescriptions on three salient dimensions for shareholder foundations

	Legacy logic	Philanthropic logic	Business logic
Board composition	Family members/friends of founder	State representatives External/Civil society experts	Firm/business executives
Influence over profit allocation	Disbursement to family (directly or through dividends)	Dividends to shareholders (notably foundation)	Reinvestment of profit/debt relief
Targets for donations	Family/founder values	Social/public needs	Core business related

Table 4.2 Selected foundations studied in Denmark

Name (founded)	Causes supported	Grants disbursed in 2016	Foundation's equity valuation in 2016	% of firm equity owned	% of firm voting rights
Novo Nordisk Foundation (1989)	R&D in medical, biotechnological and natural sciences	€565 million	€33.6 billion total, incl. €27 billion for Novo A/S	Novo Nordisk: 27.5% Novozymes: 25.5%	Novo Nordisk: 75% Novozymes: 70.9%
Carlsberg Foundation (1884)	R&D in natural sciences, social sciences and humanities for socially beneficial projects	€30 million	€4.2 billion total	30%	75%
Hempel Foundation (1948)	Education of children in need, sustainable technologies, social inclusion	€16 million	€715 million total	100%	100%

Table 4.3 Selected foundations studied in Germany

Name (founded)	Causes supported	Grants disbursed in 2016	Foundation's equity valuation in 2016	% of firm equity owned	% of firm voting rights
Robert Bosch Foundation (1964)	Health, science, society, education, international relations.	€109 million	€33.2 billion	92%	0%
Bertelsmann Foundation (1977)	Economic opportunities, education, society, culture, democracy, health	€55.6 million	€1.04 billion	69%	0%
Carl Zeiss Foundation (1889)	Education and research in the natural and engineering sciences	~€10 million	€1.4 billion	Zeiss: 100% Schott: 100%	Zeiss: 100% Schott: 100%

compare, respectively, the percentage of profit that was disbursed to family members (in many cases, as a line item in the cash flow statement), the dividends issued to shareholders (contributing to the philanthropic activities of the foundation) and finally the amount reinvested back in the company as retained earnings.[2]

---

[2] In some of the cases studied, the drafting of dividend policy occurred at the firm level rather than at the foundation level; nonetheless, in all of those firms, dividend policy had to be approved by the foundation or by its representative body.

Table 4.4 Selected foundations studied in France

Name (founded)	Causes supported	Grants disbursed in 2016	Foundation's equity valuation in 2016	% of firm equity owned	% of firm voting rights
Pierre Fabre Foundation (1999)	Access to training for health workers in developing countries	€4.2 million	Unknown	86%	0%
Christophe and Rodolphe Mérieux Foundation (2001)	Research against infectious diseases, scientific education, and training, access to care in developing countries	€0.5 million	€150 million	32%	0%
Varenne Foundation (1988)	Promotion of journalism, media education, freedom of the press, research.	Unknown	€23 million	36%	0%

For the third dimension of donation targets, we differentiated expenditures on causes: those with a direct link to the core business of the held firm were labelled as representative of a business logic. Others were deemed as "pet causes" of the founder, based on biographical information indicating more of a legacy logic in philanthropy. On occasion though, targets could have multiple labels representing both family and business logics. Any remaining expenditures that could not be categorized in either way were labelled as philanthropic targets, more directly related to a social/public need than driven by family or commercial interests.

In the second stage, we used an Eisenhardt-style multiple case comparison approach (Eisenhardt 1989) to understand how shareholder foundations responded to organizational prescriptions designated by the three institutional logics. The study firstly covered Denmark and Germany, two countries where these types of foundation have a well-established history dating back to the nineteenth century. As a counterpoint, we also explored foundations in France, where the shareholder foundation form was only recently introduced into law over the last decade. In each country, three representative foundations were selected for examination, which we describe in the following section. Given the considerable variety among foundations with respect to size, age, industry, ownership, and governance structure, we considered that the most appropriate strategy was to select highly dissimilar cases for the sample in each country and then identify points of congruence among them. In this manner, we took advantage of the inherent heterogeneity of the sample to identify similarities that could then be assigned as "typical" responses of the shareholder foundation form within each country. From there, we proceeded to compare these characteristic responses to those of foundations in other countries.

Our primary source of data was semi-structured interviews, beginning in Copenhagen, Denmark, in mid-January 2015 and continuing in Germany and France over the subsequent months, coming to a close in December 2015. We conducted 20 interviews with executive managers of the foundations and the owned firms but also with representatives of philanthropic recipients and external experts. We also supplemented our interviews with secondary documentation, based on reports and texts produced by the foundations, the held firms and the beneficiaries. In addition, given the cross-national approach, we compiled material that outlined the tax and legal codes of each country, supplemented by other sources describing the economic and cultural institutions present in each. These contextual factors are important in explaining the similarities of responses within countries as well as the variation across countries.

4.4.1 Selection of Foundations

Denmark Shareholder foundations in Denmark have played a prominent role in shaping the social and economic landscape of the country since at least the late nineteenth century. In 2013, 1350 shareholder foundations accounted for 10 percent of the capital in the Danish economy, with iconic firms like Maersk, Lego, and Carlsberg featuring foundation ownership (Thomsen 2006, 2012). Among the listing of the largest firms on the Copenhagen Stock Exchange (CSE), 68% of the market capitalization is accounted for by foundation shareholding. Their philanthropic activities are no less prolific: Each year, shareholder foundations provide an estimated €800 million toward causes deemed as "general interest."

Within Denmark, we selected three shareholder foundations considered to be leaders within their respective industries: Novo Nordisk Foundation, Carlsberg Foundation, and Hempel Foundation. These foundations varied along multiple dimensions, specifically pertaining to size, industry, age, and funding structure. More details are provided in Table 4.2.

Germany Similar to Denmark, the shareholder foundation form has a long history in Germany, with some foundations being established as early as the mid-nineteenth century. Although there are a number of other very similar models of foundation (*Stiftung* in German), those classified as shareholder foundations (*Unternehmensverbundene Stiftungen*) range between 500 and 1000 in the country,[3] with a third of this number being created since the year 2000.

As in Denmark, the endowment of a shareholder foundation is irreversible, with the charter providing binding guidelines for foundation managers to follow. Unlike their Danish counterparts, however, German shareholder foundations have no obligation to contribute to the public interest, except if they wish to benefit from a favorable tax arrangement. In fact, many smaller shareholder foundations have the sole purpose of protecting founder and family interests. Within Germany, we selected

---

[3] A precise account of the number of shareholder foundations is difficult, given that many of them are protective about their activities and organization.

three of the most prominent foundations for inclusion in our study, focusing on those with demonstrated philanthropic activities (see Table 4.3).

France In contrast to Denmark and Germany, the shareholder foundation form is very much at a nascent stage in France, as it has only been legally permissible in France for a decade. On August 5, 2005, a law was passed allowing foundations deemed as "public utility" by the French council of the state the right to own shares in commercial enterprises. The law was intended to give the heirless entrepreneur Pierre Fabre, owner of the eponymous French pharmaceutical firm, the option to bequeath all his shares to a foundation. Fabre and his advisers played a key role in influencing the legal change. Currently, there are only three shareholder foundations owning firms in France.[4] Nonetheless, these three organizations are highly different in terms of legacy, structure, and industry and, as such, form a sample that is consistent in terms of heterogeneity with those of Denmark and Germany (see Table 4.4).

4.5 Findings

4.5.1 Regulative Institutions in "Mature" Arenas: Incentives for Diverse Organizational Responses

Denmark Table 4.5 illustrates how the three foundations in our Danish sample are congruent only with respect to the treatment of the legacy logic. Across the dimensions of board composition and influence over profit allocation, there is a distinct lack of inclusion of family members on any corporate governance bodies – whether in the foundation itself, in intermediary holding entities or in subsidiaries.

Out of the three countries examined, this lack of a legacy logic is unique to Denmark. It can be attributed to a particular Danish foundation regulation stating that, subsequent to the formation of the charter, any family members after the first unborn generation can be neither involved in the governance of the foundation nor a recipient of philanthropy. This explains why two of the Danish foundations in our sample, Novo Nordisk and Carlsberg, do not disburse profits from activities of the firm to family members or heirs, either as dividends or as payments to minority interests on the cash flow statements. Here, the similarity in suppression of the legacy logic prescription is the result of a regulatory constraint.

While this accounts for the lack of family representation in two firms, it does not explain why there is no family involvement in the Hempel foundation, given that Hempel's children were alive at the time of data collection. However, a member of the executive board of Hempel A/S provided the reason for this idiosyncratic feature:

---

[4] As of 2017, a fourth foundation named Avril, owner of the agricultural conglomerate SofiProtéol, has been established. Yet this case slightly differs from the three cited above, as the family dimension is absent – the company regroups several cooperatives in which farmers are coinvestors.

Table 4.5 Organizational responses to logic prescriptions in Denmark

	Foundation	Legacy logic	Philanthropic logic	Business logic
Board composition[a]	Novo Nordisk	0	Low	High
	Carlsberg	0	High	Medium
	Hempel	0	Low	High
Influence over profit allocation[b]	Novo Nordisk	0	Medium	Medium
	Carlsberg	0	Medium	Medium
	Hempel	0	High	Low
Targets for donation[c]	Novo Nordisk	Medium	Medium	Medium
	Carlsberg	Medium	Medium	~0
	Hempel	Medium	Medium	Medium

[a]Percentage of board members representing each logic: <25% (Low); 25–49% (Med); 50–74% (Med); 75–100% (High)
[b]Percentage of profit allocated according to each logic prescription: <25% (low); 25–49% (med); 50–74% (med); 75–100% (high)
[c]Percentage of foundation budget dedicated to each logic prescription: <25% (low); 25–49% (med); 50–74% (med); 75–100% (high)

> In 1976, [J.C. Hempel's] son was impatient for his father to leave because the son wanted to do different things ... Mr. Hempel realized that the danger was the son wanted money, and would have eventually put the company on the stock exchange. His son tried to make a coup, and can you believe that out of 33 managers, no one would warn Hempel of what's coming? Hempel called everyone together, fired them all – including his son. He changed company bylaws, so that none of the family could be in the system. Dividends were paid until the third generation, and it's since been transformed into a small fixed amount. No more natural inheritors, no more physical shareholders.

The above anecdote of founder J. C. Hempel disinheriting his son also reveals that Danish laws regarding inheritance do not grant any privileges to family members, unlike the laws in France, for example. As such, they can be perceived as enabling deviation from the prescriptions of the legacy logic.

Interestingly enough, despite the lack of adherence to the legacy logic prescription in both board composition and profit allocation for the three cases, the "pet causes" of the founder are still salient across all three cases and remarkably similar in nature: For all three foundations, this expenditure entailed support and investment in Danish museums – the Natural History Museum, the Ny Carlsberg Glyptotek, and the J. C. Hempel glass museum for Novo Nordisk, Carlsberg, and Hempel, respectively. The reason for this pertains to the sanctity of the foundation charter: Although there is some flexibility in adapting the stipulations, the core of the charter (notably the core philanthropic causes) cannot be changed. The Novo Nordisk foundation, for example, must pursue a cause related to insulin – a pet cause of the founder – which is why the foundation established the Natural History

Museum as a celebration of the ninetieth anniversary of the discovery of Insulin. Although rare, a foundation can intentionally break the charter for an unrelated cause and then appeal to the state to overlook the transgression. As Professor Anker Brink Lund from Copenhagen Business School noted in an interview: "for [shareholder] foundations, it's easier to beg for forgiveness than ask for permission" (A. Brink Lund, 2015, "personal communication", 19 October).

On the other hand, there is no discernible pattern regarding the representation of corporate interests and philanthropic/state interests on the board, as well as in how profits are distributed between the two parties. Given the long history of the shareholder foundation form in this country – and indeed, of two of the three firms in our sample – the relative variety in organizational responses across these two dimensions seems to be an unusual outcome. However, according to our interviewees, these differences can be accounted for by Danish regulatory institutions that permit such diversity to occur. The first regulation relates to a requirement imposed upon foundations to pursue a mission oriented toward the common good. With respect to board composition, there are no requirements regarding the involvement of those representing corporate or philanthropic interests, outside of the constraints outlined by the founder in the foundation charter. The variety of charter stipulations explain why the boards of the Hempel and Novo Nordisk foundations have a majority of members with corporate experience, while Carlsberg features a majority of scientists.

Germany Germany, another country with a well-established history of foundation governance, has an even more heterogeneous pattern of responses compared to Denmark. Table 4.6 illustrates how diverse the German foundations are with respect to their responses to logic prescriptions across all three categories. However, this diversity can also be linked to the flexibility of the regulatory institutions of the German state and, more acutely, the decentralization of authority to different *lander* (provinces). Firstly, unlike in Denmark, there is no legal restriction on family involvement in corporate governance affairs. As a German non-profit expert – and

Table 4.6 Organizational responses to logic prescriptions in Germany

	Foundation	Family logic	Philanthropic logic	Business logic
Board composition	Bosch	Medium	Low	Medium
	Bertelsmann	Medium	Medium	Medium
	Carl Zeiss	~ 0	Low	High
Influence over profit allocation	Bosch	Low	Low	High
	Bertelsmann	Low	Low	Medium
	Carl Zeiss	0	~ Medium	Medium
Targets for donation	Bosch	Medium	Medium	Medium
	Bertelsmann	Medium	Medium	Medium[a]
	Carl Zeiss	~ 0	Medium	Medium

[a]Portfolio includes a CSR program

former manager in the Bertelsmann foundation – informed us: "There is no legal regulation on [involvement]. You can create this structure how you like: It can be all family members, it can be all corporate members." Accordingly, the family represents a strong presence on the boards of the Bosch and Bertelsmann foundations – in addition to those of the holding entities and the firms themselves – while, in contrast, there are few remnants of family legacy in the Zeiss foundation.

Similarly, with respect to the profit allocation, family members are recipients either of dividends or direct payments from the firm, with Bosch and Bertelsmann family members holding 7% and 19.1% of shares of the firms, respectively. Further compounding the diversity of responses across the three cases is the lack of a requirement that foundations pursue a goal toward the common good. A foundation in Germany can serve the interests of the family with almost no philanthropic purpose. This general lack of legal requirements for foundations, especially regarding board composition and disbursement of profit, helps to account for the diversity of responses.

As in Denmark, the only regulatory constraints are with respect to maintaining the wishes of the founder as outlined in the charter. However, in Germany, adherence to the charter is a much more stringent affair and is particularly visible regarding targets for donations. Here, the donation activities of Bosch and Bertelsmann have significant overlap with the core interests of the founder and his family, specifically with respect to the development of international relations. The outlier in this case, Carl Zeiss, features little to no involvement of family, either on the board, as a recipient or with respect to the founder's wishes. However, this is peculiarity of history: As an East German firm, the majority of Zeiss was commandeered by the Soviets following World War II, with the foundation being dismantled and reconstructed only in 1991. Nonetheless, the three foundations produce similar responses in the case of philanthropic activities (i.e. those that are not related to pet causes of the family nor to causes overlapping with the business of the firm). Except for Carl Zeiss, this is an artifact of a strict adherence to the charter; unlike in Denmark, there is no flexibility in the charter, as remarked upon by an informant from Bertelsmann:

> Once established, [the charter] is inflexible. It's not a structure that you can change, especially in the form of the civil law foundation, according to our civil code… you can only enlarge the scope of the foundation. If you contribute to the endowment you could add one or two new focus areas or increase the scope but you can't change the existing purpose or reduce the scope or abandon an existing mission because the foundation in our view as an irreversible gift.

Thus, the rigidity of the charter imposes upon the foundation a timeless obligation to pursue pet causes of the founder as well as philanthropic purposes, regardless of whether they are obsolete or not; this may help to explain why philanthropic and legacy logics are so highly represented in this dimension. However, this is the sole dimension of similarity among the German foundations; they otherwise remain highly distinct from each other.

4.5.2 Regulative Institutions in an "Emergent" Arena: Convergence Pressure Toward Homogeneous Organizational Responses

Table 4.7 outlines the responses to the prescriptions of the three logics of France, a country where the current shareholder foundation form has only been present for a decade. In such an emergent context for this type of hybrid organization, a wide variety of responses would be expected from the shareholder foundations in our study. Counterintuitively, there is a considerable amount of homogeneity, which we explain as potentially being the result of convergence pressures brought about by French regulatory institutions.

Firstly, all the foundations feature a comparable percentage (between 25% and 35%) of board members that have affective ties with the founder, whether through kinship or friendship. Secondly, they feature strong representation (between 40% and 50%) by "qualified persons" relating to service of the public interest; these are generally academics, scientists, non-profit managers, and ministry officials. While the former percentage can be attributed to the infancy of the shareholder foundation form in France – and thus the presence of foundation stewards with personal ties to the founder – the latter is the result of a regulatory imposition upon recognized public utility foundations in France to include qualified persons on the board. In addition, the combination of strong affective ties and regulation would not explain why, by itself, there is such a minority in the third category of business representatives. We attribute this low presence to the historical separation of for-profit and charitable activities in France, currently enshrined in the welfare state (Gautier 2018).

In addition, the expenditures on grants and programs have striking parallels across the three French foundations. Personal causes of the founder that are inscribed in the charter are given significant weighting in terms of expenditure; for example, almost half of expenditure of Pierre Fabre is on fighting sickle-cell anemia, one of his personal causes. Across all three, the majority of expenditure is on social causes closely related to the core business of the firms. For Pierre Fabre and Mérieux, this

Table 4.7 Organizational responses to logic prescriptions in France

	Foundation	Family logic	Philanthropic logic	Business logic
Board composition	Pierre Fabre	Medium	Medium	Low
	Mérieux	Medium	Medium	Low
	Varenne	Medium	Medium	Low
Influence over profit allocation	Pierre Fabre	0	Low	Medium
	Mérieux	Medium	Medium	Medium
	Varenne	0	Medium	~ Medium
Targets for donation	Pierre Fabre	Medium	~ 0	High
	Mérieux	Medium	~ 0	High
	Varenne	Medium	~ 0	High

entails delivery of pharmaceutical products and healthcare services in developing countries, while in the case of the Varenne Foundation, it involves supporting causes related to the promotion of the journalistic profession. The expenditure of these three foundations toward the founder's pet causes or on corporate-related causes accounts for nearly all spending on philanthropy, leaving little for other unrelated causes.

4.6 Discussion: Domestic Institutional Influence on Logic Responses

In our findings, we sought to demonstrate how domestic institutional arrangements could account for the similarities and differences in organizational responses to institutional complexity. Using the hybrid organizational form of shareholder foundations, we illustrated how organizational actors in Denmark, Germany, and France responded to a multiplicity of logics (in this case, family, commercial, and philanthropic logics). We proposed that regulative institutions in each country played a role in either constraining or incentivizing a certain type of response to an institutional prescription.

Researchers have previously indicated that the maturity of a field matters in settling institutional complexity; specifically, they note that "in more mature fields, institutional complexity at the organizational level will be lower and more predictable [compared to emergent fields], because tensions between competing logics have been worked out at the field level" (Greenwood et al. 2011). However, as our cases demonstrate, predictability of institutional demands is rather disconnected from the pattern of responses emerging across the populations of organizations. As the cases in Denmark and Germany illustrate, the maturity of a field with established "truces" among the different logics provides little prediction for the types of responses that will be taken at the level of organizations. In contrast, those organizations within an emergent field – in our case France – displayed remarkable similarity despite the nascent nature of the shareholder foundation form in that country.

We proposed that divergence and convergence of organizational responses to institutional complexity do not only relate to organizational features or individual sense-making. They also relate to institutions – specifically regulatory institutions – that exert pressure at the field or national level. While we do not directly draw causality between the establishment of a particular institution and a convergent response pattern, we do affirm that institutions, in aggregate, form a "bundle of causal patterns" (Skocpol and Somers 1980); these can at least partially account for organizational responses to institutional complexity. Future research could extend the examination of the field- or national-level institutions by examining the role played by normative and cultural-cognitive elements – for example, national culture (Scott 2014).

Although our context is based on a specific context of a foundation exercising voting rights and ownership over a for-profit enterprise, the findings can be interpreted more broadly: our findings demonstrate that responses to myriad competing institutional claims – equally present in conventional corporate foundations – can be shaped by domestic institutional arrangements. Thus, in terms of practical implications, our examination highlights how managers of foundations handle competing objectives by acquiescing to, or taking advantage of, regulatory constraints in their institutional environment.

However, our study also reveals the role of more strategic choices. The cases of Pierre Fabre and Varenne in France illustrate how appeals and lobbying efforts by founders for "special cases" can set a regulatory precedent, thus changing the regulatory landscape to favor the creation of new forms of foundation. Similarly, in Denmark representatives from the largest shareholder foundations have formed an "advisory committee" oriented toward providing feedback to the Danish state on potential foundation legislation. In this sense, foundation managers are not only recipients but also producers of the "rules of the game" that affect the legitimacy of their organizations.

References

ADMICAL. (2016). *Le mécénat d'entreprise en France Résultats complets de l'enquête Admical – CSA*. ADMICAL: Paris, France.

Battilana, J., & Dorado, S. (2010). Building sustainable hybrid organizations: The case of commercial microfinance organizations. *Academy of Management Journal, 53*(6), 1419–1440.

Battilana, J., & Lee, M. (2014). Advancing research on hybrid organizing – Insights from the study of social enterprises. *The Academy of Management Annals, 8*(1), 397–441.

Billis, D. (2010). *Hybrid organizations and the third sector: Challenges for practice, theory and policy*. New York, NY: Palgrave Macmillan.

Bundesverband Deutscher Stiftungen. (2016). Stiftungserrichtungen 1990–2015 in Deutschland. *Statistiken 2016*. Available at: https://www.stiftungen.org/no_cache/de/forschung-statistik/statistiken.html. Accessed 12 Nov 2016.

Dyllick, T., & Hockerts, K. (2002). Beyond the business case for corporate sustainability. *Business Strategy and the Environment, 11*(2), 130–141.

Eisenhardt, K. M. (1989). Building theories from case study research. *The Academy of Management Review, 14*(4), 532–550.

Foundation Center. (2014). Foundation stats. Available at: data.foundationcenter.org. Accessed 31 Oct 2016.

Friedland, R., & Alford, R. R. (1991). Bringing society back in: Symbols, practices and institutional contradictions. In P. J. DiMaggio & W. W. Powell (Eds.), *The new institutionalism in organizational analysis*. Chicago, IL: University of Chicago Press.

Friedman, M. (2007). The social responsibility of business is to increase its profits. In W. C. Zimmerli, M. Holzinger, & K. Richter (Eds.), *Corporate ethics and corporate governance* (pp. 173–178). Berlin, Germany: Springer Berlin Heidelberg.

Gautier, A. (2018). Historically contested concepts: A conceptual history of philanthropy in France, 1712–1914. *Theory and Society*. https://doi.org/10.1007/s11186-018-09335-z.

Gautier, A., & Pache, A. C. (2015). Research on corporate philanthropy: A review and assessment. *Journal of Business Ethics, 126*(3), 343–369.

Greenwood, R., et al. (2011). Institutional complexity and organizational responses. *The Academy of Management Annals, 5*(1), 317–371.

Hansmann, H., & Thomsen, S. (2013). Managerial distance and virtual ownership: The governance of industrial foundations. *ECGI—Finance Working Paper, 372*

Herrmann, M., & Franke, G. (2002). Performance and policy of foundation-owned firms in Germany. *European Financial Management, 8*(3), 261–279.

Jay, J. (2013). Navigating paradox as a mechanism of change and innovation in hybrid organizations. *Academy of Management Journal, 56*(1), 137–159.

Jensen, M. C., & Meckling, W. H. (1976). Theory of the firm: Managerial behavior, agency costs and ownership structure. *Journal of Financial Economics, 3*(4), 305–360.

Kodeih, F., & Greenwood, R. (2013). Responding to institutional complexity: The role of identity. *Organization Studies, 35*(1), 7–39.

Kronke, H. (1988). *Stiftungstypus und Unternehmensträgerstiftung: Eine rechtsvergleichende Untersuchung*. Tubingen, Germany: Mohr Siebeck.

Lounsbury, M., & Glynn, M. A. (2001). Cultural entrepreneurship: Stories, legitimacy, and the acquisition of resources. *Strategic Management Journal, 22*(6–7), 545–564.

Matten, D., & Moon, J. (2008). "Implicit" and "Explicit" CSR: A conceptual framework for a comparative understanding of corporate social responsibility. *Academy of Management Review, 33*(2), 404–424.

Pache, A. C., & Santos, F. M. (2010). When worlds collide: The internal dynamics of organizational responses. *Academy of Management Review, 35*(3), 455–476.

Pache, A. C., & Santos, F. (2013). Inside the hybrid organization: Selective coupling as a response to competing institutional logics. *Academy of Management Journal, 56*(4), 972–1001.

Porter, M. E., & Kramer, M. R. (2002). The competitive advantage of corporate philanthropy. *Harvard Business Review, 80*(12), 56–68. 133.

Prophil. (2015). *Les fondations actionnaires: Premiere etude Europeene*. Paris, France.

Reay, T. (2005). The recomposition of an organizational field: Health care in Alberta. *Organization Studies, 26*(3), 351–384.

Reay, T., & Hinings, C. R. (2009). Managing the rivalry of competing institutional logics. *Organization Studies, 30*(6), 629–652.

Scott, W. R. (2014). *Institutions and organizations: Ideas, interests, and identities*. Thousand Oaks, CA: SAGE Publications.

Sinani, E., et al. (2008). Corporate governance in Scandinavia: Comparing networks and formal institutions. *European Management Review, 5*(1), 27–40.

Skocpol, T., & Somers, M. (1980). The uses of comparative history in macrosocial inquiry. *Comparative Studies in Society and History, 22*(2), 174–197.

Suchman, M. C. (1995). Managing legitimacy: Strategic and institutional approaches. *Academy of Management Review, 20*(3), 571–610.

The Guardian. (2007). Q&A What is a corporate foundation? *The Guardian*. Available at: https://www.theguardian.com/society/2007/jun/13/societyguardian.societyguardian2

Thomsen, S. (1999). Corporate ownership by industrial foundations. *European Journal of Law and Economics, 7*, 117–136.

Thomsen, S. (2006). Industrial foundations. In K. Prewitt et al. (Eds.), *Legitimacy of philanthropic foundations: United States and European perspectives* (pp. 236–251). New York, NY: The Russell Sage Foundation.

Thomsen, S. (2012). *What do we know (and not know) about industrial foundations*. Center for Corporate Governance: Copenhagen, Denmark.

Thomsen, S., & Rose, C. (2004). Foundation ownership and financial performance: Do companies need owners? *European Journal of Law and Economics, 18*(3), 343–364.

Thornton, P. H., & Ocasio, W. (1999). Institutional logics and the historical contingency of power in organizations: Executive succession in the higher education publishing industry, 1958–1990. *American Journal of Sociology, 105*(3), 801–843.

Thornton, P.H., & Ocasio, W. (2008). Institutional logics. In *The sage handbook of organizational institutionalism* (pp. 99–129), Thousand Oaks, CA: SAGE Publications.

Werbel, J. D., & Carter, S. M. (2002). The CEO's influence on corporate foundation giving. *Journal of Business Ethics, 40*(1), 47–60.

Westhues, M., & Einwiller, S. (2006). Corporate foundations: Their role for corporate social responsibility. *Corporate Reputation Review, 9*(2), 144–153.

Zunz, O. (2012). *Philanthropy in America: A history*. Princeton, NJ: Princeton University Press.

Joel Bothello is an Assistant Professor in Management at the John Molson School of Business at Concordia University in Montréal. His research is based in organizational theory, and he investigates how alternate organizational forms (shareholder foundations, social enterprises, etc.) respond to stakeholder and institutional demands compared with traditional corporations. He has published several articles on sustainability and organizational theory.

Arthur Gautier is an Assistant Professor at ESSEC Business School, France, and the Executive Director of the ESSEC Philanthropy Chair. His research focuses on individual and corporate philanthropy, using institutional and historical perspectives. He has authored several books, articles, and reports on these topics.

Anne-Claire Pache is Chaired Professor in Philanthropy at ESSEC Business School, France. Her research focuses on the growth process of social enterprises and their relations with their institutional environments. She has authored several books and articles in top-tier management journals.

Part II
Corporate Foundations in Various Institutional Contexts

Chapter 5
Corporate Foundations in Europe

Theresa Gehringer and Georg von Schnurbein

Abstract The objective is to give an insight into what we know and what we don't know about the current situation of corporate foundations. While we are able to put the spotlight on several interesting developments in the field, this chapter cannot give a comprehensive overview of corporate foundations in all European foundation sectors. As corporate foundations are predominantly public-benefit foundations and part of the nonprofit sector, it is useful to start with a brief overview of the European foundation sector. This may help to gain a first impression of the sector and possibly allows conclusions about the number and country-specific nature of corporate foundations, at least to give some indication about the environment corporate foundations act in.

Keywords Corporate foundations · Mix methods · Case study · Europe · Institutional environment

5.1 Introduction

The European foundation sector has grown rapidly in number and size since the 1980s (Anheier 2018). In Germany, for example, more than 70% of the foundations were founded after the reunification in 1990 (Bundesverband Deutscher Stiftungen 2014). In Spain, 70.65% of the active foundations existing in 2014 were less than 20 years old (Rubio Guerrero and SosvillaRivero 2016). The European foundation sector is thus mainly characterized by a young and vital foundation population (Observatoire de la Fondation de France and CERPhi 2015).

Nevertheless, valid and reliable data on foundations on a European level are limited. There are several attempts to close this knowledge gap, but still only a few studies focus particularly on corporate foundations. A comprehensive picture of *the*

T. Gehringer (✉) · G. von Schnurbein
Center for Philanthropy Studies (CEPS), University of Basel, Basel, Switzerland
e-mail: theresa.gehringer@unibas.ch

European corporate foundation sector is still not possible as the few existing studies differ in methodology and are either incomplete or outdated. Figures that allow further conclusions on the different models or functioning of corporate foundations in Europe are non-existent.

The aim of this chapter is to give an overview of the current empirical and theoretical knowledge of corporate foundations in Europe and to highlight the diversity of practical operation of corporate foundations throughout Europe. While we are able to put the spotlight on several interesting cases in the field, this paper, however, cannot give a comprehensive overview of corporate foundations in all European foundation sectors.

5.2 Foundations in Europe

5.2.1 Structure and Method

Due to limited data on corporate foundations in Europe, the issue of corporate foundations is tackled from three different perspectives. The aim is to provide a first explorative overview of the status of corporate foundations in Europe to enable an accurate understanding of this phenomenon. As corporate foundations are predominantly public-benefit organizations and thus part of the nonprofit sector, it is useful to start with an aggregated view on the European foundation sector. This helps to gain a first impression of the environment corporate foundations operate in and possibly allows drawing conclusions about their number and country-specific nature. In Sect. 5.3, we present the results from our qualitative survey that was conducted with experts on corporate foundations from academia and representatives of national foundation associations. Due to the limited information, we continue with a micro-level perspective in Sect. 5.4 by using the case of the Vodafone Foundation.

Although this approach has several limitations, for example, a low response rate of the interviewed experts, the combined perspectives offer a first insight into the status quo of corporate foundations in Europe that will extend our understanding of these types of organizations.

For the first perspective, we sent out an open-ended questionnaire with 14 questions to researchers from universities and research centres in 20 European countries in October 2016. These institutions are considered having a current research focus on corporate foundations and an overarching point of view of the country-specific foundation sector. As there are only a few academic experts in this field within Europe, we chose purposive sampling as an appropriate and effective method. This sampling method is used for non-random selections where the researcher wants to ensure the presence of specific individuals in the final sample as he is already aware of the cases with the unique and important knowledge on the research topic that is needed (Robinson 2014). We received nine useable answers either with a full survey or with references to helpful reports or both.

For the second perspective, due to the low rate of survey responses, we sent an adapted open-ended questionnaire with five questions to representatives from national foundation associations in a first round in December 2016 and a second round in May 2017. Representatives of national foundation associations are specialists in their country's foundation sector and provide expert knowledge from a practical point of view. We contacted 18 national associations and received seven useable answers (a complete list of all interview partners can be found in the Appendix A). Combined, the two sources allow us to examine corporate foundations in 16 European countries.

For the third perspective, we used the Vodafone Foundation as case study to illustrate on a cross-country level the diverse approaches and settings of corporate foundations in Europe. The Vodafone Foundation was chosen as a case study for several reasons. First, Vodafone foundations exist in 14 European countries and thus offer a broad coverage of the continent. Second, by restricting the cases to one company, we limit the influence of different business cultures and processes that might also influence the role and functioning of a corporate foundation. Finally, Vodafone Group Plc offers the same services in all countries, for example telecommunications. These are highly standardized services, similar in all countries. Thus, the connection of foundation activities to the core business is expected to remain the same in all countries and does not change due to different products or company positioning. Data collection was conducted through desktop research on corporate websites and other open Internet sources. Additionally, representatives of the Vodafone foundations in the UK and Germany were contacted for further information. The following information was collected for all 14 European Vodafone foundations: logo and mission statement, year of establishment, size of the board and annual payout for 2015. For further analysis on the situation of the economic situation in each country, we collected public social spending in % of GDP and public social expenses per capita in EUR for 2015.

5.2.2 Public-Benefit Foundations in Europe

Foundation law in Europe varies from country to country and sets the context in which the respective foundation sectors evolve. In addition, the diverse cultural and fiscal tradition of the European member states and the fact that there is no harmonization of foundation law within Europe contribute to substantial differences in the definition of foundations across the continent (EFC 2015). Legal requirements concern the purposes of foundations, their minimum amount of assets for establishment, their governing organs, financial and activity reports and so forth (EFC 2015). Despite this great variety of legal definitions, Hopt et al. (2009, p.13–14) found a solution through a functional definition that combines the lowest common characteristics of a foundation. According to them, a foundation is "an independent organization (generally with its own legal personality), which has no formal membership, is supervised by a State supervisory authority, and serves a public benefit purpose (in some Member States: any lawful purpose), for which a founder has provided an endowment, and determined the foundation's purpose and statutes". Additionally, while having no members or shareholders, they distribute their financial resources for cultural, educational, social, religious or other public-benefit purposes. The character of their activities is either grant-making, by providing financial assistance, or operational, by carrying out their own programs (McGill 2016).

Corporate foundations are an integral part of every foundation sector and are among all other public-benefit foundations. The founding body is the company, which provides funds to the foundation either once, at the time of establishment, or in annual payments. Corporate foundations are frequently mentioned concurrent with corporate philanthropy or corporate citizenship, which will be discussed later.

There are different estimates of the total number of foundations, depending on which countries are included in the sample. On one hand, these differences exist due to the inclusion or exclusion of Russia, Turkey, Eastern European countries (such as Estonia, Latvia and Lithuania) and European microstates (such as Malta and Liechtenstein). On the other hand, some countries do not have reliable figures on the exact number of public-benefit foundations, as in the case of Denmark. There are around 1300 industrial foundations and 10,000 non-industrial foundations in Denmark. However, there is no information available whether they have a general charitable purpose, and/or are directly involved in commercial activities, or solely support the founding family (Steen et al. 2015). Since exact information is missing, Denmark is not included in our total number of public-benefit foundations. The same calculation problems apply to corporate foundations, as shown in Sect. 5.4.

Our findings from 25 European countries indicate that there are 152,057 registered public-benefit foundations in Europe (DAFNE 2017; ERNOP 2017a; McGill 2016; Observatoire de la Fondation de France and CERPhi 2015; Mernier and Xhauflair 2017; Rubio Guerrero and SosvillaRivero 2016; Strečanský 2012). The range extends from 35 foundations in Ireland to 20,200 foundations in Germany. The countries with the largest foundation sectors are Germany, Poland, Hungary and Sweden.

An earlier study from October 2016 estimates 147,932 registered public-benefit foundations in 24 European countries (McGill 2016). Other data compiled by the Observatoire de la Fondation de France and CERPhi (2015) estimates 106,630 foundations in ten European countries.

Comparing the current figures with previous studies (Table 5.1) shows a steady development and ongoing increase in the number of foundations, as already mentioned in the introduction. For example, an analysis from 2005, using data from before the fifth enlargement of the European Union, estimated 62,000 foundations in the old 15 member states (EFC 2005). Another study from 2009 that already included 25 European countries found that the number of foundations in Europe ranges between 90,000 and 110,000 foundations (Hopt et al. 2009).

Reasons for the rapid development and the growth in economic importance are manifold but are either of contextual nature or due to internal transformations in the foundation sector (Anheier 2018; Toepler 2018). First, demographic factors caused the transfer of private money from the post-war generation to the next generation

Table 5.1 Comparison of key variables over time

	Number of countries studied	Number of public-benefit foundations	Pool of assets (EUR billion)	Expenditure (EUR billion)
Own study (2017)	25	152,057	1856.14 (17 of 25)	59.9 (19 of 25)
McGill (2016)	24[a]	147,932	511.3 (17 of 24)[b]	59.5 (18 of 24)[c]
Observatoire de la Fondation de France and CERPhi (2015)	10[d]	106,630	426 (10 of 10)	53.7 (10 of 10)
Hopt et al. (2009) (data from 2005)	25[e]	90,000–110,000	1000 (25 of 25)	153 (25 of 25)
EFC (2005) (data from 1999–2003)	15[f]	62,000	174.3 (8 of 15)	51.0 (9 of 15)

[a]Austria, Belgium, Bulgaria, Croatia, Czech Republic, Finland, France, Germany, Hungary, Ireland, Italy, Liechtenstein, Netherlands, Norway, Poland, Portugal, Russia, Slovak Republic, Spain, Sweden, Switzerland, Turkey, Ukraine, the UK
[b]Data were not available for the following six countries: Belgium, Bulgaria, Croatia, Poland, Portugal and Ukraine.
[c]Data were not available for the following seven countries: Austria, Bulgaria, Croatia, Hungary, Liechtenstein, Russia and Ukraine.
[d]Belgium, France, Germany, Italy, Netherlands, Poland, Spain, Sweden, Switzerland, the UK.
[e]Austria, Belgium, Cyprus, Czech Republic, Denmark, Estonia, Finland, France, Germany, Greece, Hungary, Ireland, Italy, Latvia, Lithuania, Malta, Netherlands, Poland, Portugal, Romania, Slovakia, Slovenia, Spain, Sweden, the UK.
[f]Austria, Belgium, Denmark, Finland, France, Germany, Greece, Ireland, Italy, Luxembourg, Netherlands, Portugal, Spain, Sweden and the UK.

and increasingly to organizations with a public benefit. Second, this development and the overall giving behaviour in society are pushed due to escalating levels of private wealth and general levels of prosperity (Schuyt 2010). Third, as a consequence of the economic recession in 2008/2009, many governments cut down their public funding in areas such as arts and culture. Private initiatives such as foundations became more needed and important partners for topics where the state couldn't invest effectively or sufficiently (Observatoire de la Fondation de France and CERPhi 2015; von Schnurbein and Perez 2018). Fourth, the national foundation laws or taxation laws were reformed in almost every Central and East European member state in the past years, for example, in Belgium in 2002 and Spain in 1994 and 2003, allowing more flexibility and including fewer requirements (Hopt et al. 2009). Another reason for the growth may be a higher awareness of citizenship and self-responsibility, which resulted in individuals and enterprises considering setting up a foundation, making an endowment, or a donation (Schuyt 2010). This is especially true as the philanthropic commitment of companies became popular and promoted next to a company's corporate social responsibility (CSR) activities, although the relation of both concepts is highly debated in academia (von Schnurbein et al. 2016). One result of this development was the establishment of many corporate foundations in recent years. In addition, the foundation sector itself has become aware of its role in society and has actively begun to promote its work in the public, which may have led to further establishments of foundations, or at least an increase in donations (Observatoire de la Fondation de France and CERPhi 2015).

Looking at the rise of CSR and corporate philanthropy in Europe more closely, one sees that the concepts are strongly supported on a European level. The European Commission, the European Parliament, business networks and other stakeholder jointly promote a European CSR agenda (European Commission 2011). Other than the EU authorities, several organizations, such as the business network CSR Europe, work in particular on the improvement of the European CSR strategy (CSR Europe n.d.) and in general on the long-term implementation of the CSR agenda and on the promotion of companies' positive impact on society through their CSR activities.

A first conclusion of this section is that data on foundations are scarce and hardly comparable. However, apart from this limitation, it becomes clear that foundations are of great importance in society and are a relevant phenomenon in Europe. In addition, if these trends are replicated in the corporate social responsibility sphere, then corporate philanthropy and corporate giving through foundations as strategic commitment by businesses play an increasingly important role with a noticeable impact on society.

How do we expect this to have an influence on corporate foundations? Since corporate foundations are in the majority of countries' public-benefit foundations and part of the foundation sector, the four indicators may give a hint which approximate figures can be expected with regard to corporate foundations. For example, Germany is one of the countries with the highest number of public-benefit foundations. We could assume therefore that it's among those countries with the highest number of corporate foundations. A comparison will be given in the following section.

5.3 Corporate Foundations in Europe

Some studies exist on a global level, such as the one by corporate citizenship (CC 2016), which explored the different strategies of corporate foundations in delivering long-term social impact by using a survey of 70 individuals representing corporate foundations from more than 20 countries around the world. However, the study does not allow a focused view on just the corporate foundations in Europe.

A study by European Research Network on Philanthropy (ERNOP) gives at least some indication about corporate giving, either directly or through a foundation, in 20 European countries. Lower bound estimations indicate that corporations contributed about USD 24,600 million to charitable purposes in 2013. This represents a share of 25% of the total amount donated of about USD 99,300 million by households, corporations, foundations and charity lotteries (ERNOP 2017b). Another study that investigated foundations in ten[1] European countries discovered

---

[1] Belgium, France, Germany, Italy, Netherlands, Poland, Spain, Sweden, Switzerland and the UK.

that individuals and families are the most prevalent type of founders that set up a foundation. Companies as founders seem especially active in France and Spain where they account for 25% and 16% of the total number of founders. In Belgium, however, only 1% of the founders are companies (Observatoire de la Fondation de France and CERPhi 2015).

If national foundation associations look into this topic, they mostly provide basic information on the number and size of corporate foundations. The Polish Donors Forum, for example, has now published a report on corporate foundations in Poland for the third time in a row (previous studies took place in 2007 and 2012). According to the latest report, Poland has a total of 189 corporate foundations, of which 74 participated in an online survey and ten in qualitative interviews. The study gives information on funding areas, beneficiaries, finances as well as employment and volunteering (Polish Donors Forum 2017). Other notable but occasional studies were conducted in France (EY and Les entreprises pour la Cité 2016) and Spain (Fundación PricewaterhouseCoopers 2016).

5.3.1 Numerical Overview

The received responses of the country-specific experts made it possible to compile the following table with figures on corporate foundations for 16 European countries. Although we are focusing on a limited number of organizations, some of the corporate foundations are both large and relevant. The numbers are based on those corporate foundations that are generally known, as in the case Latvia and Liechtenstein, or those that took part in a study, as in the case of Belgium (Mernier and Xhauflair 2017), missing out foundations from small or medium size companies that are less visible in the public. The number of corporate foundations is therefore in most countries a rough estimation and a lower bound of the actual values (Table 5.2).

The case of Austria is one of the exemplary countries, where the general framework of the foundation sector significantly determines the existence of corporate foundations. Most of the 3310 foundations are private foundations in order to prevent a breaking up in course of a generational transfer of a company. Public-benefit foundations are not very common – only 701 exist – and therefore also charitable corporate foundations are rare. According to the Austrian expert, the 60–70 existing corporate foundations are mainly from the banking and insurance sector and are hardly present in the public perception. Among NPOs, they are regarded as companies, rather than non-profit organizations. Similar to Denmark, there are several foundations that are strategic owners of a business and next to their prime concern of asset preservation major funders of science, art and the social sector. Well known are the "Erste Stiftung" and the 34 regional "Sparkassestiftungen" which are the major shareholders of the "Erste Bank" and the "Sparkassen" banks, which donated USD 24 million in 2015 for charitable causes (Fundraising Verband Austria 2016).

The same applies for Slovakia, where the majority of corporate foundations were established between 2004 and 2008 after the introduction of a 2% tax assignation

Table 5.2 Comparison of public-benefit and corporate foundations

	Number of public-benefit foundations (PbF)	Number of corporate foundations
Austria	(2014 total) 3310 (2014 PbF) 701	(2017) 60–70
Belgium	(2015 total) 1751 (2015 PbF) 573	(2015) 6–x
Denmark	–	(2016, FoBs) 1320 (2016, FoBs with public-benefit purpose) ~ 600–700
France	(2016 total) 4759[a] (2016 PbF) 2506	(2016, corporate foundations) 360 ("fondation sous égide") 116 ("reconnues d'utilité publique") 34 (endowment funds) 207
Germany	(2015) 20,200	(2011) 100–300
Hungary	(2016) 15,995	(2012) 50–1500
Ireland	(2016) 35	(2016) 6
Italy	(2013) 6220	(2016) 44
Latvia		(2016) 7–x
Liechtenstein	(2014) 1239	(2017) 5–x
Netherlands	(2013) 7500	(2016) 75–100
Poland	(2015) 18,135	(2017) 189
Slovak Republic	(2010) 426	(2011) 85
Spain	(2013 total) 14,196 (2013 active) 8866	1000 (~11% of total active foundations)
Switzerland	(2016) 13,172	(2017) 160–200
UK	(2013) 12,400	(2013) 140

[a]The figure includes an unknown number of state foundations

mechanism. The Slovak tax law provided corporate taxpayers the possibility to donate 2% of their taxes to any eligible non-profit organization or civic association in the country. As a consequence, especially large companies founded a corporate foundation and assigned their 2% tax to them. In 2010 six of the top ten recipients of 2% tax funds were apparently corporate foundations. In 2014, even 12 corporate foundations were among the top 20 recipients. The mechanism, however, was subject to several adjustments, so today companies may designate 2% of their income tax if their donations from profits exceed 0.5% of the tax. If that is not the case, the percentage drops from a 2% to a 1% level of corporate tax designation (Blaščák 2016; Strečanský 2012).

In the case of France, the number of foundations with the legal status of a corporate foundation amounted to 360 in 2016. In addition, a number of other foundations have to be counted which have another legal status but are nevertheless founded by a company. These include 116 "fondation sous égide" (foundations under aegis), 34 foundations "reconnues d'utilité publique" (recognized for public utility) and 207 endowment funds. In total, 20% of all foundations in France are considered to be corporate foundations (EY and Les entreprises pour la Cité 2016).

Based on the information of the Danish expert, most companies in Denmark do philanthropy as part of their CSR or marketing activities, for example sponsorship, and not by setting up a formal foundation. Denmark has a long tradition of foundation-owned businesses (FoBs), also called industrial or shareholder foundations, where a philanthropic foundation is endowed with either a majority or full voting rights of the founding company. Today 1320 foundations of this kind are officially registered; about half of them use their dividends to supplement their business activities with public-benefit purposes. However, Denmark is home to major corporations such as Maersk, Lego, and Novo Nordisk. In the case of Maersk, the A.P. Møller Foundation supports various charitable causes and owns more than 50% of the voting share in the company A.P. Møller – Mærsk A/S, one of Denmark's leading transport and logistics companies (AP Møller and Wife Chastine MC-Kinney Møller's Fund for General Purposes 2017).

5.3.2 Finances

The expenditure and pool of assets of corporate foundations has not been analysed so far, with the exception of three countries – France, Spain and Poland. One possible reason for the missing data, according to the experts, might be the fact that they are funded in many different ways. Most of the foundations are funded on a 1–3-year basis through investment income on assets given by the company, regular donations by the company, an endowment linked to the company, money donated by the company's employees or customers and donations of in-kind gifts. Getting a full picture of the total expenditures of corporate foundations is similarly impossible as they often have no mandatory reporting requirements on their cash giving.

The first exception is a study that analysed 70 company-created foundations (65) and endowment funds (5) in France (EY and Les entreprises pour la Cité 2016). According to the findings, the annual average budgets add up to USD 1.4 million, which is an increase of 7% since 2014. Thirty-four percent of the analysed corporate foundations thereby have a budget of more than USD 1.1 million, 22% have a budget between USD 1.1 million and 570.000, 30% between USD 110.000 to 570.000 and 14% have less than USD 110.000 at their disposal (EY and Les entreprises pour la Cité 2016). The second available study examined the 133 most relevant corporate foundations in Spain estimating that about 1000 exist (Fundación PricewaterhouseCoopers 2016). The sum of their budgets is more than 1 billion Euros per year, which is equivalent to 0.1% of the Spanish GDP. Fifty-four percent of these foundations also manage voluntary activities of employees of the companies. If the volunteer hours and thus the economic impact of the companies would be included in this amount, the relevance of the foundations would be even greater. Interestingly, there is a large budget concentration in the sense that the biggest five corporate foundations account for 75% of the budget invested. The report therefore assumes that there is a direct link between the size of the corporation and the likelihood of having a foundation due to two reasons: First, 75% of the corporations in the Spanish stock exchange have a foundation; second, among those 75%, it seems the larger the corporation, the larger the likelihood of having a foundation. The third existing study on the finances of corporate foundations in Poland shows that the average budget of 69 foundations in 2016 was USD 200.000. Funds provided by the founding company are the most important source of budget for the foundations. In the case of half of the foundation, funds from the founder constitute at least 80% of the total annual budget. In every third foundation, donations from the founder cover at least 95% of the organization's annual budget. Donations from employees of the founding company are less common, although slightly more than every fourth foundation receives this support. However, their overall importance is small as they constitute only 1% of the corporate foundation's budget (Polish Donors Forum 2017).

5.3.3 Legal Models and the Relation of Corporate Foundations to Civil Society

No study looked at the legal and fiscal framework for corporate giving or corporate foundations in particular, but there is one study we can refer to that analysed the regulatory and tax conditions for charitable giving in 193 countries on the globe (Quick et al. 2014). One of their key findings is that 77% of 177 analysed UN member states offer some form of incentive for companies to donate money. Looking on a continental level, 88% of the countries in Europe offer tax incentives for corporate giving. Interestingly, Norway is the only European country that offers tax incentives for individual donors but not for corporate ones. The relationship between the availability of tax incentives and the proportion of donated money is not clear, according to the study, but one could assume at least an enabling environment for philanthropic giving if tax incentives are in place.

In most countries, the legal status of corporate foundations is the same as for public-benefit foundations if their mission is dedicated to the public good. An interesting exception is Ireland where the legal status of a corporate foundation is normally considered a company limited by guarantee with charitable status; thus, all usual corporate laws apply in addition to compliance with charity regulation. As corporate foundations are counted among the group of public-benefit foundations, some national foundation associations published guidelines and recommendations explicitly for corporate foundations that pay attention to the special situation and needs of corporate foundations. Among them are the national foundation associations of Germany (Bundesverband Deutscher Stiftungen 2016), Poland (Polish Donors Forum 2015) and the UK (ACF and Ellis, F. 2010, 2016; Charity Commission for England and Wales 2009). These are intended to apply supplementary to general recommendations such as the Swiss Foundation Code that offers generally applicable principles of good governance practice for public-benefit foundations. As the first of its kind in Europe, the Swiss Foundation Code offers detailed guidance on the topics of the establishment of foundations, their organization, management and supervision as well as on finance and investment policy for grant-making foundations, based on three main principles and 29 recommendations (Sprecher et al. 2016).

From a scientific perspective, there are different drivers which explain variability in good governance practices by foundations. A study by Rey-Garcia et al. (2012) looks into this topic and proposes a tool that contains six variables, for instance self-regulation, societal pressure caused by scandals and so forth, for assessing accountability and transparency of corporate foundations. By discussing the framework in the context of the Spanish foundation sector, they try to explain variations across different institutional settings and over time.

In the view of our experts, there are different modes of how corporate foundations see themselves in relation to civil society and the economic sector. Some consider themselves as a part of the non-profit landscape and work independently of the company alongside other foundations and non-profit organizations on a national or international level. These are more aware of their civil society identity. Others see themselves rather on the intersection of market and civil society, as they are closely linked to the company on several levels, for example regarding their own mission, funding and infrastructure, but have their own purpose. Some consider themselves as part of the company despite their separate legal status. These are more aware of their market identity. While both identities are always present, their weighting leads to different modes of corporate foundations. By taking the case of a Danish corporate foundation, Herlin and Pedersen (2013) conducted a study on the role of corporate foundations in relation to cross-sector partnerships, for example nongovernmental organizations. Their findings offer interesting insights on the role of corporate foundations and their actual potential for building bridges and enabling collaborative action between both civil society and the economic sector.

5.3.4 *Public Perception*

The general public perception of corporate foundations is problematic, according to the experts surveyed, even if this subgroup is relatively small compared to the total number of public-benefit foundations in most countries. This is the case because only a few corporate foundations actively communicate with the general public. For example, the Lloyds Bank Foundation for England and Wales and the Vodafone Foundation in the UK are extremely well-known and highly valued for their grant-making programs. Others still seem to avoid wider publicity and communicate only within the foundation sector or their very specific beneficiary group. For example, the Erste Foundation and the Velux Foundation are highly respected by the third sector in Hungary but hardly known by the public. Additionally, differences in the public perception or in a foundation's reputation are often more influenced by the reputation of their corporate founder than by the performance and achievements of the foundation itself.

5.3.5 Main Activities

The interviewees consider the activities of corporate foundations to be mainly grant-making. This is particularly the case in Ireland, Italy, Poland and the UK. Other interviewees suggest that their country's foundations to have both grant-making programs and own operational activities in play. This is particularly true for the countries Denmark, Hungary and the Netherlands.

The involvement of corporate resources for in-kind giving, for example skills, technology, etc., is on the advance. Particularly corporate volunteering is becoming more popular. This is the case for Ireland, Italy and even more for the Netherlands, where most corporate foundations already have extensive volunteering programs for the employees of the founding company or are in the process of establishing them. Payroll giving programs also seem to become popular as companies realize that they can contribute to the employees' meaningfulness and find new ways to contribute to solving societal problems. Organizing and managing volunteer projects distinguish these foundations from traditional grant-making foundations that solely distribute their financial means. The most popular causes corporate foundations support are very similar to the issues that the majority of public-benefit foundations addresses in each respective country. For example, in France these are education, social action towards disadvantaged and professional integration; in Hungary corporate foundations fund education, health and social issues; in the UK they fund education, community/social welfare and children and young people; in Switzerland social affairs, arts and culture and last education are the main funding areas. In Poland, at least half of the corporate foundations are involved in education and upbringing or health prevention and social assistance. It can be assumed that the activities of some corporate foundations are in line with the business and CSR strategies of the founding company and are used for reputational purposes or brand building by the founding company. In the case of Poland, 36% of the surveyed foundations stated that they were active in the same subject area as their funding company (Polish Donors Forum 2017). This view has been also reiterated by Purtschert et al. (2007) in the case of Switzerland, where many corporate foundations use their support for business-related activities such as training and research in a more strategic way. Often, corporate foundations serve as a corporate communication tool for the founding company to increase the company's involvement in society.

5.3.6 Trends

According to the responses of the interviewed experts from academia and national associations, any trends applying to the foundation sector in general affect corporate foundations in the same way. The relationship to the founding company (including issues of independence and integration) and best practice in employee engagement are the topics which are nowadays increasingly debated with regard to corporate foundations. Other topics such as impact measurement, the process of finding beneficiaries, evaluation, reporting and capacity problems regarding staff are as relevant to corporate foundations as they are to any other public-benefit foundation.

5.4 Case Study Vodafone Foundations

In this section, we use a unique case study to compare the role of corporate foundations in different European countries. As previously shown, the information on corporate foundations in European countries is scarce, and comparative analysis is difficult. Thus, we concentrate on the foundations of one company in order to analyse differences among these foundations in terms of governance, objectives, payouts and economic importance. Vodafone Group Plc has organized its social engagement on a global level with 27 foundations of which 14 are based in European countries. Applying the theory of social origins (Anheier and Salamon 1998) explained below, we seek to understand the influence of the societal and political environment on the structure and activities of corporate foundations in Europe.

5.4.1 The Social Origins Theory

Based on a comparative study of non-profit sectors worldwide, Anheier and Salamon (1998) developed the social origins theory. The idea of social origin addresses the emergence and complexity of social phenomena as result of institutional choices and complex interrelationships within societies (Esping-Andersen 1990). Thus, the roles and importance of non-profits can be explained through the society they are active in and the driving social forces. Anheier and Salamon (1998) distinguished four different types of non-profit regimes by two key dimensions. The first key dimension covers the extent of government social welfare spending; the second captures the scale of the non-profit sector. The liberal model, with low government social welfare spending and a relatively large non-profit sector, describes a society with a preference for voluntary approaches instead of public welfare securities. Driving social forces are middle class elements that keep traditional elite and working-class movements low. The social-democratic model is the opposite model to the first one. Welfare securities are delivered by the government and covered by high taxes. According to the social origin theory, working-class movements have an effective political power. As a consequence, the non-profit sector is limited to supportive activities, especially in the social services. In the corporatist model, state and non-profit sector work closely together. Social welfare protections are organized in joint processes and through joint decision making. Finally, the statist model describes a dominant state in many policy areas. However, low social welfare protections do not transform into private action through non-profits and, as a consequence, both forms of activities remain limited.

The four models have been discussed in many studies and the classification of specific countries was contested by different authors. In the following, we build on the original work by Anheier and Salamon (1998) and a very recent analysis by Einolf (2015) on the categorization of non-profit sectors (Table 5.3).

5.4.2 Case Description

Vodafone Group Plc is one of the largest global telecommunication companies with activities in 81 countries on four continents reaching 462 million users. The first corporate foundation with the mission to "connecting for good" was established in UK in 1989, the home country of Vodafone Group Plc. As of 2016, Vodafone Group Plc has 27 corporate foundations globally, of which 14 are located in European countries (Vodafone Group Plc 2016). Table 5.4 summarizes the information on the 14 foundations in the sample. Each foundation is an independent legal entity in the specific country with close connections to the local branch of the company. However, the foundations are financed through different revenue streams. One is the local branch of the company, another is local employees, and finally the UK-based foundation transfers financial resources to the national foundations. The legal type of the foundations may vary according to national law. For instance, the German Vodafone Foundation is organized as limited liability corporation ("Stiftungs GmbH") instead of the legal type of a foundation.

The 14 countries in the sample cover all four basic models of the social origins theory. The UK is the only country in the sample of the liberal model, the Netherlands and Italy represent the social democratic model, Germany, Ireland, Spain, Portugal and Malta fall into the corporatist model, and the statist model is represented by Greece, Romania, Hungary, the Czech Republic, Albania and Turkey. In the following, we analyse if the structure and functioning of the foundations in the four regime types show similarities or if there are other explaining factors.

Table 5.3 Models of non-profit sector regimes (Anheier and Salamon 1998)

		Non-profit scale	
		Small	Large
Government social welfare spending	Low	Statist	Liberal
	High	Statist	Liberal

5 Corporate Foundations in Europe

Table 5.4 Categorization of Vodafone foundations in European countries

Regime	Liberal	Social democratic		Corporatist					Statist					
Country	UK	NED	IT	GER	IRE	SP	POR	MAL	GRE	RO	HUN	CZ	ALB	TUR
Criteria														
Year of establishment	1989	2002	2002	2003	2003	2002	2001	2003	2002	1998	2003	2006	2007	2007
Board size	11	4	8	8	n.a.	10	4	4	n.a.	7	5	5	5	8
Payouts in 2015 (EUR million)	44.4	0.632	4.4	4.5	0.666[a]	4.8	1.3	0.230	0.300[a]	2	0.266[a]	0.039	0.384	7
Revenue Vodafone group in 2015/2016 (EUR million)	8428	1890	6008	10,626		4959	973		848					2959
Public social spending in % of GDP (2015/2016)	21.5	22.0	28.9	25.3	16.1	24.6	24.1	18.2	27.0	14.8	20.6	19.4	nn	13.5
Public social expenses per capita in EUR (2015)	9595	12,166	7987	10,494	8623	5661	4470	3593	4242	1114	2121	2927	nn	1102

[a]Estimated amounts based on multi-year reporting

5.4.3 Results

Almost all fourteen foundations have a logo with the signet of Vodafone Group Plc and the name "Vodafone foundation" plus the country's name in the national language (except for the Netherlands and Albania with English names). Despite small differences in the arrangement of the logo, there is high brand recognition across all foundations and a clear connection to the parent company. Only foundations in the corporatist model have slogans differing from the overall slogan "connecting for good". The different slogans in Germany ("Menschen und Ideen fördern"), Portugal ("Por um Mundo Melhor") and Malta ("mobilizing the community, mobilising social change") focus on different key aspects which may be the result of national expectations.

Except for the two foundations in the UK and Romania, all foundations were established in the years 2001–2007. The foundations are rather young, which may be to a larger extent explained by company decisions on corporate social responsibility than local needs. The purpose of the Vodafone foundations has a general linkage to the core business of the company. The overarching idea is to give access to technology. The foundation in the UK has defined four main goals (Vodafone Group 2016): "transforming societies globally", "changing women's lives through mobile", "energy innovation" and "young skills and jobs". These aims are identical with the social responsibility aims of the parent company. One way to fulfil the first aim is the establishment of foundations in other countries.

Another interesting aspect of the structure of the foundations is the size of the board of trustees and number of corporate board members. The range of board size is between 4 and 11 persons. Foundations with higher payouts tend to have more board members, with the UK foundation on top of the list, but there is no clear distinction between the different welfare regime types. Corporate board members are in the majority in the UK foundation, whereas in most other foundations they are the minority – as far as this information was available.

The purposes of the foundations in the two social-democratic regimes focus on a general aim to leverage quality of life through the use of mobile technology. The foundations in countries with statist regimes focus highly on education and relief. Additionally, in Turkey the situation of women in society is mentioned. Among the corporatist regime countries exists the greatest divergence of purposes. The German and Irish foundations deal with education only, whereas the Spanish foundation engages in help for disabled persons and elderly people. The foundations in Portugal and Malta aim at solving social ills in the countries.

Except the UK foundation with a global perspective, all foundations focus on social and educational aspects on national levels. All purposes fall into the four major aims defined by the parent company and the UK foundation, but they each address only parts of it.

Finally, we analyse the payouts of the foundations. The payout of the UK foundation is by far the largest, but this foundation has a global focus and supports all other foundations. These foundations are also funded by the local corporate branches. The payouts of the other foundations differ widely from USD 45,000 to 7.9 million. The reasons for the differences are manifold. First, the size of the country and, thus, the market size for the company vary. Additionally, the engagement of the local branch of the company may differ. Finally, the field of activity may lead to different amounts necessary to fund projects.

In order to check for business or public influences, we compared the foundations' payouts with the national revenue of Vodafone Group Plc and the public social expenses of the countries. Unfortunately, revenues are not published for all European countries separately. One can see that the social origins theory does explain differences in the public social expenses. The social democratic countries tend to have the highest public social expenses per capita, followed by corporatist countries and statist countries. Only the high public social expenses in the UK do not support the theory. Where accessible, the revenues of Vodafone Group Plc show a different structure. The most important markets for Vodafone Group Plc are Germany, the UK, Italy and Spain. These countries also account for most of the highest foundation payouts in the countries. One exception is Turkey with very high payouts at reasonable business revenues.

5.4.4 Discussion

This case study was aimed to add to a better understanding of the role and importance of corporate foundations in European countries. By focusing on the foundations of one parent company, we were able to keep the influence of the business constant and focus on different welfare state regimes. The fourteen foundations covered all four regime types proposed by Anheier and Salamon (1998) and further discussed by Einolf (2015). This result already highlights the different public influences corporate foundation face in European countries. In our result we find little reasoning for consistency of foundations in one regime type. The foundations in social democratic and corporatist regime countries were established within a short period of time, whereas the foundations in statist regime countries have a range of over 20 years. However, the reasons for the year of establishment are more likely the result of a business decision than of societal influences. In respect of the mission, only some foundations in corporatist regime countries differ in their aims. However, all of the aims lie within the overarching purpose of the main foundation in the UK. We also find some overlap between the public social expenses and the welfare regimes, but we cannot find a clear picture of the welfare state regimes in terms of board size and payouts. In conclusion, the role and structure of the corporate foundations seem to be much more influenced by the parent company than the welfare state regime they are active in. Vodafone Group Plc deploys parts of its corporate citizenship activities through foundations in every country. By financing these foundations in parts through the UK foundation, they ensure that the national foundations are linked to this corporate strategy. Nevertheless, adjustments to national realities are possible.

5.5 Conclusion

In this paper we offered an overview on the state of art of corporate foundations in Europe. Although statistical data on foundation has improved in recent years, data available on corporate foundations is scarce. As a first finding, we can affirm that the interest of research and practice for corporate foundations has not yet developed strongly. Only few scientific articles so far have focused on corporate foundations in Europe and other reports or studies are also rare. This does not mean that corporate foundations have no societal significance. In some countries such as Poland or the UK, profound studies or code of conducts for corporate foundations exist. In other countries such as France or Denmark, there is a special interest in different kinds of corporate-related foundations, including shareholder foundations and corporate foundations. In countries such as Spain, Germany or Switzerland, studies on corporate foundations are in progress and promise new insights in the near future.

Our second finding is that, compared to the overall number of European foundations, the number of corporate foundations is small. Companies seem to channel their corporate responsibility through other forms, such as corporate giving or corporate volunteering. One explanation can be found in higher institutional consequences of setting up a corporate foundation. In most European countries, a corporate foundation cannot be easily erased once it is established. Hence, a corporate foundation needs a long-term commitment by the parent company, whereas corporate giving is more flexible and adjustable to economic developments. Future research might build on the alignment theory (Chorn 1991) to further elaborate on the relationship between the corporate foundation and the parent company (Bethmann and von Schnurbein, Chap. 3).

As a third finding, we conclude that there is no specific field of activity of corporate foundations. Moreover, they are well integrated in the larger field of grant-making foundations with similar aims and activities. Corporate-related fields such as research, education or general social issues are more important in some countries, whereas a few countries set legal boundaries that corporate foundations' activities have to be distinct from the core business. Anheier (2018) calls for further comparative research on foundations for a better understanding of their advantages and disadvantages for society.

Building on the results from the case study of Vodafone Group Plc, we state that European corporate foundations rely primarily on their parent company and not on their social environment. Applying the social origins theory, we find that there are no clear differences between the countries in different welfare state regimes. Although the national corporate foundations of Vodafone Group Plc vary in terms of purpose, payout or board size, these differences cannot be explained by societal influences. Instead, they seem to be the result of the company's strategy and business success in each country.

To conclude, corporate foundations in Europe cover both the role of a grant-making foundation and the function as corporate responsibility tool. Thus, they have the potential to build new linkages and connections between the civil society and the business world.

Appendix A

Researchers	National foundation associations	Vodafone foundations
1. Denmark: CBS Center for Civil Society Studies
2. Italy: University of Verona/Chiara Leardini
3. Latvia: Foundation of the University of Latvia/ Laila Kundziņa-Zvejniece
4. Portugal: Coimbra Business School/Maria Madalena Eça Guimarães de Abreu
5. Spain: University of A Coruña/Marta Rey-Garcia
6. Switzerland: Center for Philanthropy Studies
7. The Netherlands: Erasmus University Rotterdam/Lonneke Roza
8. UK: The Researchery/ Catherine Walker	1. Austria: Gemeinnützige Privatstiftung Philanthropie Österreich/Günther Lutschinger
2. France: Centre Français des Fonds et Fondations
3. Germany: Bundesverband Deutscher Stiftungen/Anke Pätsch and Birgit Radow
4. Hungary: Hungarian Donors Forum/Valeria Kojnok
5. Ireland: Philanthropy Ireland/ Eilis Murray
6. Liechtenstein: Association of Liechtenstein Charitable Foundations e.V./Damar Bühler-Nigsch
7. UK: Association of Charitable Foundations (ACF)/David Emerson	1. Albania: Vodafone Albania Foundation
2. Czech Republic: Nadace Vodafone Ceskà republika
3. Germany: Vodafone Stiftung Deutschland
4. Greece: Vodafone Foundation
5. Hungary: Vodafone Magyarorszàg Alapitvàny
6. Ireland: Vodafone Ireland Foundation
7. Italy: Fondazione Vodafone Italia
8. Malta: Vodafone Malta Foundation
9. The Netherlands: Vodafone Netherlands Foundation
10. Portugal: Fundação Vodafone Portugal
11. Romania: Fundatia Vodafone Romania
12. Spain: Fundaciòn Vodafone España
13. Turkey: Türkiye Vodafone Vakfi
14. UK: Vodafone UK Foundation

References

ACF (Association of Charitable Foundations), Ellis, F. (2010). *Good practice for corporate foundations.* [pdf] London: Association of Charitable Foundations. Available through: http://www.acf.org.uk/policy-practice/practice-publications/good-practice-for-corporate-foundations/. Accessed 6 Mar 2017.

ACF (Association of Charitable Foundations), Ellis, F. (2016). *Good practice guide for corporate foundations.* [pdf] London: Association of Charitable Foundations. Available at: http://www.acf.org.uk/downloads/publications/ACF121_Guide_to_Corporate_Foundations_Digital_SP.pdf. Accessed 6 Mar 2017.

Anheier, H. K. (2018). Philanthropic foundations in cross-national perspective: A comparative approach. *American Behavioral Scientist, 62*(12), 1591–1602.

Anheier, H. K., & Salamon, L. M. (1998). Social origins of civil society: Explaining the nonprofit sector cross-nationally. *Voluntas: International Journal of Voluntary and Nonprofit Organizations, 9*(3), 213–236.

AP Møller and Wife Chastine MC-Kinney Møller's Fund for General Purposes. (2017). *About the fund*. [online] Available at: https://www.apmollerfonde.dk/om-fonden.aspx. Accessed 2 June 2017.

Blaščák, F. (2016). The case of corporate percentage tax designation in Slovakia. In B. Strečanský & M. Török (Eds.), *Assessment of the impact of the percentage tax designations: Past, present, future* (pp. 62–65). Vienna: ERSTE Foundation.

Bundesverband Deutscher Stiftungen. (2014). *Zahlen, Daten, Fakten zum deutschen Stiftungswesen*. [pdf] Berlin: Bundesverband Deutscher Stiftungen. Available at: https://shop.stiftungen.org/media/mconnect_uploadfiles/z/d/zdf_ebook_final_webgr_e.pdf. Accessed 6 Mar 2017.

Bundesverband Deutscher Stiftungen. (2016). *Zehn Empfehlungen für gemeinnützige Unternehmensstiftungen*. [pdf] Berlin: Bundesverband Deutscher Stiftungen. Available at: https://www.stiftungen.org/fileadmin/stiftungen_org/Verband/Was_wir_tun/Veranstaltungen/AK-Unternehmensstiftungen/Zehn-Empfehlungen-Unternehmensstiftungen-2016.pdf. Accessed 28 Feb 2017.

CC (Corporate Citizenship). (2016). *The game changers – Corporate foundations in a changing world*. London: Corporate Citizenship. Available through: http://corporate-citizenship.com/our-insights/game-changers-corporate-foundations-changing-world/. Accessed 28 Feb 2017.

Charity Commission for England and Wales. (2009). *A guide to corporate foundations*. [pdf] London: Charity Commission for England and Wales. Available at: https://www.gov.uk/government/uploads/system/uploads/attachment_data/file/351134/corporate-foundations-guide.pdf. Accessed 28 Feb 2017.

Chorn, N. (1991). The "Alignment" theory: Creating strategic fit. *Management Decision, 29*(1), 20–24.

CSR Europe. (n.d.) *Bringing the European CSR strategy to the next stage 2015–2019. CSR Europe's Memorandum*. [pdf] Brussels: CSR Europe. Available at: http://www.csreurope.org/sites/default/files/publications/Memorandum_to_the_European_Commission.pdf. Accessed 12 June 2017.

DAFNE (Donors and Foundations Network Europe). (2017). *Country profiles*. [online] Available at: http://DAFNE-online.eu/country_profile. Accessed 13 Mar 2017.

EFC (European Foundation Center). (2005). Foundation facts & figures across the EU – Associating private wealth for public benefit. [pdf] Brussels: European Foundation Center. Available at: http://www.centre-francais-fondations.org/fondations-fonds-de-dotation/le-secteur-europe-et-monde/etudes-sur-les-fondations-en-europe/donnees-chiffrees-sur-les-fondations-de-lunion-europeenne-en-2005/at_download/file. Accessed 29 May 2017.

EFC (European Foundation Center). (2015). *Comparative highlights of foundation laws. The operating environment for foundations in Europe*. [pdf] Brussels: European Foundation Center. Available at: http://efc.issuelab.org/resource/comparative_highlights_of_foundation_laws_the_operating_environment_for_foundations_in_europe_2015. Accessed 22 May 2017.

Einolf, C. J. (2015). The social origins of nonprofit sector and charitable giving. In F. Handy & P. Wiepking (Eds.), *The Palgrave handbook of global philanthropy* (pp. 509–529). London: Palgrave Macmillan.

ERNOP (European Research Network on Philanthropy). (2017a). *Countries*. [online] Available at: http://ernop.eu/countries/. Accessed 13 Mar 2017.

ERNOP (European Research Network on Philanthropy). (2017b). *Giving in Europe. The current state of research on giving by households, corporations, foundations and charity lotteries in Europe*. [pdf] European Research Network on Philanthropy. Available at: http://ernop.eu/wp-content/uploads/2016/12/Factsheet-7-HR.pdf. Accessed 14 Mar 2017.

Esping-Andersen, G. (1990). *The three worlds of welfare capitalism*. Princeton: Princeton University Press.

European Commission. (2011). *Communication from the commission to the European Parliament, the Council, the European Economic and Social Committee and the Committee of the Regions. A renewed EU strategy 2011–14 for Corporate Social Responsibility*. [pdf] Brussels: European Commission. Available at:http://eur-lex.europa.eu/LexUriServ/LexUriServ.do?uri=COM:2011:0681:FIN:EN:PDF. Accessed 12 June 2017.

EY (Ernst & Young Société d'Avocats), Les entreprises pour la Cité. (2016). *Panorama des fondations et des fonds de dotation créés par des entreprises mécènes – 2016. Peut-on concilier performance et intérêt général?*. [pdf] Paris: Ernst & Young Société d'Avocats, Les entreprises pour la Cité. Available at: http://www.ey.com/Publication/vwLUAssets/ey-panorama-2016-des-fondations-et-des-fonds-de-dotation-crees-par-des-entreprises-mecenes/$FILE/ey-panorama-2016-des-fondations-et-des-fonds-de-dotation-crees-par-des-entreprises-mecenes.pdf. Accessed 14 Mar 2017.

Fundación PricewaterhouseCoopers. (2016). *Fundaciones corporativas. El alma de las empresas*. [pdf] Fundación PricewaterhouseCoopers. Available at: http://www.pwc.es/es/fundacion/assets/fundaciones-corporativas-alma-empresas.pdf. Accessed 21 Mar 2017.

Fundraising Verband Austria. (2016). *Gemeinnützige und nicht-gewinnorientierte Stiftungen als wichtiger Wirtschaftsfaktor*. [pdf] Wien: Fundraising Verband Austria. Available at: http://www.fundraising.at/LinkClick.aspx?fileticket=5oPOG2BKxZs%3D&tabid=394&language=de-DE. Accessed 31 May 2017.

Herlin, H., & Pedersen, J. T. (2013). Corporate foundations – Catalysts of NGO-business partnerships? *Journal of Corporate Citizenship, 50*, 58–90.

Hopt, K. J., von Hippel, T., Anheier, H. K., Then, V., Ebke, W., Reimer, E., & Vahlpahl, T. (2009). *Feasibility study on a European Foundation Statute*. [pdf] Heidelberg: Centre for Social Investment. Available at: http://ec.europa.eu/internal_market/company/docs/eufoundation/feasibilitystudy_en.pdf. Accessed 20 Mar 2017.

McGill, L. T. (2016). *European foundation sector report 2016*. [pdf] Brussels: Donors and Foundations Network Europe. Available at: http://DAFNE-online.eu/wp-content/uploads/2016/10/PBF-Report-2016-9-30-16.pdf. Accessed 13 Mar 2017.

Mernier, A., & Xhauflair, V. (2017). *Les fondations en Belgique. Rapport 2017*. [pdf] Liège: Centre d'Economie Sociale de HEC Liège. Available at: http://labos.ulg.ac.be/philanthropie/wp-content/uploads/sites/3/2017/02/Fondations-en-Belgique.pdf. Accessed 09 June 2017.

Observatoire de la Fondation de France, Centre d'Etude et de Recherche sur la Philanthropie (CERPhi). (2015). *An overview of philanthropy in Europe*. [pdf] Paris: Observatoire de la Fondation de France, Centre d'Etude et de Recherche sur la Philanthropie. Available at: http://efc.issuelab.org/resource/an_overview_of_philanthropy_in_europe. Accessed 13 Mar 2017.

Polish Donors Forum. (2015). *Standards for corporate foundations. Polish Donors Forum's handbook for board members and employees of corporate foundations*. [pdf] Warsaw: Polish Donors Forum. Available at: http://www.forumdarczyncow.pl/docs/standards_for_corporate_foundations_polish_donors_forum_2015.pdf. Accessed 20 Mar 2017.

Polish Donors Forum. (2017). *Fundacje Koroporacyjne W Polsce*. [pdf] Warsaw: Polish Donors Forum. Available at: http://www.forumdarczyncow.pl/docs/news/fundacje_korporacyjne_w_polsce_2017_raport_forum_darczyncow.pdf. Accessed 18 Dec 2017.

Purtschert, R., von Schnurbein, G., & Beccarelli, C. (2007). Switzerland. In H. K. Anheier & S. Daly (Eds.), *The politics of foundations. A comparative analysis* (pp. 307–323). New York: Routledge.

Quick, E., Kruse, T. A., & Pickering, A., (2014). *Rules to give by a global philanthropy legal environment index*. [pdf] Washington: Nexus Network International, McDermott, McDermott Will & Emery LLP, Charities Aid Foundation. Available at: http://www.nexusglobal.org/wp-content/uploads/2014/12/RULES-TO-GIVE-BY-FINAL-Print.pdf. Accessed 09 June 2017.

Rey-Garcia, M., Martin-Cavanna, J., & Alvarez-Gonzalez, L. I. (2012). Assessing and advancing foundation transparency: Corporate foundations as a case study. *The Foundation Review, 4*(3), 77–89.

Robinson, O. C. (2014). Sampling in interview-based qualitative research: A theoretical and practical guide. *Qualitative Research in Psychology, 11*(1), 25–41.

Rubio Guerrero, J. J., & SosvillaRivero, S. (2016). *El Sector Fundacional en España: A tributos fundamentales (2008–2014)*. [pdf] Madrid: Asociación Española de Fundaciones. Available at: http://www.fundaciones.org/EPORTAL_DOCS/GENERAL/AEF/DOC-cw585d042d56ecf/ElsectorfundacionalenEspaNa-Atributosfundamentales-2008-2014.pdf. Accessed 09 June 2017.

Schuyt, T. (2010). Philanthropy in European welfare states: a challenging promise? *International Review of Administrative Sciences, 76*(4), 774–789.

Sprecher, T., Egger, P., & von Schnurbein, G. (2016). *Swiss Foundation Code 2015 – Principles and recommendations for the establishment and management of grant-making foundations.* Basel: Helbing Lichtenhahn Verlag.

Steen, T., Poulsen, T., & Børsting, C. (2015). *Denmark country report. EUFORI study.* [pdf] Luxembourg: Publications Office of the European Union. Available at: http://euforistudy.eu/wp-content/uploads/2015/07/Denmark.pdf. Accessed 24 May 2017.

Strečanský, B. (2012). *The situation of the third sector in Slovakia, the impacts of crisis, trends, mainstreams and challenges.* [pdf] In Nizák, P., Csongor, A., Kákai, L., Péterfi, F., Sebestény, I. (Eds.), *Civil Szemle* (pp. 75–93). Budapest: Civil Szemle Alapítvány. Available at: http://www.cpf.sk/files/files/Pages%20from%20Civil_Szemle_2012_3.pdf. Accessed 18 July 2017.

Toepler, S. (2018). Toward a comparative understanding of foundations. *American Behavioral Scientist, 62*(13), 1956–1971.

Vodafone Group Plc. (2016). *Sustainable business report 2015/2016.* [pdf] Newbury: Vodafone Group Plc. Available at: http://www.vodafone.com/content/dam/vodafone-images/sustainability/downloads/report2016.pdf. Accessed 18 Feb 2017.

von Schnurbein, G., & Perez, M. (2018). Foundations in Switzerland: Between the American and the German cases. *American Behavioral Scientist, 62*(13), 1919–1932.

von Schnurbein, G., Seele, P., & Lock, I. (2016). Exclusive corporate philanthropy: Rethinking the nexus of CSR and corporate philanthropy. *Social Responsibility Journal, 12*(2), 280–294.

Theresa Gehringer, MSc studied business administration and sustainable development at the University of Bayreuth and the University of Basel. Since 2015, she has been working at the Center for Philanthropy Studies (CEPS) in Basel as a PhD student and research assistant in research, further education and teaching. Her research focuses on corporate philanthropy, corporate foundations and NPO sustainability.

Georg von Schnurbein is associate professor for foundation management at the Faculty of Business and Economics and founding director of the Center for Philanthropy Studies (CEPS) at the University of Basel. He serves in several functions in boards in the field of international research on philanthropy and has co-authored the latest edition of the Swiss Foundation Code and published in several impact journals such as *Nonprofit & Voluntary Sector Quarterly* and *European Management Journal.* His research interest is on non-profit governance, financial health of non-profits and impact measurement.

Chapter 6
Corporate Foundations in the United States

Joannie Tremblay-Boire

Abstract In the United States, corporate foundations are seen as part of the foundation sector and of the nonprofit sector more generally. They began to emerge after World War II. In the early years, corporate philanthropy was purposely detached from business interests, a trend that changed staring in the 1980s. Although there are no regulations targeted specifically toward corporate foundations in the United States, they are subject to regulations as private foundations by tax authorities. According to the Foundation Center, as of 2014, about 3 percent of American foundations were corporate foundations (2521 out of 86,726). One estimate suggests that 40 percent of corporations in America have a corporate foundation. They tend to give locally, to relatively uncontroversial causes, and to many grantees—such a strategy creates goodwill from the community, a better trained workforce, and a loyal customer base. Ironically, as corporate foundation officials are pressured to maintain a strategic connection to the parent corporation, they often struggle to find support for the foundation's activities from their peers inside the parent corporation. This tension between serving the greater good and advancing the interests of the corporation is a challenge that no other type of foundation is facing.

Keywords Corporate foundations · United States · Institutional environment

6.1 State of Research on Corporate Foundations in the United States

Academic research on foundations more generally is limited in the United States. As of today, the scholarship on philanthropic foundations has been almost exclusively qualitative, which means that we know little about the population of foundations in the United States beyond large, general-purpose foundations. There have been many works on individual foundations, the motivations of their creators,

---

J. Tremblay-Boire (✉)
University of Maryland, College Park, MD, USA
e-mail: jboire@umd.edu

and their achievements since their creation (especially works on large, well-known, independent foundations such as Carnegie (Lagemann 1989), Rockefeller (Brown 1979), and Ford). Philanthropic historians and social scientists have also produced detailed historical accounts of the contributions of foundations and the controversies surrounding them since the nineteenth century in America (Weaver 1967; Karl and Katz 1981; Sealander 1997; Anheier and Hammack 2010; Hammack and Anheier 2013). But the great majority of this limited body of research, although it may touch on corporate foundations, is not focused on them specifically.

Information on the legal framework for foundations in the United States is available on the website of the Internal Revenue Service (IRS), the main federal regulator of foundations, as well as from state attorney generals. Organizations such as the Council on Foundations and the Foundation Center conduct research and provide general information, reports, and descriptive statistics about foundations. All foundations in the United States must make their tax filings publicly available. The Foundation Center uses the information from these tax filings to provide us with descriptive statistics about the sector.

To be fair, if we were to adopt a comparative perspective, the data and research on corporate foundations in the United States are probably much more developed than in other countries. Americans have a long tradition, dating back to the nineteenth century, of creating foundations to solve public problems. Nevertheless, despite foundations' economic clout (which some would argue is growing with the advent of mega-foundations like the Bill and Melinda Gates Foundation or the Walton Family Foundation), the (critical) attention foundations have received from elected officials throughout their history, and foundations' unique position in the system (outside of the state and outside of the market), academic research on foundations remains much more limited than one might expect. Even as the nonprofit/ nongovernmental organization literature has exploded in the United States in recent decades, and as universities have created dozens of programs dedicated completely to the study of nonprofit organizations, the study of foundations as one particular type of nonprofit has lagged.

6.2 A Brief History of Foundations in the United States

Although most Americans would consider the beginning of the twentieth century as the defining moment for American foundations (with the creation of the Russell Sage Foundation in 1907, Carnegie Corporation of New York in 1911, and Rockefeller Foundation in 1913), historians trace the birth of the foundation in America to much earlier (Marts 1953; Smith 1999; Hammack and Anheier 2013). Hammack and Anheier (2013, p. 20), for example, note that if we accept the current legal definition of a foundation as a "fund of money held by a trust or corporation, with principal and income to be applied over time to charitable purposes," endowed charities meeting this definition already existed in Pennsylvania and Massachusetts at the time of writing of the Constitution (1787). These charitable endowments tended to be small and for a single or a few defined purposes. In contrast, the new foundations of the twentieth century were larger general-purpose organizations and focused on efficiency and innovation ("scientific" philanthropy) rather than on fulfilling religious purposes (although plenty of other foundations at the time continued to pursue more traditional aims) (Bremner 1988).

After World War II, Congress and the public became increasingly suspicious of foundations. Critics notably argued that foundations were used for tax evasion (President Truman said as much in 1950) and for improper political influence (e.g., see investigations by the Cox and Reece Committees in the House of Representatives in the 1950s) (Hall 2002; Kiger 2000). The hostility toward foundations culminated in the Tax Reform Act (TRA) of 1969. The TRA gave us the first explicit definition of a "private foundation." The Act also created a set of stricter rules for private foundations: it established an excise tax on investment income; it required nonoperating foundations to distribute a minimum amount of money for charitable purposes each year (the payout rule); it reduced the percentage of an individual's income that could be deducted for donations to private foundations compared to other charities; and it limited self-dealing, among other rules (for a more complete description of the regulations regarding foundations in the 1969 TRA, see Labovitz (1973) and Smith and Chiechi (1974)). Frumkin (1998) argues that the 1969 TRA was a turning point for private foundations in America because it led to the bureaucratization and homogenization of the field, stifling its creativity and future impact.

John D. Rockefeller III, worried about the criticisms of foundations that had fueled the provisions of the 1969 TRA, created the Commission on Private Philanthropy and Public Needs in 1973 (better known as the Filer Commission) to study philanthropy in America. The Commission produced more than 80 studies and generated hundreds of pages of recommendations. Its most notable contribution was that it suggested that the nonprofit/voluntary sector is a distinct and important sector in America (Billitteri 2000).

Historical accounts about foundations focus mostly on independent foundations (and on community foundations, such as the Cleveland Foundation, to some extent). If we examine corporate philanthropy specifically (through both foundations and giving programs), we can probably trace the earliest examples in America to the post-World War II period (e.g., Ford Motor Company Fund in 1949 and GE corporate gift-matching program of 1954). Legally, corporate philanthropy had been considered beyond the authority of the company (ultra vires principle) since the 1880s (see, e.g., the *Old Colony Railroad* and the *Wes Cork Railway* court cases). In the early twentieth century, corporations made charitable donations, but the donations had to benefit the corporation directly in some way (Cousens 1949). They were not donating in an attempt to further the greater good, but rather to benefit their workers (and ultimately the company itself) (Sharfman 1994). With World War I, some states began to allow corporations to make donations that were not business-related (Sharfman 1994). Then, in 1953, in the case of *A. P. Smith Mfg. Co. v. Barlow*, the Supreme Court of New Jersey held that the A. P. Smith Manufacturing Company was allowed to make a $1500 donation to Princeton University, despite its stockholders' protests to the contrary. The Supreme Court refused to hear the case, which legitimated the argument that a corporation's role went beyond maximizing profits for shareholders, and included a broader "duty to society" (Gramm 1961). The ruling paved the way for corporate philanthropy as we know it in the United States. By 1960, 46 states and territories had written legislation explicitly allowing corporate philanthropy (Sharfman 1994). According to McClimon (2004), in that period:

> "Grants were often made to not-for-profit organizations that had close ties to the CEO and other senior executives or they were spread among many organizations in small amounts, often for unrestricted operating support. For the most part, these companies didn't want publicity or recognition; they simply wanted to give something back to their communities and to enhance life in the communities where their employees and customers lived and worked."

Smith (1994) notes that, at that time, corporations would make donations to charitable organizations as unrelated to their business endeavors as possible in an attempt to keep the two sectors distinct and avoid perceptions of impropriety. Then, starting in the 1980s, corporations shifted to more "strategic" philanthropy, linking their charitable behavior more closely to their business interests. The AT&T Foundation is seen as a model of this shift. Reynold Levy, the head of the foundation, "argued that the foundation staff should be 'Janus-faced'—one face serving the community, the other serving AT&T's business units" (Smith 1994). In more recent years, however, American corporations have been facing an important dilemma: how can they justify continuing their charitable giving while laying off employees and/or losing their competitive edge to overseas corporations that give much less?

6.3 Models of Corporate Foundations

In the United States, the nonprofit sector is regulated primarily through the federal tax code, more specifically through section 501(c), which deals with tax-exempt organizations. Organizations must send a tax exemption application to the Internal Revenue Service (IRS). The great majority of tax-exempt organizations in the United States are 501(c)(3) organizations, commonly known as charities. In 2015, three-quarters of all nonprofits registered with the IRS (about 1.2 million organizations) were 501(c)(3)s.[1] Foundations, including corporate foundations, are part of that group. To become tax-exempt under section 501(c)(3) of the tax code, a nonprofit must operate for the public interest (as opposed to private/mutual interests). It must also be created for specific purposes: religious, charitable, scientific, testing for public safety, literary, educational, and/or prevention of cruelty to children or animals. It may not participate in political campaigns and may only conduct insubstantial lobbying.

---

[1]The National Center for Charitable Statistics compiled this information. For the exact numbers, please see http://nccsweb.urban.org/nonprofit-overview.php

Although there are no taxation regulations targeting corporate foundations specifically in the United States, they are subject to regulations as private foundations. Federal tax law divides tax-exempt organizations described in the 501(c)(3) section of the tax code into two groups: "private foundations" and "public charities." The IRS automatically considers any organization that qualifies for tax exemption under section 501(c)(3) of the tax code a "private foundation." In order to receive the status of "public charity," organizations must pass an additional test: the public support test. The public support test determines if the organization receives a substantial portion of its income from the general public. Most corporate foundations do not qualify as "public charities" because they do not receive contributions from many different sources. They generally receive all of their funds from a few or single source, their parent corporation. However, if a corporate foundation received financial support from an array of sources like government and the public, it could hold the status of "public charity" instead of "private foundation" in the United States.

Within the "private foundation" category, the IRS distinguishes between operating and non-operating (also called grant-making) foundations. Operating foundations primarily conduct their own charitable activities (such as running a library or a research facility), while grant-making foundations disburse funds to other nonprofits to conduct their activities. Grant-making foundations are required to pay out at least 5 percent of their assets in grants each year. The American foundation literature generally categorizes grant-making private foundations as corporate, family, or independent foundations (and community foundations as public charities) based on the foundations' asset source and governance structure. However, these categories are not legal categories. The IRS does not distinguish between corporate, family, and independent foundations. They are all considered private foundations.

As opposed to public charities, private foundations may include a majority of related parties on their board of directors and are not required to receive a significant portion of their revenue from the public. However, private foundations face stricter regulations and receive fewer tax benefits than public charities: their tax filling (990-PF) is more exhaustive (e.g., they must disclose all grants and grantees, which a public charity—like a community foundation—is not required to disclose); they must disburse 5 percent of their non-charitable assets annually; they are subject to an excise tax of 2 percent on net investment income; and they are subject to an excise tax if the foundation and its insiders (or "disqualified persons") combined hold more than 20% of the voting stock of any corporation. The IRS defines disqualified persons as substantial contributors to the foundation (contribute more than 2 percent of the foundation's total contributions and bequests), foundation managers, owners of more than 20 percent interest of an organization that is a substantial contributor to the foundation, family members of any of the abovementioned individuals, entities in which any of the persons described above own more than 35 percent together, private foundations that are effectively controlled by the same individuals who control this foundation, and government officials (please see https://www.irs.gov/irm/part7/irm_07-027-020.html for more details).

Corporations cannot deduct more than 10 percent of their pre-tax net income as charitable contributions, and they are prohibited from self-dealing with their foundation. Potential individual contributors to charities and foundations are also treated differently: a contributor can deduct up to 50 percent of their adjusted gross income for donations to a public charity on their income tax, but only 30 percent for donations to a private foundation (except for private operating foundations, for which they can deduct 50 percent).

In addition to federal laws, foundations are also subject to state laws. In general, nonprofit organizations must be registered with their state first before they can seek tax-exempt status with the federal government. Laws can vary quite a bit from state to state, and foundations should consult the law for the state where they operate. Under state law, the two major options to structure private foundations are charitable trusts or not-for-profit corporations, but the most common is the not-for-profit corporation. On the one hand, trusts are more restrictive than corporations if one wants to make changes to the governing structure and/or charitable purpose. Trustees must go through court proceedings or get approval from the state's attorney general to amend a trust, whereas the board of directors of a corporation can usually make such changes through a simple vote. On the other hand, it is usually more time-consuming (and expensive) to set up a not-for-profit corporation, and states tend to impose more formal requirements on corporations (e.g., on keeping minutes of meetings, on bylaws, on state filings, and so on). However, directors in not-for-profit corporations are generally better protected against personal liability than trustees of a charitable trust. An additional point that may be important for some foundations is that, if the foundation is structured as a trust, contributions from a corporation are only deductible for charitable purposes *within* the United States. There is no such limitation on international activities for not-for-profit corporations.

6.4 Statistical Data

Guthrie (2010) estimates that about 40 percent of American companies have a corporate foundation. He writes (2010, p.187):

> "Over 39 percent of corporations in the United States own such institutions [corporate foundations or funds]. Among them, almost 63 percent fund projects for the underprivileged, 46 percent fund arts projects, and around 40 percent donate to health-related programs. Other foundations focus on other purposes such as special events (36%), infrastructure (34%) and research projects (29%)."

According to the Foundation Center, as of 2014, about 3 percent of American foundations were corporate foundations (2521 out of 86,726), and they held 3 percent of foundations' total assets ($26.7 B out of $865 B) (Foundation Center 2017). Yet, they contributed 9 percent of all giving by foundations ($5.1 B out of $60 B) (Foundation Center 2017). In general, corporate foundations are set up as grant-making foundations in the United States. Interestingly, however, some pharmaceutical companies are choosing to establish operating foundations to distribute medicine to those in need (Foundation Center 2012).

In 2010, the largest corporate foundations in the United States (192 foundations) focused their grant-making in the sectors of human services (23 percent of grant dollars), education (21 percent), and public affairs/societal benefit (20 percent) (Foundation Center 2012). More than 30 percent of grant dollars were spent on program support, and about 15 percent were spent on operating support (Foundation Center 2012). Some readers may be interested in comparing corporate foundation giving by sector to overall corporate giving by sector. The Committee Encouraging Corporate Philanthropy (CECP), in its 2016 *Giving in Numbers* report, finds that, among the 272 companies it surveyed (88% of which are in the United States), about 29% of total giving went to education (higher and K-12), 26% went to health and social services, and 13% went to community and economic development (CECP 2016). Although the percentages (and the terminology used in the two reports) are slightly different, there seems to be a clear common emphasis on social services, education, and community benefit across corporate giving overall and corporate foundation giving. Intuitively, this finding makes sense since we would expect corporate foundations to want an educated workforce and to want to give back to their local community.

The top five corporate foundations by giving in 2010 were Sanofi-Aventis Patient Assistance Foundation, Novartis Patient Assistance Foundation, Bank of America Charitable Foundation, Walmart Foundation, and JPMorgan Chase Foundation (Foundation Center 2012). By 2014, only three of the top five corporate foundations by giving were the same. The top five included Novartis Patient Assistance Foundation, Wells Fargo Foundation, Bank of America Charitable Foundation, Walmart Foundation, and JPMorgan Chase Foundation (Foundation Center 2017). Interestingly, the Foundation Center re-categorized the Sanofi-Aventis Patient Assistance Foundation as an "operating" foundation instead of a "corporate" foundation. If it had remained in the corporate foundation category, it would still be considered the largest. The banking and finance sector accounted for the greatest number of corporate foundations (at 465 or 17.1 percent) and the largest percentage of corporate foundation giving (22.1 percent) in 2010 (Foundation Center 2012). According to the Federal Reserve Bank of St. Louis, the finance, insurance, and real estate industry accounts for about 20% of the GDP in the United States. As such, the proportion of corporate foundations from banking and finance appears proportional to the sector's overall impact outside of the philanthropic realm. Financial institutions also struggle to maintain good reputations with the public, which may encourage them to start initiatives like foundations. Interestingly, the pharmaceuticals sector, while representing only 1 percent of all corporate foundations, still contributed more than 17 percent of total corporate foundation giving, second only to banking and finance (Foundation Center 2012). Many pharmaceutical foundations are "patient assistance" foundations, which means that they provide financial assistance to customers who cannot afford the co-pay amount on their drugs. In 2016, the Department of Justice began an investigation of these foundations out of a concern that pharmaceutical companies are using the foundations to boost the sales and prices of the drugs they produce (McCambridge 2016).

In terms of locations, the states of New York (210 corporate foundations), California (181), Illinois (163), Pennsylvania (136), Massachusetts (122), Ohio (119), and Wisconsin (113) each held 5 percent or more of the American corporate foundation population as of 2014. New York, California, Illinois, and Ohio consistently rank at the top of the list of states with the most Fortune 500 companies, which is consistent with having more corporate foundations (Texas also ranks very highly in terms of Fortune 500 companies and follows Wisconsin with 107 corporate foundations in the state). The prominence of Pennsylvania, Massachusetts, and Wisconsin could be explained in other ways. Pennsylvania has a rich philanthropic history (started with Andrew Carnegie), and Pittsburgh still has one of the most active philanthropic communities in the United States. Massachusetts is a wealthy state and can attract major businesses through the city of Boston and its internationally acclaimed universities. Wisconsin, according to Bernardo (2017), is the fifth most charitable state in America, which may also translate to more corporate generosity. Of course, there may be other important reasons for these states to have so many corporate foundations (for instance, they may be attractive to businesses because of their tax climates, or the composition of their workforce, or their resources).

A study of giving for elementary and secondary education by the corporate foundations of Fortune 500 companies in the United States (Morsy 2015) found that corporate foundations tend to focus their giving at the individual school, city, or district levels, which is consistent with the claim that corporate foundations tend to focus their giving in their local communities to generate some goodwill and train their future workforce (Porter and Kramer 2002; Fernandez and Hager 2014). They also make grants to "well-received, mainstream topics in education that are also relatively safe and allow little room for contention" (e.g., avoiding the school choice debate), which is consistent with the argument that corporate foundations' giving is, at least in part, an attempt to legitimize the company (Morsy 2015, p.1523). Koushyar et al. (2015) find that corporate foundations tend to spread their funds across more grantees (making their grants smaller on average) and are less likely to continue funding the same grantees year after year than their independent foundation counterparts. These findings are also consistent with the argument that corporate foundations are trying to address the interests of as many company stakeholders as possible to generate community goodwill.

6.5 Context and Activities

In the United States, corporate foundations are clearly seen as part of the foundation sector and the nonprofit sector more generally. Hammack (2006, p. 52) notes that foundations are "an integral part of the nonprofit, nongovernmental sector." Not only are foundations nonprofits themselves by law, but they are also a major source of support for other nonprofits' activities and missions.

Foundations generally have been the target of much criticism in the United States. They have often been in the public eye, and their legitimacy and privileged position questioned by Congress as well as scholars. On the one hand, some argue that foundations have a place within a democracy because they can supply public goods that the government cannot or will not supply (Prewitt 2006a); they support higher-risk, innovative projects and advocacy efforts (Karl and Katz 1981; Lagemann 1989; Hammack and Anheier 2013); and they act as a vehicle for voluntary consumption (i.e., if I am allowed to buy a car with my money, why can't Bill Gates donate to charities?) (for a point/counterpoint analysis, see Anheier and Leat (2013)).[2] Foundations also exist "outside" of the state and of the market, providing them with an opportunity to address state and market failures (Prewitt 2006b). In a theory that is now widely used by nonprofit scholars, Weisbrod (1975) argued that nonprofits, such as foundations, emerged to provide goods and services that the government could not or would not provide (government failure) and that the private sector would not provide (market failure). On the other hand, some highlight foundations' lack of transparency and accountability (Frumkin 2006), their boards composed often exclusively of the elite and the wealthy (Domhoff 2002; Roelofs 2003), the tax benefits their founders enjoy, the dangers of a consensus mentality where nonprofits (and other actors like governments or international organizations) just follow the mega-foundations' agenda (e.g., see Rushton and Williams (2011) for a discussion of mega-foundations' agenda setting in global health policy), and so on.[3] Foundations are also secretive and mysterious, which can make people uncomfortable and lead to distrust. Scholars often refer to foundations as "black boxes" (Diaz 1999; Faulk et al. 2012; Reich 2013) because we know little about them. My own experience interviewing foundation officials has shown me that they tend to be suspicious of scholars and what we might write about them (Tremblay-Boire 2015; see also Katz 2016).

Of course, corporate foundations are subject to these overall criticisms. But there also seems to be some additional skepticism about corporate foundations specifically. Some question their "intentions": are they only using their foundations to bolster their reputation/brand, for marketing purpose, or to recruit employees ("window dressing") or do they really want to improve their communities (CoF 2012; Morsy 2015; Frumkin 2006; Porter and Kramer 2002; Prewitt 2006a)? Corporate foundations have also been criticized for diverting corporation resources, acting as a sort of "tax on shareholders" (Karnani 2010; Masulis and Reza 2014). In a study of Fortune 500 companies between 1997 and 2006, Masulis and Reza (2014) find that CEOs use corporate giving for their personal benefit. They also find that the agency

---

[2] The Boston Review (2013) published a forum of prominent scholars on the place of foundations in a democratic system, available at http://bostonreview.net/forum/foundations-philanthropy-democracy (accessed 10 February 2019). The arguments discussed above mirror some of the points raised by these scholars.

[3] Again, I invite readers to read the nuanced arguments presented by the scholars in the Boston Review forum (available at http://bostonreview.net/forum/foundations-philanthropy-democracy) to get a better sense of the overall debate.

problem is worse in corporate foundations than in direct corporate giving programs to charities: "CEOs also appear to opportunistically transfer contributions to foundations, and these large transfers reduce shareholder cash flow rights significantly" (Masulis and Reza 2014, p.37). The authors conclude that corporate giving, including corporate foundations, decreases firm value and benefits the CEO's pet charities at the expense of the shareholders. In sum, critics put corporate foundations in the United States in an awkward position, criticizing them at once for not being sufficiently charity-oriented and for not being sufficiently profit-oriented.

6.6 Relation to Funding Company

Legally, in the United States, corporate foundations are separate entities; they are not a part of their parent corporation. They receive their assets from a corporation, as opposed to an individual or family (e.g., Bank of America Charitable Foundation, GE Foundation, ExxonMobil Foundation). Corporate executives also usually serve on the board of trustees. Corporate foundations can have an endowment, but often receive annual contributions from the parent corporation. Corporations can contribute more to the foundation in more profitable years and less in leaner years, using the endowment to shield the corporation from business cycles over the longer term. In contrast, in-house corporate giving programs are not separate legal entities. They are not subject to IRS laws governing tax-exempt organizations (see "Models of Corporate Foundations") and do not have to disclose their information to the public. They generally do not have an endowment.

Although conventional wisdom holds that corporate foundations tend to have smaller endowments than other types of foundations in the United States (or no endowment at all, which is known as "pass-through" foundations), the data does not appear to support this assertion overall. Koushyar et al. (2015), in a study of 471 foundations (independent and corporate foundations matched by location and year of founding), find that, although the endowments of corporate foundations are slightly smaller than the endowments of independent foundations in their sample, the difference is not statistically significant. They do find, however, that corporate foundations in the sample raise roughly three times more funds per year than their independent counterparts (Koushyar et al. 2015). Similarly, aggregate Foundation Center data for 2014 shows that the average assets of corporate foundations (about $10.6 million/foundation) are slightly lower than the average assets of operating foundations (about $11.9 million/foundation) but slightly higher than those of independent foundations (about $8.9 million/foundation). The outlier here is community foundations, with average assets of about $103 million per foundation. As such, we may need to revisit the "lack of endowment" as a defining feature of corporate foundations, at least in the United States.

A 2006 report on the expenses of the 10,000 largest foundations in the United States found that far fewer corporate foundations compensate their employees and trustees than independent and community foundations (16% of corporate foundations vs. 34% of independent foundations and 61% of community foundations) (Boris et al. 2006). And among the foundations that do compensate, the average compensation per foundation is the lowest for corporate foundations (Boris et al. 2006). However, please keep in mind that we do not know how many employees/ trustees are being compensated at each foundation. It is possible that corporate foundations have fewer employees, but pay each of them more comparatively. Intuitively, the finding that corporate foundations compensate less than other types of foundations makes sense since companies may be assuming some of the foundations' expenses, including staff pay, administrative costs, and infrastructure costs. However, the fact that the companies are in all likelihood paying at least some of corporate foundations' expenses makes it very difficult to know how much corporate foundations are really spending on administrative costs and compensation in the United States.

Which corporations will choose to create a separate corporate foundation? As noted above, one estimate (Guthrie 2010) is that about 40% of American corporations have their own foundation. Brown et al. (2006) compare Fortune 500 companies that have foundations (83.9% of their sample) to Fortune 500 companies that do not. They find that older companies and companies with more employees are more likely to have established a corporate foundation. They tend to have larger boards and lower debt ratios. And they are "much more likely to involve corporate officers in the management of their giving programs [than companies without foundations]" (Brown et al. 2006, p. 865). Yet their amount of giving is not significantly different.

The Council on Foundations (2012) produced a report, titled "Increasing Impact, Enhancing Value," where it consulted with, conducted workshops, and interviewed corporate philanthropy professionals and leaders from the United States. Findings on the relationship between foundations and their parent companies raised some interesting points. For instance, participants highlighted that corporate philanthropy is viewed differently across the field: by "those who believe philanthropy should be strictly about 'charity' and separate from the business and those who think it should be integrated with the business to create value for the business and society" (CoF 2012, p. 6). In turn, that has led to many different structures: from foundations managed completely independently from the parent company, often by employees with nonprofit experience, to foundations completely managed within the corporate responsibility unit of the parent corporation, by people with business experience, and integrated closely with the business plan. These different approaches and structures have led many to ask what role(s) their own corporate foundation should perform. Respondents also noted that, despite increasing pressure to align the foundation's philanthropy more closely with the business, many of them felt that their peers inside the company were dismissive toward them because they saw the foundation's role as only tangential to the business (CoF 2012).

In terms of decision-making, the literature is unclear on who has more influence on grant-making decisions in corporate foundations. One argument for creating a separate corporate foundation is that it reduces CEO discretion over the philanthropic endeavors of the company, thus preventing CEOs from pursuing their own self-interest at the expense of the corporation (Masulis and Reza 2014; Werbel and

Carter 2002). Yet, some find that the parent company's CEO is often the main decision-maker at the foundation (Himmelstein 1997; Barnard 1997), while others find that foundation presidents/executive directors are the primary decision-makers (Morsy 2015). Werbel and Carter (2002) find mixed evidence of company CEO influence over the giving priorities of the corporate foundation, but they do find that the giving priorities of the CEO become less important when the CEO is not on the board of trustees of the foundation.

6.7 Discussion and Outlook

The foundation landscape in America is vibrant, and corporate foundations are no exception. One estimate suggests that 40 percent of corporations in America have their own corporate foundation. Despite constituting a small portion of the overall foundation population (3 percent), corporate foundations contribute more than their share of foundation giving (9 percent). Their grants are varied in focus, but the business interests of their parent corporations are never forgotten. Corporate foundations tend to give locally, to relatively uncontroversial causes, and to many grantees—such a strategy creates goodwill from the community, a better trained workforce for the corporation, and a loyal customer base. Ironically, as corporate foundation officials are pressured to maintain a strategic connection to the parent corporation, they often struggle to find support for the foundation's activities from their peers inside the parent corporation. This tension between serving the greater good and advancing the interests of the corporation is really a challenge that no other type of foundation is facing. As such, it would be interesting to see more research on how foundations officials/employees/volunteers respond to this challenge. A comparison with corporate giving programs on this issue may also be warranted, as the giving programs' position inside of the company (as opposed to a separate legal entity) may lead to different behaviors and strategies.

As readers may have noticed, this chapter has discussed broader criticisms of foundations, in general, and of corporate foundations, in particular, but we have not really discussed foundations from the perspective of their nonprofit recipients. Social movement and nonprofit scholars argue that institutional donors (mainly foundations and governments) coopt nonprofits by providing them with critical financial resources. According to the literature, nonprofits' dependence on external funding affects their ability to choose projects based on beneficiaries' needs, to speak out against donors, and even to fulfill their mission as they prioritize quantitative reporting to donors over qualitative impact (Brulle 2000; Dowie 2001; Ebrahim 2005). As such, perhaps we should not expect nonprofits to give us honest assessments of the foundations that fund them (or refuse to fund them)—you do not bite the hand that feeds you (or that you hope will feed you in the future). But an understanding of foundations from the perspective of their partners may shine a different light on these organizations. With the movement toward professionalization and more "business-like" practices in the nonprofit sector, it would be interesting to compare corporate foundations' interactions with grantees to those of other types of foundations to determine if corporate foundations are fostering more "business-like" behavior than their counterparts. Such a line of inquiry then has implications for debates surrounding what the nonprofit sector should look like and should accomplish in America.

One of the key issues with the academic literature on foundations in the United States is that most of our findings only apply to a limited set of foundations and not to the entire population. Qualitative research has understandably tended to focus on larger, more well-known foundations. Because of time-consuming data gathering, quantitative research tends to focus on small samples, often of the largest foundations at the time (or, in the case of corporate foundations, of foundations affiliated with Fortune 500 companies or publicly traded companies), and often rely on self-reporting by foundations. The problem with such an approach is that we cannot know if there are systematic differences between how the under-researched foundations and the oft-researched foundations operate. Our understanding of philanthropic foundations may be flawed (maybe even deeply flawed) because of our biased samples. Future research needs to focus on including populations of foundations that are often neglected because of their size or because of a lack of information. However, gathering data on such populations of foundations will likely be quite difficult and may not ultimately show us a different picture of the foundation landscape.

6.8 Practical Relevance and Recommendations

Overall, this chapter aimed to give the reader an overview of what we know about corporate foundations in the United States based on statistical data (e.g., from foundations' tax filings) and academic research. However, some practical recommendations also arise for existing corporate foundations, or for companies aiming to start a corporate foundation in the United States, from this chapter.

First, the section entitled "A Brief History of Foundations in the United States" above noted that self-dealing is prohibited in foundations in the United States. This prohibition on self-dealing in federal law is especially critical for corporate foundations since corporations often choose staff members as board directors and volunteers. These individuals have to define clearly when they are acting on behalf of the corporation and when they are acting on behalf of the foundation. Corporations also may not use the foundation's assets for their own benefit. However, being too careful about self-dealing can also create problems by isolating the foundation more and more from the business and thus losing the connection between the foundation and the business strategy. I would recommend that corporate foundation staff and officers get legal counsel to understand fully what self-dealing means and what the rule entails.

Second, although the chapter has not focused on this issue explicitly, we know that collaboration can be a challenge for nonprofits more generally and has been a challenge for foundations as well. Organizations that enter into a collaborative effort or partnership do not always share the same goals or values. Collaborative efforts often require at least some changes in the organization, and staff/volunteers may resist those changes. Power dynamics may create frictions among the different partners. But research suggests that collaboration may be especially challenging for corporate foundations because they may be reluctant to cooperate with business competitors (CoF 2012). Yet, leaders of corporate foundations do understand the large contributions that collaborations can make. Business leaders are also acutely aware that many of the problems when are facing today, be they social, environmental, or other, are increasingly complex and cannot be solved by single actors. As such, I am optimistic that they will find ways to engage in more, and more meaningful, collaboration with their peers.

Third, research mentioned in the chapter (Koushyar et al. 2015) suggests that corporate foundations make smaller, more numerous grants than independent foundations in a given year and are less likely to repeat grants to the same nonprofits in subsequent years. Although such a practice makes sense from a business perspective (creating a rapport with large segments of the community), I would encourage corporate foundations to also think about the possibly larger impact on society that their funds could make if they supported a smaller set of nonprofits more substantively and consistently. Foundations need to find a balance in their grant-making: small grants to ever-changing recipients cannot produce significant results, just as large grants to the same small group of recipients can create dependence and complacency. Corporate foundations have to find their place somewhere in the middle.

Fourth and finally, although this chapter did not mention other giving vehicles, corporations must decide carefully whether a private foundation is the appropriate vehicle to achieve their goals or whether other vehicles, such as direct giving or donor-advised funds, may be more advantageous in reaching their business and societal goals.

References

Anheier, H. K., & Hammack, D. C. (Eds.). (2010). *American foundations: Roles and contributions.* Washington, DC: Brookings Institution Press.

Anheier, H. K., & Leat, D. (2013). Philanthropic foundations: What rationales? *Social Research: An International Quarterly, 80*(2), 449–472.

Barnard, J. W. (1997). Corporate philanthropy, executives' pet charities and the agency problem. *New York Law School Law Review, 41*, 1147–1178.

Bernardo, R. (2017). 2017's most charitable states. *WalletHub* [online]. Available at: https://wallethub.com/edu/most-and-least-charitable-states/8555/. Accessed 30 Nov 2017.

Billitteri, T. J. (2000). Donors big and small propelled philanthropy in the 20th century. *The Chronicle of Philanthropy*, January 13.

Boris, E. T., Renz, L., Barve, A., Hager, M. A., & Hobor, G. (2006). *Foundation expenses & compensation.* Washington, D.C.: The Urban Institute, the Foundation Center, and Philanthropic Research, Inc..

Bremner, R. H. (1988). *American philanthropy* (2nd ed.). Chicago, IL: The University of Chicago Press.

Brown, E. R. (1979). *Rockefeller medicine men: Medicine and capitalism in the Progressive Era.* Berkeley: University of California Press.

Brown, W. O., Helland, E., & Smith, J. K. (2006). Corporate philanthropic practices. *Journal of Corporate Finance, 12*(5), 855–877.

Brulle, R. J. (2000). *Agency, democracy, and nature: The U.S. environmental movement from a critical theory perspective.* Cambridge, MA: MIT Press.

CECP. (2016). *Giving in numbers* (2016th ed.). New York, NY: CECP.

Council on Foundations (CoF). (2012). *Increasing impact, enhancing value.* Arlington, VA: Council on Foundations.

Cousens, T. W. (1949). How far corporations may contribute to charity. *Virginia Law Review, 35*(4), 401–424.

Diaz, W. A. (1999). The behavior of grantmaking foundations. In H. K. Anheier & S. Toepler (Eds.), *Private funds, public purpose: Philanthropic foundations in international perspective* (pp. 141–154). New York, NY: Kluwer Academic.

Domhoff, G. W. (2002). *Who rules America?: Power and politics.* Boston, MA: McGraw.

Dowie, M. (2001). *American foundations: An investigative history.* Cambridge, MA: MIT Press.

Ebrahim, A. (2005). Accountability myopia: Losing sight of organizational learning. *Nonprofit and Voluntary Sector Quarterly, 34*(1), 56–87.

Faulk, L., Lecy, J., & McGinnis, J. (2012). *A partial theory of nonprofit success in grant markets.* Presented at the annual conference of the Association for Research on Nonprofit Organization and Voluntary Action (ARNOVA), Indianapolis, Indiana.

Fernandez, K. M., & Hager, M. A. (2014). Public and private dimensions of grantmaking foundations. *Public Administration Quarterly, 38*(3), 405–439.

Foundation Center. (2012). *Key facts on corporate foundations.* New York: Foundation Center. Available at: http://foundationcenter.org/gainknowledge/research/nationaltrends.html?_ga=1.68574232.841823220.1459433112. Accessed 31 Mar 2016.

Foundation Center. (2017). *Foundation stats.* [online] Foundation Center. Available at: http://data.foundationcenter.org/. Accessed 20 Dec 2016.

Frumkin, P. (1998). The long recoil from regulation: Private philanthropic foundations and the Tax Reform Act of 1969. *The American Review of Public Administration, 28*(3), 266–286.

Frumkin, P. (2006). *Strategic giving: The art and science of philanthropy.* Chicago: University of Chicago Press.

Gramm, C. J. (1961). Corporate donations to religious and educational bodies. *Notre Dame Law., 37*(2), 206–219.

Guthrie, D. (2010). Corporate philanthropy in the United States: What causes do corporations back? In E. S. Clemens & D. Guthrie (Eds.), *Politics and partnerships: Voluntary associations in America's political past and present* (pp. 183–204). Chicago, IL: University of Chicago Press.

Hall, P. D. (2002). *"Inventing the nonprofit sector" and other essays on philanthropy, voluntarism, and nonprofit organizations.* Baltimore, MD: Johns Hopkins University Press.

Hammack, David C. (2006). American Debates on the Legitimacy of Foundations. In: K. Prewitt, M. Dogan, S. Heydemann, and S. Toepler, eds., The Legitimacy of Philanthropic Foundations: United States and European Perspectives. New York, NY: Russell Sage Foundation, pp.49–98.

Hammack, D. C., & Anheier, H. K. (2013). *A versatile American institution: The changing ideals of realities of philanthropic foundations.* Washington: Brookings Institution Press. Hill.

Himmelstein, J. L. (1997). *Looking good and doing good: Corporate philanthropy and corporate power.* Bloomington: Indiana University Press.

Karl, B. D., & Katz, S. N. (1981). The American private philanthropic foundation and the public sphere 1890–1930. *Minerva, 19*(2), 236–270.

Karnani, A. (2010). The case against corporate social responsibility. *The Wall Street Journal*, August 23.

Katz, S. N. (2016). Does philanthropy threaten democracy? *Stanford Social Innovation Review, Fall*, 70.

Kiger, J. C. (2000). *Philanthropic foundations in the twentieth century*. Wesport, CT: Greenwood Press.

Koushyar, J., Longhofer, W., & Roberts, P. W. (2015). A comparative analysis of corporate and independent foundations. *Sociological Science, 2*, 582–596.

Labovitz, J. R. (1973). 1969 Tax reform reconsidered. In F. Heinman (Ed.), *The future of foundations* (pp. 101–131). Englewood Cliffs, NJ: Prentice Hall.

Lagemann, E. C. (1989). *The politics of knowledge; the Carnegie Corporation, philanthropy, and public policy*. Middletown, CT: Wesleyan University Press.

Marts, A. C. (1953). *Philanthropy's role in civilization: Its contribution to human freedom*. New York, NY: Harper & Brothers.

Masulis, R. W., & Reza, S. W. (2014). Agency problems of corporate philanthropy. [online] *ECGI – Finance Working Paper No. 370*. Available at SSRN: https://ssrn.com/abstract=2234221. Accessed 10 Jan 2017.

McCambridge, R. (2016). Philanthropy of pharmaceutical companies under DOJ scrutiny. *Nonprofit Quarterly* [online]. Available at: https://nonprofitquarterly.org/2016/08/02/philanthropy-pharmaceutical-companies-doj-scrutiny/. Accessed 10 Dec 2017.

McClimon, T. J. (2004). The shape of corporate philanthropy yesterday and today. *GIA Reader, 15*(3). Available at: https://www.giarts.org/article/shape-corporate-philanthropy-yesterday-and-today.

Morsy, L. (2015). Corporate philanthropic giving practices in US school education. *Voluntas: International Journal of Voluntary and Nonprofit Organizations, 26*(4), 1510–1528.

Porter, M. E., & Kramer, M. R. (2002). The competitive advantage of corporate philanthropy. *Harvard Business Review, 80*(12), 56–68.

Prewitt, K. (2006a). Foundations. In W. W. Powell & R. Steinberg (Eds.), *The nonprofit sector: A research handbook* (pp. 355–377). New Haven, CT: Yale University Press.

Prewitt, K. (2006b). American foundations: What justifies their unique privileges and powers. In K. Prewitt, M. Dogan, S. Heydemann, & S. Toepler (Eds.), *The legitimacy of philanthropic foundations: United States and European perspectives* (pp. 27–48). New York, NY: Russell Sage Foundation.

Reich, R. (2013). *Forum: What are foundations for? – Opening*. [online] Boston Review. Available at: http://bostonreview.net/forum/foundations-philanthropy-democracy. Accessed 10 Jan 2017.

Roelofs, J. (2003). *Foundations and public policy: The mask of pluralism*. New York, NY: Albany.

Rushton, S., & Williams, O. (Eds.). (2011). *Partnerships and foundations in global health governance*. London, UK: Palgrave Macmillan.

Sealander, J. (1997). *Private wealth and public life; Foundation philanthropy and the reshaping of American social policy from the progressive era to the new deal*. Baltimore, MD: The Johns Hopkins University Press.

Sharfman, M. (1994). Changing institutional rules: The evolution of corporate philanthropy, 1883–1953. *Business & Society, 33*(3), 236–269.

Smith, N. C. (1994). The new corporate philanthropy. *Harvard Business Review, 72*(3), 105–114.

Smith, J. A. (1999). The evolving role of American foundations. In C. T. Clotfelter & T. Ehrlich (Eds.), *Philanthropy and the nonprofit sector in a changing America* (pp. 34–51). Bloomington, IN: Indiana University Press.

Smith, W. H., & Chiechi, C. P. (1974). *Private foundations: Before and after the Tax Reform Act of 1969*. Washington, DC: American Enterprise Institute. State University of New York Press.

Tremblay-Boire, J. (2015). *International grantmaking by American foundations*. PhD. University of Washington.

Weaver, W. (1967). *U.S. Philanthropic foundations: Their history, structure, management and record*. New York: Harper and Row.

Weisbrod, B. A. (1975). Toward a theory of the voluntary nonprofit sector in a three-sector economy. In S. Rose-Ackerman (Ed.), *The economics of nonprofit institutions* (pp. 21–44). New York, NY: Oxford University Press.

Werbel, J. D., & Carter, S. M. (2002). The CEO's influence on corporate foundation giving. *Journal of Business Ethics, 40*(1), 47–60.

Joannie Tremblay-Boire is Assistant Professor in the School of Public Policy at the University of Maryland, College Park. Her research centers on nongovernmental organizations, nonprofits, and foundations. Her work has appeared in *Public Administration Review*, *Nonprofit and Voluntary Sector Quarterly*, and *Voluntas*, among others.

Chapter 7
Do Chinese Corporate Foundations Enhance Civil Society?

Lijun He and Qun Wang

Abstract Corporation foundation is one of the most popular tools for Chinese corporations and entrepreneurs to carry out their charitable activities. However, do these foundations play a role in the development of Chinese civil society and in what ways? Followed by a brief introduction on the history, regulations, and rational of the establishment of Chinese corporate foundations, the major body of work aims to appraise the aforementioned topic under the framework of roles of nonpoint organizations (i.e., service, value guardian, advocacy, and social capital), with a focus on service and social capital dimensions. Our empirical data analysis shows that Chinese corporate foundations have been enhancing the civil society through its mission centrality on the pressing societal issues, larger expenditure on charitable activities, and adequate equity and lower amounts on administrative costs in carrying out their missions. A public space is being created through the commitment of corporate foundations to expressing pluralism, volunteer mobilization, and an ever-growing ability to attract donations. However, its role to civil society can also be limited due to modest numbers of full-time staff and their relatively low performance ratings or accountability.

Keywords Corporate foundations · China · Quantitative research · Institutional environment

---

The authors wish to thank Yifan Tang, Hanwen Zheng, and Yushi Chen for their research assistance.

L. He (✉)
Center of Corporate Social Responsibility Development Center, Shenzhen, China

Institute of Public Service, Seattle University, Seattle, WA, China

Q. Wang
Indiana University, Bloomington, IN, USA
e-mail: qunwang@iu.edu

7.1 Introduction

Much attention has been focused on the rapid development of China's philanthropic sector, both at home and abroad. The number of foundations, especially nonpublic foundations, has more than doubled in the past 5 years; charitable donations soared in response to the massive Sichuan earthquake in 2008 and mounted to 15.75 million USD (or RMB 99.2 million[1]) in 2015; ten million Chinese participated in volunteer activities in 2015 (Yang 2016). Persistent, restrictive regulatory hurdles began to be dismantled with the debut of China's first Charity Law in 2016, a law that aims to expand a space in civil society for more people to act by lowering the threshold for nonprofit registration and fundraising (*The Wall Street Journal* 2016). Chinese corporations and entrepreneurs are the key drivers of this robust growth and dramatic change. China's most successful businessmen, including Jack Ma, the chairman of the board at Alibaba, fund and govern philanthropic foundations like One Foundation, support research and educational institutions that study philanthropy, encourage dialogue between Chinese philanthropists and the international community, and establish foundations that support the capacity building of local nonprofits and social entrepreneurs. These new forms of entrepreneurial philanthropy are "disruptive" (Horvath and Powell 2017) to long-standing government-controlled philanthropic organizations in China: private philanthropy brings alternatives for the public to make charitable donations (the One Foundation is a case in point here); philanthropists and nonpublic foundations "seek to shape civic values in the image of funders' interest" (Horvath and Powell 2017, p. 2) and empower control of their own charitable donations through newly legalized charitable organizations.

It is unclear, however, the extent to which the overall corporate foundation plays a role in the development of Chinese civil society. This question is worth examining because previous research findings have primarily focused on regarding the link between the motivation of philanthropists and the acquisition of political capital through philanthropic giving by Chinese entrepreneurs and business firms (Estes 1998; Conference Board 2012; Wang and Qian 2011). Admittedly, corporate giving, just like any kind of giving, is best understood as an act motivated by the convergence of altruism and self-interest. However, the public goods created by corporate foundations should be assessed because it grants policy makers and civic leaders insights into the power of business and contributions of corporate foundations. More importantly, such an assessment helps illuminate the business' potential to delivery social services, "fortify civic participation worldwide," and "defend for civic space" that is increasingly curtailed (Niehaus 2016).

This chapter includes five parts. The first one is dedicated to the historical development trajectory of the Chinese corporate foundations, the legal definition and concepts of corporate philanthropy and corporate foundations, and the benefits of establishing corporate foundations. The second part reviews the literature on the role of civil society and corporate foundations and identifies the theoretical

---

[1] This paper uses 1:6.3 as the US dollar to Chinese renminbi (RMB) exchange rate.

framework for analysis, in addition to describing our research method. The third part provides descriptive data on the overall development of Chinese corporate foundations. The fourth part examines the role of Chinese corporate foundations in the development of civil society from service and civic engagement perspectives. The final part discusses the findings, practical implications, and future research.

7.2 Definition and Legal Regulations

7.2.1 Background

Starting in the late Ming Dynasty, Chinese merchants gave generously through local governments, trade associations, and benevolent societies (Fuma 1997). With the establishment of the People's Republic of China (PRC), direct corporate giving can be traced back to reforms of the 1970s when the PRC embraced a policy of opening-up and reform. For more than two decades, until the 2000s, almost all the corporate direct giving went to government-endorsed foundations, which started during the 1980s. Corporate social responsibility (CSR) was introduced in the early 1990s by foreign firms in China (Zu and Song 2009).

With the development of China's market economy, the emerging private business began to give through local governments and quasi-government agencies (Shue 1998). In a 1995 national survey of 2870 Chinese private entrepreneurs, 87% replied affirmatively to having made donations in the past. The median of the cumulative contributions was 1163 USD, with a maximum of 1.3 million USD (Ma and Parish 2006). However, the number of corporate foundations was stagnant from 1990 to 2004, during which no foundation was established. Not until the 2004 *Regulations on Foundation Administration* (hereafter referred as *Regulations*) was enacted did corporate foundations come into existence. They have grown ever since. In the past decade, Chinese corporate foundations have grown from six foundations in 2004 to 183 in 2011, and the number reached 610 by the end of 2015 (China Foundation Center 2016).

7.2.2 Rules and Regulations Related to Corporate Foundations

According to the *Regulations*, foundations in China are divided into two major categories: public and nonpublic foundations. On one hand, a public foundation is eligible to raise funds from the public and is mandated to spend no less than 70 percent of the total revenues of the previous year; a nonpublic foundation, on the other hand, cannot raise funds from the public and is required to spend no less than 8 percent of the remaining funds from the previous year. Public foundations in China primarily usually consist of government-endorsed foundations (such as China Foundation for Poverty Alleviation). Nonpublic foundations are usually comprised of corporate, community, university, independent, and family foundations. To establish a nonpublic foundation, the *Regulations* require that "the original funds of nonpublic foundations should be not less than 317,460 USD (or RMB 2 million); and they must retain those funds in their current account" (Article 8, MoCA 2004). Quasi-government agencies or government units established the majority of public foundations. For instance, China Red Cross Society established China Red Cross Society Foundation, and State Council Poverty Alleviation and Development Office established China Foundation for Poverty Alleviation. Only a few exceptional individuals have been able to register their foundations as public foundation. The establishment of public foundations has stricter and higher minimum thresholds: no less than 1.3 million USD (or RMB 8 million) for establishing a national public foundation, and no less than 634,921 USD (or RMB 4 million) for establishing a regional public foundation. Additionally, foundations with initial funds exceeding 3.18 million USD (or RMB 20 million) and national foundations are mandated to register with and receive supervision of the Ministry of Civil Affairs and receive supervision under the said agency (Article 6, MoCA 2004). As of December 31, 2016, China has 5545 foundations, including 1565 public foundations and 3980 nonpublic foundations (Yang 2017). Corporate foundations account for 19.17 percent (763) of all the foundations (China Foundation Center 2016).

A corporate foundation also needs to abide by various regulations on governance, expenditures on administration, tax exemptions, and reporting, in addition to meeting the minimum charitable spending (payout) and funding requirements as discussed above regarding the nonpublic foundations. We now discuss the five areas in particular relevance to corporate foundation under the regulations for nonpublic foundations.

Governance According to Articles 20 to 24 in the *Regulations*:

- The board of directors must include 5–25 members, who serve for a term of no more than 5 years.
- No more than one-third of board members may be family members in a nonpublic foundation.
- The chair of the board, who is the legal representative of the foundation and the chief executive director, should not be simultaneously employed by the state.

Expenditure on Administration Article 29 of the *Regulations* limits the annual expenditure on salaries and office administrators to no more than 10 percent of total expenditures.

Tax exemption Foundations are not automatically qualified for tax-exempt status upon registration; instead, they need to apply for a certificate. Chinese nonprofits are required to submit different applications to the tax bureau for tax deduction and tax exemption. In the case of the tax deduction permit,[2] the nonprofit will be able to

---

[2] The Department of Finance and Tax grants permits to nonprofits to issue tax-deduction receipts if the donation is directed to disaster relief, poverty alleviation, education, science, culture, health, environmental protection, public infrastructure, or other social welfare causes.

issue receipts to donors for their income tax deductions. With tax exemptions,[3] the nonprofit can be exempted from income tax obligations. The Ministry of Finance and State Administration of Taxation issued *Notification on Nonprofit Organization's Tax Exemption* in 2009. It stipulates the following as tax-exempt income:

- Donations from individuals and organizations
- Government subsidies, excluding government payments for purchasing services
- Membership fees stipulated in relevant government regulations
- Income with tax exemption and its interest from savings in banks

It should be noted that foundations currently have to pay income tax on investments at the same rate as for-profit organizations (25%) (the Conference Board 2012).

Reporting Articles 34 to 39 of the *Regulations* requires foundations to submit annual reports to their supervisory unit and department. The annual report contains basic organizational, financial, and project information. The annual report must be audited by a certified accounting firm and published on government-designated media platforms after inspection.

7.2.3 Concepts and Definitions

A corporate foundation is usually a nonpublic foundation established by a for-profit corporation. Separate from the parent company, a corporate foundation receives funding mainly through donations from the parent company, and its governing board is mainly under the control of the parent company (Anheier and List 2005). In the context of an emerging economy like China's, business entrepreneurs sometimes provide the sources of funding in the name of the firm and blend his or her personal charitable foundation into a corporate foundation. Corporate foundations are the fastest growing category among all nonpublic foundations (China Foundation Center 2016).

7.2.4 Benefits and Motivations of Establishing Corporation Foundations

In China, the establishment of corporate foundations is also driven by various benefits that come with it. First, a corporate foundation can glean benefits that corporate giving may not achieve. Generally speaking, corporate direct giving and corporate foundations have different legal, financial, and managerial implications

---

[3] The Department of Finance and Tax grants nonprofits with tax-exemption status. According to the Regulations on the Implementation of the Enterprise Income Tax Law of the People's Republic of China, the term "qualified not-for-profit organizations" refers to an organization that concurrently meets provisions, including complete registration, public interest, profit constraints, and administrative costs within legal requirements.

for a company. From a legal perspective, Chinese corporate foundations, once established, can apply for tax deductions or exemptions (Council on Foundations 2016). The benefit of the corporate foundation is that foundations allow firms to optimally time their tax reporting for charitable contributions when tax rates are high without obligating them to pay the reported donations in the same period (Webb 1994; Smith 1993). From a financial management perspective, a firm may record the expense related to charitable contributions on the income statement in any period it chooses by moving funds to the foundation, as long as it has enough funds to cover necessary payouts (Petrovits 2006). Additionally, a corporate foundation separates a firm's corporate social responsibilities (CSR) department from managers, reducing managers' use of the corporate budget to serve their own interests. Other benefits for corporations that establish foundations include fulfilling their role as good citizens, being perceived as more neutral and objective than purely profit-oriented corporations and improving public communications and identity (see Westhues and Einwiller 2006).

Other than benefits of establishing a corporate foundation, we identified the following three motivations of corporations for the emergence of corporate foundations. First, corporate foundations play a role in helping Chinese corporations carry out charitable activities strategically. By strategically, we mean corporations in pursuit of both economic and societal returns (Porter and Kramer 2002). Such strategic activities could improve stakeholder relations or focus on areas that are both beneficial for the company and society. Some Chinese firms view corporate foundations as an extended arm for improving stakeholder relations. "Establishing a corporate foundation can strategically help increase cohesion of our tens of thousands of direct sales persons across the country through their charitable events and donations," notes the former director of the Amway Foundation China. "Moreover, our suppliers and corporate partners are also willing to donate to our corporate foundation and support our child nutrition project" (Kuang 2015). Also, empirical research shows that Chinese entrepreneurs whose business interests interact with charitable welfare activities are more likely to establish a foundation than those whose business do not (He 2015). Additionally, Chinese entrepreneurs also indicate that they mainly make contributions when disaster strikes. Establishing a foundation can help a corporation carry out well-planned and sustainable philanthropy on a regular basis (An 2015).

Second, a corporate foundation as an entity separate from the corporation can pursue charitable projects that go beyond the scope of corporate interest and business. For example, corporations that specialize in volunteer management for mass sports events may have to decline the offer to help government agencies or other nonprofits share such expertise due to its peripheral nature of such services compared to their core business activities. With a corporate foundation, the corporation can offer such professional services as its programs (Kuang 2015). In other words, the corporate foundation helps maximize discretionary managerial behavior.

Third, the establishment of a corporate foundation in China can be a result of political influence. Studies show that Chinese corporate and entrepreneurs' donations tend to be supportive of social and political conformity (Fuma 1997; Chen and Touve 2011; Ma and Parish 2006; Zhao et al. 2014). Simply put, some corporations establish foundations because the government asks them to (The Conference Board 2015). Faced with tight financial budgets, for example, local governments often solicit donations from leading entrepreneurs and corporations. Guangdong Poverty Alleviation Day is a case in point. On this day, many corporations are invited to make donations to governmental charities. The reason that the government encourages corporations and entrepreneurs to establish foundations is for government to solicit donations more easily. Additionally, empirical research finds that Chinese entrepreneurs with political affiliations (e.g., membership with the People's Congress or Chinese People's Political Consultative Conference) are more likely to establish foundations sooner than those without such affiliations (He 2015).

7.3 Literature Review, Theoretical Framework, and Method

As discussed above, the benefits of and motivations for establishing corporate foundations are multifold, beginning first with an economic agenda. At the same time, since a corporate foundation is registered as a charitable organization, its donors will be eligible to enjoy tax deductions. To justify such a public subsidy, it is important for corporate foundations to advance societal development. In this section, we will examine the existing literature on corporate foundations and civil society as well as identify the theoretical framework for this chapter.

7.3.1 Literature on Corporate Foundations and Civil Society

Corporate direct giving, especially as a common form of CSR in China, has been extensively analyzed, with a focus on the association between corporate giving and corporate financial performance, values, public reputations, or government relations (Song and Wang 2010; Wang and Qian 2011; Zhang et al. 2016).

In contrast, corporate foundations, as a nonprofit entity, are inadequately investigated by either business or nonprofit scholars in China. The existent research on corporate foundations primarily focuses on governance issues (He 2015). Other research reports on corporate foundations come from the China Foundation Center, for instance, *Report on the Development of Corporate Foundations 2016*. It provides an overview of the status of corporate foundations and raises concerns about their transparency (China Foundation Center 2016).

Additionally, a report conducted by CSR Asia outlines the challenges of developing corporate foundations in China. The challenges include the following (D'Ath and Berger 2012):

- Chinese corporate foundations demonstrate a lack of organizational capacity to support or implement community development due to limited staff and limited knowledge of communities.
- Chinese corporate foundations have difficulties navigating government regulations that allow foundations to grow in the areas of organizational registration, donations, and investments.
- Foundations lack independence from parent companies.
- Foundations have limited ability to build effective partnerships and sustainable community investments.
- Foundations lack transparency and credibility.
- Foundations lack tools and infrastructure to monitor and evaluate programs.
- Foundations find it challenging to build positive relations with government bodies to implement community development project successfully.

There are a limited number of studies of corporate or entrepreneur contributions to civil society. For example, Cumming et al. (2016) synthesize efforts by Chinese corporations with respect to environmental sustainability. Kennedy (2009) finds that Chinese corporations have been engaged in active policy advocacy through their industry associations; in response to constraints placed on them by central party–state regulation of social activism, industry associations have developed lobbying vehicles, such as direct lobbying and efforts to influence the media and to seek greater autonomy. Both Xiao (2013) and Yang (2012), from different perspectives, utilize an ethnographic approach to document and provide insights about the philanthropic involvement of a group of top Chinese entrepreneurs in environmental protection in Inner Mongolia. They contend that emerging Chinese entrepreneurs are experimenting with democratic practices through philanthropic engagement that includes membership in environmental organizations, thus creating a new space for encouraging Chinese democracy on a wider scale. Generally speaking, the majority of research on corporate philanthropy and entrepreneurs' engagement in philanthropy tends to be less about their "voluntary" nature (Fuma 1997; Chen and Touve 2011) and more supportive of social and political conformity (Ma and Parish 2006). To sum up, the role of corporate foundations and civil society has yet to be examined systematically, and this chapter hopes to close the gap in the literature.

7.3.2 Theoretical Framework

Civil society, a space for action by individuals, families, and various types of organizations to strive for a common/public good, is strengthened and redefined by the organized initiatives of private and voluntary organizations. Salamon and Anheier (1999) pinpoints the role of nonprofit organizations to enhance civil

7 Do Chinese Corporate Foundations Enhance Civil Society?

Table 7.1 Role of nonprofit organizations in contribution to civil society

Roles	Description
Service	Nonprofit organizations are the frontline respondents to social or economic problems. Nonprofit organizations also provide collective goods that are difficult to supply through the private market due to lack of public trust (Hansmann 1987). In this situation, nonprofits have the potential to provide higher-quality collective goods, greater equity, and lower cost/higher efficiency services (due to volunteers and charitable support) (Salamon et al. 2000)
Value guardian	Nonprofit organizations are an important arena for protecting a sphere of private actions through which individuals can express their values and individuality and exercise freedom of expression (Salamon and Anheier 1999). Through this expressive role, nonprofit organizations are instrumental on the promotion of pluralism and diversity of society (Salamon et al. 2000)
Advocacy	Nonprofit organizations rally people with shared concerns and mobilize public attention to address social problems and needs, serving as conduit between individuals and the broader political process to push for social policy or broader social change (Salamon et al. 2000)
Social capital	Nonprofit organizations unify and integrate individuals and communities through encouraging social interaction, fostering trust and reciprocity, and building participatory democracy (Salamon and Anheier 1999; Salamon et al. 2000)

society, including value guardians, service providers, advocates, and builders of social capital. A description of the roles of nonprofit organizations in enhancing civil society is summarized in Table 7.1:

This chapter will mainly focus on the service and social capital roles of nonprofit organizations delineated in Table 7.1 as a framework to examine the role of Chinese corporate foundations in civil society.

Service is measured by the extent to which organizational mission is devoted to greater equity, commitment to expenditures on charitable projects, and service provision capacity. A nonprofit's capacity, as represented by professionalism, ability to provide services or attract donations, quality of services, and financial sustainability, not only directly affects how it discharges its mission but also reflects whether it serves as an "agent" of change. A nonprofit that is professionally operated, highly accountable, and financially healthy enhances civil society. Financial sustainability, an important indicator of service capacity, is measured by the adequacy of equity, administrative expenses, and operating margins. Nonprofits with relatively small amounts of equity may be less able to replace lost revenue following a financial shock than those with relatively large amounts of equity (Greenlee and Trussel 2000). Nonprofits with high administrative expenses can adjust to revenue reductions by taking steps to cut costs (Trussel and Parsons 2008). According to Tuckman and Chang (1991), a nonprofit with a higher operating margin has a greater potential surplus on which to draw during financial difficulties.

Social capital accumulation is measured by examining a corporate foundation's volunteer engagement. Table 7.2 is a summary of measures of the role of civil society with a focus on service and social capital.

Table 7.2 Measures of civil society with a focus on service and social capital dimension

Role in civil society	Measures	
Service	Mission centrality:	Whether the corporate foundations provide services to the most needy of society
	Mission commitment:	Percentage of expenditure to public affairs
	Ability to provide services:	Number of full-time employees
	Ability to attract donations:	Types of tax benefits obtained
	Quality of services:	Evaluation grade received
	Financial sustainability:	
	Adequacy of equity	$\dfrac{\text{Net asset}}{\text{Total asset}}$
	Administrative cost ratio	$\dfrac{\text{Administrative expenses}}{\text{Total expenses}}$
	Operating margin	$\dfrac{\text{Total revenues} - \text{total expenses}}{\text{Total revenues}}$
Social capital	Volunteer engagement:	Number of volunteers mobilized

7.3.3 Methodology for Data Collection

Empirical data for this analysis comes primarily from the archival data of Research Infrastructure of Chinese Foundations (RICF). The database consists of two major types of data: organizational information (i.e., year of establishment, mission statement, board members, supervisors, staff, etc.) and financial information (i.e., donations, revenue sources, expenditures, etc.). Several scholars have utilized this dataset and produced publications on Chinese foundations (Ma and DeDeo 2017; Wang and He 2018; Wei 2016).

Sample size: Data from 2014 and 2016 serve as the focus of major analysis for this chapter in Part III and IV, respectively. The 2016 database, consisting of 621 corporate foundations, provides the most recent (as of October 2016) overview of Chinese corporate foundations.[4] The 2014 database, which consists of 560 corporate foundations and 3681 noncorporate foundations (including both public and nonpublic foundations), provides an in-depth analysis of each measure identified above to examine the contributions of Chinese corporate foundations to civil society.

---

[4] Please note that the actual number of foundations by the end of 2016 is more than 621. This research project uses 621 foundations as of October of 2016 as sample.

7.4 Overview of Chinese Corporate Foundations

7.4.1 Foundation Size, Location, and Scope

As of October 2016, there are 621 corporate foundations in China in total. Most Chinese corporate foundations (93%) are registered at the regional level, with only about 7 percent being registered at the national level through the Ministry of Civil Affairs. Corporate foundations, at regional or national levels, are understood in terms of the geographical scope of their charitable activities at the local level or nationwide. The majority of corporate foundations (78%) are registered at the provincial level of Department of Civil Affairs.

The number of corporate foundations appears to align well with regional economic activity in China. Guangdong province, which tops the GDP list among Chinese provinces, has the largest number of corporate foundations, with 138 or 22 percent of all corporate foundations in China. Jiangsu province, which ranks second in terms of GDP, has the second largest number of corporate foundations, with 68 or 11 percent of the total. Other high GDP areas, such as Beijing and Zhejiang, also have a large number of corporate foundations. Overall, corporate foundations are heavily concentrated on the East Coast and sparsely developed in China's hinterland (see Fig. 7.1). Three major reasons account for the distribution: market mechanisms, regulatory environments, and civil society. The East Coast of China has a high density of companies. Studies of diffusion patterns find that a practice adopted by socially proximate firms (such as firms in the same industry or in the same area) will be more quickly adopted by the local firm because of the ease of obtaining information, the perceived relevance of the practice, and the pressure associated with being left behind (Davis and Greve 1997). Furthermore, provincial governments on the East Coast embrace a more relaxed regulatory environment. For example, Guangdong province has exempted nonpublic foundations from the registration eligibility requirement of identifying a government-sponsoring organization. Lastly, civil society organizations are active in the East Coast, possibly creating a more organic system for corporate foundations.

The charitable activities of Chinese corporate foundations are wide ranging and include the following: education, health, arts, civil society development, environment protection, women and children, public safety, disaster relief, heroic behavior awards, volunteering, and scientific research.

China has witnessed a steady growth of corporate foundations since 2004, when the *Regulations* was enacted. Majority of corporate foundations are young, with 47 percent being newly established between 2012 and 2016 and 45 percent were established between 2007 and 2011. The growth took off in 2009, likely due to massive Sichuan earthquake donations and the consequent Red Cross scandal (He 2015). The growth also reflects the maturation of Chinese philanthropy, a shift from predominantly emergency-driven individual giving to rational institutional giving.

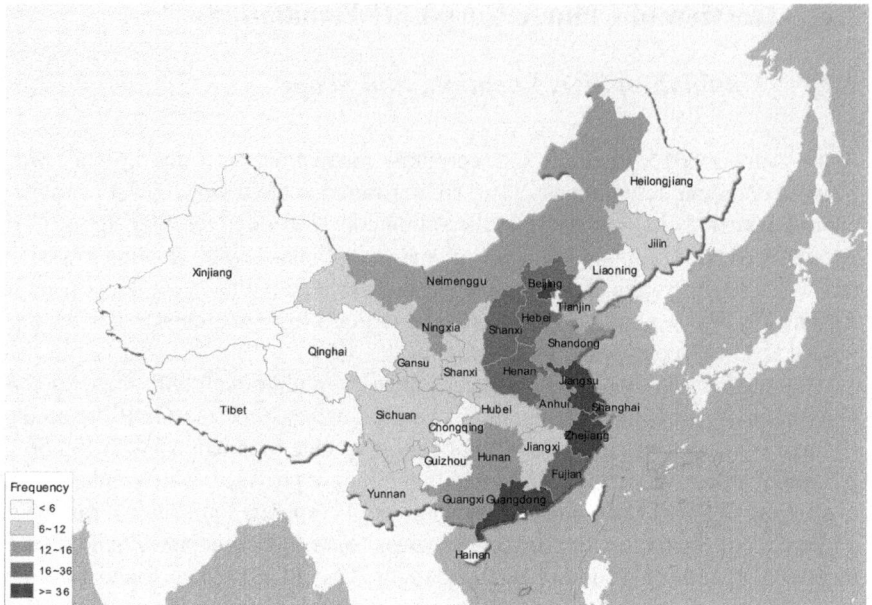

Fig. 7.1 Geographic distribution of Chinese corporate foundations

7.4.2 Resources and Financial Assets

Original Assets Most Chinese corporate foundations choose to register their foundation at the 317,460 USD (or RMB 2 million) level, the lowest minimal fund requirement for registration at a local Department of Civil Affairs. The median and mode of initial assets set up by Chinese corporate foundations are both 317,460 USD (or RMB 2 million).

Net Assets The average net assets of Chinese corporate foundations are 3,174,363 USD (or RMB 19,998,487), and the median is 475,163 USD (or RMB 2,993,528).

Annual Income The average annual income for Chinese corporate foundations is 1,284,523 USD (or RMB 8,092,501), but the distribution is much more positively skewed because the median annual income is only 153,502 USD (or RMB 967,066).

Annual Expenditures Annual expenditures by Chinese corporate foundations vary widely. The average annual expenditure of Chinese corporate foundations is 879,978 USD (or RMB 5,543,860), with a minimum of 0 USD and maximum of USD 36,728,884 (or RMB 231,391,975).

7.5 Contributions to Chinese Civil Society

This section will focus on the contributions of Chinese corporate foundations to civil society. We used data from year of 2014 to examine the above-stated theme, because the necessary variables were relatively complete in 2014, and data from the same year provided consistency. In this section's data analysis, 560 corporate foundations and 3681 noncorporate foundations were included. We will examine the contributions of corporate foundations to civil society in comparison to noncorporate foundations in China. As delineated earlier in the chapter, the contributions were measured according to service and social capital dimensions.

7.5.1 Service

Mission Centrality We measured mission centrality by examining the extent to which corporate foundation missions deviated from the overall major mission declarations of all foundations in China. The service roles assumed by Chinese corporate foundations did not differ from the overall pattern for all the Chinese foundations and noncorporate foundations. Specifically, the top five mission areas for all types of Chinese foundations were education, poverty alleviation, culture, science and research, and elder care. Chinese corporate foundations prioritized education, poverty alleviation, disaster relief, health aid, and elder care. These areas, to a great extent, reflected corporate foundation motivations for giving, that is, public relations enhancement through meeting immediate and widely recognized societal needs and social and political conformity by responding to the government's call for donations to address emergency needs and social welfare. Interestingly, the top five mission areas for noncorporate foundations were almost the same as the overall pattern of all foundations, except that they exclude elder care. Similar to corporate foundations, many noncorporate foundations also focused on health aid, but disaster relief was distinct to corporate foundations.

Mission Commitment We examined Chinese corporate foundation service roles by examining their financial commitment to charitable activities, that is, the percentage of expenditures on charitable activities out of the total annual expenditures. Our data analysis showed the average percentage of expenditure by Chinese corporate foundation was about 90.2 percent and the median was 95.6 percent, which is high. Compared to noncorporate foundations, the difference was not significant ($p = 0.6$).

Ability to Provide Services Studies find that employee size is used as a measure of organizational capacity because human capital is considered a major constraint on an organization's capacity building (The Conference Board 2015). Although Chinese foundations generally have a low capacity with a limited number of full-time staff (as shown in Table 7.3(a)), corporate foundations have significantly lower number of staff members. More than half of corporate foundations we identified had 0–4 full-time employees, and only about ten corporate foundations had more than 10 employees. A t-test was conducted to further compare the number of employees found in corporate foundations and other types of foundations. There was a significant difference between the two types of foundations ($p = 0.0001$). This finding can be interpreted in two ways: First, Chinese corporate foundations take advantage of corporate resources to provide services. Corporate foundation employees usually come from the corporation to minimize administrative costs. Second, corporate foundations appear to provide limited direct services, tending to outsource their services to other nonprofit or government agencies.

Ability to Attract Donations We measured the ability to attract donations by looking at the types of corporate foundation tax benefit. Although there are significant tax benefits for Chinese nonprofits in theory, only a small number of nonprofits applied and obtained approval due to the unclear processes and inconsistent guidelines (Council on Foundations 2016). Table 7.3(b) shows the distribution of types of tax benefits obtained by all Chinese foundations and corporate foundations. Corporate foundations represented 12.4 percent of all Chinese foundations that received tax deductions or have been granted permission to issue tax deductions for donation receipts. Twenty-three corporate foundations, or 18.7 percent of the total number of Chinese foundations, received income tax exemptions, having been granted an income tax exemption license. A similar number of corporate foundations have obtained both tax deductions for donations and income tax exemption licenses. Only 107 corporate foundations out of 996 foundations, or 11 percent, had yet to obtain either of the two tax benefits. Fisher's exact test was conducted to determine whether the differences between corporate and noncorporate foundations were significant. The result was that corporate foundations differ significantly from noncorporate foundations in terms of obtaining income tax-exemption status ($p = 0.04$). No significance was found with respect to other tax-benefit categories.

Quality of Services Foundations are usually evaluated every 5 years (they can apply for a more frequent evaluation if preferred). The Department of Civil Affairs conducts evaluations of foundations and other social organizations for the purpose of promoting healthy, legal, and high-quality social organizations. Four components are evaluated, including basic infrastructure, internal governance and management, work performance, and public opinion. A foundation is ranked according to five levels based on the score they receive. The highest level is 5A, and the lowest level is 1A. Table 7.3(c) illustrates the evaluation results for all Chinese foundations and corporate foundations. As is seen, corporate foundations with 5A or above accounted for 8.5 percent, 4A with 11.6 percent, and 3A with 13.3 percent. A one-way ANOVA (analysis of variance) was conducted, demonstrating that age and evaluation grade were significantly correlated ($p < 0.01$). A Pearson's chi-squared test was conducted, and the results show corporate foundations were not significantly different from noncorporate foundations on the evaluation grade ($X^2 = 6.3642, p = 0.27$).

Table 7.3 Full-time employees, tax-benefit type(s), evaluation grades, and volunteers of Chinese corporate foundation vs. all foundations

(a) Ability to provide services: Measured by number of employees

Number of full-time employees	Frequency (corporate)	Frequency (all)	Percentage (corporate/all foundations)
≥25	1	35	3%
20–24	1	18	5.60%
15–19	2	29	6.90%
10–14	6	124	4.80%
5–9	50	514	9.70%
0–4	314	2203	14.30%
Missing data	186	1183	15.70%

(b) Ability to attract donations: measured by tax benefits obtained

Tax-benefits type	Frequency (Corporate)	Frequency (all)	Percentage (corporate/all foundations)
Tax deduction for donations only	165	1371	12.40%
Income tax exemption only	23	123	18.70%
Both tax deduction and exemption	120	643	18.70%
None	107	996	11%
Missing data	145	1108	13%

(c) Quality of services: evaluation grade received

Evaluation grade	Frequency (Corporate)	Frequency (all)	Percentage (corporate/all foundations)
1A	4	42	9.50%
2A	4	61	6.60%
3A	52	390	13.30%
4A	35	302	11.60%
5A	16	188	8.50%
Not applicable*	259	1968	13.16%
Missing data**	190	1290	14.70%

*Not applicable = not evaluated in the last 5 years or the foundation is established less than 2 years

**The absence of evaluation result does not mean they were not evaluated in the past; it could simply mean they were not evaluated in the last year

(d) Volunteer engagement: number of volunteers mobilized

Number of volunteers	Frequency (Corporate)	Frequency (all)	Percentage (corporate/all foundations)
0	175	1576	11.10%
1–500	179	2950	6%
>500	23	110	21%
Missing data	183	1181	16%

Financial Sustainability A nonprofit's financial sustainability determines whether the nonprofit can fulfill its mission effectively. For example, the adequacy of equity and operating margin indicate whether a nonprofit has enough net assets and surplus to deliver its services without interruption; the administrative cost ratio indicates the nonprofit's operating efficiency (Tuckman and Chang 1991). Table 7.4 displays statistics about equity, administrative ratios, and operating margins found in Chinese corporate foundations. Overall, they had adequate equity to fulfill their missions although the advantage was not significant in comparison to noncorporate foundations. The administrative ratio of Chinese corporate foundations was low, with a mean of 4.2 percent and median of 1.3 percent. This was significantly below the required 10 percent administrative ratio mandated by the Chinese government. In comparison to noncorporate foundations, Chinese corporate foundations had significantly lower administrative cost ratios than noncorporate foundations ($p = 0.008$). The low administrative cost could mean the Chinese corporate foundations may have difficulty in adjusting to revenue reductions via taking steps to cut costs (Trussel and Parsons 2008), but it could also mean, in the Chinese context where low administrative cost is desired by government and public, that corporate foundations currently possess an advantage over other foundations since corporate foundation staff's salary and office expenses are usually covered by the parent company. Operating margin minimums were largely negative in value. The negative ratios confirm overspending as a common practice among Chinese corporate foundations. Due to a number of foundations with large negative operating margin ratios, all the average operating margin ratios skew to the negative. The median value for Chinese corporate foundation operating margins was 1 percent, which shows the limited surplus available to carry out projects sustainably. The low operating margin seems, however, to run across all types of foundations, and corporate foundations were not significantly lower than other types of foundations in terms of their operating margins.

7.5.2 Civic Engagement

Volunteer Engagement Nonprofit organizations traditionally build bonds of social trust and reciprocity by making connections between individuals, groups, and communities. Corporate foundations can contribute to civil society by mobilizing volunteers, especially company volunteers, to serve in the local community, thus creating a network of social trust between volunteers, the company, and the community. Social trust and social networks are pivotal for democracy and address social problems through collective action (Backman and Smith 2000). Table 7.3(d) displays volunteer engagement of corporate foundations in China. It shows that 179 (or 6 percent) corporate foundations reported to have engaged between 1 and 500 volunteers each year. Interestingly, 23 corporate foundations out of 110 of all Chinese foundations (21%) reported they engage 500 or more volunteers each year.

Table 7.4 Financial sustainability of Chinese corporate foundations

	Observations	1st Quartile	Median	Mean	3rd Quartile	Min	Max	Standard deviation
Equity	430	0.99	1	1.05	1	−10.17	267.5	4.65
Administrative cost ratio	430	0.003	0.0131	0.042	0.03	−1.17	1	0.13
Operating margin	430	−0.2	0.1	−505.1	0.5	−1,552,069.5	40.3	27,309.18

Note: The maximum and minimum equity ratios are expected to be 1 and 0, respectively. The unusual maximums and minimum shown in Table 7.4 are a result of the fact that a foundation's liability is negative, meaning other people or organizations owe the foundations. The negative minimums in the table are due to negative net assets in some foundations

7.6 Discussion and Outlook

Do Chinese corporate foundations contribute to civil society and if so, in what way? We examined this question through an analysis of service and social capital dimensions. Among the various measures, we found the following: Chinese corporate foundations are devoted to addressing major issues in civil society, such as education, heath aid, poverty alleviation, and disaster relief; they committed about 90 percent of their annual expenditures on charitable activities, received significantly more permits for income tax exemption, maintained adequate equity to carry out missions, spent significantly lower amounts on administrative costs, and engaged large numbers of volunteers. Although the motivations for these contributions were not purely altruistic, it was still laudable that Chinese corporate foundations could provide complementary services and engage their stakeholders to address societal needs through a strategic alignment of their economic goals and the development goals of society at large.

Chinese corporate foundations, however, may inhibit the enhancement of civil society due to modest numbers of full-time staff and their relatively low evaluation grades. Current law prohibiting foundations from spending more than 10 percent on salaries and administration severely hinders nonprofit organizations from developing talent, providing competitive compensation, and developing professional management structures. Without commitment to nurture a qualified workforce, China's civil society will "continue to face challenges to advancing and professionalizing their operations" (Conference Board 2012, p. 20). We anticipate that Chinese corporate foundations may boost their quality of services as they mature. Currently, many corporate foundations have only recently been established and may not have filed for evaluation or are finding it difficult to meet evaluation requirements. Furthermore, Chinese corporate foundation operating margins are low. This can be improved by long-term corporate budget planning, attracting diverse donors, or creating endowments.

These findings are mostly consistent with previous professional industry reports on Chinese corporate foundations. For example, the role of Chinese corporate foundations in civil society is restrained by their lack of dedicated full-time staff (D'Ath and Berger 2012; China Foundation Center 2016) and difficulties with income sustainability (China Foundation Center 2013).

We also discovered, however, a public space is being created through the commitment of corporate foundations to address societal problems, volunteer mobilization, and an ever-growing ability to attract donations. Moreover, we argue that Chinese entrepreneurs and corporate foundations have begun to bring pluralism to their role as value guardians and to service provisions, although certainly not yet at a large scale or among the majority of entrepreneurs. In this chapter, we find that corporate foundations give priority to missions that meet the pressing needs of Chinese society or advance the government's agenda (Ma and Parish 2006). There is, however, a diverse but rising interest in supporting arts and culture, environmental protection, nonprofit sector capacity building, and research institutions. These interests, to a certain extent, reflect the multiple motivations of Chinese entrepreneurs and the founders of corporate foundations for giving, a shift from purely political, moral, and strategic priorities to personal enrichment and plural "imaginations" of the public good. From the value guardian perspective, Chinese entrepreneurs use their corporate foundations to reflect their philosophical and religious beliefs and revive Chinese traditional culture. In the past 30 years, most Chinese people have been enthusiastically chasing after money and materialistic gain. The allure of capitalism, however, can lead to disorientation. Spiritual fulfillment is a growing need for wealthy people in China. In the search for spiritual fulfillment, some have developed artistic, cultural, and outdoor interests, leading to their philanthropic support for the arts and museums, poetry, environmental protection, and social justice. As we discussed earlier, the mission priority of corporate foundations focuses on education and other immediate need areas, which can reflect the role of corporate foundations in expressing and preserving traditional Chinese values and cultures.

Nonetheless, this chapter also has a few limitations in addressing the contributions of corporate foundations to civil society. The data utilized were purely quantitative, and a lack of qualitative data to provide in-depth understanding about their contributions limits our findings. There is also insufficient information on foundation projects and partners, such as advocacy roles, which could add more insight to their contributions to civil society. These limitations mainly result from the nascent stage of the development of China's nonprofit sector infrastructure (D'Ath and Berger 2012) as well as the early life cycle of corporate foundations. Constrained by an authoritative Chinese political environment and highly compliant culture, Chinese corporate foundations are rarely engaged in controversial social or political issues; thus, advocacy that challenges the state is limited. Future research could focus on case studies of outlier corporate foundations that engage in advocacy.

Despite of these limitations, the findings of this research still provide practical implications for policy makers and the sector professionals.

- For policy makers, two areas can be addressed to promote the effectiveness of corporate foundations on civil society enhancement in China.

  - Corporate foundations' low evaluation grade implies room for strengthening their accountability.
  - Corporate foundations, like the overall Chinese foundations, could benefit from the favorable government policy regarding removing 10 percent cap of administrative cost to allow them to attract professional talents and operate professionally with diminishing interference from parent companies.

- For sector professionals, efforts should be afforded to engage corporate foundations in the nonprofit realm so as to release its many potentials for advancing civil society. For example:

  - Corporate foundations can be transformed from direct service providers to grant-makers, given that the number of full-time staff of Chinese corporate foundations is very low and corporate foundations are significantly more interested in obtaining tax-exempt status.

- Corporate foundations can also be very good partners for charitable projects that have a strategic fit with corporations due to entrepreneurs' increasingly plural civil charitable interests, high alignments with overall social development areas, and strong capacity of engaging volunteers.
- Corporate foundations can be a great addition to Chinese civil society in terms of increasing pluralism and encouraging more donor engagement through their own powerful social networks. A step to doing so requires obtaining legal permission to issue tax-deductions receipts for their donors.

- For scholars studying corporate philanthropy and corporate social responsibilities, it would be of particular interest to separate corporate giving into two entities: giving through corporate social responsibility (CSR) and giving through corporate foundations. As stated earlier in the chapter, the motivations, rationale, and structures for the two types of giving are distinct. Corporate foundations arguably create more credibility and reputation for the companies compared to a regular CSR program. Corporate foundations fall into the realm of the nonprofit world. Here, they subject themselves to a more democratic process, diverse boards, and stricter public scrutiny. Based on these unique facts, there are several theoretical perspectives to be potentially applied to Chinese corporate foundations:

  - Agency theory: As a separate entity from the corporate, the manager of a corporate foundation could further exercise his/her discretionary behavior against the company. Future research could examine the discretionary behaviors of corporate foundations and examine how they differ from CSR managers.
  - Resource dependency theory: Some Chinese corporate foundations are able to raise significant donations from the parent company's partners, supply chains, customers, and employees. Do the corporate foundations that accept more donations tend to be more transparent than those with less donations?
  - Instrumental stakeholder theory: This theory emphasizes that a firm's fulfillment in its economic and social purpose is motivated by its survival and continuing profitability. This motivation is also likely to be reflected in other business practices that demonstrate responsibility, such as the provision of a high level of financial transparency to investors. Namely, are companies with corporate foundations associated with corporate financial transparency and misconduct?
  - Type of ownership and corporate foundation: It is well known that state-owned enterprises (SOEs) are distinct from non-state-owned enterprises (non-SOEs) in China. Both types of companies actively contribute to the robust growth of Chinese philanthropy. How different are corporate foundations established by SOEs and by non-SOEs in terms of board structure, organizational capacity, accountability, civic engagement, mission diversity, expenditures, project partners, fundraising capabilities, etc.?

- Future research question can also explore charitable choices by Chinese corporations and entrepreneurs. For corporations, what factors affect establishing a foundation versus giving directly to the needy, implementing its own projects, or directly partnering with charitable organizations? For entrepreneurs, what factors influence decisions to form a family, corporate, or independent foundation? Possible factors include degree of agent control (e.g., family in line to succeed the entrepreneurs, family members as board members in foundations, shares of stocks in the company) and community characteristics (e.g., ties with government, ties between entrepreneurs and existing foundations, cohesiveness of local elites, reports from watchdogs or media on nonprofit misdeeds).

References

An, P. (2015). The founder of Midea: Be a world-class family foundation, *China Philanthropists Magazine*. [Online] Available from: http://www.icixun.com/2015/1019/5180.html. Accessed 5 Aug 2017.

Anheier, H. K., & List, R. A. (2005). *A dictionary of civil society, philanthropy and the non-profit sector*. London: Routledge.

Backman, E. V., & Smith, S. R. (2000). Healthy organizations, unhealthy communities? *Nonprofit Management & Leadership, 10*(4), 355–373.

Chen, Y., & Touve, D. (2011). Conformity, political participation, and economic rewards: The case of Chinese private entrepreneurs. *Asia Pacific Journal of Management, 28*(3), 529–553. [Online] Available from: https://doi.org/10.1007/s10490-009-9171-2.

China Foundation Center. (2013). Report on development trend of corporate foundations established by public-listed companies. *Report on development trend of corporate foundations established by public-listed companies*.

China Foundation Center. (2016). Report on the Development of Chinese Corporate Foundations. Beijing: The Author.

Conference Board. (2012). Corporate philanthropy in China: A practitioner's guide for foreign donors. Beijing: The Author.

Council on Foundations. (2016). *USIG country note-China*. [Online] Available from: http://www.cof.org/content/china. Accessed 5 Aug 2017.

Cumming, D., Hou, W., & Lee, E. (2016). Business ethics and finance in Greater China: Synthesis and future directions in sustainability, CSR, and fraud. *Journal of Business Ethics, 138*(4), 601–626. [Online] Available from: https://doi.org/10.1007/s10551-016-3288-2.

D'Ath, E. & Berger, M. (2012). *Corporate foundations in China: Recommendations for effective investment*. [Online] Available from: http://www.csr-asia.com/download_files/CSR_Asia_CF_in_ChinaFINAL.pdf

Davis, G. F., & Greve, H. R. (1997). Corporate elite networks and governance changes in the 1980s. *American Journal of Sociology, 103*(1), 1–37.

Estes, R. J. (1998). Emerging Chinese foundations: The role of private philanthropy in the new China. *Regional Development Studies, 4*, 165–180.

Fuma, S. (1997). *A study of benevolent societies and benevolent halls in China*. Kyoto: Dōhōsha Shuppan.

Greenlee, J. S., & Trussel, J. M. (2000). Predicting the financial vulnerability of charitable organizations. *Nonprofit Management & Leadership, 11*(2), 199–210.

Hansmann, H. (1987). Economic theories of nonprofit organizations. In W. Powell (Ed.), *The nonprofit sector: A research handbook*. New Haven: Yale University Press.

He, L. J. (2015). What drives change? Examining wealthy Chinese entrepreneurs' creation of foundations: An institutional entrepreneurship theory perspective. Doctoral dissertation, Indiana University-Purdue University-Indianapolis. [Online] Available from: https://scholarworks.iupui.edu/bitstream/handle/1805/7384/He_iupui_0104D_10035.pdf?sequence=1. Accessed 5 Aug 2017.

Horvath, A., & Powell, W. (2017). Contributory or disruptive: Do new forms of philanthropy erode democracy? *Stanford Social Innovation Review*. Available from https://ssir.org/articles/entry/disruptive_philanthropy. Accessed 9 Jan 2017.

Kennedy, S. (2009). Comparing formal and informal lobbying practices in China: The capital's ambivalent embrace of capitalists. *China Information., 23*(2), 195–222. [Online] Available from: https://doi.org/10.1177/0920203x09105125.

Kuang, J. N. Interviewed by: He, L J (15th November 2015).

Ma, J., & DeDeo, S. (2017). State power and elite autonomy in a networked civil society: The board interlocking of Chinese non-profits. *Social Networks*, 1–12.

Ma, D. L., & Parish, W. L. (2006). Tocquevillian moments: Charitable contributions by Chinese Private Entrepreneurs. *Social Forces, 85*(2), 943–964. [Online] Available from: https://doi.org/10.1353/sof.2007.0016.

Niehaus, M. (2016) Fortifying civic participation worldwide. *Stanford Social Innovation Review*. [Online] Available from: https://ssir.org/articles/entry/fortifying_civic_participation_worldwide. Accessed 5 Aug 2017.

Petrovits, C. M. (2006). Corporate-sponsored foundations and earnings management. *Journal of Accounting and Economics, 41*(3), 335–362. [Online] Available from: https://doi.org/10.1016/j.jacceco.2005.12.001.

Porter, M. E., & Kramer, M. R. (2002). The competitive advantage of corporate philanthropy. *Harvard Business Review, 80*(12), 56–58, 133.

Salamon, L. M., & Anheier, H. K. (1999). *Defining the nonprofit sector: A cross-national analysis*. Manchester: Manchester University Press.

Salamon, L. M., Hems, L. C., & Chinnock, K. (2000). *The nonprofit sector: For what and for whom?* Baltimore: Johns Hopkins Center for Civil Society Studies.

Shue, V. (1998). State power and the philanthropic impulse in China today. In E. A. Icchman (Ed.), *Philanthropy in the world's traditions* (pp. 332–354). Bloomington: Indiana University Press.

Smith, H. W. (1993). *To have or have not: a corporate foundation*. New York: Council for Aid to Education.

Song, L., & Wang, J. (2010). Market reactions and corporate philanthropy: A case study of the Wenchuan Earthquake in China. *Modern Economic Science., 32*(6), 82–88.

The Conference Board (2015). *Corporate philanthropy in China*. [Online] Available from: https://www.avpn.asia/wp-content/uploads/2013/01/Corporate-Philanthropy-in-China.pdf. Accessed 5 Aug 2017.

The Wall Street Journal. (2016). The good and bad about China's new Charity Law. *The Wall Street Journal*. 16 March 2016. [Online] Available from: http://blogs.wsj.com/chinarealtime/2016/03/16/the-good-and-bad-about-chinas-new-charity-law/. Accessed 5 Aug 2017.

Trussel, J. M., & Parsons, L. M. (2008). Financial reporting factors affecting donations to charitable organizations. *Advances in Accounting, 23*, 263–285.

Tuckman, H. P., & Chang, C. F. (1991). A methodology for measuring the financial vulnerability of charitable nonprofit organizations. *Nonprofit and Voluntary Sector Quarterly, 20*(4), 445–460. [Online] Available from: https://doi.org/10.1177/089976409102000407.

Wang, H., & Qian, C. (2011). Corporate philanthropy and corporate financial performance: The roles of stakeholder response and political access. *Academy of Management Journal, 54*(6), 1159–1181. [Online] Available from: https://doi.org/10.5465/amj.2009.0548.

Wang Q. & He, L. J. (2018) Are the wealthy also healthy? An empirical evaluation of the financial health of Chinese Foundations. *Chinese Public Administration Review, 9*(1) http://dx.doi.org/10.22140/cpar.v0i0.155

Webb, N. J. (1994). Tax and government policy implications for corporate foundation giving. *Nonprofit and Voluntary Sector Quarterly, 23*(1), 41–67. [Online] Available from: https://doi.org/10.1177/0899764094231004.

Wei, Q. (2016). From direct involvement to indirect control? A multilevel analysis of factors influencing Chinese foundations' capacity for resource mobilization. *VOLUNTAS: International Journal of Voluntary and Nonprofit Organizations*, 1–17.

Westhues, M., & Einwiller, S. (2006). Corporate foundations: Their role for corporate social responsibility. *Corporate Reputation Review, 9*(2), 144–153.

Xiao, J. (2013). *Eco-conservation democratic experiment: A travelogue through Alxa League*. Beijing: Social Science Academic Press.

Yang, P. (2012). *Democracy in Philanthropy: The organization governance journey of Social Entrepreneur Ecology*. Beijing: CITIC Publishing Group.

Yang, T. (2016). *Bluebook of Philanthropy 2017*. Beijing: Social Science Academic Press.

Yang, T. (2017). *Bluebook of Philanthropy 2016*. Beijing: Social Science Academic Press.

Zhang, J. J., Marquis, C., & Qiao, K. (2016). Do political connections buffer firms form or bind firms to the government? A study of corporate donations of Chinese firms. *Organization Science, 6*, 18–25.

Zhao, S. M., Bai, X. M., & Zhao, Y. X. (2014). A study of Chinese entrepreneurs and philanthropic behavior. In M. L. Taylor, R. J. Storm, & D. O. Renz (Eds.), *Handbook of research on entrepreneurs' engagement in philanthropy* (pp. 234–267). Edward Elgar Publishing, Cheltenham.

Zu, L., & Song, L. (2009). Determinants of managerial value on corporate social responsibility: Evidence from China. *Journal of Business Ethics, 88*, 105–117.

Lijun He is the China Advisor of the Omidyar Network (San Francisco). She also serves as the US Senior Advisor for Center of Corporate Social Responsibility Development Center of Shenzhen, China, and adjunct faculty at the Institute of Public Service at Seattle University. Previously, she was an assistant professor in Nonprofit Management at Pace University in New York (2015–2018). Her research interests include entrepreneurship and philanthropy, impact investment, philanthropic ethics, and strategic philanthropy.

Qun Wang is PhD candidate in public policy and associate instructor at the School of Public and Environmental Affairs, Indiana University. His research interests include foundations, government-nonprofit relationship, and comparative politics.

Chapter 8
Corporate Foundations in Russia: Overview of the Sector

Irina Krasnopolskaya

Abstract Corporate social responsibility (CSR) is not as new a phenomenon for Russia as it is considered to be. Despite the prevalence of CSR among Russian corporations and considerable budgets, the number of corporate foundations is limited to a few tens. This chapter develops explanations for a narrow prevalence of corporate foundations as a tool of CSR. The chapter is based on the available statistical information, corporate social reports and interviews with representatives of the corporate foundations. Three aspects are examined. The first is a statistical portrait of the subsector of corporate foundations: its size, funding models, payouts, projects being funded, etc. The second point is an institutional context: the current legislation on foundations and CSR, and the tax regulations. The third aspect to be covered is a hybrid role of corporate foundations, their operation in the social policy and the non-profit sector. The chapter concludes with a discussion on comparative advantages and weaknesses of corporate foundations in an emerging Russian market.

Keywords Corporate foundations · Russia · Quantitative research · Desk research · Institutional environment

8.1 Introduction

Corporations currently play a significant role in the social sector and made considerable contributions to social infrastructure during the Soviet period (Abramov 2005). However, despite the prevalence of CSR practices among Russian corporations, as

---

Support from the Basic Research Program of the National Research University Higher School of Economics is gratefully acknowledged.

I. Krasnopolskaya (✉)
National Research University Higher School of Economics, The Centre for Civic Initiatives Assessment, Moscow, Russia
e-mail: ikrasnopolskaya@hse.ru

well as substantial CSR budgets, the number of corporate foundations is limited to a few dozen.

Knowledge and data on corporate foundations are scarce and inconsistent for several reasons, including their small overall numbers and the absence of a distinct legal form, to name but a few. No comprehensive survey of corporate foundations has ever been conducted in Russia, and they have not been covered in Russian academic literature. Further, they have never become a subject of research in academic publications, and there are literally no publications with the keyword "corporate foundation" in the Russian language (EBSCO database, 2017). They have, however, received some attention from academics in the literature on CSR (Polischuk 2009), but mostly from practitioners. Most of the existing Russian publications on CSR are descriptive and present the results of CSR rankings (Ochareva 2016; Liborakina 2003). The majority of them were published in the early 2000s. Some of those publications investigated the social role of CSR (Peregudov 2003); others examined CSR connections with the government (Chirikova et al. 2005), while others reported poll results showing the public's perception of CSR. Notably, what the existing literature has not provided thus far are insights into the nature of corporate foundations, their relations with their respective parent enterprises and the division of responsibilities with CSR.

This chapter aims to provide an overview of the state of corporate foundations in Russia and to develop an explanation for the scarcity of the distribution of corporate foundations as vehicles for corporate philanthropy in comparison with CSR, which is operated through the company itself. For these purposes, the chapter first examines the available census of corporate foundations, patterns of relationships with the parent enterprise, and the level of independence. Second, we present a brief overview of the non-profit sector, of which corporate foundations are a subgroup, their geography, the specifics of their prevalence and typical features. Third, the chapter considers the historical and social factors which influenced the hybrid nature of corporate foundations, with their significant penetration into the social sector, and the important social role they have assumed.

This study is based on secondary and primary data. Since the number of corporate foundations in Russia is limited, it has been possible to examine secondary data from almost all corporate foundations. The annual reports of corporate foundations, together with their constitutions, were analysed, and several interviews were conducted with the representatives of both the corporate foundations and representatives of the national foundation umbrella association.

8.2 Spectrum of Operational Structures

Corporate foundations operate under the legal status of non-profit organisations (NPOs). However, Russian legislation does not provide a distinct definition for them. All types of foundations operating as NPOs share the same legal status, meaning that philanthropic, private, corporate and fundraising foundations are subject to the same federal laws. Federal laws No. 135 "On philanthropic activity and philanthropic organisations" (11 August 1995) and No. 7 "On non-profit organisations" (12 January 1996), both with several amendments, regulate the activities of foundations.

Corporate foundations, therefore, appear to be a subdivision of non-profit organisations from the statutory perspective, as well as a form of institutional CSR and corporate philanthropy from the everyday practice, among both CSR and non-profit practitioners. A corporate foundation is a legally independent entity, a non-profit organisation established and financially supported by an enterprise or a group of enterprises to implement philanthropic and social programmes – this is a commonly accepted definition used in CSR and the non-profit sector. The founder is always a company or a group of companies, and the main stream of finance to the foundation is supplied by the enterprise. We found no corporate foundations that own a controlling block of shares of a founder company. This sets Russian corporate foundations apart from Dutch and Danish practices, whereby foundations typically exercise control of the founder company.

There is a broad scope for making the decision whether or not to set up a corporate foundation. Current legislation offers no tax deductions or other incentives for corporate foundations, corporations implementing CSR or philanthropic activities. Private donations, but not those made by juristic persons, are eligible for a tax refund.

Tax incentives per se do not have a direct correlation with the volume of corporate philanthropy, but they contribute to the shaping of a favourable environment for CSR development in general. Since there are no financial or legal incentives to establish a foundation, its establishment is a matter of arbitrary decisions made by a company's management. It may depend on the volume and character of their objectives in the social sector, which will be delegated to the corporate foundation, and on the flexibility of the enterprise's organisational structure to redistribute some competences to an external organisation.

Normally, corporate foundations are established by large enterprises which present themselves as bearing a high level of social responsibility and trying to satisfy additional social requirements and demands for good citizenship (Longsdon and Wood 2002; Waddock 2004). Corporate foundations are seen to dovetail with the concept of corporate citizenship. They aim to concentrate internal and external resources to solve selected social problems and are a means for more proficient and focused performance. Creating a corporate foundation is always the second step in pursuing CSR objectives, after the enterprise has gained considerable expertise in solving certain social issues and plans to boost its outcomes in the area. A foundation is thought to have enough of its own professional and organisational resources and level of expertise to work successfully on the social problem. This conclusion regarding the one focus issue of corporate foundations is also supported by the fact that most of the corporations we researched also have a CSR department, which organises the corporation's regular external and internal CSR activities. Enterprises continue to fulfil their commitments to employees and in some cases continue external social programmes. Indeed, a corporate foundation is not a means to limit and outsource the fulfilment of social obligations but is rather a step in the professionalisation of one particular set of social programmes among other ongoing CSR projects.

The influence of multinational corporations and the requirements for their Russian branches to follow head office strategy in social responsibility also constitute stimuli. Thus, the local branches of global corporate foundations such as Alcoa, Amway, Deloitte and Auchan started their operations and became a kind of trendsetter. This process is very similar to the development of the Russian non-profit sector once new legal forms were created in the immediate post-Soviet period. Non-profits were then joined by a sizable upsurge of new institutions formed during the 1990s, many of them supported by foreign governments and foundations, and operating in new spheres of advocacy, as well as service delivery and organisational capacity (Henderson 2002; Skokova et al. 2018).

The second rationale for the development of corporate foundations is the decision of an owner or senior management to focus on a particular social issue or a set of issues and devote its efforts to tackling it. Doing so, a company outsources the management of its social programmes or the entire corporate philanthropy to a separate entity.

Creating a corporate foundation, or indeed any other kind of foundation, can be facilitated by the organisational support and expertise provided by professional associations. The non-profit partnership "Donors Forum" operates to a certain extent as an umbrella organisation and serves the needs of the CSR and foundations' communities without discriminating between the types of foundations or CSR itself. It includes representatives of business, private, corporate and endowment foundations and CSR managers and provides organisational, legal, and research expertise.

8.3 Overview of the Non-profit Sector and Corporate Foundations in Russia

The current section briefly introduces the available statistical data on the state and scope of the non-profit sector and provides a simplified picture of the array of corporate foundations in Russia.

The Russian non-profit sector is relatively young and weak and is still largely lacking the civic participation and the support of local communities, business and local governments (Mersiyanova et al. 2017; Skokova et al. 2018). The sector grew after the collapse of the Soviet Union in 1991 and acquired some organisational and managerial capacities due to the support of foreign donors (Sundstrom 2006). The first key regulatory provision, Federal Law №7 "On Non-profit Organisations", was adopted in 1995 and is still in force, with numerous amendments. That said, the non-profit sector in Russia is currently developing into a prominent actor in public service provision (Ljubownikow and Crotty 2016). About 60% of the approximately 224,000 registered non-profit organisations (Jan. 2017, Ministry of Justice) are active in the social sector, including education, social services, welfare and health

(Wathen and Allard 2014; Tarasenko 2015), complementing the services provided by government bodies. Alongside this, the sector is still relatively small in terms of its share of the economy, accounting for only 0.9% of GDP and contributing a workforce of about 1.2% of the economically active population (Salamon et al. 2015).

Legally, there are no less than 18 official legal forms of NPOs in Russia, including foundations, associations, consumer cooperatives, religious organisations, trade unions, and many more (2019). The foundations constitute a subgroup of the non-profit sector organisations. This subgroup consists of approximately 7500 philanthropic foundations (2017), and only about 25 of which are corporate foundations. Reliable statistical information on corporate foundations is absent in Russia, as the Federal State Statistics Service does not consider corporate foundations a separate type of entity. Another limitation to our data is that not every corporate foundation publishes annual reports or provides accurate information on its website. Small- and medium-sized enterprises are mainly left unobserved. We, therefore, rely on expert estimations and desk research data, which enables us to present only very rough estimations.

The number of corporate foundations might appear surprisingly small, taking into account the steady increase in the number of socially responsible enterprises in Russia, together with the fact that more than 150 enterprises systematically implement CSR programmes on a professional basis and enjoy significant financial resources.

Despite that only large-sized businesses' CSR is visible and reported in Russia, small- or medium-sized businesses are actively involved in CSR practices, just not being named as such. Small and medium enterprises intensively support local communities, often in forms of traditional philanthropy, monetary and in-kind support. The support is directed to schools, kindergartens, orphans, elderly people, and churches (Chernysheva 2016). Businesses reply to personal requests from the needy or from behalf of the regional and municipal policymakers. No financial data are available on size or scope of social activity of small and medium businesses; meanwhile experts estimate it as widespread (more than 60% of Russian enterprises conduct some socially responsible activity) and a significant practice across Russia.

Unlike large businesses, small- and medium-sized enterprises are not separable from an entrepreneur; the latter performs simultaneously as an economic actor and a community member. Economic activity is thus heavily rooted in social networks and local background and relies on formal and informal relationships with stakeholders. Philanthropy of small and medium businesses, in this case, fulfils a facilitation role in terms of access to and integration into financial, material and social capital networks.

Analysis of the available data demonstrates that there is no drastic inconsistency in the numbers of corporate foundations established at different periods. Approximately one-third of corporate foundations were established in 1990 and the mid-2000s by industrial (mainly mining, oil, and mineral processing) enterprises. For instance, LUKOIL and MMK (OJSC Magnitogorsk Iron and Steel Works) established their corporate foundations in 1993, NLMK (Novolipetsk Steel) in 1999, Joint-Stock Financial Company Sistema in 2003, RUSAL (aluminium mining and production) in 2004, Severstal (steelworks) in 2005, and Renova (a group of investment and asset management companies) in 2007. Two-thirds of corporate foundations were established in the early 2010s in line with and due to CSR development. At that time, non-industrial companies, mass market producers, and financial enterprises introduced their corporate foundations, as the common understanding was that they were a more advanced means to run CSR activities.

Financial data on CSR and corporate philanthropy programmes is very limited and hard to access. Many companies keep their financial information confidential for various reasons, including security. However, companies behaving transparently with their financial data spent at least 20 billion rubles (US$328 million) in 2015 on philanthropic and social support programmes (Boldureva 2016). External CSR constitutes a reasonable part of social welfare provision, taking into account that, for example, the budget allocation of the Russian Federation for health in 2017 was 378 billion rubles (US$6.2 billion). As private philanthropy is mostly of an informal nature in Russia, corporate philanthropy constitutes a major share (up to 75%) of overall philanthropic donations (Mersiyanova et al. 2015). This is very different from European practices, whereby private donations constitute a significant contribution to the total volume of collected charitable funds (CAF World Giving Index 2017). Small- and medium-sized enterprises also conduct a lot of mostly informal and irregular CSR-related activities. The aforementioned factors explain the insufficiency and inconsistency of statistical data about CSR and corporate foundations, respectively.

In 2015, at 2.055 billion rubles (over US$32 million), the total budget of corporate foundations amounted to a little more than one-fifth (22%) of the cumulative budgets of all foundations (9.38 billion rubles) (Ochareva 2016). The open access data which we analysed in this chapter show that the volume of resources spent on corporate foundations' philanthropic activities in 2015 was 3.2 billion rubles (about US$52.5 million). Foundations with an industrial parent enterprise possess significantly higher budgets than those with mass market of financial origins (Fig. 8.1). Maybe the industrial foundations are related to heavy industry (mining, etc.), while mass market relates to consumer goods and services.

Staff numbers in corporate foundations are increasing slowly. This figure ranged from 1 to 26 employees per foundation in 2013. The overall number of staff positions in 2013 was 133, having grown from 111 in 2012.

The geographic reach of a corporate foundation is fully determined by the geographic presence of its corresponding parent enterprise. Equal numbers of foundations operate nationally and at the regional or local levels. Operating at the federal level is more typical for mass market corporations, which have wide regional coverage. The corporate foundations of mining and mineral processing enterprises, by contrast, usually operate in the regions of the company's presence. International operations are very rare; only a few corporate foundations support international programmes, such as providing humanitarian help and supporting cultural programmes, within the regions of their overseas operations.

Corporate foundations do not have their distinctive image in the eyes of the public, tending to be lumped together with philanthropic foundations more than with

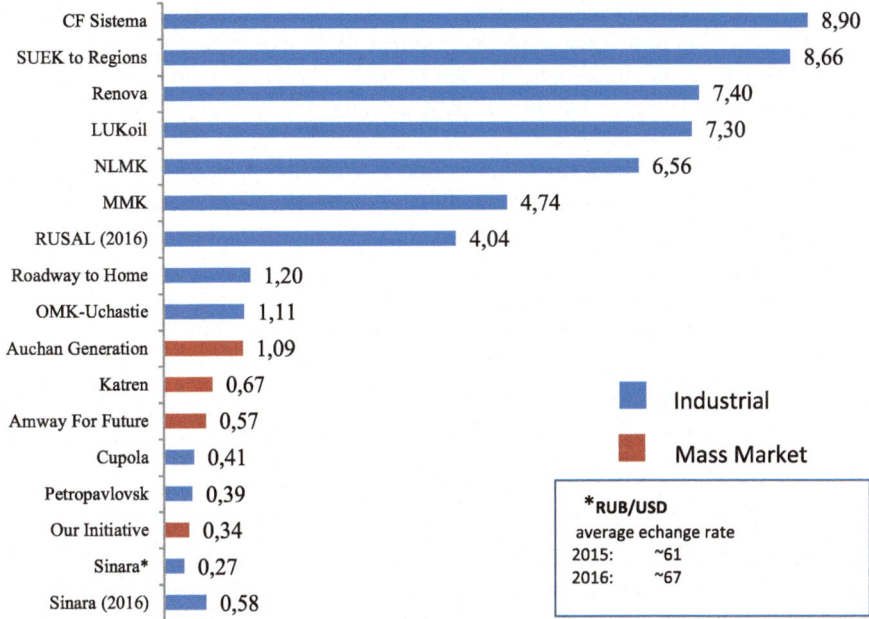

Fig. 8.1 Foundations' budgets for the focused activities, *Industrial* vs. *Mass market*, mln USD*

CSR. Indeed, issues of philanthropy and CSR have gained much attention from mass media in the last few years due to intensive federal efforts to boost the third sector, volunteering and philanthropy. By 2012, the number of mass-media publications on philanthropy had more than doubled since the previous year (86,321 publications in 2012 vs. 30,756 publications in 2011; Ochareva 2016). Most of the messages were positive (58%), covering issues of help and how it was provided. Corporate foundations were mentioned in only 1% of publications, remaining stable during the whole examined period. Fundraising and private foundations gained the most attention in the mass media (13% and 19% of publications, respectively). Therefore, corporate foundations constitute a small but financially significant group among foundations and the non-profit sector in general.

8.4 Relationship with the Parent Enterprise

The particularities of a foundation's operational structure are significantly determined by its nonfinancial background, the flexibility of the parent corporation's organisational structure and budget allocation. Establishment of a corporate foundation requires modification of the corporate governance system and the active involvement of senior managers. In the current study, we classified corporate foundations in accordance with the differences in their operational structures. The baseline criteria were operational independence from the parent enterprise and budget allocation. At one end of the spectrum is an "independent" corporate foundation model and, at the other, an "integrated" model. In both cases, corporate foundations are independent legal entities, but they differ in their degrees of autonomy from the parent corporation.

The "independent" corporate foundation is established by the allocation of a special budget, separate from budgets for CSR, advertisement or communications. These foundations are established by transferring a part of the corporate budget out to the foundation. In this context, a corporate foundation is able to set its agenda and budget and is relatively independent from the enterprise in terms of operation. "Integrated" foundations, on the other hand, are established with a high degree of financial and management subordination to the CSR, advertising or PR departments. In such a case, the enterprise does not allocate a separate budget for its corporate foundation operations; the budget may come, for example, from part of the company's CSR budget. An integrated foundation's agenda and purposes are thus significantly determined or even developed by the CSR department. About half of the foundations examined may be considered to fall within the "integrated" category (Ochareva 2016).

The influence of a foundation board generally corresponds to the model of a foundation and its relationship with the organisational structure, that is with other departments of the enterprise. On the other hand, the composition of the board itself does not have a major impact on the independence or the degree of integration of the foundation. As mentioned above, a corporate foundation might be either subordinate to the internal CSR or other departments, or it may be able to set its mission and programmes relatively independently from CSR management. In the first case, the board and executive management of the foundation follow the CSR strategy of the parent company. In the second, the foundation's mission takes priority. For instance, "The Dome" Foundation (Kinross Corp., gold mining) has its mission and programmes and operates independently from the CSR department, with few joint practices and events. On the other hand, the "Center of Social Programs" RUSAL (aluminium mining and works) foundation operates under the supervision of its CSR department and is subordinate to it, both in operations and planning.

With very few exceptions, a foundation's board members, just like members of the supervisory boards or councils and inspection committees, are comprised of representatives of the enterprise or business group, including top managers, owners and executive staff of the parent enterprise. Very few corporate foundations are significantly open to stakeholders and include representatives of regional and municipal authorities or representatives of local community groups in the board or executive committee. This practice might take place within foundations with large community development programmes, as they have to coordinate with the regional or municipal programmes in the social sector and with collaborative community projects. All surveyed foundations disclosed information about the members of the board, executive directors or the executive committee.

Irrespective of a degree of autonomy in terms of mission and operations, corporate foundations are very dependent on their parent enterprises for financial backing.

Russian corporate foundations rely on the same funding model, with slight variations. The biggest share of the budget, and often its entirety, is provided exclusively by the enterprise. Annual commitments from the parent company constitute a predominant part of the foundations' revenue structure. These commitments are quite flexible and vary across different foundations, while only a few corporations have established a fixed funding formula for a foundation, for example as a certain percentage of the net profit. As a general rule, budget is set annually, and its size differs, depending on the corporation's financial circumstances. However, annual fluctuation is not significant and budgets tend to increase. Even during the global economic crisis starting in 2008, corporations did not significantly shrink the budgets for their foundations. Corporate foundations can attract other resources via fundraising and establish an endowment or for-profit activities on a much smaller scale than other types of foundations, since the majority of them do not experience a significant budget deficit. Donations from external stakeholders arrive via joint projects or programmes implemented together with other non-profits or with local or regional authorities. However, such joint projects are relatively rare. In some cases, the foundations receive a profit and, in the absence of an endowment, use it to provide additional support to the beneficiaries.

Most of the examined corporate foundations enjoy a vast variety of services provided free of charge, by the parent enterprises. As a rule, foundations use the office space, media relations and communications resources and occasionally the transportation and logistics capacities of the parent enterprise. The foundation's performance is usually reflected in the parent enterprise's annual reports. Coverage of the administrative costs by the enterprise is also a typical practice among foundations. However, information about the financial value of these services from the parent enterprise is scarce and inconsistent.

8.5 Operation: Areas and Patterns

Russian legislation does not impose any restrictions on the interrelation or connections between the business goals of an enterprise and the activity of a corporate foundation. Foundations might have a direct connection to the business purposes of an enterprise and/or perform their activities in an unrelated field. Despite receiving almost, if not all, of their funding from a parent enterprise, most corporate foundations do not have a direct connection to the business interests of the parent. Rather, their activities are related but separate.

Russian corporate foundations also implement a community development model. This perspective is highly sensitive to the geographic areas and markets of operation, indicating communities and local areas as immediate beneficiaries. This approach is based on a combination of corporate philanthropy, CSR programmes and the owner's personal interests in the social sector. Therefore, a significant share of the current programmes implemented by corporate foundations focuses on education, support and protection for socially vulnerable groups, including for childhood,

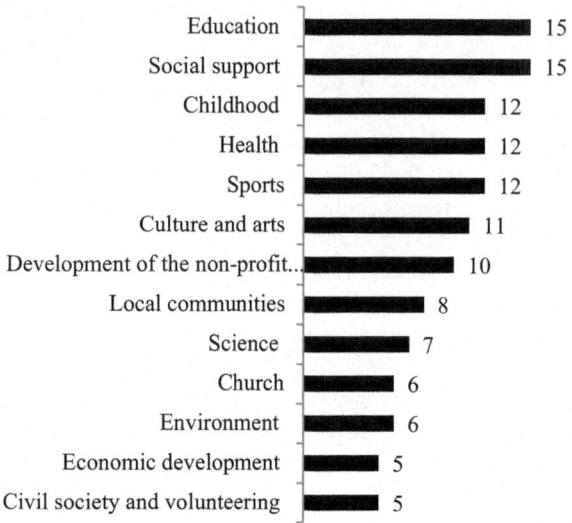

Fig. 8.2 Main areas, which are supported by corporate foundations ($n = 16$, 2016) (Boldureva 2016)

healthcare, sports, culture and the arts (Fig. 8.2). There are certain exceptions when corporate foundations implement programmes with a clearer focus, such as those targeting current or potential groups of both customers and employers. These are social investment or social entrepreneurship programmes, courses developing financial competences, etc. (for instance, the programmes run by the Sberbank Foundation).

Most of Russia's corporate foundations implement a grant-making pattern, distributing grants to civil society organisations in the areas of a company's geographical presence. Approximately two-thirds of the foundations examined predominantly practise this model, while the remaining one-third are operating foundations and run programmes with their staff. Foundations usually combine operational and grant-making activities. Beneficiaries can be natural persons, non-profits or public bodies. Philanthropic help on request has not been found in the examined foundations, although charitable support within the framework of the existing programmes was observed quite frequently. Desk research and interview data revealed that operational corporate foundations are mostly of the "independent" type and therefore enjoy a higher degree of autonomy and freedom to set and implement their programmes.

Grant competitions are usually quite open and transparent at the stages of authorisation and administration and, in some cases, at the assessment phases (Beam and Conlan 2002). The foundation is responsible for the distribution of the information, training of applicants, collection and evaluation of proposals, selection of winners and evaluation of the completed programmes. The competition committee consists of the representatives of the governing body and, if present in the governing body, representatives of stakeholders, local government or community groups. In some cases, the foundations choose one non-profit organisation to run the grant competition and collaborate with them. We have not found any strict requirements with regard to grant distribution. The negative selection of grant recipients was not unusual – the corporate foundations did not support extremist activities or political parties. However, the foundations do not have any restrictions with regard to the support of "GONGOs" (government-organised NPOs) or other types of organisations.

We observe a certain correlation between the industry/sector of a parent enterprise and a profile of areas or sets of areas being supported by the foundation. The "industrial" group consists of foundations established chiefly by the biggest mining and processing corporations. Mining companies operate in Russia's remote regions, often in small towns, where they are often one of the biggest or the only employer and a corporate taxpayer in the corresponding region. Such industries are city-forming, which makes their CSR and corporate foundations vital for the municipality of the region. More often than other corporate foundations, "industrial" types take on a number of social responsibilities for the support and restoration of the social and/or transportation infrastructure of the region within the framework of their CSR or corporate foundation programmes. This can include the building or restoration of objects belonging to the municipality, along with projects in education, healthcare, and support to vulnerable groups. Few examples of such programmes are presented next in the text.

> Industrial foundation of a regional scale: Charitable Foundation "Kupol" ("The Dome") (Kinross Gold Corporation). Main activity – contribution of the foundation to the socio-economic development of the region and assistance in solving problems of the residents of Chukotka, which involves programmes to support the traditions of indigenous peoples, including traditional methods of managing natural resources, healthcare, education and training and the sustainable development of small- to medium-sized enterprise.
>
> Industrial, inter-regional foundation: Foundation of the socio-economic support of the regions "SUEK – to the regions" (SUEK JSC). The activity of the foundation is aimed at increasing the standard of living in the areas of the company's presence. The programmes include education, improvement of the local government, affordable housing, improvement and development of infrastructure, environment, healthcare, sports and healthy lifestyles, development of social and entrepreneurial activities of the population and leisure and culture.
>
> Industrial federal foundation: Charitable foundation "Sistema" (AFK Sistema PAO). Foundation works to support and develop science, education; culture and arts; healthcare and social care; and fitness and sports.

The "industrial" corporate foundations work closely with the local authorities and representatives of local groups of beneficiaries, for instance, in an association of indigenous peoples, to develop joint projects to be supported. Such projects are beneficial both to the region, due to their contributions to the social budget, and to corporate foundations themselves, as they achieve their social objectives and provide help to beneficiaries. The representatives of CF who were interviewed declare voluntary and partner nature of cooperation with local authorities concerning objects of infrastructure and social projects to be supported. No explicit pressure was reported about, although it is less likely to depict the alignment of forces adequately. We examine enterprise and corporate foundation relations with local authorities from the perspective of isomorphism and demand-side pressure (Campbell 2007; Brammer et al. 2012) in the next section.

The other group of corporate foundations consists of those with mass market and/or finance origins and are established by both Russian and international corporations. Corporate foundations in this group do not operate in or liaise directly with the home region, unlike the "industrial" foundations. Further, they are usually named after the parent enterprise, while "industrial" foundations frequently are known by the name of the dominant programme. "Mass market" corporate foundations are considered one of the PR strategies of the parent enterprise. Therefore, these foundations, more so than others, tend to support social projects with a clear positive image and try to "avoid" controversial or complex projects such as palliative care, support to marginalised groups of adults, etc. Such limitations result in a certain randomness or skewness of the selection of projects to be supported.

> Mass-market foundation of a federal scale: Charitable foundation "Our initiative" (M-Video). Charitable projects aimed at social support, including the support of children growing up in troubled homes or living in institutional care homes such as orphanages, as well as the veterans of World War II.

> Mass market foundation on a federal scale: the charitable foundation Beautiful children in a beautiful world (M-Video). The Foundation provides organisational and financial assistance for healthcare services and environmental campaigns.

Corporate foundations establish partnerships with other companies or with the representatives of authorities in order to work in certain areas. The partners, including the authorities, cofinance the projects and activities of the foundation in areas of mutual interest. However, joint projects are likely to be an exception rather than a rule. "Industrial" foundations might undertake joint projects in the area in which they are present within the framework of a socio-economic collaboration agreement with the municipal and regional authorities. They work with objects of transport and social infrastructures and support educational and healthcare institutions, etc. By contrast, "mass market and/or finance" foundations more often conduct joint projects with other enterprises. These projects often concern charitable help and voluntary activities, including corporate volunteering and environmental campaigns. The employees of enterprises are actively involved in these projects as volunteers or donors. These projects are likely to contribute to the reputation of philanthropy – namely, the positive image of enterprise in the eyes of the general public and the local authorities.

8.6 Discussion

Corporate social responsibility is, in many respects, the assumption of responsibility by the business for problems that were traditionally dealt with by the state (Gainer 2010). Corporate foundations provide a vivid illustration of this.

CSR blurs the boundaries between the state and the market and implies a different allocation of responsibilities between public and private actors (Davies et al. 2016). As such, corporations become one of the hybrid institutional actors linking the state, the market, and society (Haufler 2008; Bruyn 1999). This trend is pronounced in the Russian context, and we believe that several social variables are responsible for it: The first is the peculiar social role of enterprises during Soviet period; the second is the current poor socio-economic conditions in Russia's regions and public expectations of social security, while the third is local authorities' expectations of social contributions from business. Corporate foundations are a tool of enterprises to fulfil social commitments, responding to isomorphic pressure from both authorities and citizens. Isomorphism enhances the organisation's legitimacy and facilitates external stability and access to local markets.

8.6.1 Social Role of Enterprises During the Soviet Period

The social commitment and CSR activities of enterprises are not as new in Russia, as they are often considered to be. The literature suggests that social responsibility was not invented after 1991 but rather drew upon and adapted from earlier practices and traditions (Davies et al. 2016). The Soviet Union was an industrialised country, and the role of industry in the social structure was extremely important. Soviet enterprises were burdened with a number of social obligations to employees, their families and the region, especially if the enterprise was the one around which the town had been formed and which had remained the biggest employer in the region. Social commitments included the creation of social infrastructure, kindergartens, schools and other educational institutions, health centres, recreational areas, etc. Soviet enterprises provided a certain level of social security and, therefore, social stability for citizens – both current and future employees and their families.

With the collapse of the Soviet Union and the introduction of privatisation, a significant number of the largest industrial enterprises were "released" from direct governmental control, social obligations and governmental contracts. The industry was unprepared to make the transition from the planned to a market economy, resulting in rapid economic decline. Populations in a number of regions were living in severe material and emotional hardship. State social activities and support virtually ceased, failing to provide even the most basic social security. Given the low geographic and professional mobility of citizens, enterprises remained the only employers in local labour markets. This is especially true for mono-industrial towns (94 out of the total of 319 towns were in very poor socio-economic circumstances in 2016, ICSS 2017). Thus, corporations stepped in to restore at least some social obligations in those regions.

8.6.2 Expectations of Local Authorities

The socio-economic status of Russia's regions is still rather weak (Zubarevich 2015) but was much worse during the 1990s and 2000s, by which time social security at the regional level had largely been broken down. Local authorities, therefore, approached enterprises in an attempt to secure the budget for the social sector and infrastructure. In some cases, authorities delegated part of their social responsibilities to companies. Studies have revealed both formal and informal pressure exerted by local or federal authorities on corporations (Chirikova et al. 2005). The resources of enterprises, in addition to officially established taxes, became in some cases a source of replenishment for regional budgets (Peregudov and Semenenko 2009). From this perspective, social responsibility and corporate philanthropy are both an indicator of loyalty to the state (Chebankova 2013: 107) and an attempt to meet officials' expectations in order to gain legitimacy and permission to operate in a particular territory (Matten and Moon 2008; Campbell 2007).

8.6.3 Public Satisfaction with the Social Sector and Public Expectations of Social Security

Expectations of social security, as an inheritance of the Soviet period, are highly pronounced among Russians. Indeed, education, healthcare, social services, recreation and sports to some extent remain "free" for the general population in modern Russia. Privatisation after the collapse of the Soviet Union was conducted with serious violations, and the majority of Soviet enterprises were privatised at low prices (Leonard and Pitt-Watson 2013). The public is confident that privatisation was unfair. Social stratification and income inequality rose exponentially, especially in contrast with the "flat" and equal Soviet social stratification structure (Denisova et al. 2012). The Gini coefficient increased from 0.260 in 1991 to 0.409 in 1994 and 0.379 in 1998 (Statistical Yearbook of Russia, Official documents, 1999, p. 141, 155). Serious public discontent emerged in the early to mid-1990s, and citizens demanded that enterprises "share" and redistribute "unjustly obtained" wealth in order to restore a minimal level of personal wellbeing and social justice (Polishchuk 2006).

The current state of the social sector in Russia is rather poor, and the population is largely dissatisfied with the state of healthcare and education. Thus, there are certain expectations, firstly, of the government and, secondly, of the enterprises to provide a minimal level of social security. This is especially pronounced in the areas where mining companies are present, as they play a crucial role in local labour markets.

Thus, the social responsibility of companies is, in many respects, much more determined by societal factors than by market or direct economic benefit considerations. Social responsibility, in the forms of both CSR and corporate foundations, follows several strategies. The first strategy is to modify current socio-economic agreements in areas of an enterprise's business interest. Multinational corporations and the biggest Russian corporations tend to create new rules, which would lead to a favourable socio-political climate for business activity in the future (Zhao 2012). The actual partnership has not yet been developed, since business–government relations for the majority of companies are of a short-term nature and are inefficient (Chirikova 2012). The second strategy is to obtain direct advantages and resources within the current arrangements. Corporations participate in social projects which are close to government interests and which are, at the same time, in the business interests of corporations themselves. This provides opportunities to propose new business projects in these areas and to be rewarded with additional government support for them. The third strategy is a philanthropic one, which is not obviously related to the explicit business interests of an enterprise. Philanthropy boosts the status of an enterprise in its communications with authorities. Corporations can be rewarded with more prestigious political status and protection from inspections and from direct political interference in exchange for such voluntary philanthropic commitments. Thus, corporate social responsibility is inevitably correlated with attempts to develop partnership relations with the government in order to gain economic or political advantage. The ultimate objective might be a "fixed" division of areas of social responsibility between the state and corporations. Corporations thereby take responsibility for some social infrastructural objects in the region, while officials assist them in solving business issues.

8.7 Conclusion and Outlook

Corporate foundations in Russia constitute a distinct group of non-profit organisations, founded and predominantly financed by their parent company. They are not, however, viewed as a special type of foundation from the point of view of law and taxation. Furthermore, corporations do not have any obvious financial incentives to establish a foundation. The decision to form one is determined, to a large degree, by a parent company's wish to focus on the implementation of certain charitable and social programmes at an advanced level.

The number of corporate foundations in Russia was about 25 at the end of 2016, but their contribution to social and charitable activity is significant, relative to the cumulative budget of the overall foundation sector. Corporate foundations are mainly supported by their parent enterprises, and the revenue structure of a foundation is not particularly diverse. Despite this, the majority of the foundations enjoy autonomy from the financing parent organisation with regard to activity, missions, and objectives. The majority of the programmes are related to but separate from the corporation's commercial activities. Two-thirds of corporate foundations award grants, while the rest are operational. Foundations pursue several aims, with social support for vulnerable groups, education, health, and local community development being the most prominent.

The activities of corporate foundations, as well as CSR, generally involve a significant local component, with their patterns of operation being influenced and determined by context. Despite their small numbers, corporate foundations make a large contribution to the total volume of philanthropic and social programmes. Hence, corporate foundations can be understood as a tool to meet the expectations of external requirements from the public and local authorities and to obtain legitimacy and access to operate in their respective area (of interest). Their Soviet background, budget limitations, and government–business relationships provided a platform for the growth of CSR and the establishment of corporate foundations.

Corporate foundations' activities are unlikely to decline in the future. Russia has generated a favourable climate for non-profit activities and for the charitable activities of its citizens. Recently, the Russian state has made a lot of effort to involve non-commercial organisations in the provision of services in the social sector (Benevolenski and Toepler 2017). In addition, citizens' philanthropic activities are actively supported, and efforts are made to stimulate it and to develop formal philanthropy in contrast to informal practices widely spread nowadays. In the meantime, the state of the social sector remains unsatisfactory. Consequently, it is likely that the state's interest in maintaining a partnership with commercial organisations regarding joint social projects will continue. The legal form of a corporate foundation is sometimes more convenient for these purposes, as well as for professionalisation and tackling a variety of social problems. At the same time, in the absence of financial and tax incentives, an explosion in the number of corporate foundations is unlikely.

The chapter contributes to research and practice in several aspects. First, in line with the practical issues, the chapter brings some basic research data on corporate foundations, being previously under the research focus both internationally and in Russia. The sector of corporate foundations becomes somehow visible, as the chapter provides information on the estimated scope and financial size of the sector in relation to a broader CSR.

Second, research contribution relates to the conceptual discussion on actual roles and advantages or disadvantages of corporate foundations in broader aspects of CSR, the non-profit sector, public service provision (Anheier 2018; Toepler 2018) and the role stakeholders play in CSR activities. The chapter provides some insights on capacity-building of corporate foundations and the role they have in developing of the non-profit sector in Russia. Foundations are examined from the institutional perspective, elaborating on particular determinants that lead to the role of CSRs and foundations as a kind of revenue source for state institutions and welfare projects.

References

Abramov, R. (2005). Corporate social responsibility as an example of organizational isomorphism in the conditions of globalization. *Journal of Social Policy Studies, 3*(3), 327–347.

Anheier, H. K. (2018). Philanthropic foundations in cross-national perspective: A comparative approach. *American Behavioral Scientist, 62*, 1591–1602.

Beam, D., & Conlan, T. (2002). Grants. In L. Salamon (Ed.), *The tools of government: A guide to the new governance*. New York: Oxford University Press.

Benevolenski, V., & Toepler, S. (2017). Modernising social service delivery in Russia: Evolving government support for non-profit organisations. *Development in Practice, 27*(1), 64.

Boldureva A. (Ed.) (2016). All about the leaders of 2016: On the materials of the project "leaders of corporate philanthropy – 2016. Donors Forum.

Brammer, S., Jackson, G., & Matten, D. (2012). Corporate social responsibility and institutional theory: New perspectives on private governance. *Socio-Economic Review, 10*, 3–28.

Bruyn, S. T. (1999). The moral economy. *Review of Social Economy, LVII*(1), 25–46.

CAF World Giving Index. A global view of giving trends (2017). Charities Aid Foundation 2017. Avaliable at: https://www.cafonline.org/docs/defaultsource/about-us-publications/cafworldgivingindex2017_2167a_web_210917.pdf

Campbell, J. L. (2007). Why would corporations behave in socially responsible ways? An institutional theory of corporate social responsibility. *Academy of Management Review, 32*, 946–967.

Chebankova, E. (2013). *Civil society in Putin's Russia*. London: Routledge.

Chernysheva, M. (2016). Charity of small- & medium-sized businesses in a Russian small town: An empirical analysis. *Journal of Economic Sociology., 17*(4), 129–163.

Chirikova, A. (2012). State and business: Interaction on the field of social policy in modern Russia. *Russia Reforming*, 11: Yearbook / ans. M. K. Gorshkov (Ed.). (The new chronograph).

Chirikova, A., et al. (2005). Biznis kak Subjekt Sotsial'noj Politiki (Business as s Social Policy Actor) (In Russian). Moscow: HSE Publishing House.

Davies, J. S., Holm-Hansen, J., Kononenko, V., & Røiseland, A. (2016). Network governance in Russia: An analytical framework. *East European Politics, 32*(2), 131–147.

Denisova, I., Eller, M., Frye, T., & Zhuravskaya, E. (2012). Everyone hates privatization, but why? Survey evidence from 28 post-communist countries. *Journal of Comparative Economics, 40*(1), 44–61.

Gainer, B. (2010). Corporate social responsibility. In R. Taylor (Ed.), *Third sector research*. New York: Springer.

Haufler, V. (2008). Civil society, corporate social responsibility, and conflict prevention. In J. W. Walker & A. S. Thompson (Eds.), *Critical mass: The emergence of global civil society* (p. 169). New York: Wilfrid Laurier University Press.

Henderson, S. L. (2002). Selling civil society: Western aid and the nongovernmental organization sector in Russia. *Comparative Political Studies, 35*(2), 139–167.

Leonard, C. S., & Pitt-Watson, D. (2013). *Privatization and transition in Russia in the early 1990s'*. New York: Routledge.

Liborakina, M. (Ed.). (2003). *City and business: Creation of social responsibility of Russian companies*. Moscow: Foundation Institute for Urban Economics.

Ljubownikow, S., Crotty, J., & Rodgers, P. W. (2013). The state and civil society in Post-Soviet Russia: The development of a Russian-style civil society. *Progress in Development Studies, 13*(2), 153–166.

Ljubownikow, S., & Crotty, J. (2016). Nonprofit influence on public policy: Exploring nonprofit advocacy in Russia. *Non-Profit and Voluntary Sector Quarterly, 45*(2), 314–332.

Longsdon, J., & Wood, D. (2002). Business citizenship: From domestic to global level of analysis. *Business Ethics Quarterly, 12*(2), 155–158.

Matten, D., & Moon, J. (2008). "Implicit" and "explicit" CSR: A conceptual framework for a comparative understanding of corporate social responsibility. *Academy of Management Review, 33*, 404–424.

Mersiyanova, I., Jakobson, L., & Krasnopolskaya, I. (2015). Giving in Russia: The difficult shaping of the new nonprofit regime. In P. Wiepking & F. Handy (Eds.), *The Palgrave handbook of global philanthropy*. New York: Palgrave Macmillan.

Mersiyanova, I. V., Kononykhina, O., Sokolowski, W., & Salamon, L. M. (2017). Russia: A classic statist model. In L. M. Salamon (Ed.), *Explaining civil society development: A social origins approach.* (chap. 14) (pp. 223–236). Baltimore: Johns Hopkins University Press.

Ochareva, O. (2016). Report on the status and development of foundations in Russia, 2015. Donors Forum.

Overview of Russian Mono-Industry Towns (2017). Analytical Report. An Institute for Complex Strategical Research. Moscow.

Peregudov, S. (2003). *Corporations, society, state: Evolution of relations.* Moscow: Nauka Publishers.

Peregudov, S., & Semenenko, I. (2009). Business and the state in the social sphere: Confrontation or partnership? *World Economy and International Relations, 6*, 58–66.

Polischuk, L. (2009). Corporate social responsibility or government regulation: An analysis of institutional choice. *Problems of Economic Transition, 52*, 73–94.

Polishchuk, L. (2006). Businessmen and philanthropists. *Pro et Contra, 1*, 59–73.

Salamon, L., Benevolenski, V., & Jakobson, L. (2015). Penetrating the dual realities of government-nonprofit relations in Russia. *VOLUNTAS: International Journal of Voluntary and Nonprofit Organizations, 26*(6), 2178.

Skokova, Y., Pape, U., & Krasnopolskaya, I. (2018). The non-profit sector in today's Russia: Between confrontation and co-optation. *Europe-Asia Studies, 70*(4), 531–563.

Sundstrom, L. (2006). *Funding civil society: Foreign assistance and NGO development in Russia.* Stanford: Stanford University Press.

Tarasenko, A. (2015). Russian welfare reform and social NGOs: Strategies for claim-making and service provision in the case of Saint Petersburg. *East European Politics, 31*(3), 294.

Toepler, S. (2018). Toward a comparative understanding of foundations. *American Behavioral Scientist, 62*(13), 1956–1971.

Waddock, S. (2004). Parallel universes: Companies, academics and the progress of corporate citizenship. *Business and Society Review, 109*, 5–42.

Wathen, M., & Allard, S. (2014). Local nonprofit welfare provision: The United States and Russia. *Public Administration Issues*, (5), 7.

Zhao, M. (2012). CSR-based political legitimacy strategy: Managing the state by doing good in China and Russia. *Journal of Business Ethics, 11*(4), 439–460.

Zubarevich, N. (2015). The relations between the center and the regions. In M. Lipman & N. Petrov (Eds.), The State of Russia: What comes next? Palgrave Pivot, London.

Irina Krasnopolskaya is a research associate at the National Research University Higher School of Economics, The Centre for Civic Initiatives Assessment. Irina studies the non-profit sector, volunteering and corporate volunteering and also focuses on social innovations and social innovation measurement.

Chapter 9
Corporate Foundations in Latin America

Marta Rey-Garcia, Michael D. Layton, and Javier Martin-Cavanna

Abstract This chapter provides an overview of the evolution, context, current characteristics, and future perspectives of corporate foundations in Latin America (Central and South America). The number of corporate foundations has grown considerably during the last three decades, against a backdrop of historical prevalence of informal expressions of generosity under the clout of Catholic charity and State paternalism and of a mostly unfavorable legal and fiscal framework for philanthropy. This growth has run in tandem with the advances of CSR and civil society in the region under the forces of democratization and economic liberalization, and with the encouragement of foreign donors, particularly from the USA. Due to a scarcity of data and the lack of a single legal or fiscal definition for corporate foundations, we first offer a definition reflective of regional traits and then approach corporate foundations through three case studies of Brazil, Mexico, and Colombia – the region's most populated countries – constructed from multiple sources, including our own database of 262 corporate foundations. We identify six regional commonalities and also important variations between countries, including Brazil leading in terms of sector institutionalization, Mexico staying in close proximity to the US grantmaking model, and an idiosyncratic Colombian pattern of involvement in community development. We close the chapter with practical and research implications.

Keywords Corporate foundations · Latin America · Corporate social responsibility · Quantitative research · Desk research · Institutional environment

M. Rey-Garcia (✉)
University of A Coruña, A Coruña, Spain
e-mail: marta.reyg@udc.es

M. D. Layton
Inter-American Foundation, Washington, DC, USA

J. Martin-Cavanna
Fundacion Compromiso y Transparencia, Madrid, Spain
e-mail: jmcavanna@compromisoempresarial.com

9.1 Introduction

The number of corporate foundations has considerably grown in Latin America (Central and South America) during the last three decades, parallel to the growth of direct social investment programs of companies and in the context of the overall advance of corporate social responsibility (CSR) in the region (Villar 2015). The goal of this chapter is to provide an overview of the evolution, context, current characteristics, and future perspectives of corporate foundations in Latin America. If research on institutional philanthropy in the region is in its very infancy, research on corporate foundations is almost nonexistent, with two landmark studies that approach them in the broader context of philanthropy (Sanborn and Portocarrero 2006) and private social investment (Villar 2015). Most countries in the region lack an updated census of the population of foundations including financial data, and only a few disaggregate corporate ones. A relevant source for identifying the main corporate foundations consists of publicly available directories of members of the associations and networks of philanthropic and private social investment organizations. Though none of them gathers exclusively corporate foundations, some of these infrastructures – notably Mexico's CEMEFI as the oldest and largest one – are leading the process of institutionalization of corporate philanthropy in the region (see Table 9.1). Regarding the best estimates of the volume of their assets and expenditures, they come from voluntary registries and surveys, which are by nature limited in scope by the willingness of the institutions to participate. One exception is Mexico, whose tax law requires all tax-exempt organizations to place detailed financial data (such as income, assets, and most importantly grants made) on a

Table 9.1 Main civil society infrastructures leading institutionalization of corporate foundations in the region (author's elaboration)

Country	Infrastructure	Founded	Membership
Brazil	GIFE Grupo de Institutos Fundaçãos e Empresas / Group of Institutes, Foundations, and Corporations	1995	125 members including corporate foundations (53%), firms (18%), family foundations (17%), and independent or community foundations (12%) (Velasco et al. 2015)
Mexico	CEMEFI Centro Mexicano para la Filantropía / Mexican Center for Philanthropy	1988	341 members including associations, foundations, companies, and individuals as of February 2017 (Cemefi n.d.)
Colombia	AFE Asociación de Fundaciones Empresariales / Association of Corporate Foundations	2008	71 corporate and family foundations as of February 2017 (AFE n.d.)
Argentina	GDFE Grupo de Fundaciones y Empresas / Group of Foundations and Corporations	1995	24 corporate and independent foundations and 14 corporations as of February 2017 (GDFE n.d.)

public transparency website (Layton 2016): this transparency provision has made it possible to identify grantmaking foundations in this country.

With these limitations in mind, we have approached the challenge of mapping corporate foundations in Latin America through three case studies of Brazil, Mexico, and Colombia. Criteria for selecting these countries are twofold. First, they are the three largest countries in the region in terms of population. Secondly, these countries offer the most thorough data on corporate foundations, as some exploratory studies and partial census have been recently undertaken, though of limited comparability (Velasco et al. 2015 for Brazil – the GIFE Census; Layton 2013; Villar et al. 2014, 2017 for México; Fundacion Promigas and DIS 2012 for Colombia). The case of Argentina, the fourth most populated country in the region, remains unexplored. Although corporate foundations are estimated to account for 75% of all foundations in this country, available studies do not classify corporate foundations separately (Villar 2015). Due to severe data scarcity, we have combined the aforementioned studies with multiple sources including available scholarly works, but also practitioner reports, that address broader phenomena at a regional level – philanthropy, corporate social responsibility, social investment, and the like – and sometimes include marginal though valuable insights on corporate foundations. In the case of Brazil and Colombia, reference studies have been combined with the elaboration of own databases constructed from GIFE and AFE directories of members and primary data from corporate and foundation websites and available annual reports. However, before empirically mapping corporate foundations in these countries against their historical, social, and legal background, it is imperative to discuss the regional traits that shape the conceptualization of this type of foundation in the following section.

9.2 Conceptualizing Corporate Foundations in the Region

The prevailing approach to explaining cross-country variation of foundations mostly originated from social origins theory. Under this approach, the economic dimensions of public policies and third sectors shape diverse third sector regimes, which in their turn host different foundation models characterized according to the size of foundation populations and their relation with public and third sector policies (Salamon and Anheier 1998; Anheier and Daly 2007). More recently, institutional research's tradition of categorizing and classifying organizational forms has been used to propose an integrative framework of foundation types based on contextual, organizational, and strategic categories (Jung et al. 2018). However, the lack of systematic empirical evidence prevents rigorous application of these theoretical approaches to Latin American foundations.

In the particular case of corporate foundations, conceptual approaches originating from other regional contexts should not be imposed upon an emerging and mutating reality that is deeply embedded in the local context and its unique conditions. The philanthropic engagement of businesses and their owners and managers was pivotal for the recent emergence of family and corporate foundations that were both independent from Catholic charity and the State. However, it has been challenging to impose upon the region what Salamon (2010) terms the "MBA mindset" (p. 42) typical of corporate philanthropy in the USA. Traditional approaches – reflecting the long-standing influence of paternalistic philanthropic charitable giving or merely focusing on public relations returns – coexist with innovative types of corporate engagement that are shaped by the specific regional context.

Given this combination of lack of evidence with signs of a rapidly transitioning state, and in order to advance comparative research on corporate foundations in Latin America, two pressing needs must be addressed: a consistent conceptualization and the establishment of a standardized set of descriptors to structure data collection efforts. Thus, our first step consists of proposing an operational definition of a corporate foundation for the region, as on the one hand there is no single legal or fiscal definition that applies across the board (Layton 2010), and on the other hand, the legal form of nonprofits may be irrelevant for tax exemption purposes (Nexus et al. 2014).

Furthermore, we argue that the US model that has inspired conceptualization of corporate foundations internationally is of limited application in Latin America. In the US model, the foundation receives its assets and/or annual gifts from its founder, a standalone and generally listed private business corporation – the Chandlerian paradigm of the large-scale, multi-unit, bureaucratically structured, professionally managed, vertically integrated business firm (FC 2012). Moreover, foundations are not allowed to be the main shareholder of businesses since the 1969 Tax Reform, and entrepreneurial families tend to endow their own family foundations independent from the family business, its CSR strategies and its corporate foundation (Rey-Garcia and Puig 2013).

Corporate foundations consistent with this US-inspired model coexist in Latin America with other different typologies. In fact, regional particularities of business ownership have important implications for the nature of corporate foundations. First, a majority of firms in the region are small and medium size, are not listed, and/or are family owned. Family businesses are predominant in Latin America, with a dual effect: Many corporate foundations are connected to family firms, and the boundaries that usually separate corporate and family philanthropy are unclear. Second, business groups – often closely linked to families – are a prevalent ownership structure in the region (Barbero and Dávila 2009). A business group is defined as "legally independent firms, operating in multiple (often unrelated) industries, which are bound together by persistent formal (e.g., equity) and informal (e.g., family) ties" (Khanna and Yafeh 2007: 331). Many corporate foundations are connected to business groups, rather than to stand-alone firms, and receive contributions from several affiliates. Third, state-owned enterprises (SOEs), that is, enterprises where the state has significant control through full, majority, or significant minority ownership, are also relevant regional players. Their share of the revenue of the largest listed companies (Fortune Global 500) in Brazil, Colombia, Mexico, and Venezuela has substantially grown between 2005 and 2014, their prevalence being second to Asia among world regions (PwC 2015). Some large corporate foundations in the region are controlled by SOEs. Fourth and last, foundations that own significantly influencing shareholdings of firms ("controlling foundations") are allowed in some countries. Just to underline these distinct features, recent studies in Brazil, Mexico, and Colombia use the term enterprise foundations (*fundaciones empresariales*) rather than corporate foundations (*fundaciones corporativas*).

Thus, we adopt a definition that is inclusive of these regional traits, as it conceptualizes a corporate foundation as a nonprofit organization (with its own legal personality, under a non-distribution constraint, and with public benefit purposes) that (1) is governed under corporate control (is controlled by one or several corporations, be they private businesses or state-owned enterprises, stand-alone firms, business groups, or associations); and/or (2) obtains the majority of its resources from one or several corporations, be they donations or dividends (Rey-Garcia et al. 2018: 517). This conceptualization is based on organizational governance theory and resource dependency theory and acknowledges three sources of distinctness for a corporate foundation, regardless of who founded it or its legal form: (1) its complex connectedness to the company beyond its dependency on corporate resources, (2) its hybrid business–nonprofit nature, and (3) its instrumental character for the pursuit of public benefit goals by corporations (Rey-Garcia et al. 2018). Thus, a foundation will be corporate if one or several companies are its main resource provider and/or one or several firms are ultimately responsible for its governance, that is, the systems and processes concerned with ensuring its overall direction, control, and accountability (Cornforth 2012).

This conceptualization has implications for the identification of populations to be studied in comparative research. First, corporate foundations would include not only company-established foundations that are created by a decision of its board of directors, or company-sponsored foundations that operate as a pass-through for corporate contributions, but also foundations that were originally established by individual entrepreneurs or entrepreneurial families, and currently obtain the majority of resources from the family firm, and/or are governed under corporate control to the extent that business owners and managers occupy key positions as trustees or directors. In these cases, the interests of the entrepreneurial family and those of the business are difficult to unravel, particularly if the foundation is endowed with shares of the family business. In fact, in Brazil, some corporate foundations act also as a vehicle for family philanthropy, to the extent that "many powerful families [choose] to conduct their philanthropy through their company, instead of structuring a family foundation" (Monteiro et al. 2011: 39). Secondly, controlling or shareholder foundations – those owning part of the shares of a commercial firm in a portion sufficient to grant, directly or indirectly, control or dominant influence over it (Rey-Garcia and Puig 2013) – would be also considered as corporate insofar dividends from the companies they own represent the majority of resources of the foundation. This type of corporate foundation is used as a vehicle to preserve the firm into the future and to transfer its control in a tax-efficient way. Although minority in the region and a rarity in Mexico, it is illustrated by large, relatively old, and highly influential examples in the case of Colombia and Brazil. Thirdly, our definition is inclusive of foundations that are funded and/or controlled by groups of entrepreneurs or groups of enterprises. Fourth and last, our conceptualization is not dependent on country-specific legal forms. In fact, 62% of GIFE members complying with our operational definition are legally incorporated as nonprofit associations, and 38% are incorporated as private foundations – versus 53–47% for family ones (Velasco et al. 2015). The members of these associations (sometimes self-identifying as "corporate NGOs") are most frequently a small number of firms or executives belonging to the same business group or enterprise, who in the end control the resulting corporate foundation and/or provide the majority of its resources.

9.3 Historical, Social, and Legal Context

An examination of the historical, social, and legal context of philanthropy in the region goes a long way in explaining the relatively limited development of corporate foundations (Layton 2010). Beginning in the sixteenth century, the Spanish conquistadors and the Brazilian colonizers brought with them their Catholic faith and the corresponding philanthropic values and practices, which have proven quite durable in fomenting paternalistic and informal expressions of generosity (Sanborn and Portocarrero 2006). With independence in the nineteenth century, many governments took control of charitable activities from the Church as a key aspect of state-building (Thompson and Landim 1998). Through most of the twentieth century, Latin America was characterized by populist or authoritarian regimes. "The state defined itself as the source and arbiter of all social goods," and the development of private philanthropy was inhibited (Thompson and Landim 1998: 364). As that century came to a close, globalization, expressed in the region through the phenomena of democratization and economic liberalization, had a dominating influence. Political reform brought with it the flowering of civil society and economic reforms engendered the creation of great private wealth: these transformations, combined with encouragement from foreign donors, all encouraged greater philanthropy in the region (Sanborn and Portocarrero 2006).

The first modern corporate philanthropy departing from Church or State paternalism originated from the initiatives of large, local, family-controlled business groups, most of which had close connections with American firms and foundations. The Venezuelan Mendoza Group is a case in point. Its founder, Eugenio Mendoza, always acknowledged the influence of North American philanthropy, particularly the Rockefeller Foundation, on his own corporate philanthropy. Starting in the early 1940s, he mobilized the support of other local businessmen for collective CSR initiatives such as the creation of the Dividendo Voluntario para la Comunidad Foundation, an affiliate of United Way International, with around 500 corporate members in the late 1960s (Puig 2016).

At a key historical moment in 1968, the Russell Sage Foundation published *Philanthropic Foundations in Latin America*, the first attempt to catalog these relatively new institutions in 18 Latin American nations (Stromberg 1968). Stromberg ascribes the rise of private foundation to "an awakening on the part of businessmen to the possibilities and advantages which foundations offer" and to the "private sector's growing sense of social responsibility" (p. 5). She could categorize a total of 300 foundations; 225 of them were created to support a "specific purpose" –a particular institution or cause – and 25 were corporate (9–10). The book also includes a brief essay, "Corporate Responsibility in Social Progress," by Ivan Lansberg Henriquez the then president of Dividendo Voluntario Para la Comunidad in Venezuela. Lansberg argues that "corporate leaders have awakened to the challenging fact that social progress in deeply unbalanced societies like ours cannot be considered an affair of government alone." He goes on to argue, "Corporate giving should never be looked on as mere charity. It is a long-range investment," and to predict that one day every company will have a "Department of Social Investment" (Lansberg Henriquez 1968: 183–185).

The data shared in the following section and the case studies show that the flourishing of corporate foundations in the region coincided with the period of intense engagement and investment in philanthropic infrastructures by a bevy of foreign donors, particularly from the USA, including Business for Social Responsibility, Inter-American Foundation, Ford and Kellogg Foundations, Synergos Institute, and Avina, with regional networks such as Forum Empresa and RedEAmerica (Puig 2016). Companies became more socially minded in the context of globalization, which enhanced their visibility and legitimacy to tackle social problems and facilitated the creation of transnational networks that integrated local entrepreneurial families, large multinationals, and civil society organizations (Rey-Garcia and Puig 2013).

Despite increasing CSR and philanthropic initiatives in the region, and growth in the number of corporate foundations, perceptions that corporate philanthropy is self-interested and tax benefit-driven only, and distrust of NGOs remain (Monteiro et al. 2011); so do pressing social problems. Economic growth in the region has been substantial – Brazil, Mexico, Argentina, and Colombia occupy positions 9, 15, 21, and 39, respectively, in World Bank's GDP ranking (2016) – but poverty, marginalization, and inequality persist. Latin America retains the dubious distinction of being the most unequal region in the world (Bárcena Ibarra and Byanyima 2016). In this context, pressures by relevant stakeholders on corporate actors to account for the impact of their philanthropy in truly tackling social problems tend to increase.

Ironically, despite the frequent claim that tax benefits drive corporate philanthropy, the legal and fiscal framework for philanthropy in the region is often unfavorable. In general, the policy context for nonprofit and philanthropic activity is characterized by complexity, and its enforcement is often marked by hostility (Appe and Layton 2016). Tax law, which is the most common manner to regulate and incentivize philanthropy, is quite inconsistent across countries, with many nations offering no incentives, and those who do narrowly selecting the beneficiaries of private generosity (Layton 2010). Endowed foundations are not common, as in most countries there are few incentives for establishing an endowment, and protection of assets is limited (Hauser Institute 2016). Thus, the use of fiscal incentives to encourage philanthropy – a tool of choice around the world – is weak in the region (Nexus et al. 2014). Paradoxically though it may seem, the United Nations' Economic

Commission for Latin America and the Caribbean (ECLAC) describes the region's tax system as poorly designed and riddled with avoidance and evasion (Bárcena Ibarra and Byanyima 2016), meaning that fiscal incentives that do exist are unlikely to have much impact on corporate donors.

To summarize, a strong tradition of religiously motivated charity has influenced Latin American business leaders to be generous, and the influence of globalization politically and economically, combined with international encouragement, has led to an important growth in corporate foundations, as will be described in the following section.

9.4 Characterization of Corporate Foundations in the Region: Available Empirical Data

The universe of corporate foundations in Latin America is unknown, as no publicly available, updated census of (active) corporate foundations, including their main characteristics, is available across the region. Best available data for Brazil come from our own database of 65 corporate foundations, constructed from multiple sources upon the list of GIFE members. Slightly over 50% of a total of 129 GIFE members as of February 2017 comply with our operational definition (GIFE n.d.-a). This database has been combined with data from the latest available GIFE "Census" (GIFE n.d.-b). This publication, which is based on survey responses from its members, started in 2001; was updated in 2004, 2006, 2008, 2010, 2012, and 2015; and turns Brazil into the only country with historical data on foundations. In 2015 GIFE obtained 113 responses out of a total of 125 members, both corporate and independent (Velasco et al. 2015). In the case of Mexico, best available data comes from combining a study based on 64 survey responses from a directory of 131 foundations originating from multiple sources (Villar et al. 2014), with an analysis of all the nation's grantmaking foundations – the predominant type – including 135 corporate ones, based upon information from the tax authority (Villar et al. 2017). In the case of Colombia, best available data come from Fundacion Promigas & Fundacion DIS (2012) survey responses from 129 corporate foundations, in combination with a database of 62 corporate foundations who are AFE members constructed by authors from multiple sources (AFE n.d.). It is reasonable to assume that overall data presented in this chapter encompass a substantial portion of the corporate foundation sector of the three countries, though a bias should be acknowledged in the case of Brazil and Colombia as foundations belonging to collective infrastructures tend to be more professionalized. Key data sources used in our research are summarized in Table 9.2.

It should be noted that available country studies are hardly comparable insofar as they adopt different conceptualizations. In Colombia, the reference study defines corporate foundations as those "created, oriented, controlled, and funded by firms, business groups, groups of entrepreneurs or entrepreneurial families" (Fundación

Table 9.2 Key data sources used to approach corporate foundations (CFs) (author's elaboration)

Country	Secondary sources		Primary sources	
	Study	Sample size	Source	Sample size
Brazil	Velasco et al. (2015) – The GIFE Census	113 corporate and independent foundations that are GIFE members	Own database of CFs that are GIFE members as of February 2017 + multiple sources	65 CFs
Mexico	Villar et al. (2014)	64 CFs		
	Villar et al. (2017)	135 grantmaking CFs identified from the public transparency website		
Colombia	Fundación Promigas and Fundación DIS (2012)	129 CFs	Own database of CFs that are AFE members as of February 2017 + multiple sources	62 CFs

Promigas and Fundación DIS 2012: 17). In Mexico, however, a corporate foundation is restrictively defined as that created by one firm (which would be the case for only 54% of corporate foundations in the Colombian study). Thus, a foundation that is mostly funded and/or controlled by several firms or groups of entrepreneurs is not considered as a corporate foundation, but rather as a community foundation (Villar et al. 2014). In the case of Brazil, corporate "foundations and institutes" are largely defined as "nonprofit organizations created and supported by a firm or its shareholders. They are governed by people connected to the supporting firm" (Velasco et al. 2015: 67). It should be noted that of the 65 GIFE members that are corporate foundations according to our operational definition, 27 are called "fundação empresarial" (corporate foundation), and 38 are branded as "instituto empresarial" (corporate institute). This second brand has gained in relevance since the 1980s, until almost replacing the term "foundation" (27 out of the 32 corporate foundations created after 2011 that are GIFE members are labeled as "institutes"). As "institutes" are not a legal form in Brazil, they are most frequently incorporated as nonprofit associations.

Back to the need for setting a research agenda on corporate foundations in the region, the second research priority – the first was consistent conceptualization – consists of establishing a standardized set of descriptors that structures data gathering efforts, integrates regional traits, and allows for cross-country comparison. Basic descriptor variables proposed by Rey-García and Alvarez (2011) for the first census of the Spanish foundation sector include legal form, age, size, geographic scope, type of founder, area of activity according to the International Classification of Nonprofit Organizations (ICNPO), type of beneficiaries (individuals or organizations), sources of funding, model of activity (grantmaking, operating or service providing, advocacy), assets, revenues, or expenditures. At this point, there is no systematic data gathering on these variables for Latin American foundations, with the notable exception of GIFE's surveys to its members. Furthermore, in the case of corporate foundations, these basic descriptors should be supplemented with additional variables that characterize in further depth the relationship between the corporate foundation and the supporting firm(s) across different dimensions. As an illustration, they may include the following descriptors:

Type of Corporate Funding Annual contributions of the company/dividends, detailing in this case whether the foundation is controlling or non-controlling.

Characteristics of Founder(s) Firm/business group/individual entrepreneur/ entrepreneurial family/group of entrepreneurs.

Board Composition Owners of the enterprise/executives of the enterprise/ independent.

Features of Supporting Company Listed/privately held; foreign multinational/ multilatina/national/regional/local; private family owned/private nonfamily owned/ State-owned enterprise; sector or industry where it operates.

Degree of Strategic Alignment Between the Foundation and the Company Areas of activity/geographic scope/type of beneficiaries of the foundation.

Some available evidence allows us to roughly estimate the age and relative size of the corporate foundation sector in the three countries that are the object of our analysis. The sector is predominantly young, particularly in Mexico, where 94% of corporate foundations were created after 1991. In Colombia and Brazil, there is a relatively larger tradition, with 35% and 33% of corporate foundations, respectively, created before 1991 (see Table 9.3). Regarding size in terms of number of organizations, corporate foundations, though latecomers to the philanthropic landscape, have grown in numbers relatively faster and represent a majority share of the overall foundation sector in Brazil and Colombia. In 2011/2012 corporate foundations represented 67% of all foundations in Brazil (down from 82% in 2009/2010), 65% in

Table 9.3 Age (year of creation) of corporate foundations in the region

Brazil	<1960	1961–1970	1971–1980	1981–1990	1991–2000	>2000	Total
	5	2	3	11	12	32	**65**
	8%	3%	5%	17%	18%	49%	100%
Mexico	<1970		1971–1990		1991–2001	2001–2013	Total
	0		8		30	93	**131**
	0%		6%		23%	71%	100%
Colombia	<1970		1971–1980	1981–1990	1991–2000	2001–2011	Total
	13		13	19	36	48	**129**
	10%		10%	15%	28%	37%	100%

Author's elaboration from own database of Brazilian corporate foundations, Fundacion Promigas and Fundacion DIS (2012) and Villar et al. (2014)

Colombia, and 33% in Mexico (Villar 2015: 37). Villar et al. (2017) found that of 336 grantmaking foundations identified in 2013 in Mexico, 135 (40%) were classified as corporate, the single most numerous category, and another 12 (4%) represented associations of businesses.

Regarding size in terms of expenditures, data from tax authorities are only available for Mexico. Of a total of $371 million USD in grantmaking by foundations in 2013, corporate foundations accounted for $132 million USD (36%) and business associations nearly $13 million (3%). Four of the top 10 grantmaking foundations in Mexico, ranked in terms of annual grantmaking, are corporate foundations (Vizcarra, FEMSA, Televisa, and Wal-Mart de México) (Villar et al. 2017). However, in the context of overall corporate philanthropic expenditures, corporate foundations are a minor player. The case of multilatina companies, a major philanthropic actor, is illustrative of the paucity of corporate foundation expenditures in comparison with direct corporate investments. Multilatinas are multinational companies headquartered in Latin America, controlled by shareholders based in the region and maintaining significant operations within it. They have been one of the main drivers for recent economic growth in the region, with 2.1 million employees and approximately $780 billion in annual revenue (2012). A 2012 study estimated their annual direct social investments and philanthropic contributions in a range of $224–569 million, mostly motivated by community relations and provided through cash contributions. 67.3 percent of the contributions of the 100 largest multilatinas in Latin America and the Caribbean focused on education, targeting local schools and NGOs, and teachers and adolescents, with Brazil and Colombia topping the list of beneficiary countries. However, less than one-fifth (18%) of the total cash and in-kind contributions of multilatinas originated from corporate foundations. Instead, the companies invested the bulk of resources from their business budgets (Van Fleet et al. 2012).

9.5 The Case of Brazil: Corporate Social Investing, Collaboration, and Institutionalization

Historically, philanthropy understood as private, lay initiatives for the public good, did not belong to Brazilian corporate culture. The State acted as guardian of the sporadic, unsystematic charitable giving of local entrepreneurs in the social realm, consistent with their broader dependence on State intervention in the economy. It was not until the democratic transition of the 1970s and, particularly, the globalization of the economy in the 1980s that firms started to participate in the social development of the country (De Melo Rico 2004).

The construction of a "third sector" in Brazil started in the early 1990s. The number of foundations tripled between the mid-1990s and 2010. During those early years, aid from the US foundations such as Ford, Kellogg or Mott, or other foreign actors such as Avina – itself a regional player – was key to develop an infrastructure for the emerging voluntary sector, most notably GIFE, which took part in meetings in the American Chamber of Commerce, Instituto Ethos, and IDIS (Monteiro et al. 2011).

GIFE is the only infrastructure for philanthropy in the region publishing economic data of foundations, gathered through a biannual survey since 2001 (Mexico's economic data do not come from CEMEFI but from the public tax agency). Other relevant country infrastructures are Instituto Ethos, founded in 1998 to promote CSR among firms based in Brazil, and IDIS, founded in 1999 to promote private social investment, defined as a voluntary and strategic allocation of private resources – whether financial, monetary, human, technical, or managerial – for public benefit.

Local business actors played a leading role in this process of sectoral construction through GIFE, Ethos, and IDIS, together with the Johns Hopkins Comparative Nonprofit Sector Project – another US import – the World Bank and other multilaterals, and administrative reform promoted by the Federal Government. In this context, corporate philanthropy endorsed a business approach to social problems – progressively consolidating the idea of corporate social investing, the first country trait – and was a driver for the professionalization of nonprofits. The distinct feature of this new institutional space for civic engagement was cross-sector collaboration, rather than opposition to the other two societal sectors – the second country trait (Aguilar Calegare and Silva Junior 2009).

In the absence of a census, the 65 corporate foundations that are GIFE members have been used as a proxy for the current population of corporate foundations in Brazil. The first characteristic of Brazilian corporate foundations is that their missions are very broadly stated, with sustainable development – particularly at a local level in the communities where the enterprises operate – and education, particularly of the youth, being the most prevalent areas of activity. Once again, the ideal US-based definition of a corporate foundation is rarely to be found in Brazil (Schommer and Fischer 1999). For instance, 6% of corporate foundations are related to State-owned enterprises: 2 of the oldest ones originated from SOEs that were then privatized in the 1990s, 1 was created right after the privatization took place, and another one is still controlled by a SOE. Also, 45% of corporate foundations are connected to business groups, with heterogeneous origins and sometimes complex governance structures. Some were founded and/or are funded by all firms affiliated to the business group; others were created and depend on resources provided by the holding company. Another portion was created with specific goals by the founding entrepreneur (e.g., building a hospital for his hometown), but currently channels CSR initiatives of a (sometimes family-held) business group all across the board. In the case of family-held business groups, corporate foundations become another governance organ of the group, together with the boards of directors of the affiliate companies and the family counsel (e.g., Instituto Votorantim).

Regarding the geographic origin of the controlling/founding corporation, two-thirds are Brazilian, with only 29% of corporate foundations originating from foreign enterprises – including 2 from other Latin American countries, 2 from Spain, and 1 from Portugal. Regarding the geographic scope of the controlling/founding corporation, 43% are global multinationals, 26% are multilatinas, and 30% are national in scope. Regarding the sector or industry where the enterprise operates, 52% belong to sectors with large environmental impacts at a local level (e.g., mining, iron and steel, equipment, paper, agriculture, energy, automotive, construction, building materials, real estate), and 25% depend on public regulators and supervisors or public contractors (banking, telecom, and transportation infrastructures).

These features explain the drive for collaboration with local nonprofits and particularly with the government that impregnates the undertakings of corporate foundations in Brazil. Not by chance, 57% of corporate foundations have achieved the governmental declaration as "Organização da Sociedade Civil de Interesse Público" (OSCIP), and 35% have obtained a federal certificate of public utility (Velasco et al. 2015), which allow their private donors to access tax benefits for their giving and/or facilitate partnering with the public sector through agreements, contracts, and public funding.

In fact, there is some controversy regarding the appropriation of the third sector by corporate foundations. On the one hand, their model of activity is mostly operating (Table 9.4), and their actual goals, plan of activities, and expected outcomes are established by the enterprise, inspiring a public discourse of victory and self-accomplishment (Borges et al. 2007). On the other hand, they rarely are fully endowed and therefore tend to have a considerably diversified income structure (Table 9.4). Thus, they compete with their own programs against other third sector organizations for both private resources and public subsidies (Bastos de Paula and Morilha Muritiba 2014).

In any case, and similar to Colombia, Brazil hosts a few relevant examples of fully or substantially endowed corporate foundations, some including controlling shares. In fact, the largest Brazilian foundations in terms of endowment are corporate foundations (formerly) connected to financial enterprises, as can be seen in Table 9.5.

Of the three countries analyzed, Brazil shows the highest degree of institutionalization in terms of scale and scope of professionalization and sectoral debates – the third country trait. During recent years GIFE has been putting a strong focus on

Table 9.4 Model of activity and sources of income of Brazilian corporate foundations

Model of activity	Operating only	45%
	Grantmaking only	7%
	Mixed	48%
Source of income (% over total income)	Contributions from related enterprise(s)	34%
	Investment returns (returns on endowment and other assets)[a]	43%[a]
	Government funding (subsidies and contracts)	10%
	Sales of products or services	7%
	Other private donors	5%
	Other sources	1%

Author's elaboration from Velasco et al. (2015)
[a]If data from one large, fully endowed outlier is excluded, the percentage of total income originating from returns on own assets falls to 17%, and the source consisting of donations from the related enterprise(s) goes up to 51%

Table 9.5 Largest endowed foundations in Brazil

Foundation	Founded	Related enterprise	Endowment estimate in Brazilian Real (R$) in millions
Fundação Bradesco	1956	Banco Bradesco	R$ 34,500
Itaú Social	2000	Itaú Unibanco	R$ 2400
Instituto Unibanco	1982	Itaú Unibanco	R$ 1000
Fundação Maria Cecília Souto Vidigal	1965	Shareholder of former Banco Mercantil de São Paulo, founded by the Vidigal family	R$ 400
Instituto Alana	1994	Shareholder of Itaú Unibanco supported by the income from an endowment fund since 2013	R$ 280
Fundação Banco de Brasil	1986	Banco do Brasil	R$ 137

Author's elaboration from own database and Levisky Negócios e Cultura (2017)

governance and transparency issues, and on overall strategic reflection, coherent with sectoral challenges identified by IDIS in 2011: (1) lack of transparency, monitoring, and performance evaluation; (2) lack of family philanthropy tradition; (3) community leaders' lack of knowledge of the potential of local philanthropy; (4) lack of focus on grantmaking; and (5) lack of commitment of donors with social transformation (Monteiro et al. 2011). In its *Guide of Best Practices for the Governance of Corporate Foundations*, GIFE recommends the existence of a formally constituted board in strategic and monitoring roles, and including independent members. Furthermore, it is endorsing eight strategic agendas among its members around the following themes: (1) alignment between social investment and public policies, (2) alignment between social investment and business, (3) a move toward grantmaking, (4) evaluation, (5) communication, (6) strengthening of civil society organizations, (7) governance and transparency, and (8) social impact businesses (GIFE and IBGC 2014).

However, the 2014 GIFE Census shows corporate foundations lagging behind some of these recommendations. Only 19% of board members are independent vs. 42% in family and 61% in community foundations. While 51% of the resources of corporate foundations are deployed in operating their own programs, only 25% go to grantmaking other nonprofits, and 24% correspond to administrative costs. Concerning the alignment with their supporting firms, it is surprisingly low as reported by foundations: 48% of corporate foundations take into account business activities only occasionally when defining their areas of activity, and 12% never take them into account. Also, 28% take corporate activities into account only occasionally when choosing their target beneficiaries, and 33% never consider them at all. In addition, 42% of corporate foundations rarely have business interests in mind when defining their geographic scope. On the contrary, 80% of corporate foundations perceive they influence the principles and values of their supporting firms,

77% feel they contribute to corporate dialogue with stakeholders, and 63% perceive they influence corporate communication with the public in general. Perceived influence on core business aspects (productive processes, client or supplier procedures), however, is relatively lower (Velasco et al. 2015).

9.6 The Case of Mexico: Local Tradition and International Influence

In 2002 Manuel Arango, one of Mexico's leading philanthropists, noted "a growing awareness of the value of CSR" and "an institutionalization and professionalization of CSR practices and programs," alongside "a long-standing tradition of giving." This "tradition" was being transformed into "programs [that] are being expanded to incorporate a broader definition of social investment that goes beyond checkbook philanthropy" (Arango 2002). First came corporate donations and then came notions of CSR, which is turn helped to spur the creation of corporate foundations.

The emergence of expanded corporate philanthropy has both domestic and international roots. Domestically, "philanthropic activity has emerged as governments become less effective and support of societal needs by churches is not as prevalent as in earlier times" (Viesca-Sada 2004: 13). Internationally, Mexico has a particularly open trade policy and receptivity to foreign investment, epitomized by the North American Free Trade Agreement and the related US–Mexico Income Tax Convention, which has a specific article to encourage cross-border philanthropy (USA–Mexico Foundation 2013: 42). Its proximity to the USA has resulted in a particularly strong influence of US corporate and philanthropic practices.

The bulk of corporate foundations were created after 1991, and 71% were founded after 2001 (see Table 9.3). Perhaps the most remarkable finding is that more than half of all Mexican corporate foundations (56%) were established between 2002 and 2008 (Villar et al. 2014). While the other cases also saw the greatest growth in this sector during the twenty-first century, neither Brazil nor Colombia had a spike in growth like Mexico's. No corporate foundations were identified in Mexico before 1970, and only 6% were established by 1990, in contrast to Brazil where nearly 30% were established by then and Colombia that had 45% established. How can one reconcile Arango's observation that Mexico has a long tradition of giving with these numbers? Early on Mexican philanthropy was not channeled via the institutional form of corporate foundations but through the establishment of private, secular universities (e.g., Tec de Monterrey and the Autonomous Technological Institute of Mexico or ITAM), other types of foundations (e.g., Mexican Rural Development Foundation), and direct donations (Logsdon et al. 2006). Beginning in 1990, many of the same actors who promoted the growth of corporate foundations in Brazil also played an important role in Mexico, collaborating with Arango's own project, the Mexican Center for Philanthropy

Table 9.6 Model of activity of Mexican corporate foundations

Foundation budget (US$)	Grantmaking only (%)	Mixed (%)	Operating only (%)
> $ 235 k	25%	64%	11%
$ 79–235 k	25%	75%	0%
$ 21–78 k	50%	50%	0%
Up to $ 20 k	0%	0%	100%
All levels	28%	61%	11%

Adapted from Villar et al. (2014)

launched in 1988, which in turn created AliaRSE, an alliance to promote CSR via the annual event of the Seal of Business Responsibility, which recognizes the importance of corporate philanthropy as one aspect of CSR (Holz and List 2009).

Two recent publications give a detailed view of corporate foundations in Mexico, one via a survey of 64 foundations (Villar et al. 2014) and the other via an analysis of publicly available tax data on the nonprofit sector, which places corporate philanthropy in a comparative context with other foundations (Villar et al. 2017).

Perhaps the single most important decision for a foundation is whether to make grants, operate programs, or do both. In Mexico, Villar et al. (2014) found that 89% of the corporate foundations make donations, and 72% operate programs; at the next level of detail, 28% only make donations, 11% only operate programs, and the bulk (61%) are hybrids. As shown in Table 9.6, this decision is heavily influenced by the size of the foundation's budget.

When asked how businesses supported their affiliated foundations, foundation representatives responded: 88% provide annual contributions, 83% provide staff support; two-thirds offer in-kind contributions (from office space to the donation of goods), 44% make contributions to an endowment, and 28% seek donations from their own employees. When tallied up, the contributions made by the businesses constitute three-quarters of foundation resources. The bulk of Mexico's corporate foundations have five or fewer employees (58%), while 19% have between six and ten, and 24% have more than ten (Villar et al. 2014).

In a more recent study of Mexico's grantmaking foundations, and drawing upon the US-based National Taxonomy of Exempt Entities, the priority areas for grantmaking are philanthropy and volunteerism with $39 million USD (27%), human services with $26 million (18%), education with $20 million (14%), health with 13 million (9%), and $8 million to government institutions, together accounting for over $107 million USD, for nearly three-quarters of all corporate foundation grants. Corporate foundations are heavily concentrated in three states: There are 76 in Mexico City (52% of the total); 18 in the northern state of Nuevo Leon (12%), with most in the economic hub city of Monterrey; and 12 in Jalisco (8%), home to another major city, Guadalajara. These three states alone account for nearly three-quarters of all corporate foundations. Of the remaining 29 states, 17 have between one and five corporate foundations and 12 have none (Villar et al. 2017).

9.7 The Case of Colombia: A Long-Standing Tradition of Corporate Foundations Operating Programs in Connection with Church, Family, and Communities

Colombia stands out in the region due to the number, seniority, and significance of its local corporate foundations. Contrary to literature considering Venezuela as the leading country in terms of corporate philanthropy, and pointing out toward the role played by the US foundations in the development of corporate foundations in the region (Puig 2016), the Colombian model is clearly autochthonous and dates back to the 1960s, when two of the most relevant corporate foundations in the country were created: Fundacion Carvajal (1961) and Fundacion Social (1965, but originating in 1911 as workers' circle).

Both are relevant cases of corporate foundations of the controlling type, which head a business group. The case of Fundacion Social additionally exemplifies the notable influence of the Catholic tradition of charity upon regional philanthropic institutions. This organization was created as a workers' circle by a Galician Jesuit priest in 1911, was transformed into a philanthropic foundation in 1965, remained under control of the Jesuit order until 2001, and currently heads the 13th largest business group in Colombia, including Banco Caja Social and another five financial companies, with 5330 million dollars in assets and over 5.1 million clients (Dávila et al. 2014). The foundation funds its nonprofit, charitable activities with returns from its business subsidiaries.

Fundacion Carvajal is representative of corporate foundations of the controlling type connected to family business groups. The Carvajal Group, founded in 1904 in Cali, diversified from the printing and editing business into a variety of services and is now a family-controlled multinational extending its activities to several Latin American countries, the USA and Spain. The Carvajal Foundation was endowed in 1961 by the Carvajal family with 40% of their stakes in the Group, thus becoming its main shareholder. It currently holds 23% of its shares. Not by chance, the governance of the foundation – goals, board, and executive chairman – is detailed in the protocol that governs the family business, which aims toward integrity of the business group and unity of the family (corporate and foundation web sites; IFC 2011; Martin-Cavanna 2008a, b).

Fundacion Carvajal embodies the three main features of the Colombian model, as an operating foundation with strong ties with the community, closely interlocked to an entrepreneurial family and its business group, and of Christian inspiration. The mission of the foundation is to improve the well-being of the excluded populations in Cauca Valley, Colombia; and its vision is based on the Christian values of charity and social justice sponsored by the Carvajal family. It has pioneered micro-entrepreneurship and community development programs in the area, with a comprehensive approach to social interventions, and developed 88 projects in collaboration with 48 partners in 2015. Its innovative character has turned it into a reference for other corporate foundations in the region (Martin-Cavanna 2008a, b; Carvajal 2016).

Colombia is probably the country where the frontier between corporate and family foundations is more difficult to draw. Some of the AFE members characterized by the association as "family foundations" are in fact corporate foundations according to our definition, as they were originally endowed with a significant share of the family business and belong to the controlling type (the case of Fundacion Carvajal or Fundacion Sadarriaga Concha), or alternatively they are funded with corporate contributions that are allocated on an annual basis by decisions of the family council that governs the family business (e.g., Fundación Corona and Fundación Mario Santo Domingo). Out of 71 AFE members, 62 comply with our definition and 9 are family foundations.

Among 62 corporate foundations who are AFE members, 22 are connected to publicly listed companies. Regarding the geographic scope of the related company, 20 are national, 14 regional, 15 multilatinas, and 7 foreign multinationals. 6 AFE members have been created by groups of firms operating with different geographic scopes. Only 4 corporate foundations in AFE belong nowadays to the controlling type, with either significant or majority shareholdings of the related firms. In the first subcategory are Fundación Carvajal and Saldarriaga Concha foundation, which owns 12% of the Orbis Group. In the second subcategory are Fundacion Social and Fundacion WWB, with 85.7% of the WWB Bank, a microfinance institution lending to microentrepreneurs.

Regarding other descriptors of Colombian corporate foundations, we will use as a reference the largest sample available (the one elaborated by Promigas & DIS in 2011, with 129 corporate foundations). The majority of corporate foundations are related to companies of large size for country standards. In fact, 35% of the 200 largest Colombian firms have a corporate foundation, and the portion increases with company size, 7 of the 10 largest having one. The majority of corporate foundations were created by a firm (54%), followed by those created by an entrepreneurial family (18.4%), a business group (12.6%), and a group of entrepreneurs (12.6%). Between 1960 and 1980, corporate foundations created by entrepreneurial families or groups of entrepreneurs predominate; from 1980 onward, the portion of corporate foundations created by firms or business groups increases significantly. This shift is coherent with the concurrence of the popularity of CSR and the internationalization of Colombian economy through the entrance of multinationals in the 1990s, resulting in the creation of corporate-sponsored foundations by both local and foreign companies (Fundacion Promigas & Fundación DIS 2012).

Regarding their model of activity, it is mostly mixed, and an overwhelming majority consider themselves as mainly operating. Though 51.7% of corporate foundations receive returns from an endowment, a majority is not substantially endowed and depends on corporate contributions that tend to consist of cash donations, dividends, product donations, or asset donations. Corporate foundations created before 1991 tend to receive dividends in a larger proportion, while most of those created after that date depend on annual contributions. Coherent with social inequalities prevalent in the country, the main areas of activity of corporate foundations are education, community, and economic development (Table 9.7). Regarding board characteristics, 60.9% of corporate foundations include external

Table 9.7 Model of activity, sources of income, and areas of activity of Colombian corporate foundations

Model of activity	Operating only	29.9%
	Grantmaking only	5.7%
	Mixed	64.4%
Source of income (% over total income)	Contributions from founding firm(s)	57.8%
	Investment returns	20.3%
	Contributions from founding family	5.5%
	International cooperation	4.5%
	Government funding	4.2%
	Individual donors	3.0%
	Non-family shareholders	2.4%
	Suppliers	1.6%
	Employees	0.7%
Main areas of activity	Education	80.5%
	Community development	60.4%
	Economic or business development	59.8%
	Environment	42.5%
	Social integration	37.9%
	Human rights	36.8%
	Art, culture, and sports	35.6%
	Nutrition	33.3%
	Health	32.2%

Author's elaboration from Fundacion Promigas and Fundacion DIS (2012)

members in their board, but these independent members represent the majority of members only in 28% of corporate foundations (Fundación Promigas and Fundación DIS 2012).

9.8 Conclusions

There is no strong tradition of institutional philanthropy in Latin America, understood as voluntary private action for the public good that is independent of State and Church and is formalized through ad hoc organizations. The historical record is rather of informal charity, mainly based on the Christian culture prevalent in the region, the strong presence of the Catholic Church in the field of social welfare, and the related initiatives of local elites. However, during the last 30 years, a reconceptualization of civil society and a new understanding of the roles state, market, and civil society play unfolded. A role for NGOs and other civil society organizations, including foundations, emerged, and competition for funding led them to become increasingly entrepreneurial. Societal expectations upon local and foreign firms also evolved as the pressure to behave responsibly and commit themselves with community development and environmental sustainability increased.

We have tried to conceptualize, contextualize, and characterize corporate foundations as hybrid creatures – business tools of nonprofit nature where radically different institutional logics coexist – born out of this emerging role for enterprises in Latin American society. Results of this exploration point toward some general traits at a regional level:

1. Latin American corporate foundations are positioned as a distinct, though not prevalent, vehicle for private social investment, and as ancillary elements of broader CSR strategies.
2. Although instrumental for enterprises and resource-dependent on them, corporate foundations are highly heterogeneous organizations and are connected to business groups and entrepreneurial families to a larger extent than their US counterparts.
3. They participate in philanthropic infrastructures together with firms and/or family foundations, rather than networking among themselves or promoting foundation or nonprofit-only associations.
4. Their primary role within the third sector does not consist of funding civil society organizations, but rather on managing corporate relations with relevant stakeholders, most notably public and community actors, through a mixed operating-grantmaking model.
5. Endowed corporate foundations are a minority, and annual corporate contributions are the main revenue source in the context of diversified income structures.
6. Institutional proximity of corporate foundations to the government – not only as supervisor, but also as funder or partner – is noteworthy.

Against this common background, important country differences emerge from our three country studies. The relevance of international support, especially from the USA, for the process of emergence and growth of corporate foundations in the broader context of the construction of a third sector is evident in Brazil and Mexico. However, the impact of that support does not diminish the importance of national traditions and practices of philanthropy, as well as local leadership. Brazilian corporate foundations have tended to camouflage themselves as operating nonprofits. Mexico is the only country where the US model of grantmaking foundation has taken root. Colombia has followed a more idiosyncratic path, with corporate foundations working as a distinct type of civil society organization on community development.

The case of Brazil clearly stands out in terms of institutionalization of corporate philanthropy, GIFE being a reference for further data collection efforts in the region. In the case of Mexico, the public availability of data from the tax authority provides a reliable and detailed look at the flow of donations and a comparative perspective on the scope and size of corporate foundations compared to other types. AFE has been the main responsible for the increased visibility of corporate foundations in Colombia, inextricable from entrepreneurial families and family foundations.

Our exploration depicts an emerging, heterogeneous, and very rich landscape where different understandings, models of operations, and societal expectations upon corporate foundations coexist. It also suggests implications for both academia and practice. From a research perspective, this limited evidence does not diminish the need to get at some of the key descriptors identified in this chapter, particularly disaggregated financial data, and to illuminate critical issues in the relationship between the sponsoring business and the corporate foundation (e.g., how the sponsoring firm governs and funds the foundation or how the characteristics and strategy of the firm influence foundation governance and activities, among others). However, further data collection and categorization efforts should not only pursue systematic description of corporate foundations and their relationship with supporting firm(s), but also try to assess the evolutionary stage of corporate engagement they belong to as civil society actors. The "Five P Framework" developed by Salamon (2010) – Proliferation, Professionalization, Partnering, Participation, and Penetration – offers a promising venue to assessing the effectiveness of corporate foundations in tackling social problems.

From a practical perspective, corporate foundations are emerging against a background of lack of trust of civil society – the public and other nonprofits – vis-à-vis large corporate actors. This trust deficit may hinder innovative developments and must be factored out by firms or entrepreneurial families when funneling their philanthropic engagement through a corporate foundation, and also by foundation managers. As hybrid organizations, corporate foundations face a wider range of competing demands from external stakeholders, including different forms of accountability for different conceptions of performance. Latin American corporate foundations embody the difficult equilibrium between corporate instrumentality and civic engagement.

References

Aguilar Calegare, M. G., & Silva Junior, N. (2009). A "construção" do terceiro setor no Brasil: da questão social à organizacional. *Revista Psicologia Política., 9*, 17.
Anheier, H. K., & Daly, S. (Eds.). (2007). *The politics of foundations. A comparative analysis.* Oxon: Routledge.
Appe, S. M., & Layton, M. D. (2016). Government and the nonprofit sector in Latin America. *Nonprofit Policy Forum, 7*(2), 117–135.
Arango, M. (2002). Philanthropy in Mexico: Challenges and opportunities. *ReVista: Harvard Review of Latin America, 1*(3). http://revista.drclas.harvard.edu/book/philanthropy-mexico. Accessed 17 Dec 2017.
Association of Corporate and Family Foundations of Colombia (AFE). (n.d.). http://afecolombia.org/es-es/InformacionEstadistica. Accessed 26 Dec 2016.
Barbero, M. I., & Dávila, C. (2009). Introduction: A view from Latin America. *Enterprises et Histoire., 54*(1).
Bárcena Ibarra, A., & Byanyima, W. (2016). Latin America is the world's most unequal region. Here's how to fix it. World Economic Forum. https://www.weforum.org/agenda/2016/01/inequality-is-getting-worse-in-latin-america-here-s-how-to-fix-it/. Accessed 8 Jan 2017.
Bastos de Paula, M., & Morilha Muritiba, P. (2014). Influencia dos Fundadores na Cultura Organizacional das Fundacões de Direito Privado. *Revista de Governança Corporativa, 1*(1).

Borges, J. F., Miranda, F., & Valadão Júnior, V. M. (2007, , October–December). O Discurso Das Fundacões Corporativas: Caminhos de uma "Nova" Filantropia? *RAE-Revista de Administração de Empresas*.
Carvajal. (2016). Informe Social y Ambiental 2015. http://www.carvajal.com/informes/SocialAmbiental2015.pdf. Accessed 22 Dec 2016.
Cemefi. (n.d.). ¿Qué es Cemefi? https://www.cemefi.org/archivos/mision.pdf. Accessed 8 Jan 2017.
Cornforth, C. (2012). Nonprofit governance research: Limitations of the focus on boards and suggestions for new directions. *Nonprofit and Voluntary Sector Quarterly, 41*(6), 1116–1135.
Dávila, J. C., Dávila, C., Grisales, L., & Schnarch, D. (2014). *Business goals and social commitment: Shaping organizational capabilities – Colombia's Fundación Social* (pp. 1984–2011). Bogotá: Ediciones Uniandes.
De Melo Rico, E. (2004). A responsabilidade social empresarial e o Estado: uma aliança para o desenvolvimento sustentável. *São Paulo em Perspectiva, 18*(4).
Foundation Center (FC). (2012). *Key facts on corporate foundations*. New York: FC. http://foundationcenter.org/gainknowledge/research/pdf/keyfacts_corp2012.pdf. Accessed 17 Dec 2017.
Fundación Promigas & Fundación DIS. (2012). *Las fundaciones empresariales en Colombia: Una mirada a su estructura y dinámicas*. Bogotá: Asociación de las Fundaciones Empresariales de Colombia.
Grupo de Fundaciones y Empresas (GDFE) (n.d.). Los socios GDFE. http://www.gdfe.org.ar/los-socios-gdfe. Accessed 26 Dec 2016.
Grupo de Institutos, Fundações e Empresas (GIFE) (n.d.-a) Associados. http://gife.org.br/associados/. Accessed 28 Feb 2017.
Grupo de Institutos, Fundações e Empresas (GIFE) (n.d.-b). Censo GIFE Online. http://censo2012.gife.org.br/bloco1.asp?st=80&c=empresarial&f=&vi=&a=&aa=. Accessed 26 Dec 2016.
Grupo de Institutos, Fundações e Empresas (GIFE) & Instituto Brasileiro de Governanca Corporativa (IBGC). (2014). *Guia das melhores práticas de governanca para fundacões e institutos empresariais*. 2 ed. São Paulo: IBGC e GIFE. http://gife.org.br/agendas-estrategicas/. Accessed 30 Dec 2016.
Hauser Institute for Civil Society at Harvard University. (2016). *From prosperity to purpose: Perspectives on philanthropy and social investment among wealthy individuals in Latin America*. UBS.
Holz, M., & List, R. (2009). Centro Mexicano para la Filantropia, AC (CEMEFI). In H. K. Anheier & S. Toepler (Eds.), *International encyclopedia of civil society*. New York: Springer Science & Business Media.
International Finance Corporation (IFC). (2011). Manual IFC de Gobierno de Empresas Familiares. http://semanaeconomica.com/familiasac/wp-content/uploads/sites/94/2015/09/FamilyBusinessGovernance_Handbook_Spanish-1.pdf. Accessed 22 Dec 2016.
Jung, T., Harrow, J., & Leat, D. (2018). Mapping philanthropic foundations' characteristics: Towards an international integrative framework of foundation types. *Nonprofit and Voluntary Sector Quarterly, 47*(5), 893–917.
Khanna, T., & Yafeh, Y. (2007). Business groups in emerging markets: Paragons or parasites? *Journal of Economic Literature, 45*(2), 331–372.
Lansberg Henriquez, I. (1968). Corporate responsibility in social Progress. In A. Stromberg (Ed.), *Philanthropic foundations in Latin America* (pp. 183–187). New York: Russell Sage Foundation.
Layton, M. D. (2010). Philanthropy in Latin America. In H. K. Anheier & S. Toepler (Eds.), *International encyclopedia of civil society*. New York: Springer Science & Business Media.
Layton, M. D. (2013). Entidades Donantes Empresariales. In J. Butcher García-Colín (Ed.), *Generosidad en México: Fuentes, cauces y destinos*. México: Porrúa. Centro de Investigación y Estudios sobre Sociedad Civil, Instituto Tecnológico y de Estudios Superiores de Monterrey.
Layton, M. D. (2016). Regulation and self-regulation in the Mexican nonprofit sector. In A. Dunn, O. Breen, & M. Sidel (Eds.), *Regulatory waves: Comparative perspectives on state regulation and self-regulation policies in the nonprofit sector*. London: Cambridge University Press.

Levisky Negócios e Cultura. (2017). Conceitos e benefícios dos endowments como mecanismo de financiamento à cultura. *Guía do I Fórum Internacional de Endowments. Culturais*, com a parceria da Edelman Significa, IDIS e PLKC Advogados (June). http://www.leviskycultura.com.br/forum#guias

Logsdon, J., Thomas, D., & Van Buren, H. J. V. I. (2006). Corporate social responsibility in large Mexican firms. *Journal of Corporate Citizenship*, (21, 6), 51–60.

Martin-Cavanna, J. (2008a). Historia de una imprenta. In *Viaje a la otra orilla. Historias de los que trabajan por una América Latina mejor* (pp. 209–251). Bogotá: Edit. Norma.

Martin-Cavanna, J. (2008b, Mayo-Junio). Fundación Carvajal. Historia de un compromiso familiar, *Compromiso Empresarial*.

Monteiro, H., Kisil, M., & Woods, M. (2011). *Private social investment tendencies in Latin America*. São Paulo: IDIS – Instituto para o Desenvolvimento do Investimento Social.

Nexus Network International, McDermott, Will & Emery and Charities Aid Foundation (CAF). (2014). *Rules to give by: A global philanthropy legal environment index*.

Price Waterhouse Coopers (PwC). (2015). *State-owned enterprises: Catalysts for public value creation?* Public Sector Research Centre. www.psrc.pwc.com. Accessed 2 Dec 2016.

Puig, N. (2016). The origins of modern family foundations in Spanish – Speaking countries: A preliminary study. In P. Fernández Pérez & A. Lluch (Eds.), *Evolution of family business: Continuity and change in Latin America* (pp. 57–74). Cheltenham: Edward Elgar Publishing and Fundacion BBVA.

Rey-García, M., & Alvarez, L. I. (2011). Foundations and social economy: Conceptual approaches and socio-economic relevance. *CIRIEC-España, Revista de Economía Pública, Social y Cooperativa, 73*, 61–80.

Rey-Garcia, M., & Puig, N. (2013). Globalisation and the organisation of family philanthropy: A case of isomorphism? *Business History, 55*(6), 1019–1046.

Rey-Garcia, M., Sanzo, M. J., & Alvarez, L. I. (2018). To found or to fund? Comparing the performance of corporate and non-corporate foundations. *Nonprofit and Voluntary Sector Quarterly, 47*(3), 514–536.

Salamon, L. M. (2010). *Rethinking corporate social engagement: Lessons from Latin America*. Bloomfield: Kumarian Press.

Salamon, L. M., & Anheier, H. K. (1998). Social origins of civil society: Explaining the nonprofit sector cross-nationally. *VOLUNTAS: International Journal of Voluntary and Nonprofit Organizations, 9*(3), 213–248.

Sanborn, C., & Portocarrero, F. (Eds.). (2006). *Philanthropy and social change in Latin America* (David Rockefeller Center on Latin American Studies) (Vol. 16). RCLAS: Cambridge, MA.

Schommer, P. C., & Fischer, T. (1999). Cidadanía Empresarial no Brasil: os dilemas conceituais e a ação de três organizações baianas. *Organizações & Sociedade, 6*(15), 99.

Stromberg, A. (1968). *Philanthropic foundations in Latin America*. New York: Russell Sage Foundation.

Thompson, A. A., & Landim, L. (1998). Civil society and philanthropy in Latin America: From religious charity to the search for citizenship. In W. Ilchman, S. Katz, & E. Queen (Eds.), *Philanthropy in the world's traditions* (pp. 355–370). Bloomington: Indiana University Press.

U.S.-Mexico Foundation. (2013). Shared destiny, shared responsibility: Growing binational philanthropy for a stronger U.S.-Mexico partnership.

Van Fleet, J. W., Zinny, G. S., & Besharati, S. (2012). *Corporate social investments in education in Latin America & the Caribbean: Mapping the magnitude of Multilatinas' private dollars for public good*. Washington, DC: Brookings Institution. Center for Universal Education Working PAPER 5.

Velasco, A. C., Silva, A. L., De Império Lima, A. L., Szazi, E., Santiago, G., Moraes, M., Oliva, R., & Andrade, S. (2015). *Censo Gife 2014*. São Paulo: GIFE.

Viesca-Sada, A. (2004). The current state of philanthropy in Mexico and Central America. *Philanthropic Fundraising, 2004*(46), 13–25. https://doi.org/10.1002/pf.80.

Villar, R. (2015). Private funds for social transformation: Philanthropy and social investment in Latin America Today. Group of Foundations and Corporations in Argentina (GDFE), Group of Institutes, Foundations and Corporations of Brazil (GIFE), Association of Corporate and Family Foundations of Colombia (AFE) The Mexican Center for Philanthropy (Cemefi).

Villar, R., Butcher, J., Gandini, L., & Sordo, S. (2014). *Fundaciones Empresariales en México: un estudio exploratorio*. México, D.F.: Centro de Investigación y Estudios sobre Sociedad Civil en el Instituto Tecnológico de Monterrey y Centro Mexicano para la Filantropía.

Villar, R., Sordo, S., & Layton, M.D. (2017). Las Fundaciones Donantes: principales entidades donantes en México. In: Butcher García-Colín, J. (Ed.). *Generosidad en México II: Fuentes, cauces y destinos*, chapter 4. México, D.F.: Editorial Porrúa, Centro de Investigación y Estudios sobre Sociedad Civil, Instituto Tecnológico y de Estudios Superiores de Monterrey.

World Bank. (2016). GDP ranking. http://databank.worldbank.org/data/download/GDP.pdf. Accessed 22 Dec 2016.

Marta Rey-Garcia is Associate Professor of Management at the University of A Coruña, Spain. Her research focuses on civil society organizations, nonprofits, and philanthropy – particularly comparative studies on foundations. Her work has appeared in *Nonprofit and Voluntary Sector Quarterly, American Behavioral Scientist, Nonprofit Management and Leadership, Journal of Comparative Policy Analysis: Research and Practice and Management Decision*.

Michael D. Layton is one of the foremost experts on philanthropy and the nonprofit sector in Mexico. He currently serves as a Senior Program Specialist for the Inter-American Foundation.

Javier Martín-Cavanna is director of Fundacion Compromiso y Transparencia. He is the promoter and (co)author of the annual reports on transparency and good governance of business and family foundations in Spain.

Part III
Stakeholder Perspectives on Corporate Foundations

Chapter 10
Outsourcing of Corporate Giving: What Corporations Can('t) Gain When Using a Collective Corporate Foundation to Shape Corporate Philanthropy

Stephanie Maas

Abstract Recent years witnessed a diversification of the how of corporate philanthropy. The chapter distinguishes between in-house (direct) corporate giving and outsourced (indirect) corporate giving, bringing corporate philanthropy back to a make-or-buy decision. In addition, corporate donors can go down a collaborative path and participate in collective corporate foundations (CCFs): a corporate foundation serving the interests of multiple corporate donors simultaneously. The chapter examines the rationales of and consequences for corporations outsourcing corporate philanthropy by means of a CCF. The study entails a single instrumental case study in Rotterdam, the Netherlands. Primary data stems from 19 interviews with various stakeholders, including (former and non-) donor organizations. The study finds two rationales guiding corporate decision-makers facing the make-or-buy decision of corporate philanthropy: (1) available resources and (2) need for efficiency. Second, the study finds three consequences for corporations from utilizing a CCF for corporate giving: (1) loss of control, (2) loss of involvement, and (3) fewer organizational one-on-one residues. Third, the study identifies a trade-off between the identified rationales and consequences. The chapter concludes by relating the rationales back to a strategic management and an economic view on outsourcing and by discussing the study's limitations as well as the implications for corporate decision-makers and beyond.

Keywords Outsourcing · Qualitative research · Collective giving · Corporate philanthropy

---

S. Maas (✉)
Rotterdam School of Management (RSM), Erasmus University Rotterdam, Rotterdam, The Netherlands
e-mail: s.a.maas@rsm.nl

10.1 Introduction

> Imagine: [Corporation A] is setting up their own foundation, then [Corporation B] will set one up too, and [Corporation C] will do the same. (...) Nonetheless, there are only a few large corporations who can actually make that happen. A few who have the manpower, the knowledge, and the capital to do so (Representative B, partner organization).

Recent years witnessed a diversification of the "how" of corporate philanthropy. Over time, the landscape of corporate philanthropy grew increasingly more crowded, as more and more organizational forms and philanthropic practices came to populate the terrain and became part of the giving repertoire. Traditionally, corporations make direct grants to nonprofit recipients. The responsibility for corporate giving then resides with a company agent such as the CEO or a member of top management (Gautier and Pache 2015), or philanthropic responsibilities are carried out by a particular department that structures, unifies, and smoothens corporate giving (e.g., CSR, public affairs, corporate or external communications department) (Altuntas and Turker 2015; Husted 2003). Nowadays, more and more corporations make voluntary donations through separate (outside) vehicles. A frequently used vehicle are corporate foundations, also called company-sponsored or company foundations (Gautier and Pache 2015; Petrovits 2006; Webb 1994). The corporation then indirectly gives to nonprofit organizations and uses a corporate foundation as an intermediary vehicle that grants final donations to nonprofit recipients.

The diversification of the how of corporate philanthropy enables us to make a distinction between in-house (direct) corporate giving and external or outsourced (indirect) corporate giving. In-house (direct) corporate giving entails organizing and managing corporate philanthropy by particular individuals or departments within the corporation. External, outsourced (indirect) corporate giving entails organizing and managing corporate philanthropy by legal separate vehicles such as various types of corporate foundations or third-party providers. The distinction brings corporate giving back to a make-or-buy decision, as outsource decisions have their origin in the existence of make-or-buy alternatives. According to Greer, Youngblood, and Gray Greer et al. (1999), outsourcing refers to the performance of tasks that otherwise would be performed in-house by outside parties on a recurring basis. Following the definition on outsourcing by Turnbull (2002), I define outsourcing in the context of corporate philanthropy as placing responsibility for various elements of corporate philanthropy with legal separate entities and/or third-party providers. Outsourcing is comparable to governmental contracting out, where governments can decide to delegate the delivery of services to private organizations, instead of delivering the services themselves (Ferris and Graddy 1986).

Various vehicles exist for corporations to organize and manage a corporation's giving externally. These include for example third-party intermediaries (Lee 2015) or corporate foundations (Rey-Garcia et al. 2012). Besides shaping, organizing, and managing corporate giving individually, corporations can go down a collaborative path with like-minded corporations and combine their corporate philanthropy. One could expect corporations to even have a more fundamental impact on societal issues when opting collective giving strategies, as one can argue collective business efforts have comparative advantages over individual efforts in various areas (i.e., pooling resources, ruling out any suspicion on individual gains, reaching scale and critical mass, demonstrating common commitment) (e.g., Fourie and Eloff 2005). Porter and Kramer (2002, p. 11) state that "corporate philanthropy is ripe for collective activity," as "collective action will often be more effective than a solo effort in addressing context and enhancing the value created" (2002, p. 16). Corporate foundations and other corporate philanthropic vehicles are increasingly promoting and adapting combined or collective giving strategies. For instance, corporate foundations serving the interests of multiple corporate donors simultaneously came to populate the corporate philanthropic landscape. Within the study, I focus on these multiple-donor corporate foundations and label them as collective corporate foundations (CCFs). CCFs are thereby an example of an outsourced (external) and collective corporate giving practice.

10.1.1 Study Purpose and Case Context

The research question in the study is: What are the rationales of and consequences for corporations outsourcing corporate philanthropy by means of a CCF? Hereby, I dive into the rationales that guide corporate decision-makers in the make-or-buy decision of corporate giving as well as the decision between individual or collective giving strategies. Furthermore, I wonder what the implications are of a corporation's[1] choice when it decides to indirectly donate to nonprofit organizations through a collective separate entity. The study finds two rationales guiding corporate decision-makers facing the make-or-buy decision of corporate philanthropy and opting for collective giving strategies: (1) the amount of available resources and (2) the need for efficiency. These rationales relate to a strategic management and an economic view on outsourcing. The strategic management view follows a resource-based view on the firm and the resource dependency theory. The economic view on outsourcing entails transaction cost economics and agency theory (Lee et al. 2000). Second, three main consequences of outsourcing corporate philanthropy to a CCF are identified: (1) a loss of control, (2) a loss of involvement, and (3) fewer organizational one-on-one residues.

I find these rationales and consequences by means of a single instrumental case study (Stake 1995), concerning a corporate foundation located in the port of Rotterdam, the Netherlands. DeltaPORT Donation Foundation finds its origin in 1974 and is established by an industry association: the predecessor of Deltalinqs.[2] The foundation embodies a corporate foundation for the port's industry and

---

[1] Within this study, "corporations" are personified as the term is used as if corporations undertake actions themselves. Nevertheless, I acknowledge that corporations operate through people.

[2] Deltalinqs is the ports' industry association and is active in the joint interests of industrial companies in the port of Rotterdam.

established to give something to the local community and to compensate for the industry's hindrance caused to the local community. The foundation provides small monetary donations to nonprofit organizations located in 17 municipalities surrounding the port active in sports, culture, and well-being. The foundation constitutes a vehicle for corporations to engage in and shape (collective) corporate giving. Currently 82 corporations contribute to the foundation (i.e., donor organizations). Donations constitute a fixed amount based on the number of employees ($13 per employee) or an amount agreed upon with the founding industry association. The foundation's operating budget ($400.000) comes from two main sources: (1) donor organizations (55%) and (2) the foundations official partner[3] (45%) (DeltaPORT Donatiefonds 2016). Some corporate representatives of donor organizations also serve as board members of the foundation as representatives of the industry. Where a corporate foundation generally has a single corporate donor, this foundation has multiple. Thereby the foundation serves multiple corporate donor interests simultaneously. Given its structure, functioning, and multiple served donor interests, the foundation provides a collective voice for corporate philanthropy.

10.1.2 (Collective) Corporate Foundations

The boundary of what is considered a corporate foundation is blurry and can be disputed. Within the limited literature on corporate foundations, there is no single accepted definition (Rey-Garcia et al. 2012). There are a few characteristics differentiating corporate foundations from other types of foundations. First, corporate foundations are separate legal entities and are often founded by a corporation whose name is frequently part of the foundation's name. Second, a corporate foundation obtains the majority of its operating income and other resources from a (founding) firm's generosity. Third, the foundation's board often includes owners, directors, or top managers from the founding corporation (Rey-Garcia et al. 2012). Following a more subjective definition, the foundation should self-identify as a corporate foundation (see also the characteristic of a family foundation from Moody et al. (2011)). Although not founded by a for-profit corporation, DeltaPORT Donation Foundation fulfils most of the differentiating characteristics (i.e., operating income, board composition). Self-identification as a corporate foundation is an important aspect with respect to the DeltaPORT Donation Foundation, as it is depicted as a corporate foundation for the ports' industry. The foundation differs from a community foundation, as the foundation is not accessible to every (corporate) donor. Only corporations located in the port area, and member of the founding industry-association, can donate to the foundation.

---

[3] In 2007, Deltalinqs approached the Port of Rotterdam Authority (PoR) to become a partner of the foundation. The PoR is a publicly owned but corporatized port-development company.

CCFs are a relatively new emerging phenomenon and are still in its infancy. Similar initiatives are collective (corporate) foundations established or supported by the collective efforts of multiple corporations, serving multiple donor interests simultaneously. Existing examples of these initiatives are found globally and arise from specific industry clusters or industry associations. The Toy Industry Foundation (TIF), for example, constitutes the focal point for the philanthropic efforts of the North American toy industry, where corporations can accomplish philanthropic goals by donating funds (Toy Association n.d., Toy Industry Foundation, n.d.). Another example of a CCF is the Industrial Fabrics Foundation in the USA, as this foundation constitutes "the philanthropic voice of the specialty fabrics industry for nearly 20 years" (Industry Fabrics Foundation n.d.). Another example is the SBF Foundation established by the Singapore Business Federation. "The SBF Foundation is a collective foundation of the business community, serving the needs of the local community" in Singapore (SBF Foundation 2015, p. 1). Although still at its infancy, the potential to collectively fund or found a separate corporate multiple-donor foundation is tremendous. For instance, both small or large business and industry clusters[4] could go down a collaborative path in their corporate philanthropy. Business clusters such as Silicon Valley or small-scale clusters could give a collective voice to their corporate giving. For example, small-scale retailer associations could give collectively by setting up a CCF for retailers in a specific region.

10.1.3 Contributions

The bulk of current corporate giving literature deals with various facets of direct corporate giving for individual corporations (e.g., motivations, determinants, processes, outcomes) (Gautier and Pache 2015; Liket and Simaens 2015). Moreover, scant research examines the rationale behind establishing a corporate foundation (Petrovits 2006; Webb 1994). Academics, however, hitherto ignore when and why corporations engage in indirect, collective giving strategies and use a CCF as a vehicle to shape corporate giving. In doing so, academics insufficiently articulated what differs indirect giving from direct giving, as well as individual versus collective corporate giving strategies. Hereby, scholars also ignore the consequences of the various corporate giving channels resulting from these decisions. The inductive study intends to overcome this lacuna by providing explorative insights on the above topics. The novelty of the study lies in the effort to conceptualize corporate giving as a make-or-buy decision and as an individual or collective corporate giving decision. As such, the chapter aspires to make a contribution to the corporate philanthropy literature by examining the rationales and consequences related to the make-or-buy decision as well as the individual or collective decision of corporate

---

[4] A business or industry cluster is a geographic concentration of interconnected businesses, suppliers, or institutions in a particular region or field (Porter 2000).

giving. An enhanced understanding helps corporate decision-makers to identify where they should focus their philanthropic endeavors and guides them in the decision between in-house or outsourced giving channels as well as individual versus collective giving strategies. Meanwhile, findings assist CCFs (and other collective or multiple-donor vehicles) to enhance the quality of its operations. This in return helps foundations to attract more funding from corporations outsourcing corporate philanthropy. Likewise, the findings apply to other external multiple donor foundations (e.g., community foundations) or collective giving efforts (e.g., giving circles), as the rationales of and consequences for donors might be comparable.

10.2 Methodology

10.2.1 Data Collection

As I focus on one bounded case to illustrate the topic of interest, the study entails a single instrumental case study (Stake 1995). I build an in-depth, contextual understanding of the case, relaying on multiple data sources (Yin 2003). Primary data were gathered from a sample of (former) donor organizations, representatives of the founding industry association and partner organization, and (former) board members of the foundation. Furthermore, corporations able to donate to the foundation, but who rather keep their corporate giving in-house or individually were also selected (i.e., non-donor organizations). The CEO of Deltalinqs formally consented with the research. The researcher in cooperation with the CEO purposefully selected the final sample. The sample includes individuals available and willing to participate and experienced with the phenomenon of interest (Creswell and Plano Clark 2011). Six telephone interviews and 13 face-to-face interviews at the interviewee's place of work gathered the primary data. All 19 interviews were semi-structured, meaning that a list of high-level themes and key questions as a checklist was composed beforehand. Key themes included among others rationales for various forms of corporate giving (i.e., in-house versus outsourced and individual versus collective corporate giving), differences between various forms, as well as advantages and disadvantages in respect to one another. The intent was to come to a real conversation with the interviewee, allow deviations, and explore issues that were not thought about prior to the interview. Questions were continuously adapted in accordance with the role of the interviewee. Nineteen respondents were formally interviewed for the current study, including three current and two former board members, three and two representatives of the founding association and the partner organization, and respectively four, three, and one corporate decision-makers within donor organizations, former donor organizations, and non-donor organizations. All interviewees were responsible for corporate philanthropy within their organization, except for three board members of the CCF who served the board as community representatives (e.g., mayors, public relations expert). All other interviewees held positions as CEO, middle manager (i.e., corporate communication, external affairs, or public affairs manager), or management assistant. I include several stakeholders to capture a holistic view with regard to the subject of analysis, whereas this triangulated use of multiple interviews ensures greater trustworthiness of the data. Interviews took place in April and May 2017 and ranged in length between 30 and 70 minutes. Interviews amounted to a total of over 14 hours. All interviews were recorded and transcribed verbatim, which formed the input for the data analysis.

Additionally, I gathered publicly available information via websites and CSR reports from donor organizations. Documentary evidence was used to understand the context of the case study, permitting more perceptive exchanges with interviewees, and support findings from primary data.

10.2.2 Data Analysis

Data analysis followed a strategy of thematic analysis (Braun and Clarke 2006). Thematic analysis offers an accessible and theoretically flexible approach for analyzing qualitative data that searches for themes and patterns (Braun and Clarke 2006). As this study explores rationales, a realist/essentialist paradigm was taken, in order to enable the researcher to report experiences, meanings, and the reality of the interviewees (Braun and Clarke 2006). Using an inductive approach, the themes identified are data-driven and are strongly linked to the data itself. Furthermore, the researcher used semantic themes. With a semantic approach, "the themes are identified within the explicit or surface meaning of the data and the analyst is not looking for anything beyond what a participant has said" (Braun and Clarke 2006, p. 13). The analysis included reading transcripts completely through to get a sense of the entire data set. This was followed by re-reading and coding segments, and re-coding and grouping codes into broad clusters of similar topics or nodes, primarily around the research question.

10.3 Case Findings

The research seeks to identify outsourcing rationales and consequences by means of a CCF. Five central themes emerged from the data analysis, resulting in two rationales for and three consequences of outsourcing collective corporate philanthropy to a collective initiative. Table 10.1 presents a description of the five primary themes with illustrative comments. Below I will indicate why these rationales and consequences exist.[5]

---

[5] Each interviewee has a unique label (e.g., board member A; representative B partner organization; CEO former donor organization C) that refers to the type of interviewee, the function of the interviewee in his organization (e.g., board members, founding association representatives, partner organization representatives, (former donor organizations, and non-donor organizations), and the alphabetic letter assigned to the interviewee within each group.

Table 10.1 Illustrative comments supporting case findings

Rationale or consequence	Description	Key representative comments
Amount of available resources	The amount of available corporate resources to organize corporate philanthropy is often limited as it constitutes a noncore activity. A collective corporate foundation enables corporations – both SMEs as well as MNEs – to shape corporate giving in a low-threshold manner	*"Imagine: [Corporation A] is setting up their own foundation, then [Corporation B] will set one up too, and [Corporation C] will do the same. (...) Nonetheless, there are only a few large corporations who can actually make that happen. A few who have the manpower, the knowledge, and the capital to do so"* (Representative B, partner organization)
Efficiency	The collective corporate foundation enables corporations to receive a high return for philanthropic endeavors from a philanthropic perspective, compared to a relatively small investment of resources	*"You can do things that corporations cannot do on an individual basis. Both financially, as organizational"* (CEO, donor organization B)
Loss of control	When outsourcing corporate giving to a collective corporate foundation, a corporation is giving the foundation control over its philanthropic endeavors and activities	*"So yes, you do not exactly know in the end where you donate to, but you assume that that happens in good faith by (the foundation)"* [CFF] (CEO, donor organization D)
Loss of involvement	Indirect corporate philanthropy places corporate giving at arms' length from the corporation compared with direct corporate philanthropy. Given that the corporation is uninvolved in policy or decision-making, corporations are to a lesser extent involved, engaged, and committed toward their philanthropic endeavors	*"Certainly in times when things are rough that corporations say: 'Well, not right now'. The decision to stop is easily and perhaps more likely made, when corporate giving takes places on a distance, compared to when you are participating in it, and when you are very actively involved"* (Representative C, partner organization)
Fewer organizational one-on-one residues	With a collective corporate foundation serving multiple corporate donors simultaneously, corporations are unlikely to receive organizational one-on-one residues from philanthropic endeavors	*"On the moment you are doing it directly, it is much clearer. Then it is directly from us [corporation] to the initiative"* (CEO, donor organization B) *"The direct visibility, however, is less, because those who make a request to the foundation might not obtain a direct association with [the corporation]"* (CEO, donor organization B)

10.3.1 Rationales

Amount of Available Resources An important rationale for outsourcing corporate philanthropy via a CCF is the amount of corporate resources corporations have available for corporate giving. Corporations receive many requests for donations on a weekly, or even daily, basis. Small- and medium-sized enterprises (SMEs) often lack capacity to handle those requests in terms of personnel, time, and money. Board member B explains:

> There are many small corporations in the port that are not small in the amount of work or transshipment they do, but small in terms of organizational form. (...) These corporations do not have the ability to engage in communication activities with the local environment or whatever. For those corporations, this [CCF] poses a solution.

The same rationale applies to subsidiaries of multinationals. Subsidiaries located in the port are operational subsidiaries with limited budgets and resources to engage in peripheral activities such as corporate giving (representative C founding association). Headquarters in home countries take on peripheral activities, and subsidiaries in host countries are more focused on performing core activities:

> Local management is limited in terms of policy development, communication, and stakeholder management. These corporations are focused on the core activities. So they do the operations, a bit of risk management and safety management. But they do not possess the CSR managers. (Representative B, partner organization)

The headquarters keep the resources to organize corporate philanthropy, whereby subsidiaries in the host countries possess limited resources to organize philanthropic activities. The CCF constitutes a vehicle that enables subsidiaries to shape and engage in local corporate community involvement and corporate philanthropy in a low-threshold manner. Thus, organizing corporate philanthropy externally enables corporations to give. When outsourcing corporate giving via the foundation, donor organizations can refer incoming donor requests to the foundation. The foundation hereby presents a vehicle to channel donation requests (board member C). As board member E clarifies, it goes beyond the matter of handling requests:

> If you organize it individually you have to spend a lot more time on it. You have to account for it, you have to set up your own policy, when do you grant a request, when do you reject one. You take care of the entire implementation. And that also has to be controlled.

Corporations, oftentimes unaware of community needs and issues (representative A, partner organization), are said to be unable to make adequate decisions regarding donation requests. When a corporation decides to organize corporate philanthropy in-house, there is a need to open up continuous dialogues with the community in order to make well-informed decisions (CEO former donor organization C). If corporations shun this dialogue, a corporation may end up with supporting pet causes of a company agent (representative B, founding association). Engaging in such a dialogue, however, is a time-consuming activity with high participation[6] or opportunity costs of people's time. The CCF has the capacity to adequately take care of donor requests, due to its board composition. With its community representatives, the foundation has all associated knowledge to make well-informed and adequate decisions (CEO, donor organization A). As there is a need for specialized expertise, there is a need for outsourcing. In this way it is rational to outsource corporate giving, given that someone else can perform the activity better.

Interviewees moreover explained that especially subsidiaries of MNEs need to invest significant resources to establish relationships with the local community to become knowledgeable about community needs. This requires an investment of resources subsidiaries often lack for peripheral activities (representative B, partner organization). Outsourcing corporate philanthropy by means of a CCF allows the subsidiary to buy itself into the local community:

> We also have large international corporations where headquarters are located in America. And these corporations don't know the local community that well. Also the corporation's personnel are becoming more and more international. So by becoming part of the [CCF], I think it enables you to maintain that local feeling. (Representative C, partner organization)

It is unrealistic to assume that every corporation has the resources and capacity to organize philanthropy in-house or through an individual corporate foundation (representative B, partner organization). Economic pressures force many corporations to consider outsourcing as an alternative for corporate giving. A CCF enables corporations to concentrate resources on core business activities where the corporation has expertise and is likely to do best. The CCF thus brings new money to the philanthropic table, given that SMEs and subsidiaries of MNEs are unable to organize corporate giving themselves in some instances due to limited resources.

Efficiency Efficiency is another critical construct for understanding the make-or-buy and individual or collective corporate giving decisions of corporate giving. External collective giving strategies represent a relatively small investment that provides corporations with a high (social) return. The efficiency rationale for outsourcing corporate philanthropy is indicated in at least three different ways.

First, shaping corporate giving by means of a CCF enables donor organizations to refer donation requests to the foundation. Oftentimes, donor organizations avoid taking requests into consideration themselves but refer them to the foundation instead. Board member A explains:

> We see it oftentimes that corporations say to individual requests, 'Sorry, we organize our corporate philanthropy in the context of [the CCF], so please go there to get your share', so it saves you a lot of small donation-requests, and work.

The foundation thereby provides an efficient way for organizations to channel incoming requests. Representative C of the founding association clarifies:

> It entails also some efficiency for corporations, because these corporations do not have to take care of many requests. As a corporation you receive many requests, and if you want to

---

[6] One interpretation of participation costs is that it is simply the time involved in making organizational decisions.

handle them neatly, you have to give them an answer. (...) Anyway, someone in your corporation is spending time on it.

Second, it is found that by means of a CCF, the donations of donor organizations result in a high (social) return for corporations from a philanthropic perspective. The CCF entails a collection of philanthropic endeavors, meaning the total operating budget is accumulated. This means in total more money can be donated compared with the budget individual corporations have available when organizing corporate giving individually in-house. This indicates that nonprofit recipients requesting high donations can be met. CEO donor organization B explains:

> Initiatives can also be supported easier and on a bigger scale being [the CCF], compared to what you are capable of. I mean, you sometimes see initiatives that make you say, 'I would like to contribute to that', but as a small corporation you cannot participate infinitely.

In addition, given that the total operating budget is larger of collective giving initiatives, more donation requests are honored, and thereby more nonprofit organizations are reached by corporations. An individual corporation, for example, now supports the local football association, the local tennis club, the rotary club, the ice-skating range, and the card association, and so forth (CEO donor organization B; representative B, founding association). The philanthropic endeavors of the CCF result in more visibility for one's philanthropy within the local community. The power of corporation's philanthropic endeavors is thus magnified, and corporations gain a broader range of supported charitable organizations. Likewise, the foundation enables corporations to make donations year round (representative B, founding association B), whereas individual corporations with a limited budget may run dry quickly.

Third, using a (outside) foundation to organize corporate philanthropy allows corporations to mitigate risk and liabilities. Outsourcing creates opportunities for corporations to shift the risk and uncertainty associated with the activity of giving to a third party. First, when a donation request is declined, it is never the corporation rejecting the request. The CCF is the rejecting party, indicating that critique about the rejection is directed toward the foundation in lieu of donor organizations (representative C, founding association). Second, when a wrong decision is made (e.g., initiatives are supported that should have been supported or vice versa), the CCF is held accountable.

10.3.2 Consequences

Loss of Control Corporations donating indirectly via a CCF experience a loss of control given their philanthropic endeavors. As representative C of the founding association explains:

> With [the CCF] you relinquish the choice of where your donation will go to, to the board. So thereby you make it indirect. By a direct choice you are the one making the decisions.

A principle-agent problem is created, given that donor organizations (principles) formally delegate the authority of corporate philanthropy to the foundation (agent). Corporations support the foundation in good faith, trusting the board to make decisions that are in line with the corporation's philanthropic interests (CEO donor organization D). Additional agency costs may occur to monitor and control the foundation. The loss of control creates the possibility that donor organizations support nonprofit organizations that insufficiently comply with the norms and values of the donor organizations. If insufficiently in line with corporate interests, corporations may decide to reorganize philanthropy in-house (management assistant, former donor, organization B). In-house corporate philanthropy enables corporations to gain more control over the corporation's philanthropic spending and to shape and adjust corporate giving to the needs and wants of the own corporation (CEO of former donor organization C).

Loss of Involvement Indirect collective corporate giving places giving at a distance or at arm's length of the corporation. Hereby corporations are to a lesser extent committed to the philanthropic activities as compared with in-house individual philanthropy. When corporations need to cut costs, the outsourced philanthropic endeavors are one of the first things corporations will most likely stop doing (representative C, partner organization).

Second, in this particular case context, corporations engage in a passive way of giving (e.g., limited to the activity of simply writing a checkbook). Because corporations shape corporate giving by such a passive activity instead of making their own policy and decisions, using a CCF may also be seen as an easy way of shaping corporate philanthropy and as an easy way to deal with donation requests (middle manager, non-donor organization A). Given donor organizations are to a lesser extent involved with the foundation and its activities, it limits a corporation's feelings of ownership toward the foundation and its operations (representative C, partner organization). Documentary evidence shows that only 3 out of 82 donor organizations (3.6%) mention the CCF on corporate websites or within CSR reports solely, and 4 (4.9%) in conjunction with in-house giving programs. In addition, 22 donor organizations (25.6%) only mention their own direct giving programs, whereas 54 donor organizations (65.9%) suppress giving behavior at all.

Fewer Organizational One-on-One Residues Outsourcing corporate philanthropy places corporate philanthropy on a distance from the corporation. As the CEO of donor organization B explains:

> When you organize corporate philanthropy via [the CCF] the link with our own corporation is less, compared with when you directly organize things yourself with the local community. That is the difference.

This indirectness affects the perceived residues by donor organizations in relation to their corporate giving. Corporations receive more organizational one-on-one residues from direct individual corporate giving programs compared with external giving through a CCF. Honored donation requests made through the multiple-donor foundation are made under its umbrella name. Hereby, it is unlikely for donor organizations to receive one-on-one residues from the philanthropic endeavors as corporations are not mentioned by name. These include residues such as differentiation from competitors, brand awareness, or brand recognition. Receiving nonprofit organizations, as well as the community at large, are unaware of the donor organizations supporting the foundation:

> In the moment you are doing it directly, it is much clearer. Then it is directly from us [corporation] to the initiative. (CEO, donor organization B)

> If something nice would be donated with a sign indicating: 'This piece of art is donated by [the CCF], I do not think a lot of people will visit Google on their computer and see what [the CCF] entails and who supports it, and think by themselves 'I am thankful to [corporation A] and I am thankful to [corporation B] for providing us this piece of art. (Board member C)

Indirect and collective giving is more invisible or hidden compared with in-house and individual corporate giving. Outsourcing collective corporate giving is thus inappropriate if corporation's desire to use corporate philanthropy to serve marketing-related purposes or as a means for differentiation. A direct and individual corporate giving program is far more beneficial in that perspective. On the other hand, when donor organizations are unable to receive one-on-one residues for their philanthropic endeavors, giving is perceived as more neutral and legitimate. As indirect collective corporate giving is more hidden and invisible, corporations are not able to showcase corporate philanthropy to serve hidden agendas (middle manager of donor organization C).

10.4 Discussion

A central theme within the study is to understand the factors that guide corporate decision-makers in the make-or-buy and individual or collective corporate giving decisions and to identify the rationales and consequences of these decisions. Figure 10.1 vertically shows various channels of philanthropy on a horizontal continuum, ranging from pure direct or in-house giving to corporate giving via hybrid channels (i.e., corporate foundation linked to one corporation) toward pure indirect or outsourced corporate giving. Figure 10.1 also illustrates the rationales (depicted in light grey) and consequences (depicted in dark grey).

Corporate decision-makers consider a CCF for various (overlapping) perceived benefits and rationales. First, it allows corporations to concentrate resources on core business activities. Second, it allows corporations to organize corporate giving as efficient as possible. Corporations refer donation requests almost effortless to a knowledgeable third party that can do the activity better than the corporation; corporations collectively honor more and higher donations year-round; it allows corporations to mitigate risks and liabilities to a third party. This is all based on the belief that the collective strategy of a CCF is an efficient way to engage corporate donors

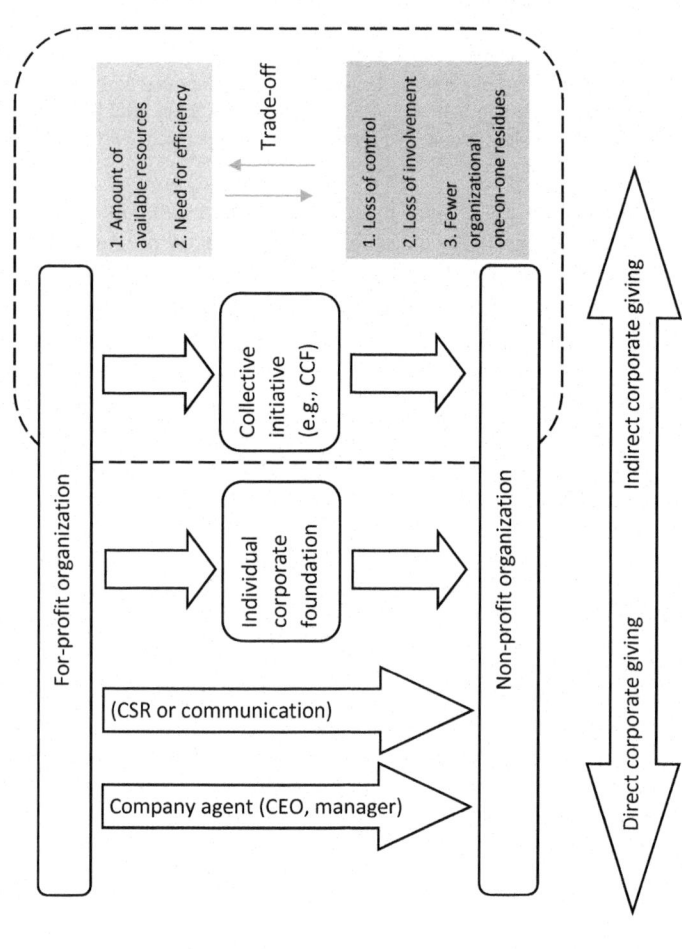

Fig. 10.1 The make-or-buy decision of corporate philanthropy

in corporate giving who cannot do individually and in-house, gain exposure to a broader range of nonprofit recipients, and provide an effective service desired by corporate donors. In doing so, a CCF for corporate giving is comparable to federations as vehicles for private giving (i.e., secular federations such as United Way or religiously grounded federations). Frumkin (2010, p. 147) indicates that at the core of the federation giving model is "the argument that funds pooled together can have a greater impact and that the expert selection of recipient organizations can lead to greater community benefits." Outsourcing corporate philanthropy to a CCF is not a fad and provides certain corporate and community benefits.

My findings also provide insights into the consequences of outsourcing via a CCF: (1) Corporate donors experience a loss of control regarding their philanthropic endeavors, as the CCF makes its own decisions; (2) corporate donors are to a lesser extent involved with the CCF and its activities; (3) a CCF serving multiple corporate donors is inappropriate when corporate donors wish to use philanthropy to serve marketing-related purposes or as a means for differentiation. A trade-off exists between the aforementioned rationales and (unintended) consequences. To overcome the consequences, and to become more involved and to retain control, a larger investment of corporate resources is required (e.g., time or personnel).

10.4.1 Theoretical Explanations

Outsourcing literature uses three major theoretical perspectives to explain the make-or-buy decision: a strategic management view, an economic view, and a social view (Lee et al., 2000). The strategic management view adapts resource-based theories; the economic view focuses on the transaction cost approach; the social view focuses on the relationship between clients and service providers and adapts power-political theories and social exchange theory.

The two rationales (i.e., the amount of available recourses and efficiency) relate to the strategic management view and the economic view. Both views made valuable contributions to and influenced the study of outsourcing (McIvor 2009; Ndubisi 2011). First, the economic view entails transaction cost economics (TCE) and agency theory. TCE focuses on why firms exist (Williamson 1981). TCE specifies the conditions under which corporations should manage a function internally (i.e., within firm boundaries) and specifies the conditions that suit external exchanges (i.e., outside firm boundaries) (Williamson 1975). The outsource decision is brought back to the central question whether a transaction can be more efficiently performed internally or externally by a third party (Geyskens et al. 2006). Transaction costs relate to the level of uncertainty, the frequency of activities, and specificity (Williamson 1981). If these increase, the transaction costs for outsourcing will also increase (e.g., operational costs and contracting costs). Based on TCE, corporations engage in make-or-buy decisions to minimize costs and outsource an activity when external transaction costs are lower than the internal transaction costs (Ndubisi 2011, p. 110). External transaction costs include arranging costs, actual outsourcing cost, and monitoring and control costs (Shook et al. 2009). Consider now the transaction costs associated with the various channels of corporate giving. Outsourcing corporate giving via a CCF entails relatively low external transaction costs (e.g., simply writing a check book and referring donation request, as well as minimal monitoring and control costs). The internal transaction costs that exists when organizing corporate giving in-house are much higher (e.g., policymaking, decision-making, building and maintaining community relationships, implementation, and accountability). Outsourcing thus helps corporations to avoid high costs related to in-house corporate giving programs and helps them to gain access to specialized expertise.

Agency theory (Jensen and Meckling 1976) complements the economic view on outsourcing. Agency theory posits that when the principle delegates responsibility to the agent, the principle should monitor the agent. A corporation should outsource an activity when the agent is deemed more efficient and is trusted by the principle (for a review, see Ndubisi (2011)). The CCF is deemed to perform corporate giving more efficient and should be trusted by corporate donors to act on their behalf.

A complementary view to understand the case findings is a strategic management perspective. This perspective consists of resource dependency theory and a resource-based view (RBV) of the firm. From a resource-dependency perspective (Pfeffer and Salancik 1978), corporations seek to acquire and maintain resources and control. In doing so, corporations seek to minimize dependency on others while at the same time increase the dependency of others on the corporation. In terms of outsourcing, corporations that lack the resources to perform an activity should seek relationships with other parties to obtain those resources (Ndubisi 2011, p. 110). I found that corporations often lack the resources to organize corporate giving in-house.

As TCE focuses on why corporations exist, RBV focus on why corporations differ in performance. From the RBV a corporation is viewed as a collection of resources that can create competitive advantages (Peteraf 1993) and lead to the distinction between core and peripheral activities. From a RBV, findings inform corporations "not to outsource capabilities, functions or activities that create competitive advantage" (Ndubisi 2011, p. 110), known as the core activities. RBV argues that corporations should concentrate on their core business activities and exploit competencies based on their knowledge and expertise, rather than channel resources to non-core activities, as this is more efficient (for a review, see Carey et al. (2006)). Case findings show that SMEs as well as subsidiaries of MNEs focus on their core activities. Corporate philanthropy is seen as a peripheral activity, indicating that limited resources are channeled to corporate giving. It is plausible that some corporations outsource routine philanthropic activities (i.e., handling donation requests) to give in-house corporate giving a more strategic role (i.e., strategic giving and employee volunteering).

Based on the case findings, the following propositions are offered:

P1. Adhering to the logic of the RBV, when corporate philanthropy is more seen as a peripheral activity, the greater the likelihood corporate giving will be outsourced.

P2. Adhering to the logic of resource-dependency theory, when corporations have limited resources available to organize corporate giving, the greater the likelihood corporate giving will be outsourced.

P3. Adhering to the logic of TCE, when external transaction costs are lower than the costs associated to perform corporate giving in-house, the greater the likelihood corporate giving will be outsourced.

P4. Adhering to the logic of agency theory, when another party is deemed more efficient and is deemed trustworthy, the greater the likelihood corporate giving will be outsourced.

P5. Outsourcing corporate giving to a collective initiative or foundation will lessen the corporation's control over its corporate giving.

P6. Outsourcing corporate giving to a collective initiative or foundation will lessen a corporation's involvement with its corporate giving.

P7. Outsourcing corporate giving to a collective initiative or foundation will result in fewer organizational one-on-one residues (e.g., serve strategic and marketing purposes).

10.5 Conclusions, Limitations, and Future Research

10.5.1 Recommendations

In "the essence of strategic giving," Frumkin (2010) describes two key dimensions influencing an individual's giving style: (1) level of engagement or involvement and (2) desired public profile. Findings indicate that other and similar dimensions exist for corporate giving. Four key dimensions influence a corporation's giving style: (1) corporate philanthropy being a core or spherical activity, (2) the amount of resources or the need for efficiency, (3) level of control and involvement, and (4) the desired public profile in terms of using corporate giving as a marketing or differentiation devise. Corporate donors are thus required to make important decisions about giving as an activity, how much resources they can and want to devote, how much control and engagement they want in their giving, and what kind of and how much public exposure, visibility, or profile they desire. And, as agreed with Frumkin (2010), these choices are often shaped by the motives that underlie the philanthropic endeavors.

First, I recommend corporate decision-makers to consider the role of corporate philanthropy within their corporation. Does corporate giving constitute a core or peripheral activity? With corporate giving as a core activity, the corporation wants to excel in its giving and take a competitive advantage with its philanthropic endeavors. Being a core activity, corporate philanthropy should be kept in-house and entail individual strategies. Enough resources should be made available to organize corporate giving adequately. With corporate giving as a peripheral activity, corporate giving is neither critical nor something the corporation wants to take competitive advantage in, indicating that corporate philanthropy can be outsourced to a CCF or another external vehicle. Second, I recommend corporate decision-makers with limited resources for corporate giving and those who wish to organize corporate giving efficiently to consider outsourcing or to pursue collective giving strategies. Third, I recommend corporate decision-makers to ponder to what extent they want to control and be involved or engaged with its corporate giving. Those who do not want to relinquish control and be more involved should keep corporate giving an in-house activity. Fourth, I recommend corporations to organize giving in-house and individually that wish to use corporate giving as a marketing or differentiation device. A trade-off exists between these considerations. A corporation can obtain more control, more involvement, and one-on-one residues in exchange for larger investments, as more resources are required, affecting the amount of resources and the efficiency of corporate giving.

The enhanced understanding helps corporate decision-makers identify where they should focus their philanthropic endeavors. Moreover, it guides them in the make-or-buy decision of corporate philanthropy and in deciding between individual versus collective giving. Likewise, findings can encourage collective giving strategies and stimulate corporations to establish a CCF together when corporations lack the resources to organize corporate philanthropy in-house. Furthermore, providing empirical evidence on the impact of transactional- and organizational-related factors on the make-or-buy decision of corporate giving assists CCFs to enhance the quality of its operations. Operations can be improved as findings inform multiple-donor foundations of the factors that count heavily for corporate decision-makers. This in return might help multiple-donor foundations to attract funding from corporations outsourcing philanthropy.

10.5.2 Limitations

As every research, the study entails its own limitations. First, my research entails a case study with inherent limitations. The corporate foundation within this case study is a grant-making foundation (i.e., engaged in grant-making on significant scale), rather than an operating foundation (i.e., a foundation operating its own programs) or a mixed foundation (Anheier 2001). Grant-making foundations are only part of the philanthropic landscape. Findings might remain narrow due to the passive involvement and dynamics inherent to the narrow operations of the foundation. Thus, the transferability of the results to other settings can be questioned. Future research can examine to which extent the findings are applicable to other multiple-donor foundations (e.g., community foundations and federations) or collective philanthropic concepts (e.g., giving circles[7]). Findings might also be limited to the potential peculiarities of the Dutch system and influenced by national circumstances (e.g., depending on nonprofit or civil society regimes (Salamon and Anheier 1998) and philanthropic history and landscape).

---

[7] Where the corporate foundation connects corporations, giving circles connect individuals to pool resources and collectively decide which nonprofit initiatives will receive their donations (Eikenberry 2007), are a relatively easy way to participate in giving (Eikenberry 2007, p. 872), and provide an opportunity for more effective giving and better decision-making (Eikenberry and Breeze 2015).

Second, the study entails limitations regarding data collection and analysis. As qualitative data collection and analysis are a useful starting point for explorative research, these methods have their own limitations (e.g., interview and interviewee biases, risk of excess information, bounded to the interviewees' memory and knowledge). Moreover, as the question why corporations use a CCF as an intermediary vehicle to shape corporate philanthropy has a lot in common with the question of why corporations engage in corporate giving; interviewees might have a good idea of the desirable answers (e.g., social desirability bias). This could potentially be overcome by taking an ethnographic or holistic approach in future research. Nevertheless, the assurance of anonymity was used to encourage respondents to speak candidly. Furthermore, to get more insights into the philanthropic endeavors of donor organizations, I gathered information from publicly accessible documents from donor organizations. It is possible that only parts of their efforts are obtained, as it is imaginable that corporations might donate without publicly communicating about it. Moreover, while the research sample covers a wide range of stakeholders, the size of the sample warrants mention (i.e., 19 interviewees). Despite achieving saturation in the data collection and providing robust findings and stable patterns, it would be interesting to conduct a study with a larger sample. Additionally, the purposive selection of respondents also limits the generalizability of the study's findings. Lastly, within the thematic analysis, the researcher had an active role in identifying themes and patterns in the data set and selected those that were of interest (Taylor and Ussher 2001).

10.5.3 Future Research

I encourage future research to provide insights into other rationales that might impact the make-or-buy decision as well as the decision for individual for collective giving strategies. It might be that when a collective corporate giving vehicle is supported by prominent corporations in a certain area or industry isomorphic pressures are in play. Giving to the collective initiative can then become the norm and (friendly) competition between corporations can stimulate non-donor organizations to give. As this research focuses more on the strategic management and economic view related to outsourcing, future research might take a more social view to explore the rationales for outsourcing and collective giving strategies (see Lee et al. 2000). Likewise, some key findings raise questions for future research. First, future research can examine the contribution of corporate giving to organizational performance. Perhaps, it is not even a matter of a make "or" buy decision. Some corporations might outsource routine philanthropic activities (i.e., handling donation requests) to give its in-house corporate giving a more strategic role (i.e., focus on strategic giving and employee-volunteering). Second, CCFs might entail implications for non-profit organizations. One question to address is to what extent collective giving initiatives change the transaction costs for nonprofit recipients. For example, when corporations organize corporate philanthropy individually (and in-house), they can be addressed on an individual basis. When multiple corporations' channel corporate philanthropy by means of a CCF, I wonder if this has implications for nonprofit professionals. Will these professionals only address the CCF or also the individual corporations behind the foundation? Does this differ if the request directed at the foundation is honored or rejected? Moreover, as I conclude that both outsourcing and collective giving adds value to corporate giving process and outcomes, I wonder if it adds value to nonprofit organizations. Are decisions indeed better made in a CCF compared to individual in-house corporate giving, and how does this affect the nonprofit sector? Third, acknowledging that various types of corporate foundations and intermediary vehicles exists, it is promising to obtain an overview of the various (individual or collective) corporate philanthropy outsourcing possibilities available to corporations. Efforts might expand and deepen Fig. 10.1, as the continuum might contain more organizational forms, channels, or (corporate) philanthropic practices that came to populate the corporate giving landscape. This can be part of wider efforts to understand the corporate giving landscape and shed light on various corporate giving strategies available within the corporate giving repertoire.

References

Altuntas, C., & Turker, D. (2015). Local or global: Analyzing the internationalization of social responsibility of corporate foundations. *International Marketing Review, 32*(5), 540–557.

Anheier, H. K. (2001). Foundations in Europe: A comparative perspective. In *Foundations in Europe: Society, management and law* (pp. 35–81). London: Directory of Social Change.

Braun, V., & Clarke, V. (2006). Using thematic analysis in psychology. *Qualitative Research in Psychology, 3*(2), 77–101.

Carey, P., Subramaniam, N., & Ching, K. C. W. (2006). Internal audit outsourcing in Australia. *Accounting and Finance, 46*(1), 11–30.

Creswell, J. W., & Plano Clark, V. L. (2011). *Designing and conducting mixed method research* (2nd ed.). Thousand Oaks: Sage Publishing.

DeltaPORT Donatiefonds. (2016). *Annual report*. [Online] Available at: http://www.deltaportdonatiefonds.nl/wp-content/uploads/2011/12/Jaarverslag-2016.pdf. Accessed 19 Jan 2017.

Eikenberry, A. M. (2007). Philanthropy, voluntary association and governance beyond the state: Giving circles and challenges for democracy. *Administration and Society, 39*(7), 857–882.

Eikenberry, A. M., & Breeze, B. (2015). Growing philanthropy through collaboration: The landscape of giving circles in the United Kingdom and Ireland. *Voluntary Sector Review, 6*(1), 41–59.

Ferris, J., & Graddy, E. (1986). Contracting out: In what? With whom? *Public Administration Review, 46*(July/August), 332–344.

Fourie, A., & Eloff, T. (2005). The case for collective business action to achieve systems change. *Journal of Corporate Citizenship, 2005*(18), 39–48.

Frumkin, P. (2010). *The essence of strategic giving: A practical guide for donors and fundraisers*. Chicago: University of Chicago Press.

Gautier, A., & Pache, A. C. (2015). Research on corporate philanthropy: A review and assessment. *Journal of Business Ethics, 126*(3), 343–369.

Geyskens, I., Steenkamp, J. B. E., & Kumar, N. (2006). Make, buy, or ally: A transaction cost theory meta-analysis. *Academy of Management Journal, 49*(3), 519–543.

Greer, C. R., Youngblood, S. A., & Gray, D. A. (1999). Human resource management outsourcing: The make or buy decision. *The Academy of Management Executive, 13*(3), 85–96.

Husted, B. W. (2003). Governance choices for corporate social responsibility: To contribute, collaborate or internalize? *Long Range Planning, 36*(5), 481–498.

Industry Fabrics Foundation. (n.d.). *About us.* [Online] Available at: http://www.indfabfnd.com/about_us. Accessed 9 Sept 2017.

Jensen, M. C., & Meckling, W. H. (1976). Theory of the firm: Managerial behavior, agency costs and ownership structure. *Journal of Financial Economics, 3*(4), 305–360.

Lee, L. (2015). Understanding the role of the broker in business non-profit collaboration. *Social Responsibility Journal, 11*(2), 201–220.

Lee, J. N., Huynh, M. Q., Chi-wai, K. R., & Pi, S. M., (2000). *The evolution of outsourcing research: What is the next issue?* In Proceedings of the 33rd Annual Hawaii International Conference on System Sciences (pp. 10-pp). IEEE.

Liket, K., & Simaens, A. (2015). Battling the devolution in the research on corporate philanthropy. *Journal of Business Ethics, 126*(2), 285–308.

McIvor, R. (2009). How the transaction cost and resource-based theories of the firm inform outsourcing evaluation. *Journal of Operations Management, 27*(1), 45–61.

Moody, M., Lugo Knapp, A., & Corrado, M. (2011). What is a family foundation? *The Foundation Review, 3*(4), 47–61.

Ndubisi, N. O. (2011). Conflict handling, trust and commitment in outsourcing relationship: A Chinese and Indian study. *Industrial Marketing Management, 40*(1), 109–117.

Peteraf, M. (1993). The cornerstones of competitive advantage: A resource-based view. *Strategic Management Journal, 14*(3), 179–191.

Petrovits, C. M. (2006). Corporate-sponsored foundations and earnings management. *Journal of Accounting and Economics, 41*(3), 335–362.

Pfeffer, J., & Salancik, G. (1978). *The external control of organizations: A resource dependence perspective.* New York: Harper & Row.

Porter, M. E. (2000). Location, competition, and economic development: Local clusters in a global economy. *Economic Development Quarterly, 14*(1), 15–34.

Porter, M. E., & Kramer, M. R. (2002). The competitive advantage of corporate philanthropy. *Harvard Business Review, 80*(12), 56–68.

Rey-Garcia, M., Martin-Cavanna, J., & Alvarez-Gonzalez, L. I. (2012). Assessing and advancing foundation transparency: Corporate foundations as a case study. *The Foundation Review, 4*(3), 77–89.

Salamon, L. M., & Anheier, H. K. (1998). Social origins of civil society: Explaining the nonprofit sector cross-nationally. *VOLUNTAS: International Journal of Voluntary and Nonprofit Organizations, 9*(3), 213–248.

SBF Foundation. (2015). *Welcome address by Mrs. Therese Foo.* [Online] Available at: https://www.sbf.org.sg/images/pdf/2015/Welcome_Address_SBFF_Fundraising_Dinner.pdf. Accessed 28 Jan 2019.

Shook, C. L., Adams, G. L., Ketchen, D. J., & Craihead, C. W. (2009). Towards a strategic toolbox for strategic sourcing. *Supply Chain Management: An International Journal, 14*(1), 3–10.

Stake, R. (1995). *The art of case research.* Newbury Park: Sage Publications.

Taylor, G. W., & Ussher, J. M. (2001). Making sense of S&M: A discourse analytic account. *Sexualities, 4*(3), 293–314.

Toy Association. (n.d.). *The Toy Association.* [Online] Available at: http://www.toyassociation.org/. Accessed 9 Sept 2017.

Toy Industry Foundation. (n.d.). *Get involved.* [Online] Available at: http://www.toy-industryfoundation.org/TIF/Get_Involved/TIF/Get_Involved/Get_Involved.aspx?section=landing&hkey=3c56da97-6574-4585-a705-5e3a234339fb#.WbkIik0UnmQ. Accessed 9 Sept 2017.

Turnbull, J. (2002). Inside outsourcing. *People management: Connected HR* (pp. 10–11).

Webb, N. J. (1994). Tax and government policy implications for corporate foundation giving. *Nonprofit and Voluntary Sector Quarterly, 23*(1), 41–67.
Williamson, O. E. (1975). *Markets and hierarchies: Analysis and antitrust implications, a study in the economics of internal organization.* New York: Free Press.
Williamson, O. E. (1981). The economics of organization: The transaction cost approach. *The American Journal of Sociology, 87*(3), 548–577.
Yin, R. K. (2003). *Case study research: Design and methods* (3rd ed.). Thousand Oaks: Sage Publishing.

Stephanie Maas is a researcher at the Department of Business-Society Management, Rotterdam School of Management at Erasmus University Rotterdam. Her research interests include contemporary forms of giving, both on a private and on a corporate level. Doing so, she examines various new forms of volunteering and private donations, as well as modern corporate giving channels, such as corporate foundations, collective giving practices, and intermediary organizations.

Chapter 11
The Social Impact of Corporate Citizenship Programs on Their Beneficiaries and Society at Large: A Case Study

Marjelle Vermeulen and Karen Maas

Abstract Within their corporate citizenship program (CCP) "Future Matters," Nationale-Nederlanden (NN) runs several community investment programs. One of these programs is the Social Innovation Relay (SIR). SIR is a partnership with Junior Achievement Europe and exists of a highly developed international network of corporate volunteer employees and students. SIR aims to increase entrepreneurial competences, practical business experiences, and financial resilience of young people by entrepreneurship education. Available research about employee volunteering (EV) mainly focused on indicating and showing its positive effects in CCPs on the employee and the organization. Unfortunately, knowledge about the effect of EV on the target group and society at large is less developed. In this study, we aim to bridge this research gap by assessing the impact of the program on the SIR participants. We found that the beneficiaries of the SIR program indeed show more entrepreneurial intention, behavior, and social awareness. Our findings show that the main results are achieved during the first phase of the program. Because the skills and characteristics of entrepreneurial behavior of the beneficiaries increase during the program, we can argue that it is likely that NN creates social impact for the beneficiaries with their program.

Keywords Social impact · Corporate citizenship · Quantitative research · Experiment

M. Vermeulen (✉) · K. Maas
Impact Centre Erasmus (ICE), Erasmus University Rotterdam, Rotterdam, The Netherlands
e-mail: mvermeulen@ese.eur.nl; maas@ese.eur.nl

11.1 Introduction

Worldwide we see increasing attention for social and environmental issues. Society progressively expects organizations to take responsibility and to be accountable for the social, environmental, and economic impacts of their activities on society (Eccles and Krzus 2010; Maas 2009). Also, an increasing number of investors do not only consider the financial performance of organizations (van Duuren et al. 2016; Toxopeus et al. 2016), but also consider the behavior of organizations and, thereby, their (in)direct environmental and social impact and societal performances (Lee and Lounsbury 2011). In result, organizations must consider the needs and interests of nonfinancial stakeholders, such as employees and the community (Mahoney and Thorn 2006). The nature of market and civil society increasingly intertwine (Roza 2016), causing blurring boundaries.

Corporate social responsibility (CSR), also called by practitioners corporate responsibility (CR), has become increasingly important as the concept which frames the business responses to those blurring boundaries (Maas 2009). The organizational motivations behind CR, however, vary across firms. The profitability of CR (Idowu and Papasolomou 2007), the strengthening of stakeholder relations (Du et al. 2010), the image and reputation building (Villagra and López 2013), the health and well-being of employees (Murillo and Lozano 2006), improved employee relations, improvement of organizations' community (Muthuri et al. 2009), community engagement and the corresponding legitimacy (Chen et al. 2008), alignment with personal or organizational norms (Santana 2015), and societal impact (Maas and Liket 2016) are mentioned as motives for and expected benefits of CR practices. Similar to the different motives that are associated with CR practices, there are also different ways for organizing CR practices by organizations. For example, organizations can donate money to nonprofit organizations, as part of their corporate philanthropy strategy, they can organize in-house CR programs, as well as develop a corporate foundation (Monfort and Villagra 2016).

Corporate foundations "are philanthropic organizations that are created and financially supported by a corporation. The foundation is created as a separate legal entity from the corporation, but with close ties to the corporation" (Council of Foundation, n.d., cited by Monfort and Villagra 2016, p. 768). A corporate foundation can serve as vehicle of CR and has the responsibility to contribute to the CR missions of their parent firm. Moreover, within a corporate foundation, many organizations develop corporate citizenship programs, as an instrument for CR and/or corporate philanthropy practices.

In this chapter we focus on corporate citizenship programs and the impact they have. This chapter is structured as follows. After our introduction, we secondly will discuss existing literature concerning the social impact of corporate citizenship programs. Thirdly, we will describe our case study, an example of an organization that acknowledge the importance and the chances of a specific corporate citizenship program. Fourthly, we will explain our methodology to conduct a quantitative, empirical analysis of the social impact of the program. Fifthly, we present our results, and finally, we conclude with a discussion section describing our conclusions and suggestions for future research.

11.2 Impact of Corporate Citizenship Programs

The fundamental idea of corporate foundations, and therefore also the corporate citizenship programs that can run in those foundations, is to support and extend a firm's CR commitment (Monfort and Villagra 2016). Unfortunately, there is almost no research available yet focusing on the actual impact of corporate foundations and their programs. There is, however, an increasing body of literature about the (expected) impact of corporate and employee volunteering (e.g. Roza 2016).

Corporate volunteering is often an important element of corporate citizenship programs, as corporate volunteering influences the attitudes of employees and companies with regard to social issues, thereby creating legitimacy for the social issue the company addresses (Samuel et al. 2016). In corporate volunteering, "the companies encourage their employees to give time and expertise as volunteers, and volunteer activities can be undertaken within or outside the employee's official workload and time" (Haski-Leventhal et al. 2010, p. 148).

Available research mainly focused on the positive effects of employee volunteering in corporate citizenship programs on the employee and the organization (de Gilder et al. 2005), such as increased job motivation and job satisfaction, decreased absenteeism (van Knippenberg and Sleebos 2006), improved organizational or social skills (Geroy et al. 2000), an improved attitude toward the organization (van Knippenberg et al. 2006; de Gilder et al. 2005), increased creativity (Geroy et al. 2000), improved teamwork, and an increased sense of being useful and indispensable for the society and the employer (Geroy et al. 2000).

Unfortunately, knowledge about the effect of employee volunteering in corporate citizen programs on the target group and society at large is still in an infancy stage. Existing research mainly focus on the impact of corporate volunteering in terms of companies' perspectives, perceptions of corporate volunteers, and employee engagement (Roza 2016), but existing literature neglects the issue of beneficiaries (Samuel et al. 2016). According to Samuel et al. (2016), the statement that corporate volunteering will result in a win–win situation for all stakeholders is too simplistic, as the perspective of the beneficiary is often missing. Therefore, in this study, we aim to fill this gap by assessing the social impact of a specific corporate citizenship program on the beneficiaries.

11.3 Case Study

An organization that acknowledges the importance and chances of a corporate citizenship program is Nationale-Nederlanden (NN). In their corporate citizenship program, "Future Matters," they partner with various global and local partners with the aim to positively influence the lives of 100,000 young people in the markets where they operate by 2020. One of the initiatives organized within Future Matters together with global partner Junior Achievement Europe (JA Europe) is the Social Innovation Relay (SIR), to which NN employees voluntarily contribute their time.

Corporate citizen programs can be developed to serve the business (business logic prevails) or to serve society (social impact logic prevails). In practice we barely see a corporate citizenship program that only has a business logic or social impact logic. Instead, often we see a hybrid perspective that combines both logics (Battilana et al. 2012). Also, NN is aware of the importance of social impact and value creation, not only for society but also for their employees. As an insurance company, NN expect that social value creation is important for their long-term credibility. However, the corporate citizenship program of NN is not related to a corporate foundation. In the current practice at NN, the legal vehicle of a foundation is not a necessity to make the societal impact that they are striving for through volunteering by employees or fundraising for or donating to local charity. NN believes that none of the work with JA Europe would have been done differently in a foundation. Therefore, we believe that the results of this study also provide valuable insights in the social impact of corporate citizenship programs that are run through corporate foundations.

SIR exists of an international network of corporate volunteer employees of NN and thousands participating students from different countries. In 2016, SIR is executed in ten countries: Singapore, Poland, Netherlands, Hungary, Greece, Spain, Czech Republic, Bulgaria, Japan, and Romania. A total of 10,202 students of 213 schools participated in the project. SIR aims to address social needs, such as education, health, social inclusion, livelihood development, and sustainability of young people by educating these youngsters about (social) entrepreneurship. The underlying line of reasoning is that entrepreneurial and practical skills will be beneficial for young people indifferent of the job or business a youngster roles in. Consequently, the expectation is that these young people will be more financial resilient. This should in the end reduce the social needs of the students.

In the SIR program, NN employees educate, guide, and help the young participants to write a business plan for the start of social enterprise. The education within SIR is provided by the NN employees during the program and includes training, case support, and online quizzes. After a first introduction to the program, student groups will be formed. The groups will discuss case studies in the classroom and do an online quiz; consequently, the groups can hand in an idea for a sustainable business plan. This is the first phase of the program. After their submissions of ideas, for each country the 20 best teams are selected that will further participate in the program. This is the second phase of the program. By means of (e-) mentoring, in each country, these 20 teams are supported by a NN volunteer to strengthen and improve their draft idea of a business plan into a concrete business plan. Consequently, for every country a national final gathering will take place. Each of the 20 groups from that specific country will present their ideas and business plan. Based on those presentations, the best social business plan will be selected and gets awarded.

NN believes that through SIR, NN will have a positive impact on society, on the NN organization as well as on the employees involved. This thought is supported by Duval-Couetil (2013), who argued that entrepreneurship education programs create positive outcomes for the beneficiaries (students).

11.4 Methodology and Research Design

We analyze the impact of the corporate citizenship program of NN on the SIR participants by means of an empirical, quantitative approach. We gather data through surveys that are provided to the high school students between 14- and 18-year-old participants. Based on this data, a social impact measurement is conducted. With impact, we refer to "the portion of the total outcome that happened as a result of the activity of an organisation, above and beyond what would have happened anyway" (Clark et al. 2004). *Social* impact refers to these attributional effects on society on the three dimensions 'social', 'environmental' and 'economic' (Maas and Liket 2011). As NN does not claim to positively contribute to environmental issues, the environmental dimension is not included in the impact measurement.

11.4.1 Theory of Change

Before starting the impact measurement, and the development of the survey, we developed a Theory of Change (ToC) describing how actions of the corporate citizenship program are expected to lead to effects. A ToC runs from input to impact. This causal chain, also referred to as the "impact value chain," distinguishes between the resources used for an action (input), the action itself (also referred to as project or activity or intervention or program), the immediate quantitative synthesis of the action (output) and the direct changes in people, organizations, natural and physical environments, and social systems and institutions (outcome), along with highest order effects of the action (impact) (Clark et al. 2004; Liket et al. 2014). Systematically depicting the ToC behind SIR requires information on the process of the corporate citizenship program. Being explicit about the ToC (see Fig. 11.1) behind the implementation of SIR helps to monitor how the program works, how effective it is, and to identify opportunities for further improvement.

11.4.2 Survey Development

As Fig. 11.1 shows, the intended overall impact of SIR is to improve social needs of the participating high school students on the long term. However, unfortunately, due to restrictions such as available money and the time frame of the research, it is not possible to measure this long-term impact among the high school students. Therefore, this intended impact is not included in the impact assessment. However, within the time frame of this research, we are able to measure the effect on the ultimate outcome level. It is possible to analyze if participating students develop more entrepreneurial intentions, and exhibit more entrepreneurial behavior. Consequently, we conducted a qualitative literature review to collect academic literature about the

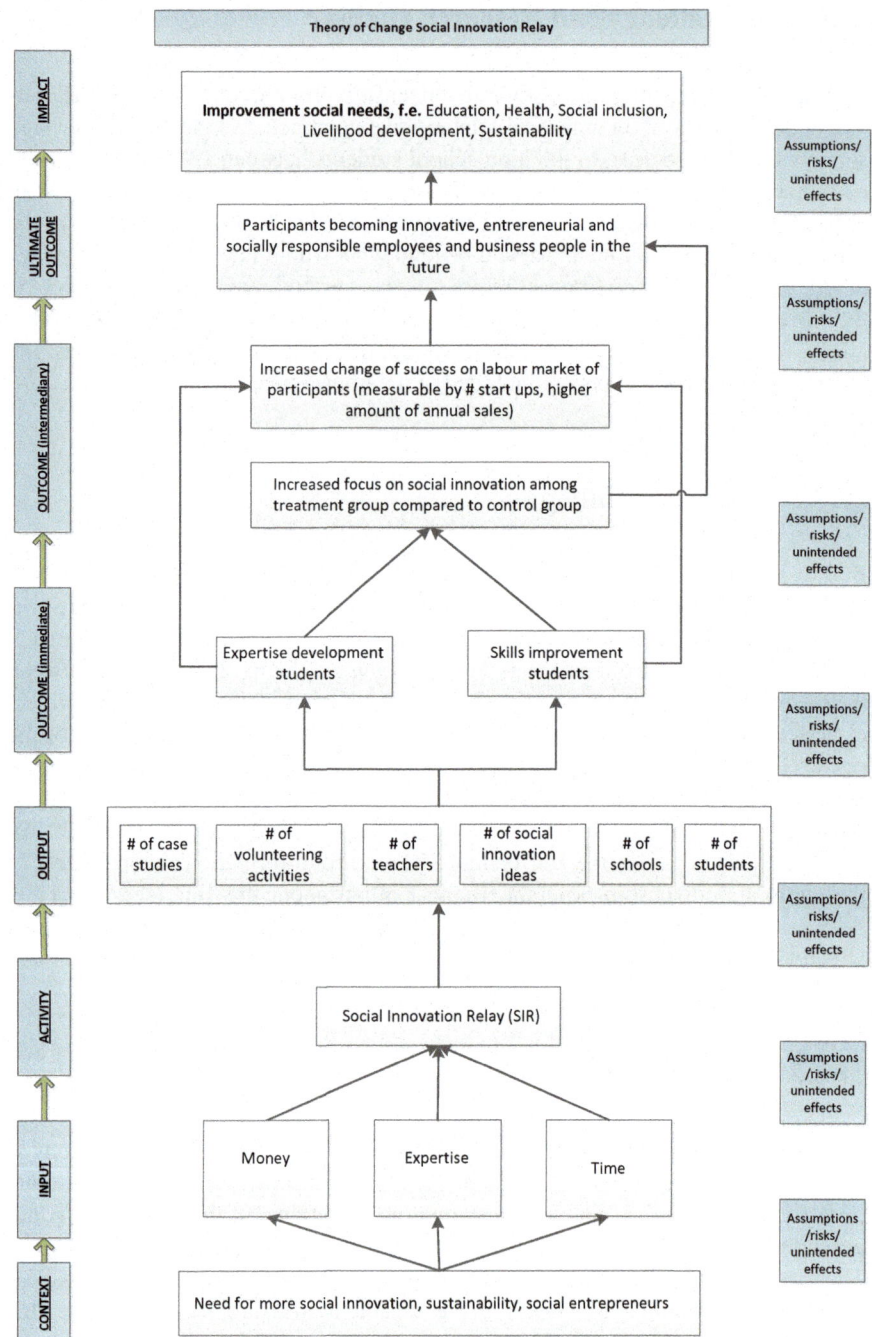

Fig. 11.1 ToC behind Social Innovation Relay

key performance indicators of entrepreneurial behavior and intention that can be used in the survey, and to analyze if there is already empirical evidence between education and training, and entrepreneurial behavior.

We decided not to specifically focus on key performance indicators of *social* entrepreneurial behavior and intention, as we see the focus of the program on *social* enterprises as a subservient issue. The main focus of the program is to stimulate entrepreneurial intention and behavior in order to improve the future economic opportunities of students, and make them more financial resilient. The benefit of this approach is that the results of this study are also useful for the research area of general entrepreneurship, or cultural entrepreneurship. However, to gain valuable, additional information concerning the social aspect of the program, we did include five questions that give insight in the social awareness of participants.

Entrepreneurship can be divided in two aspects: entrepreneurial intention and entrepreneurial behavior. While many existing validated questionnaires concerning entrepreneurship are focused on "becoming an entrepreneur" (Liñán and Chen 2009), NN also aims to stimulate students to "become more entrepreneurial." Therefore, in literature, we have looked for perceptual variables that influence entrepreneurial behavior. Perceptual variables are factors describing subjective perceptions of the individual, but do not reflect objective circumstances (Arenius and Minniti 2005). In literature, questionnaires related to entrepreneurship are framed differently. According to Wilson et al. (2007), the characteristics to become an entrepreneur are entrepreneurial self-efficacy, intention, and education. Lüthje and Franke (2003) divided entrepreneurial characteristics in six elements: risk-taking propensity, locus of control, perceived barriers, perceived support factors, attitude toward entrepreneurship, and entrepreneurial intent. This classification corresponds highly with Gürol and Atsan (2006), who see the need for achievement, locus of control, tolerance for ambiguity, innovativeness, risk-taking propensity, and self-confidence as the six characteristics for entrepreneurial behavior. Entrialgo et al. (2000) see the locus of control, the need for achievement, and tolerance for ambiguity as indicators for entrepreneurship. In the Entrepreneurial Intention Questionnaire (EIQ), personal attitude, perceived behavioral control, entrepreneurial intention, and entrepreneurial skills are important entrepreneurial characteristics (Liñán and Chen 2009). Innovativeness, autonomy, proactiveness, and competitive aggressiveness can also be seen as dimensions of entrepreneurial orientation (Lumpkin and Dess 1996). Arenius and Minniti (2005) see opportunity perception, confidence in personal ability, fear of failure, and knowing other entrepreneurs as perceptual variables for entrepreneurial behavior, while Kume et al. (2013) shape the entrepreneurial profile as locus of control, entrepreneurial self-efficacy, independence motive, and innovation motive. Lastly, Koellinger et al. (2007) analyzed six perceptual entrepreneurial behaviors: knowledge/skills, perceived unexploited opportunities, fear of failure, know someone who is entrepreneurial, trust in better business conditions in the future, and trust in better future financial situation. The different variables for entrepreneurial behavior and intention are summarized in Table 11.1.

Table 11.1 Variables that influence entrepreneurial behavior and entrepreneurial intention

Indicators for entrepreneurial behavior and entrepreneurial intention	
Need for achievement	Knowledge/skills
Locus of control	Entrepreneurial self-efficacy
Tolerance for ambiguity	Independence motive
Innovativeness	Entrepreneurial education
Risk-taking propensity	Personal attitude
Self-confidence (in skills and ability)	Autonomy
Opportunity perception	Proactiveness
Fear of failure	Competitive aggressiveness
Optimism/trust in future business conditions	Knowing other entrepreneurs
Optimism/trust in future financial situation	

Based on Gürol and Atsan (2006), Entrialgo et al. (2000), Arenius and Minniti (2005), Koellinger et al. (2007), Kume et al. (2013), Liñán and Chen (2009), Wilson et al. (2007), Lüthje and Franke (2003) and Lumpkin and Dess (1996)

Many variables overlap between the different researches about entrepreneurial intention and/or entrepreneurial behavior. Therefore, in collaboration with NN and JA Europe, we discussed which variables fits best to the objectives of SIR. We decided to follow Wilson et al. (2007), who measure entrepreneurial intention by asking participants how interested they were in different careers. Starting or owning a business is one of the choice options. We implemented questions for need for achievement, locus of control, and tolerance for ambiguity as used by Entrialgo et al. (2000), and implemented the questions concerning fear of failure and trust in better financial situation (in our analysis referred to as "optimism") from Koellinger et al. (2007). We followed the example of EIQ and include their question concerning entrepreneurial skills (Linan 2008; Liñán and Chen 2009). We did not specifically ask for self-confidence, as we believe this is already covered in the question about abilities and skills. As a control variable, we implemented the question from EIQ whether people in their environment would be proud of the students when they decided to start their own business. Moreover, we asked if they knew someone personally who owns a business (Koellinger et al. 2007). As most of these questions were previously used to survey university students or adults, we rephrased all questions in order to make the questions more understandable for teenagers. We executed a pilot with some students in the Netherlands to see if the questions were understandable. Based on this, we slightly rephrased some of the questions. Consequently, the national coordinators in each country translated the survey and guaranteed the same meaning of the questions in each country.

11.4.3 Measurement

The overarching research question of this case study is threefold. First, the intention of this study is to analyze whether the NN corporate citizenship program creates social impact for the beneficiaries. Secondly, the study will provide interesting insights whether training programs can stimulate entrepreneurial behavior and entrepreneurial intention, the two key aspects of entrepreneurship. Thirdly, this case study will provide information whether the NN corporate citizenship program stimulates social awareness among the beneficiaries.

Although this case study aims to address three different research questions, the overarching logic of these question is similar. Each question provides an answer to the question if providing *Knowledge* will lead to another *Attitude* among the beneficiaries, and consequently, will lead to a changing *Practice*. In order to find an answer on these three research questions, we developed corresponding hypotheses. This KAP approach (Knowledge, Attitude, and Practice) and the corresponding research questions are as follows (see Table 11.2):

Table 11.2 KAP approach for the research questions

	Knowledge	Attitude	Practice	Hypothesis
Research question 1	Providing knowledge and expertise through the SIR program	Is the attitude toward the skills and abilities of the beneficiaries changing?	Does the organization create social impact for beneficiaries with their program?	
Research question 2	Providing knowledge and expertise through the SIR program	Is the attitude toward entrepreneurship (intention) of the beneficiaries changing?	Do the beneficiaries show more entrepreneurial intention and behavior?	Hypothesis 1: Participation in the Social Innovation Relay program leads to increased entrepreneurial skills of the students. Hypothesis 2: Participation in the Social Innovation Relay program leads to an entrepreneurial intention of the students. Hypothesis 3: Participation in the Social Innovation Relay program leads to increased entrepreneurial behaviors of the students
Research question 3	Providing knowledge and expertise through the SIR program	Is the attitude toward social issues of the beneficiaries changing?	Do the beneficiaries show more socially responsible awareness and behavior?	Hypothesis 4: Participation in the Social Innovation Relay program leads to more social awareness of the students

To analyze whether the intended results are achieved, we implement three measurement moments in the research design. Implementing different measurement moments enables us to analyze if skills, intention, behaviors, and expertise of students develop over time. Moreover, it also helps us to analyze the effect of both the first and second phase of the program. Measurement moment T0 will take place directly after the registration. The survey will be sent to all participating students. Measurement moment T1 will take place after the submission of ideas, but before the announcement of the top 20 teams. Measurement moment T2 will take place after the national final. Less students will participate in this survey than in measurement moment T0 and T1. Lastly, we included a control group for Spain, Romania, and the Netherlands, to test if the development was causally related to the program or effected by other external activities.

11.5 Results

An important question in academic literature concerning entrepreneurship and education is whether entrepreneurs can be made or are born (Henry et al. 2005). Based on the data of the survey, an impact measurement is conducted in order to gain more knowledge on this topic. The results of our measurement provide new academic and practical insights in the area of the impact of corporate citizenship programs. The number of responses in our treatment group and control group on the different measurement moments is given in Table 11.3.

11.5.1 Analysis Hypothesis 1

Existing literature concerning the impact of training programs on entrepreneurial skills shows very different results. Oosterbeek et al. (2010) found no significant results of an entrepreneurial education program on entrepreneurial skills gained by

Table 11.3 Number of responses

Country	T0	T1	T2	Control T0	Control T2	Total
Spain	255	177	61	127	13	633
Romania	173	49	41	79	10	352
Netherlands	592	79	21	73	9	774
Japan	68	11	13			92
Hungary	279	67	7			353
Greece	122	7	0			129
Czech Republic	37	86	17			140
Bulgaria	134	62	46			242
Poland	87	129	55			271
Singapore	235	62	59			356
Total	1982	729	320	279	32	3342

the participants. In contrast, Botha et al. (2006) analyzed an entrepreneurship program focused on women. They concluded that participants of the program gained more entrepreneurial skills and knowledge. In contrast, Bilán et al. (2005) also found significant increases for some entrepreneurial skills. Because of these different research results, there is little uniformity about the question if entrepreneurs are made or born (Henry et al. 2005).

In our analysis, we conducted factor analyses in order to test if we could combine the responses of our survey questions into a few underlying factors. Consequently, based on a factor analysis, we found out that all skills related to entrepreneurship could be categorized in two components: entrepreneurial skills related to communication and network and entrepreneurial skills related to creativity and innovation. For both categories, we calculated an average score on a 5-point Likert scale to use in our analysis, measured as the sum of means, divided by the number of questions. To test our hypotheses we created tables, which enabled us to summarize our data. Our results show a significant increase between T0 and T1 in both skills related to communication and network and skills related to creativity of the treatment group students (see Table 11.4). This means that in the first phase of the SIR program, the entrepreneurial skills of the treatment group increase significantly. Between T0 and T2, we also found this significant increase. However, if we specifically focus on the second phase of the program, we do not find a significant effect between T1 and T2. Moreover, for the control group we do not find any significant results as well. This means that hypothesis 1, "Participation in the Social Innovation Relay program leads to increased entrepreneurial skills of the students," is accepted. It seems however that the main results are achieved during the first phase of the SIR program.

11.5.2 Analysis Hypothesis 2

Souitaris et al. (2007) found that entrepreneurship programs influence the entrepreneurial intentions and attitudes of science and engineering students. In line with this, Turker and Sonmez Selçuk (2009) also found that educational and structural support factors affect the entrepreneurial intention of students. Fayolle et al. (2006)

Table 11.4 Mean and significance level for hypothesis 1

Treatment group	T0 mean	T1 mean	T2 mean
Skills communication network	3.75	3.84	3.93
Skills creativity	3.73	3.84	3.91
Significance level (0.05) for treatment group	**T0**	**T1**	**T2**
	(A)	**(B)**	**(C)**
Skills communication network		A	A
Skills creativity		A	A

Results are based on two-sided tests assuming equal variances. For each significant pair, the key of the smaller category appears in the category with the larger mean
Significance level for upper case letters (A, B, C): 0.05

analyzed an entrepreneurship education program and found a strong impact on the entrepreneurial intention of students, and a positive but not very significant impact on their perceived behavioral control. These previously mentioned findings are based on university students. Our results that are based on the responses of high school students correspond with these findings. Based on a 5-point Likert scale, we found a significant increase in entrepreneurial intention of the treatment group students between T0, T1, and T2 (see Table 11.5). This means that in the SIR program, the entrepreneurial intention of student increases significantly. If we look at the specific results of the two phases, we see that especially the first phase of the program (difference between T0 and T1) shows a significant positive result. Between T1 and T2, the second phase of the SIR program, we do find an increase in entrepreneurial intention, but this increase is not significantly related to T1. Moreover, for the control group, we did not find any significant results. This means that hypothesis 2, "Participation in the Social Innovation Relay program leads to an entrepreneurial intention of the students," is accepted. It seems however that the main results are achieved during the first phase of the SIR program.

11.5.3 Analysis Hypothesis 3

It is difficult to measure the actual entrepreneurial behavior of students, as they are not entrepreneurs yet. Consequently, studies that focus on measuring entrepreneurial behavior are extremely limited. In our analysis we analyzed the change in characteristics that are associated with entrepreneurial behavior. As the characteristics locus of control, need for achievement, and tolerance for ambiguity were questioned by means of multiple sub-questions, we used factor analysis. After this factor analysis, we found out that locus of control could be categorized in two components: locus of control related to external elements that happens to be outside the sphere of influence of the individual, and locus of control related to internal elements, where the individual has direct influence. For the characteristic locus of control, tolerance for ambiguity, and need for achievement, we calculated one average score on a 5-point Likert scale to use in our analysis, measured as the sum of means, divided by the number of questions. The aspects knowledge, fear of failure, and optimism

Table 11.5 Mean and significance level for hypothesis 2

Treatment group	T0 mean	T1 mean	T2 mean
Entrepreneurial intention	3.80	3.94	4.03
Significance level (0.05) for treatment group	T0	T1	T2
Entrepreneurial intention	(A)	(B)	(C)
		A	A

Results are based on two-sided tests. For each significant pair, the key of the category with the smaller column proportion appears in the category with the larger column proportion

Significance level for upper case letters (A, B, C): 0.05

are already based on one question. Between T0 and T1, we see a significant increase in the treatment group for need for achievement, locus of control, and knowledge (see Table 11.6). In this first phase of the SIR program, we do find a significant decrease in tolerance for and for optimism. We also found a significant increase between T0 and T1 for external related locus of control. However, despite the fact that there is a significant decrease, this is a good result as the statements are "reversed." A decrease in the score between T0 and T1 means that they feel they have more control over their life and that they start believing that getting a job depends on their own skills and not just on coincidence. Moreover, Table 11.6 shows that we did not find a significant relationship between T0 and T1 for fear of failure. Moreover, between T1 and T2 we do not find any significant results at all. In the control group, we only find a significant decrease in optimism.

Summarized, hypothesis 3, "Participation in the Social Innovation Relay program leads to increased entrepreneurial behaviors of the students," is partly accepted.

Table 11.6 Mean and significance level for hypothesis 3

Treatment group	T0	T1	T2	Control group	Control – T0	Control – T2
Characteristics	Mean	Mean	Mean	Characteristics	Mean	Mean
Need for achievement	3.71	3.84	3.83	Need for achievement	3.59	3.78
Locus of control – self	3.72	3.84	3.88	Locus of control – self	3.80	3.80
Locus of control – external	2.93	2.81	2.87	Locus of control – external	2.75	2.52
Tolerance for ambiguity	3.22	3.15	3.23	Tolerance for ambiguity	3.12	2.97
Knowledge	3.53	3.63	3.76	Knowledge	3.48	3.78
Fear of failure	3.45	3.54	3.52	Fear of failure	3.38	3.38
Optimism	3.67	3.54	3.52	Optimism	3.54	2.97
	T0	T1	T2		Control – T0	Control – T2
Significance level (0.05) for treatment group	(A)	(B)	(C)	Significance level (0.05) for control group	(C)	(D)
Need for achievement		A	A	Need for achievement		
Locus of control – self		A	A	Locus of control – self		
Locus of control – external	B			Locus of control – external		
Tolerance for ambiguity	B			Tolerance for ambiguity		
Knowledge		A	A	Knowledge		
Fear of failure				Fear of failure		
Optimism		B		Optimism	D	

Results are based on two-sided tests assuming equal variances. For each significant pair, the key of the smaller category appears in the category with the larger mean
Significance level for upper case letters (A, B, C): 0.05

Participation in the first phase of the SIR program leads to a significant increase in some characteristics of entrepreneurial behavior: need for achievement, locus of control (both self-related and external), and knowledge. Moreover, for need for achievement (self-related), locus of control, and knowledge, the hypothesis is also accepted when we look at the overall program (when we compare T2 to T0). However, we found a significant decrease for the treatment group between T0 and T1 for the characteristics optimism and tolerance for ambiguity. This significant decrease in optimism could be explained by the argumentation that students develop an increased sense of reality. We cannot find any significant effects on characteristics of entrepreneurial behavior for participating in the second phase of the SIR program.

11.5.4 Analysis Hypothesis 4

Social responsibility and social awareness are highly relevant topic nowadays, nevertheless empirical research on the effects of education on the social awareness is still limited. Already 26 years ago, Elias et al. (1991) concluded that education could stimulate prosocial behavior. Our results correspond to this finding, as we see a significant increase between T0 and T1 of the treatment group on all our five statements related to social awareness (see Table 11.7). If we take a closer look at the development between T1 and T2, we only find a significant increase for the element

Table 11.7 Mean and significance level for hypothesis 4

Treatment group	T0	T1	T2
Elements of social awareness	Mean	Mean	Mean
I know what a social entrepreneur is	3.48	3.94	4.04
I understand what social innovation is	3.44	3.95	4.11
I am aware of what social issues exist in my community	3.74	3.99	4.09
I want to solve social and/or environmental issues	3.68	4.00	4.06
I am confident that I will be able to work with others to solve social issues	3.90	4.11	4.20
	T0	T1	T2
Significance level (0.05) for treatment group	(A)	(B)	(C)
I know what a social entrepreneur is		A	A
I understand what social innovation is		A	A B
I am aware of what social issues exist in my community		A	A
I want to solve social and/or environmental issues		A	A
I am confident that I will be able to work with others to solve social issues		A	A

Results are based on two-sided tests assuming equal variances. For each significant pair, the key of the smaller category appears in the category with the larger mean
Significance level for upper case letters (A, B, C): 0.05

"I know what social innovation is." In the control group, we did not find any significant results. Summarized, hypothesis 4, "Participation in the Social Innovation Relay program leads to more social awareness of the students," can be accepted. Between T0 and T1 and between T0 and T2, the social awareness of students shows a significant increase on all five elements of social awareness. Between T1 and T2, we only find a significant increase for the understanding of social innovation. This implies that the first phase of the program is most important in increasing the social awareness of participating students.

11.5.5 Other Findings

Based on all the data gathered, we were able to draw some other conclusions about entrepreneurial intention, environment, and education. These analyses do not provide information about the impact of the SIR program, but do provide valuable insights. Based on linear regression analyses, we found that the direct environment of a student is significantly related with the intention of that student to become an entrepreneur. The opinion of friends (*sig.* = *0.000*), classmates (*sig.* = *0.019*), and family (*sig.* = *0.000*) is significantly related to the entrepreneurial intention of the student. The opinion of the teacher is not significantly related to this intention (*sig.* = *0.149*). There is also a significant relationship between the entrepreneurial intention of the high school students and whether they know someone close to them who owns a business (*sig.* = *0.000*). These findings correspond to Kume et al. (2013), who argued that entrepreneurial intention is shaped by the opinion of the students' parents, family, and friends.

11.6 Conclusion and Discussion

There exists many research focusing on the impact of corporate citizenship programs on (corporate) volunteers and organization. However, information on the impact of corporate citizenship programs on beneficiaries is limited. Therefore, in this study, we aim to bridge the research gap that exists concerning the social impact of corporate citizenship programs for beneficiaries by performing a case study. We analyzed the impact of SIR on the participants, by conducting an impact measurement, including a treatment group and a control group. The results of our measurement give new insights in the area of the impacts of corporate citizenship programs.

We developed three research questions with corresponding hypotheses. We tested the hypotheses in order to answer these research question. We found that participation in the first phase of the SIR program (case studies in the classroom, online quiz, and submission of an idea for a sustainable business plan) leads to increased entrepreneurial intention, entrepreneurial skills, social awareness, and entrepreneurial behavioral aspects such as "need for achievement," "locus of control," and "knowledge." In this first phase of the SIR program, we also see a significant decrease in optimism. This might imply that students develop a sense for reality during the program. However, in the second phase of the SIR program, when the winning teams have to improve their existing business plan with the help of (e-) mentoring, we do not find many significant effects. The only significant effect is related to the understanding of social innovation.

Based on these results, we can conclude that the beneficiaries of the SIR program indeed show more entrepreneurial behavior and intention (research question 2) and social awareness (research question 3). Our findings show that the main results are achieved during the first phase of the program. Therefore, we recommend NN to talk with participants in order to find out the additional value of the second phase of the program. Moreover, focus groups with participants can help them to understand the underlying mechanisms. It can give NN information about the needs of the high school students. With this knowledge, NN can optimize the SIR program.

Moreover, because the skills and characteristics of entrepreneurial behavior of the beneficiaries increase during the program, we can argue that it is likely that NN create social impact for the beneficiaries with their program (research question 1), as the high school students can use their gained skills and knowledge to distinguish themselves in further educations, and possibly future workplace. However, we do not have direct prove for the overall social impact (improvement of social needs) of the program.

11.6.1 Implications for Corporate Foundations

How can this case study of a corporate citizenship program be of value for corporate foundations? Similar to corporate citizenship programs, corporate volunteering is an important element of corporate foundations. Both corporate citizenship programs as well as corporate foundations aim to solve a social problem. Consequently, as previously mentioned, in the current practice at NN, the legal vehicle of a foundation is not a necessity to make the societal impact that they are striving for through corporate volunteering. NN believes that the execution of the program would not have been done differently in a foundation. Therefore, we believe that these results also provide valuable insights for corporate citizenship programs that are executed corporate foundations.

Available research mainly focused on the positive effects of corporate volunteering on the employee and the organization. This case study gives an example how to gain insights in the perspective of and the effects of corporate volunteering on the beneficiaries. Corporate foundations can use this example to get a clearer picture of their corporate volunteering programs on beneficiaries.

Moreover, this case study is important for corporate foundations because it shows the importance of social impact measurements and provides a methodology to use. This case study shows how a corporate foundation can apply impact measurements in order to gain insights in the effects of their programs or activities.

It shows that measurements can be used to *prove*. It can help organizations, both corporate citizenship programs as well as corporate foundations, to legitimize their activities. It can also help them to *improve*: This kind of measurements can be useful for corporate foundations to learn and to strategically focus on more impact, and to manage and optimize the positive intended impacts.

Therefore, we recommend corporate foundations to use this case study as inspiration to start with analyzing their own social impact. On the one hand, practitioners can help creating more evidence for the social impact of corporate citizenship programs that are executed within corporate foundations. On the other hand, corporate foundations benefit from the measurement themselves as it can help them to *prove* and to *improve*. In particular, this learning perspective of the impact assessment is of high value. When corporate foundations learn from impact measurements and manage their impact based on the results, the chance of success of their activities will increase.

However, when corporate foundations decide to use this case study of NN as inspiration to start measuring their social impact themselves, it is important to keep in mind that a "one-size-fits-all" methodology does not exist. If a corporate foundation applies a "one-size-fits-all" methodology, there is a chance that it measures elements that are not relevant at all for the corporate foundation. Therefore, we recommend corporate foundations to develop a research methodology that fits to the mission, ambition, activities, and intended impacts of their specific organization.

11.6.2 Limitations and Future Research

This impact measurement focuses on a corporate citizenship program which does not relate to a corporate foundation. It is expected that none of the work done with JA Europe would have been executed differently if the program would have been linked to a foundation; similar to corporate foundations, the corporate citizenship program of NN has a mission and works together with partners (often charities) to co-create impact that is in line with this mission. Consequently, we expect that the effects of SIR would not have been different if SIR was executed by a foundation. The main difference with corporate foundations can be found in organizational elements, such as tax constructs, external board advisors, and endowments. Consequently, we believe that our measurement does provide valuable information on the potential impact of corporate foundations as well. Our results show that initiatives within corporate citizenship programs, regardless of the question if they are executed inside or outside a foundation, can be valuable not only for employees but also for society. However, with the present level of knowledge of the effect of corporate citizenship programs on beneficiaries, generalization of the results is not possible. Future research can focus on creating more evidence for the social impact of corporate citizenship programs that are executed within corporate foundations.

Regression analyses already showed that the close environment of the students shows a significant relationship with the entrepreneurial intention. However, this finding is based on our dataset and we did not implement control variables. We are aware that there are many other factors influencing the entrepreneurial intention of the students, such as the national culture of entrepreneurship. Another limitation is the construction of our control group, which is not randomized. For the construction of the control group, we were dependent on international and local coordinators of JA Europe, and on the teachers of the participating schools. Unfortunately, because of these many parties involved, we were not able to monitor the construction of the control group sufficiently. Consequently, we received a low number of responses in the control group. We also experienced huge dropout of respondents between T0 and T2. In addition, we did not ask for gender in the survey, so it is not possible to analyze the different effects for boys or girls. Future research can address this question.

Despite the limitations of our study, we do believe that this study contributes to our existing knowledge and we do hope to have paved the way for further research into the impact of corporate programs on its beneficiaries and in the end society at large.

Acknowledgments The authors would like to thank Nationale-Nederlanden for their financial support for this research and JA Europe for their coordination in this research.

References

Arenius, P., & Minniti, M. (2005). Perceptual variables and nascent entrepreneurship. *Small Business Economics, 24*(3), 233–247.

Battilana, J., Lee, M., Walker, J., & Dorsey, C. (2012). In search of the hybrid ideal. *Stanford Social Innovation Review, 10*(3), 50–55.

Bilán, S. G., Kisenwether, E. C., Rzasa, S. E., & Wise, J. C. (2005). Developing and assessing students' entrepreneurial skills and mind-set. *Journal of Engineering Education, 94*(2), 233–243.

Botha, M., Nieman, G., & van Vuuren, J. (2006). Enhancing female entrepreneurship by enabling access to skills. The International Entrepreneurship and Management Journal, 2(4), 479-493.

Chen, J. C., Patten, D. M., & Roberts, R. W. (2008). Corporate charitable contributions: A corporate social performance or legitimacy strategy? *Journal of Business Ethics, 82*(1), 131–144.

Clark, C., Rosenzweig, W., Long, D., & Olsen, S. (2004). *Double bottom line project report: Assessing social impact in double bottom line ventures. Methods catalog.* New York: Columbia Business School. Retrieved at http://www.shidler.hawaii.edu/Portals/1/resources/DoubleBottomLine.pdf.

de Gilder, D., Schuyt, T. N., & Breedijk, M. (2005). Effects of an employee volunteering program on the work force: The ABN-AMRO Case. *Journal of Business Ethics, 61*(2), 143–152.

Du, S., Bhattacharya, C. B., & Sen, S. (2010). Maximizing business returns to corporate social responsibility (CSR): The role of CSR communication. *International Journal of Management Reviews, 12*(1), 8–19.

Duval-Couetil, N. (2013). Assessing the impact of entrepreneurship education programs: Challenges and approaches. *Journal of Small Business Management, 51*(3), 394–409.

Eccles, R. G., & Krzus, M. P. (2010). *One report: Integrated reporting for a sustainable strategy.* Hoboken: Wiley.

Elias, M. J., Gara, M. A., Schuyler, T. F., Branden-Muller, L. R., & Sayette, M. A. (1991). The promotion of social competence: Longitudinal study of a preventive school-based program. *The American Journal of Orthopsychiatry, 61*(3), 409.

Entrialgo, M., Fernández, E., & Vázquez, C. J. (2000). Characteristics of managers as determinants of entrepreneurial orientation: Some Spanish evidence. *Enterprise and Innovation Management Studies, 1*(2), 187–205.

Fayolle, A., Gailly, B., & Lassas-Clerc, N. (2006). Assessing the impact of entrepreneurship education programmes: A new methodology. *Journal of European Industrial Training, 30*(9), 701–720.

Geroy, G. D., Wright, P. C., & Jacoby, L. (2000). Toward a conceptual framework of employee volunteerism: An aid for the human resource manager. *Management Decision, 38*(4), 280–287.

Gürol, Y., & Atsan, N. (2006). Entrepreneurial characteristics amongst university students: Some insights for entrepreneurship education and training in Turkey. *Education and Training, 48*(1), 25–38.

Haski-Leventhal, D., Meijs, L. C., & Hustinx, L. (2010). The third-party model: Enhancing volunteering through governments, corporations and educational institutes. *Journal of Social Policy, 39*(1), 139–158.

Henry, C., Hill, F., & Leitch, C. (2005). Entrepreneurship education and training: Can entrepreneurship be taught? Part I. *Education and Training, 47*(2), 98–111.

Idowu, S. O., & Papasolomou, I. (2007). Are the corporate social responsibility matters based on good intentions or false pretences? An empirical study of the motivations behind the issuing of CSR reports by UK companies. *Corporate Governance: The international Journal of Business in Society, 7*(2), 136–147.

Koellinger, P., Minniti, M., & Schade, C. (2007). "I think I can, I think I can": Overconfidence and entrepreneurial behavior. *Journal of Economic Psychology, 28*(4), 502–527.

Kume, A., Kume, V., & Shahini, B. (2013). Entrepreneurial characteristics amongst university students in Albania. *European Scientific Journal, 9*, 16.

Lee, M. D. P., & Lounsbury, M. (2011). Domesticating radical rant and rage: An exploration of the consequences of environmental shareholder resolutions on corporate environmental performance. *Business & Society, 50*(1), 155–188.

Liket, K. C., Rey-Garcia, M., & Maas, K. E. (2014). Why Aren't Evaluations Working and What to Do About It A Framework for Negotiating Meaningful Evaluation in Nonprofits. American Journal of Evaluation, 35(2), 171–188.

Liñán, F. (2008). Skill and value perceptions: how do they affect entrepreneurial intentions?. *International Entrepreneurship and Management Journal 4*(3), 257–272.

Liñán, F., & Chen, Y. W. (2009). Development and cross-cultural application of a specific instrument to measure entrepreneurial intentions. *Entrepreneurship Theory and Practice, 33*(3), 593–617.

Lumpkin, G. T., & Dess, G. G. (1996). Clarifying the entrepreneurial orientation construct and linking it to performance. *Academy of Management Review, 21*(1), 135–172.

Lüthje, C., & Franke, N. (2003). The 'making' of an entrepreneur: Testing a model of entrepreneurial intent among engineering students at MIT. *R&D Management, 33*(2), 135–147.

Maas, K. (2009). *Corporate social performance: From output measurement to impact measurement.* (No. EPS-2009-182-STR, ERIM Ph.D. Series). Rotterdam: Erasmus University Rotterdam.

Maas, K., & Liket, K. (2011). Talk the walk: Measuring the impact of strategic philanthropy. *Journal of Business Ethics, 100*(3), 445–464.

Maas, K. E. H., & Liket, K. C. (2016). Strategic philanthropy: A happy marriage of business and society? *Business & Society, 55*(6), 889–921.

Mahoney, L. S., & Thorn, L. (2006). An examination of the structure of executive compensation and corporate social responsibility: A Canadian investigation. *Journal of Business Ethics, 69*(2), 149–162.

Monfort, A., & Villagra, N. (2016). Corporate social responsability and corporate foundations in building responsible brands. *El profesional de la Información (EPI), 25*(5), 767–777.

Murillo, D., & Lozano, J. M. (2006). SMEs and CSR: An approach to CSR in their own words. *Journal of Business Ethics, 67*(3), 227–240.

Muthuri, J. N., Matten, D., & Moon, J. (2009). Employee volunteering and social capital: Contributions to corporate social responsibility. *British Journal of Management, 20*, 75–89.

Oosterbeek, H., Van Praag, M., & IJsselstein, A. (2010). The impact of entrepreneurship education on entrepreneurship skills and motivation. *European Economic Review, 54*(3), 442–454.

Roza, L. (2016). *Employee Engagement in Corporate Social Responsibility. A collection of essays.* (No. EPS-2016-396-ORG). Rotterdam: Erasmus University.

Samuel, O., Roza, L., & Meijs, L. (2016). Exploring partnerships from the perspective of HSO beneficiaries: The case of corporate volunteering. *Human Service Organizations: Management, Leadership & Governance, 40*(3), 220-237.

Santana, A. (2015). Disentangling the knot: Variable mixing of four motivations for firms' use of social practices. *Business & Society, 54*(6), 763–793.

Souitaris, V., Zerbinati, S., & Al-Laham, A. (2007). Do entrepreneurship programmes raise entrepreneurial intention of science and engineering students? The effect of learning, inspiration and resources. *Journal of Business Venturing, 22*(4), 566–591.

Toxopeus, H. S., Maas, K. E., & Liket, K. C. (2016). *Innovating for impact investing. Principles and practice of impact investing: A catalytic revolution* (pp. 174–187). Sheffield: Greenleaf.

Turker, D., & Sonmez Selçuk, S. (2009). Which factors affect entrepreneurial intention of university students? *Journal of European Industrial Training, 33*(2), 142–159.

van Duuren, E., Plantinga, A., & Scholtens, B. (2016). ESG integration and the investment management process: Fundamental investing reinvented. *Journal of Business Ethics, 138*(3), 525–533.

van Knippenberg, D., & Sleebos, E. (2006). Organizational identification versus organizational commitment: Self-definition, social exchange, and job attitudes. *Journal of Organizational Behavior, 27*(5), 571–584.

van Knippenberg, B., Martin, L., & Tyler, T. (2006). Process-orientation versus outcome-orientation during organizational change: The role of organizational identification. *Journal of Organizational Behavior, 27*(6), 685–704.

Villagra, N., & López, B. (2013). Analysis of values and communication of the responsible brands. Corporate Brand strategies for sustainability/Análisis de los valores y la comunicación de las Marcas responsables. Estrategias de las marcas corporativas en el contexto de la Sostenibilidad. *Communications Society, 26*(1), 196–221.

Wilson, F., Kickul, J., & Marlino, D. (2007). Gender, entrepreneurial self-efficacy, and entrepreneurial career intentions: Implications for entrepreneurship education. *Entrepreneurship Theory and Practice, 31*(3), 387–406.

Marjelle Vermeulen works as a social impact researcher at the Impact Centre Erasmus (ICE). Moreover, she is a PhD candidate at the Impact Centre Erasmus and the Erasmus School of History, Culture and Communication (ESHCC).

Karen Maas is endowed professor Accounting and Sustainability at the Open University, academic director of Impact Centre Erasmus (ICE) and scientific director of ESAA's Executive CSR education programs. She is specialized in the combination of quantitative and qualitative evaluations and impact measurements, related to CSR, impact investment and social entrepreneurship.

Chapter 12
"Capturing People's Hearts, Hands, and Wallets": Corporate Foundations as a Vehicle for Promoting Volunteering

Debbie Haski-Leventhal

Abstract This chapter aims to shed light on the role corporate foundations (CFs) play in enhancing volunteering. Due to the limited literature on the topic, we lack knowledge on the motivation for enhancing volunteering by CFs, how it is done, and what differences there are, if any, between CFs and corporate social responsibility (CSR) departments when it comes to enhancing volunteering. To develop an initial understanding of these issues, a mixed method study was conducted in Australia, which included employee survey, three in-depth case studies, and document analysis of 40 CFs and CSR reports. The findings of the study show that CFs somewhat enhance personal volunteering but mainly focus on corporate volunteering. They do so by offering paid leave for volunteering, employee-led corporate volunteering, and matching funds. Recent shifts in corporate volunteering emerged, including skill-based volunteering, international corporate volunteering, strategic CSR, and measuring social impact. The main differences between CFs and CSR departments relate to motivation and how strategic they are, although some admit the boundaries are blurred. The contribution of the findings and implications for practice are discussed.

Keywords Corporate foundations · Corporate volunteering · Mixed methods · Corporate social responsibility

12.1 Introduction

Corporate foundations (CFs) are nonprofit entities established by corporations and (usually) linked to the company through their name, funding, trustees, administration, and potential employee involvement (Westhues and Einwiller 2006). CFs are seen as boundary organizations between the mother company and the community (Herlin and Pedersen 2013). Similarly to social enterprises, CFs can be seen as

D. Haski-Leventhal (✉)
Macquarie University, Sydney, NSW, Australia
e-mail: debbie.haski-leventhal@mgsm.edu.au

hybrid organizations between for-profits and not-for-profits (Doherty et al. 2014) as many foundations focus on addressing social problems while also creating value for the mother company (Westhues and Einwiller 2006). In many places around the world, CFs are often the philanthropic arms of the mother company, aimed at increasing its corporate social responsibility (CSR); they usually involve the employees of the mother company in giving money (e.g., through payroll giving) and/or time (e.g., through corporate volunteering).

Corporate volunteering (CV) is therefore an activity that is promoted by many CFs. By volunteering, we refer to any activity in which time is given freely to benefit another person, group, or organization yet given a narrow scope to family and friends (Cnaan et al. 1996; Wilson 2000). Volunteering is at the core of civil society, and it is essential for delivering services to the community at a lower cost for individuals and governments (Wilson 2012). Specifically, corporate volunteering is a form of volunteering which is done with the support of one's employer. It takes place when employees give their time, knowledge, and/or skills to the community on company time, as part of the employer's community service (Bussell and Forbes 2008). Corporate volunteering refers to organizational support programs which are usually developed to encourage employee voluntary activities outside the organization (Kotler and Lee 2005). Rodell (2013, 2015) made a distinction between corporate volunteering and personal volunteering: While corporate volunteering is basically volunteering conducted through a company initiative, personal volunteering refers to volunteering conducted on one's own personal time.

When CFs are involved in enhancing corporate and personal volunteering of the mother company's employees and as such, they could also have a vital role to play in increasing volunteering as a third-party organization (Haski-Leventhal et al. 2010). However, we still lack the knowledge on how it is done, what the motivation of companies and CFs are to offer volunteering opportunities, and what differences there are, if any, between CFs and CSR departments when it comes to enhancing the private and corporate volunteering of employees. It is therefore the aim of this chapter to use a mixed method approach to answer the following research questions: How and why do CFs promote volunteering? Are there any differences between CFs and CSR departments in the context of promoting volunteering?

12.2 Corporate Foundations (CFs)

Petrovits (2006) defined CFs or company-sponsored private foundations as separate legal entities that are founded by companies to manage their charity acts. In order to classify as philanthropic and to determine qualification for tax exemption, CFs exclusively pursue public benefit purposes (von Schnurbein 2009) and demonstrate accountability through public disclosure and obedience to governmental or legal regulations (Grant 2012). In other words, CFs act as philanthropic arms of corporates and play a significant role in firms pursuing their interests (Brown 2006) while following the societal, legal, and governmental expectations on them.

Despite their connection with the mother company, CFs are usually separate entities, distinct from other corporate contribution or direct giving programs. The independence of the foundation secures its financial and operational solidarity when compared with an in-house CSR department. Its function as a boundary organization fosters networking abilities and comprehensive sensation of societal expectations (Herlin and Pedersen 2013). Brown (2006) argued that since CFs do not depend on electoral support and are not in direct competition with corporates for funds, they present potential to pursue interests that do not conform to those of the corporation and to take up innovative initiatives (Adloff 2009).

Anheier (2001) identified two principal models of CFs: grant making and operative. While a grant-making foundation gives financial aid to support nonprofit organizations, an operative foundation directly performs activities, including organizing corporate volunteering programs and collecting resources needed for a selected project. In addition, Ostrower (2006) classified CFs based on a range of attitudes and behaviors—proactive orientation, capacity building, and advocacy.

CFs often locate their CSR initiatives (including, but not limited to, their philanthropy) outside the mother company (Griffin 2014). O'Mahony (2008) explained that as boundary organizations with a dual responsibility, CFs can accommodate the varying interests of both business and community. This allows the firm to gain all potential benefits of philanthropy and impacts the CF's objectives and field of activities (Bronn 2009). CFs strengthen firms' commitment toward the community by distributing wealth more equally and by improving living conditions and basic services, acting as "tools" for social value creation (Westhues and Einwiller 2006). At the same time, the CF's activities are expected to legitimize the role of the firm in its environment, play an important role in economic development, and enhance culture and knowledge diffusion (Fombrun 1990). These views present CFs as institutionalized means for demonstrating firm's long-term commitment with a degree of progressive work in problem-solving, service provision, driving forward social agendas, creating new ways of thinking, and specifically consolidating corporates' CSR activities.

Several researchers linked the reason for creating a CF to reputational and enlightened self-interest (Ricks 2005). CFs communicate the corporate's commitment toward CSR to the employees and other stakeholders (Westhues and Einwiller 2006) and involve them in such efforts to increase commitment and identification with the company (Chong 2009). CFs aim at improving employees' morale and commitment to the firm by improving their engagement in activities, by providing opportunities for training and development (Ostrower 2006).

Together with the globalization of business activities, CFs and corporate philanthropy are becoming global as well. Parent companies' breadth of operations on a global scale and their reach into both developed and developing countries enable CFs to attain a global presence and the ability to deliver CSR activities over a larger geographical area (Kramer 2006). An increasing number of CFs have established subsidiaries or branches in countries where their founding companies operate. As such, some CFs offer employees opportunities to volunteer in other countries (international volunteering), particularly in other locations of the mother company (Diprose 2012).

12.3 CSR and Corporate Volunteering

There is a growing academic and managerial interest in CSR, and in the last few decades, many companies started to formally adopt CSR practices, either through a CF or a CSR department. CSR is viewed as a means to bring corporate behavior up to a level where it corresponds to currently prevailing social norms, values, and performance expectations (Aguinis and Glavas 2012; Carroll 1979). When CFs apply strategic CSR principles, they strive to align their community involvement with core business and issues that are relevant to the mother company (Werther and Chandler 2011).

Researchers identified different drivers and motivation for CSR (Aguinis and Glavas 2012). Aguilera (2007) presented a four-model framework, which includes instrumental, relational, moral, and interactional drives. In addition, there are internal drivers of CSR aimed at achieving organizational benefits, including employee engagement (Sprinkle and Maines 2010) and external drivers, which are usually based on expectations of external stakeholders (Sharma 2005).

Corporate volunteering programs are considered an effective way to include employees in CSR and enhance CSR levels in order to create and maintain a positive reputation for the (mother) company as a good corporate citizen (Grant 2012; Marquis 2007). Corporate volunteering is considered as more genuine and community-centric and therefore is more likely to yield better results than other CSR activities (Kotler and Lee 2005; Plewa 2015). Corporate volunteering is often the result of integrating policies in the professional sphere with volunteering—an activity that traditionally is seen as a personal and individual act (van der Voort 2009).

It should be noted that corporate volunteering can be perceived as a "triangle" of business, community, and employees (Lee and Higgins 2001), with all three groups benefiting for these activities. Corporate volunteering holds benefits to business, as it enables business to make a tangible contribution to the community, involve their own employees, and receive some additional benefits in the form of employee engagement, team-building, and branding (Lee and Higgins 2001). Corporate volunteering also offers benefits to the community, as nonprofit organizations and community groups receive assistance and resources—raised awareness of their cause and a strong network (Haski-Leventhal et al. 2010). Finally, corporate volunteering creates engagement, satisfaction, and meaningfulness for employees and congruence between employees and their employer (Haski-Leventhal et al. 2017; Rodell 2015).

However, it can also have negative aspects, including costs of time and money for the company and its CF, costs of time and emotional challenges for the individual employees, and cost of possible unprofessional services for the recipients and the community (Haski-Leventhal 2018). In addition, employees sometimes feel pressured or even coerced to participate in voluntary activities, and some employees prefer to see it as a personal activity that should be separated to their work (Rodell 2015).

Furthermore, corporate volunteering can be either employer initiated or employee led (Mirvis 2012). Employer-initiated corporate volunteering could be support programs developed for voluntary activities inside the companies (Kotler and Lee 2005) or outside the companies. It could also be acting as a broker to find volunteering opportunities outside the company for employees (Benjamin 2001) as part of their community service, outreach, or social responsibility activity (Grant 2012; Marquis 2007). Sometimes companies and CFs accommodate the initiatives taken by employees and allow them to volunteer independently for causes of their choosing (Sprinkle and Maines 2010). One study of US corporations revealed that most corporate volunteering programs are initiated, arranged, and implemented by employees (Wainwright 2005).

Companies (and sometimes CFs) support corporate volunteering activities in various ways, including initiating and coordinating team volunteering, providing paid leave for volunteering, matching funds for the projects, acknowledging and awarding employee participation in volunteer programs, and providing employees with release time from work while rescheduling work shifts (Basil and Erlandson 2008; Haski-Leventhal et al. 2017; Plewa 2015; Rodell 2015).

Studies on corporate volunteering distinguished the schemes of volunteering in terms of the rate of recurrence of volunteering, the mode of interaction between volunteers and service recipients, the number of volunteer participants, employees' unique roles in CSR, and their level of engagement (Muthuri 2009). As such, corporate volunteering includes episodic vs. long-term volunteering, online/virtual volunteering vs. face-to-face, team vs. individual volunteering, local vs. remote/international volunteering, and skilled vs. non-skilled volunteering (Grant 2012; Haski-Leventhal et al. 2017; Mirvis 2012; Rodell 2015).

12.4 Method

To address the aforementioned research questions and gaps in our knowledge on CFs and corporate volunteering, a mixed-methods study took place in Australia in 2016 to compare CFs to CSR departments regarding corporate volunteering activities. A qualitative method was utilized through interviews and document analysis. Semi-structured interviews (DiCicco-Bloom and Crabtree 2006) were conducted with CF and CSR managers in three organizations. In addition, document analysis was conducted using annual reports of 20 other CFs in Australia and 20 CSR departments.

In addition to the qualitative data, during February–August 2016, an online survey was distributed among employees in seven organizations in Australia to examine their personal and corporate volunteering, motivations, and CSR perceptions and attitudes. We received 522 full surveys, including 117 surveys from CF1 (see details below).

12.4.1 Sample

In order to understand how CFs enhance volunteering, a theoretical sampling methodology was employed through case studies. Theoretical sampling allows building theories from case studies by gaining a deeper understanding of analyzed cases and facilitating the development of theoretical constructs, propositions, or midrange theory from case-based, empirical evidence (Strauss and Corbin 1994).

Three CFs were included in this study. The first one (CF1) was a foundation of a relatively new Australian software giant, which works to involve employees in corporate volunteering. CF1 was set up in 2008 (the mother company was founded in 2002), and it runs a variety of initiatives as well as offers grants to charities and social organizations to further its vision. Its three goals are (1) Improving educational outcomes in developing countries, (2) Increasing skill-based volunteering, and (3) Leveraging their products for the benefit of charities and social organizations. The focus of CF1 is on education, particularly in one or two countries in the developing world. As mentioned above, 117 employees also responded to an online survey on personal and corporate volunteering.

The second CF belongs to a large financial service company in Australia (CF2). The company was founded in Sydney in 1969, and the foundation was established in 1985 (a 16-year gap). In 2016, the CF donated close to $A30 million to 1500 organizations globally, with staff also donating 46,000 hours of their time. In total, their financial donations exceeded A$270 million. One of the criteria for charities to receive money from this foundation is to have the employees of the mother company involved in corporate volunteering.

The third foundation belongs to a multinational property and infrastructure company headquartered in Sydney, Australia (CF3). This foundation was set up in 1983, 25 years after the company was founded (1958), and it is the oldest of our CFs. In 1996, the foundation started an annual day of volunteering, and over 600,000 hours of corporate volunteering were contributed since. The focus of CF3 is "on maintaining and enhancing physical, mental, and emotional well-being" for both employees and the community. The focus of their corporate volunteering is on a number of causes, including providing shelter to homeless, mentoring young people and retired military personnel, delivering educational opportunities, and helping people who are recovering from natural disasters.

In addition, one of the interviewees led another corporate foundation (CF4) for 7 years, which he also discussed in his interview. The employees of the mother company, a large airline, responded to the survey, and CF's reports were analyzed in our document analysis.

12.4.2 Procedure

Data were collected through an online survey, document analysis, and three audio-recorded semi-structured interviews, lasting 30–60 minutes each. Semi-structured interviews involve predetermined, open-ended questions, with other questions emerging during the interview based on the dialogue between the interviewer and interviewee (DiCicco-Bloom and Crabtree 2006). Interviews included questions about the foundation, its history, its relations to the mother company, its goals, and its targets. The interview then focused on how the foundation enhances corporate volunteering and private volunteering of the employees of the mother company, what programs they developed, what types of corporate volunteering programs they hold, and what kind of support they offer their employees. We further asked the CFs' representative to reflect on the differences between CFs and CSR departments when it comes to the volunteering of employees.

We then conducted document analysis (Bowen 2009) of publicly available reports of these foundations in addition to other Australian foundations, totaling 20 CFs. According to Bowen (2009), document analysis is a systematic procedure for reviewing or evaluating documents—both printed and electronic material—and it requires that data be examined and interpreted in order to elicit meaning, gain understanding, and develop empirical knowledge. Document analysis was also used to analyze reports of companies with CSR departments and compare the two.

The qualitative data analysis was conducted based on the grounded theory coding principles, particularly the constant comparison process involving simultaneous data collection and analysis (Charmaz 2008). Themes were firstly identified within cases (for each interview), followed by a theme analysis between cases and a final analysis of each case. As the interviews were conducted, some reoccurring themes emerge, particularly on recent shifts and trends on corporate volunteering (e.g., skill-based volunteering) and a focus on strategic CSR. In addition, quantitative data were analyzed to compare levels of participation in corporate volunteering in organizations where the activity is led by the CF vs. a CSR department. Open-ended questions in the survey regarding corporate volunteering were also analyzed.

12.5 Results

12.5.1 How CFs Enhance Volunteering

Most participating CFs focused on corporate volunteering, while some also included personal volunteering as part of their endeavors. Corporate volunteering is usually seen as an important part of the philanthropic responsibilities of the CF.

Higher Levels of Corporate Volunteering Through CFs vs. CSR Based on the survey, it seems that companies with CFs had higher levels of volunteering compared to companies with CSR departments only. For example, in the mother company of CF1, 75% of employees volunteered privately and 90.6% volunteered through their workplace (15.4% volunteered through their workplace very often; 25.6% volunteered often; 23.9% volunteered sometimes; 25.6% volunteered occasionally; and only 9.4% of the survey respondents never volunteered through the workplace). Compared to other companies that participated in the survey but only had a CSR department, these participation rates are much higher. For example, in a telecom company that only had a CSR department, 36% of employees never volunteered. In a multinational financial services company with well-known CSR, 26.5% never volunteered. In general, 34.7% of all survey participants never volunteered, and it can be seen that volunteering rates through CF1 are much higher than in other companies ($X2 = 108.182$, $df = 24$, $p < 0.001$).

CFs Promote a Culture of Volunteering The CFs that participated in this study discussed the importance of corporate volunteering in building and promoting a culture of volunteering in the mother company to achieve the goal of increased corporate volunteering participation. By encouraging people to volunteer, the foundation changes the culture, awareness, and even exposure to the work of the corporate volunteering. This was explained by CF1:

> In [CF1], being very young, [the goal] has been to create a culture of volunteering. We face lot of people coming here never volunteered before and finding it very daunting and very threatening. And what we want to do is to create that culture first for them to value what volunteering is (…). Even the word for volunteering, we don't call it volunteeringly, we call it "foundationly" (CF1).

In another CF, employees were volunteering through an annual volunteering day to create a culture of participation and engagement:

> For the last part of 21 years, our community day has been our main way of engaging employees in the community activities. One day is the big day in the year, 5000–6000 people on that one-day volunteer in that event. A whole organization going to one location. We also bring in our contractors and our temporary employees to attend (CF3).

Socializing Employees to Volunteering CF1 explained how important it is to recruit employees to corporate volunteering activities as soon as they join the organization. CF1 provides each employee with 5 days of paid leave to volunteer, and it is not always easy to get employees who never volunteered before to do it, and as such they start with low-skill volunteering and "move up" to skill-based volunteering:

> [Employees] get five days a year [of paid leave to volunteer], but we focus on just getting them out of the door, they have never volunteered before, they want to go into really a safe environment of volunteering. Things that people with low skill set (can do), like packing boxes, planting trees. What we find is that as employees go and do that, they come back and say that this has been great, we want to start using our skills and create more value. That naturally transfers some of them to next level which is the skill-based volunteering (CF1).

Paid Leave for Volunteering One of the things often mentioned in the literature and by practitioners as useful for increasing corporate volunteering participation is offering employees paid leave to volunteer. CF1, for example, offers all employees of the mother company 5 full days of volunteering and the flexibility to do it during working hours. As was shown above, this helps to encourage employees to volunteer. Other CFs shared similar practices and results:

> We also offer something called "well-being leave." Employees get to take one-day off or take an extra day of leave every quarter. Lot of people use it for volunteering purposes. On things like community day, then everyone gets to take day off. It is considered people's normal day of work. We do have volunteering and service leave (CF3).

On the other hand, CF2 does not offer paid leave for all employees to volunteer, but rather it is the discretion of the managers to do so:

> We don't offer paid leave. But, it is up to managers' discretion to allow staff to volunteer during work hours. Essentially we do offer paid leave because they are volunteering during work hours (CF2).

Promoting Personal Volunteering In addition to promoting corporate volunteering, CFs also promote personal volunteering, but in more limited way.

> We are not just encouraging [personal volunteering] but we are kind of supporting them. To work weekends and things like that, we like to support our employees to do that (CF3).

Another CF representative sees the transitioning of employees into volunteers as something that can last even after the employees leave the company:

> I think corporate volunteering is great for those people that have never volunteered. I think a majority never volunteered. Just get them going. And the view is like, even when they leave the company or outside the company, they turn volunteering as well (CF1).

However, some employees prefer personal volunteering to corporate volunteering. For example, in the online survey, one employee stated, "I prefer doing good outside the workplace, i.e., outside my daily job environment." By encouraging people to volunteer outside the workplace, CFs can meet this demand and increase overall volunteering rates and volunteerability.

Employee-Led Corporate Volunteering Corporate volunteering can be employer led and employee led. All the CFs that participated in this study had both and encouraged employees to come up with their own projects and volunteer initiatives:

> [Employees] can apply for funding. That particular one project we signed a partnership gave each of them for three years, out of the foundation budget (CF3). Being a staff-led foundation, we don't have key areas or a list of charities kind of support. We basically empower staff to take up activities they are passionate about, and whatever they give back through donations and fundraising or volunteering or just sitting on the board of Not-for-profits, whatever might be (CF2).

It should be noted that having employee-led corporate volunteering does not imply that the CFs does not need to organize opportunities for employees. As it was explained by the CF below, it means being active but not proactive regarding corporate volunteering:

> We promote activities that our staff are actually interested in. But, we do have a good platform that allows us to promote live opportunities to staff. So, staff required to get alerts and to be informed about volunteering opportunity available and those staff basically contact the charity and form that relationships themselves. We also have an informal board register. We collect each of the staff looking to be on the board of non-profit, and we look for opportunity in the given sector and try and connect to the interest the opportunity they are looking for. That is a kind of active, but not proactive in going on the website and searching for opportunities come across Macquarie staff (CF2).

Volunteering and Giving Oftentimes, CFs tie corporate volunteering to giving of money. This could be through grants to the organizations in which employees volunteer, matching volunteering hours with a donation, giving grants to employees to start a corporate volunteering program, and/or asking employees to donate in addition to giving time:

> First one you capture people's hearts, before you capture their hands and their head and then capture their wallet. For me, that was the ideal journey and we try to build that into an

experience I guess for volunteering. Some people naturally go straight into donating, some people go straight into skill-based volunteering, but I think there is a progression for people (CF1).

12.5.2 Recent Shifts and Trends

CFs and the nature of corporate volunteering have both undergone major shifts and changes in the last two decades. This study shows that some of the recent trends in corporate volunteering include skill-based volunteering, strategic CSR, shifting away from an annual day of volunteering to a more meaningful and ongoing corporate volunteering, measuring impact, and globalization of corporate volunteering.

Skill-Based Volunteering Skills-based volunteering occurs when employees use similar skills that they apply in their regular role to do their corporate volunteering as well. From the point of view of CFs and the mother companies, this is desirable because giving then becomes more effective and with a greater impact:

> You could have ten people out there, planting trees and there could be having a minimal impact because all employees are all good brains smart, software developers for example. Or you could have people out there operating in a skill set creating amazing impact. What do you value more? (…) Ultimate goal is to get people operating the skill sets (CF1).

This was also reflected in some of the open responses to the survey question, such as:

> [CF1] is very supportive of volunteering and supporting me to volunteer and apply my skills with NGOs.

In the reports of other foundations, we also found testimonies to skill-based volunteering that is employee led. One such example was of a CF of a large bank:

> Since 2003 staff give an increasing number of seminars on financial literacy and money skills. Notably, the two main financial literacy programs developed from staff-led initiatives; while large numbers of employees have participated in the Cape York financial inclusion initiative.

Globalization and International Volunteering With a shift toward globalization, CFs and corporate philanthropy are becoming global as well, including the growing trend of international volunteering. CF3 moved with the mother company to become global, which, in turn, affected its philanthropic activities:

> Originally when it was set up, it was only operating in Australia, obviously now we have global presence. […] We created a partnership in Japan, in an area that was devastated by Tsunami in 2010 and 2011. We have been sending volunteering groups of 30–40 people every quarter to go and continue to work with the community (CF3).

The shift toward international volunteering was also reflected in the employee survey of the mother company of CF1:

- "Last year I participated in an overseas volunteer trip. This year I was only able to participate locally."

- "I participated in a workplace coordinated trip to Cambodia to perform due diligence on [CF1]'s donations."

Strategic CSR Another shift that is taking place in both CFs and CSR departments is toward strategic CSR. Moving away from "random acts of charity" to giving that is aligned with the company's core operations and mission. CF2 reflected on how the company's philanthropy became more strategic over the years:

> So, if we look at the beginning it was less strategic, probably little bit of chairman and senior executive's [choices]. So it would be writing checks by some of the seniors to organizations they were passionate about. I think what we recognize 10–15 years ago is that aligning the foundation with the company was more powerful. It made sense to our staff. We got flip model and starting from senior people being writing checks to actually completely empowering staff and fundraising for any registered charities anywhere in the world and to allow them to matching qualities, donations they do, and also empower managers to use staff invest their skills to give back to the community organizations (CF2).

CFs developed goals that are aligned with the mother company, although the alignment may not be clear for outsiders. For example, the construction company focused a lot on safety and mental health, because mental health is a major issue in this industry:

> We have been much more focused on things like mental health, physical health […]. A recent initiative we have been much more focused on [is] mental health, implementation of mental health come through foundation. One of the main reasons for promoting that is the Foundation's mindfulness to resilience and stress and strategic management, and suicide prevention programs have all been run through and for the foundation […] There is also a lot of non-profit organizations that we work and partner with, and given the mental health example, we work with other organizations that globally look at delivering mental health program (CF3).

As such, this foundation shifted away from random acts of charity to focused and strategic philanthropy:

> Money becomes more channeled instead of making it random because it doesn't relate to people. If we start doing things just random, because either the branding or marketing profile, people won't understand and cannot relate to it and to shape causes and to have positive impact on these causes in partnership with charities and experts in that area that are trying to make a difference (CF3).

Shifting Away from an Annual Day of Volunteering Another important shift was due to the understanding that having one annual, sometimes global, day of volunteering may not be the most effective way to give. Nonprofit organizations' needs require more than one day of giving, and many employees wanted to volunteer more than once a year. CF3 shifted away from an annual day of volunteering called "Community Day" to a program called "Community 365" in which employees can volunteer any day of the year:

> The feedback [from employees] was about moving beyond the annual community day, so [employees] could do more community days. The impact of having a longer period of time rather than one day, people could help an entire school, rather than 24 hours to deliver these

projects. [Employees] wanted more time and wanted longer time partnerships so that they could really have that impact and use their skills more. Out of that feedback was born Community 365, which is about volunteering for 365 days in a year. So, we encourage volunteering outside the Community day, it is more about general volunteering. (CF3).

Measuring Social Impact There is a growing interest among CFs to measure and report on their social impact. Many CFs collect data and aim to report beyond input (i.e., number of employee hours donated) on the impact created for society. Communicating impact back to the employees could help them understand why the company does its CSR and increase participation:

> We have a whole sustainability function that looks at that impact and our foundation is just another vehicle to deliver that. We leverage our people to participate and contribute. In way they feel involved, and they feel like the part of making a difference in those spaces. And they understand why we are doing it (CF3).

To do so, this CF discusses goals with employees and nonprofit organizations in various stages and measures how these goals were achieved:

> [We discuss] measurement and evaluation in interview or survey round before the program starts to understand from our point of view our staff competencies what we are looking at to build, from the charity point of view what they are expecting from the program, at the end of the program, 6 to 12 months down the track. Say for that dual purpose of understanding what they are expecting from the program and what competencies we are looking for them to build and has the charity received the deliverables they are expecting. Six months down the track, having an impact, we track whether that is actually doing what they thought of they are doing (CF2).

However, when examining the reports of 20 CFs, we found that all of them reported on input and activities (e.g., how many employees volunteered, for how many hours, doing what and for which organizations) rather than on outcomes and impacts.

12.5.3 Motivations for Enhancing Volunteering

CFs discussed their strongest motivations to enhance volunteering. Based on the literature review above, we can see that CFs also have moral and instrumental motivations to enhance volunteering. The strongest motivation that we found was moral, focusing on being a good corporate citizen and doing the right thing:

> Some of the things are just being a good corporate citizen. It is about being a corporate that the world aspires us to be. I think [our company is] really passionate about the community where we operate in and actually reminding and encouraging staff to think about how to go above and beyond (CF3).

Another strong motivator to enhance volunteering was instrumental: To engage the mother company's employees, attract talent, and yield HRM benefits, such as commitment and performance. CF4 moved the foundations to HR to focus on employees:

> The Foundation, over the 7 years that I was there, moved from different parts, it moved from different stakeholders. It started at Finance and grant and moved it into HR. It became all

about employee engagement. So, how could we develop grant programs to engage our employees a lot more, how do we get employees involved in the foundation rather than external (CF4).

Another CF representative detailed all the benefits to the employees and the mother company as a result of offering corporate volunteering opportunities, demonstrating other instrumental motivations:

> Employees feel like they are supported, on how intensive and how much time they can have off, the more they have that flexibility, and volunteering becomes part of that. What we are trying to do is make sure that as part of flexibility they can participate in community grants, volunteering, they can apply for funding, I think it generates a sense of loyalty and people feel happy about taking on those activities even after work hours (CF3).

Other instrumental motivations included to increase employee engagement, commitment, and tenure:

> But also what we see is that [volunteering] makes people stay. They get this opportunity beyond their day job. I think my boss is reflecting in a speech on that we have a 93% approval rating. So we are now one of the most popular areas [in the company], which is nice to know (CF2).

Employee Motivation to Volunteer In addition to the organizational motivations to enhance volunteering that were detailed above, employees also expressed their own motivation to participate which was increased through the work of the CFs. Employees from CF1 and CF4 participated in an online survey and explained how the work of the CFs impacted their motivation to volunteer:

- [CF1] gives us money, resources, and time off to volunteer and get involved with social/environmental initiatives. It's a big part of their culture, so in coming here I've had the opportunity to do it a lot more than I did at my previous company.
- It was not an option in previous jobs. I also set up a long-term goal after joining [Mother Company] to volunteer for Angel Flights. At the moment I am building my required hours "in command" by sharing the cost with fellow [employees].

12.5.4 Differences Between CFs and CSR Departments

Examining the document analysis of 20 reports of CFs and 20 reports of CSR departments, we found some interesting difference, although this is not a representative sample. We found that 65% of CFs had a clear focus area for their giving and volunteering, as opposed to only 25% CSR departments. Both CF and CSR were supporting employees in their volunteering endeavors, mostly through paid leave to volunteer and matching/giving funds. Just over half (55%) of CFs mentioned skill-based volunteering compared to 25% of CSR reports. The CFs we studied offered more virtual (online) volunteering opportunities, while CSR departments offered more international volunteering programs. CFs also tended to measure and report on social impact more than CSR.

Different Motivations When discussing the differences between CFs and CSR, CF representatives mainly spoke about different motivations and how they affect actions. According to the interviewees in our study, CSR departments focus on employee engagement and marketing, while CFs are more focused on the community needs:

> What the foundation brings is a purer view toward philanthropy. So, we are creating an impact in society as opposed to "we are doing this to show we are really great brand." CSR people want to do really good, kind of "look at us, we care about our employees, intakes, and so on." I think the value that a corporate foundation adds is that it keeps philanthropy pure (CF1).

More Strategic CSR Another difference that came up in the interviews was around strategic CSR. Based on the above definition (Werther and Chandler 2011), strategic CSR is about adopting a holistic approach that is better aligned with the company's core operations. Based on this study, foundations were more aligned with the mother company's core operations and offered a more strategic CSR and strategic philanthropy. As such, CFs believe they can be more effective and successful:

> I think that foundations can actually be more successful. Definitely ours has been. And I can't specifically talk about others. I think if your organization and its CSR agenda are aligned with what your foundation wants to do and it matches the purpose of the organization then it is better. For us, it doesn't make sense that we are trying to help youth cancer (CF3).

Blurring Boundaries However, some CFs discussed the blurring boundaries between them and CSR departments, as the differences are not so great as they used to be:

> CSR is very much about business and business processes and business needs and so on like that. I think what's happening in the corporate world, especially when corporate foundations being so aligned to the business, it's a bit of blur that's happening between CSR and foundations (CF1).

12.6 Discussion

This chapter explains how CFs enhance personal and corporate volunteering. This study found that CFs, similarly to CSR departments, offer support to employees of the mother company in their efforts to volunteer. They provide paid leave for volunteering and encourage employees to volunteer inside and outside the workplace. CFs seem to focus more on employee-led corporate volunteering rather than employer led, perhaps due to their independence from the mother company (Herlin and Pedersen 2013). Due to their traditional role as grant makers (Anheier 2001), they also offer financial support for employees who want to volunteer, in terms of providing grants to allow employees to start their own initiatives or in matching employee time with dollar donations.

This study allowed us to identify some of the recent shifts and changes that are taking place in CFs when it comes to corporate volunteering. The CF representatives we interviewed discussed a shift toward skill-based volunteering instead of general volunteering. They also spoke about international volunteering aligned with the globalization of the mother company. There is a growing shift of strategic CSR—asking what the mother company is best at as well as what issues it faces in order to decide in which areas to focus (Werther and Chandler 2011). CFs seem to focus more than before and more than CSR departments on measuring impact, although most of them focused on measuring input and activities instead (Haski-Leventhal and Mehra 2016). We further found several motivations of CFs to engage employees in volunteering, and the most common ones were helping the mother company to be a good corporate citizen and employee engagement (Ostrower 2006). This is aligned with the literature on motivation for CSR and corporate volunteering in general, but it shows that although CFs are usually a spate legal entity, they can still be used to engage the employees of the mother company.

When discussing differences between CFs and CSR departments directly with the study participants as well as examining 40 reports, we did not find major differences between them when it comes to volunteering. The differences that were found related to motivation: While CFs were more focused on the community, CSR departments (according to CFs) are more concerned with the company's brand and marketing. It seems that CFs are more focused on strategic CSR than CSR departments, aligning their activities with company's mission, core operations, and related issues.

While this chapter takes a positive approach toward corporate volunteering and therefore sheds light on the role CFs play in promoting it, it is also important to remember that corporate volunteering can have some negative aspects and that promoting it, either through the CF or CSR department, is not always positive. The related costs to the company and the employees as well as the possibility of having a misfit between what the company wants to do and what the nonprofit organizations need can lead to some minor and major issues. While we did not find these negative aspects in this study, we did find that some employees were reluctant to partake in corporate volunteering and that a sense of autonomy is very important to yield the benefits to all stakeholders.

12.7 Contribution to Theory and Further Research

As this was the first study to examine such differences, it contributes to our knowledge on CFs as well as to our knowledge on corporate volunteering. In particular, it contributes to the theory of hybridity, as CFs can be seen as hybrid organizations, somewhere between for-profit and not-for-profit organizations (Doherty et al. 2014). As such, this research is important not only for the understanding of the role CFs play in promoting corporate volunteering but also as it sheds light on the dual purpose of such hybrid organizations. Further research can use institutional theory to further investigate these differences and their implication on theory and practice. We also recommend a large-scale quantitative research to determine the role of CFs in enhancing volunteering and comparisons to CSR departments. In addition, as this study was undertaken in Australia, additional research in other regions is important.

12.8 Implications for Practice

CFs have a vital role to play in enhancing personal and corporate volunteering. To do, they need to understand what the mother company stands for and what the main issues are, in order to offer corporate volunteering opportunities that are strategically aligned. Understanding recent trends in personal and corporate volunteering could help CFs offer better opportunities for employees, including employee-led corporate volunteering, skill-based corporate volunteering, and international and virtual corporate volunteering opportunities.

An important finding of this study that should be of interest to CFs is the shift away from one annual day of corporate volunteering that does not necessarily meet the needs of the nonprofit organizations, employees, and the mother company. Offering flexible and accessible corporate volunteering opportunity all year is a key for increasing employee participation in corporate volunteering. Some CFs that participated in this study also asked for employees' feedback on their corporate volunteering program. Such ongoing communication allows CFs to offer corporate volunteering opportunities that meet the needs of employees. Another important issue is measuring and reporting on social impact back to employees, which could help them understand what the CF is doing and why and what their involvement could help archive.

References

Adloff, F. (2009). What encourages charitable giving and philanthropy? *Ageing and Society, 29*(08), 1185–1205.
Aguilera, R. V. (2007). Putting the S back in corporate social responsibility: A multilevel theory of social change in organizations. *Academy of Management Review, 32*(3), 836–863.
Aguinis, H., & Glavas, A. (2012). What we know and don't know about Corporate Social Responsibility. A review and research agenda. *Journal of Management, 38*(4), 932–968.
Anheier, H. K. (2001). *Foundations in Europe: A comparative perspective*. London: Centre for Civil Society, London School of Economics and Political Science.
Basil, D. Z., & Erlandson, J. (2008). Corporate social responsibility website representations: A longitudinal study of internal and external self-presentations. *Journal of Marketing Communications, 14*(2), 125–137.
Benjamin, E. (2001). A look inside corporate employee volunteer programs. *The Journal of Volunteer Administration, 19*(2), 16–32.
Bowen, G. A. (2009). Document analysis as a qualitative research method. *Qualitative Research Journal, 9*(2), 27–40.

Bronn, P. S. (2009). Corporate motives for social initiative: Legitimacy, sustainability, or the bottom line? *Journal of Business Ethics, 87*(1), 91–109.

Brown, O. H. (2006). Corporate philanthropic practices. *Journal of Corporate Finance, 12*(5), 855–877.

Bussell, H., & Forbes, D. (2008). How UK universities engage with their local communities: A study of employer supported volunteering. *International Journal of Nonprofit and Voluntary Sector Marketing, 13*(4), 363–378.

Carroll, B. (1979). A three-dimensional conceptual model of corporate performance. *Academy of Management Review, 4*(4), 497–505.

Charmaz, K. (2008). Grounded theory as an emergent method. In S. Hesse-Biber & P. Leavy (Eds.), *Handbook of emergent methods* (pp. 155–172). New York: The Guilford Press.

Chong, M. (2009). Employee participation in CSR and corporate identity: Insights from a disaster-response program in the Asia-Pacific. *Corporate Reputation Review, 12*(2), 106–119.

Cnaan, R. A., Handy, F., & Wadsworth, M. (1996). Defining who is a volunteer: Conceptual and empirical considerations. *Nonprofit and Voluntary Sector Quarterly, 25*(3), 364–383.

DiCicco-Bloom, B., & Crabtree, B. F. (2006). The qualitative research interview. *Medical Education, 40*(4), 314–321.

Diprose, K. (2012). Critical distance: Doing development education through international volunteering. *Area, 44*(2), 186–192.

Doherty, B., Haugh, H., & Lyon, F. (2014). Social enterprises as hybrid organizations: A review and research agenda. *International Journal of Management Reviews, 16*(4), 417–436.

Fombrun, C. J. (1990). What's in a name? Reputation building and corporate strategy. *Academy of Management Journal, 33*(2), 233–258.

Grant, A. M. (2012). Giving time, time after time: Work design and sustained employee participation in corporate volunteering. *Academy of Management Review, 37*(4), 589–615.

Griffin, J. P. (2014). Corporate responsibility: Initiatives and mechanisms. *Business & Society, 53*(4), 465–482.

Haski-Leventhal, D. (2018). *Strategic Corporate Social Responsibility: Tools and theories for responsible management*. London: SAGE.

Haski-Leventhal, D., & Mehra, A. (2016). Impact measurement in social enterprises: Australia and India. *Social Enterprise Journal, 12*(1), 78–103.

Haski-Leventhal, D., Meijs, L. C. P. M., & Hustinx, L. (2010). The third-party model: Enhancing volunteering through governments, corporations and educational institutes. *Journal of Social Policy, 39*(01), 139–158.

Haski-Leventhal, D., Roza, L., & Meijs, L. C. (2017). Congruence in corporate social responsibility: Connecting the identity and behavior of employers and employees. *Journal of Business Ethics, 143*(1), 35–51.

Herlin, H., & Pedersen, J. T. (2013). Corporate foundations: Catalysts of NGO-business partnerships? *Journal of Corporate Citizenship, 2013*(50), 58–90.

Kotler, P., & Lee, N. (2005). *Corporate social responsibility: Doing the most good for your company and your cause*. Hoboken: Wiley.

Kramer, M. P. (2006). *Uncommon partners: The power of foundation and corporation collaboration*. Cambridge: John F. Kennedy School of Government, Harvard University.

Lee, L. H., & Higgins, C. (2001). Corporate volunteering: Ad hoc interaction or route to dialogue and partnership? *Journal of Corporate Citizenship, 1*(4), 79–90.

Marquis, C. G. (2007). Community isomorphism and corporate social action. *Academy of Management Review, 32*(3), 925–945.

Mirvis, P. (2012). Employee engagement and CSR: Transactional, relational, developmental approaches. *California Management Review, 54*(4), 93–117.

Muthuri, J. M. (2009). Employee volunteering and social capital: Contributions to Corporate Social Responsibility. *British Journal of Management, 20*(1), 75–89.

O'Mahony, S. A. (2008). Boundary organizations: Enabling collaboration among unexpected allies. *Administrative Science Quarterly, 53*(3), 422–549.

Ostrower, F. (2006). Foundation approaches to effectiveness: A typology. *Nonprofit and Voluntary Sector Quarterly, 35*(3), 510–516.
Petrovits, C. M. (2006). Corporate-sponsored foundations and earnings management. *Journal of Accounting and Economics, 41*, 335–362.
Plewa, C. C. (2015). The impact of corporate volunteering on CSR image: A consumer perspective. *Journal of Business Ethics, 127*(3), 643–659.
Ricks, J. A. (2005). Strategic corporate philanthropy: Addressing frontline talent needs through an educational giving program. *Journal of Business Ethics, 60*(2), 147–157.
Rodell, J. B. (2013). Finding meaning through volunteering: Why do employees volunteer and what does it mean for their jobs? *Academy of Management Journal, 56*(5), 1274–1294.
Rodell, J. B. (2015). Employee volunteering: A review and framework for future research. *Journal of Management, 42*(1), 55–84.
Sharma, S. H. (2005). Stakeholder influences on sustainability practices in the Canadian forest products industry. *Strategic Management Journal, 26*, 159–180.
Sprinkle, G. B., & Maines, L. A. (2010). The benefits and costs of corporate social responsibility. *Business Horizons, 53*(5), 445–453.
Strauss, A., & Corbin, J. (1994). *Grounded theory methodology: Handbook of qualitative research*. Thousand Oaks: SAGE Publications.
van der Voort, J. G. (2009). Managing corporate community involvement. *Journal of Business Ethics, 90*(3), 311–329.
von Schnurbein, G. (2009). Foundations as honest brokers between market, state, and nonprofits through building social capital. *European Management Journal, 28*(6), 413–420.
Wainwright, C. (2005). Building the case for corporate volunteering. Retrieved 7.12.16 from: http://www.volunteering.com.au/wp-content/uploads/2016/01/The-Business-Case-for-Corporate-Volunteering.pdf
Werther, W. B., & Chandler, D. (2011). *Strategic corporate social responsibility: Stakeholders in a global environment*. London: Sage Publications Ltd.
Westhues, M., & Einwiller, S. (2006). Corporate foundations: Their role for corporate social responsibility. *Corporate Reputation Review, 9*(2), 144–153.
Wilson, J. (2000). Volunteering. *Annual Review of Sociology, 26*, 215–240.
Wilson, J. (2012). Volunteerism research: A review essay. *Nonprofit and Voluntary Sector Quarterly, 41*(2), 176–212.

Debbie Haski-Leventhal (Ph.D., Hebrew University) is an Professor in Management and the Program Director of the Master of Social Entrepreneurship at Macquarie University, Australia. She has published widely on volunteering and corporate social responsibility and cowrote the United Nations State of the World Volunteerism Report. Her work has been published in *Human Relations, Journal of Business Ethics, Nonprofit and Voluntary Sector Quarterly (NVSQ)*, and *Voluntas: International Journal of Voluntary and Nonprofit Organizations*.

Chapter 13
Revisiting the Political Nature of Corporate Philanthropic Foundations: The Case of Sweden

Johan Hvenmark and Johan von Essen

Abstract Almost a decade ago, it was argued that scholarly knowledge largely overlooked the political nature of foundations in favor of issues related to legislation, board composition, management, and societal contributions. As this argument still seems to apply, the aim of this chapter is to explore the political nature of corporate foundations (CFs). To meet this aim, this chapter draws out the contours of an emergent social imaginary concerning welfare provision from the outlook of CFs. The analysis builds on both survey data regarding CFs in Sweden and interviews with representatives from four different Swedish CFs, concerning the interlock between organizational visions and perceived contributions to welfare in this national context. A main conclusion in the chapter relates to the intermediary position of these organizations as they straddle the boundaries of corporate contexts and a public welfare system where they have a potential to influence both these worlds simultaneously, by carrying norms, values, and practices between them. It is also here that parts of the political significance of CFs can be found—both as expressions and containers of an emergent political vision of welfare in society.

Keywords Political significance · Corporate foundations · Welfare state · Intermediary position

13.1 Introduction

Almost a decade ago, it was argued that scholarly knowledge largely overlooked the political nature of foundations in favor of issues related to legislation, board composition, management, and their contributions in society (Anheier and Daly 2007a). This argument, which still seems to apply, constitutes a crucial backdrop for this chapter, where the aim is to explore the political nature of corporate philanthropic

---

J. Hvenmark · J. von Essen (✉)
Ersta Sköndal Bräcke University College, Stockholm, Sweden
e-mail: johan.hvenmark@esh.se; johan.von-essen@esh.se

foundations.[1] To meet this aim, we are below studying the contours of an emergent social imaginary concerning the provision of welfare in Swedish society from the outlook of CFs.

The chapter includes survey data regarding Swedish CFs and an analysis of interviews with CF representatives concerning the interlock between visions of these CFs and their perceived contribution to welfare in society. The empirical work and the analysis presented below are guided by the following questions: Why do corporations behind CFs choose foundation as the organizational form? How do CF representatives perceive the relation between their organization and the founding corporation, and how do they describe the relation between their organizations and the public welfare system? Finally, how do their visions of welfare provision look like, and how do they think the responsibility for providing welfare ought to be distributed in society?

Sweden appears to be a relevant context for the exploration of the political nature of CFs since the social contract, which for larger parts of the twentieth century has dictated rules and understandings in Sweden regarding the provision of welfare, seems to be changing (Trägårdh 2012). A change largely set in motion as neoliberalism entered the Swedish scene in the late 1980s, which brought with it everything from privatizations and contracting out of welfare services to an increased faith in market solutions, social entrepreneurship, and CSR initiatives (Hartman 2011; Hvenmark 2013; Svedberg and Olsson 2010). Parallel to this change and at odds with earlier dominating conceptions, foundations seem to become more visible, influential, and accepted as they gain an increased legitimacy in Sweden (Wijkström 2007). Yet, although Swedish CFs have attracted attention before (cf. Wijkström and Einarsson 2004), our knowledge regarding this particular type of foundation in relation to social issues and the provision of welfare services seems scarce.

13.2 Analytical Framework

The modern Swedish society was heralded by the popular movements during the latter part of nineteenth century and then realized by the social democratic political vision of "the strong society" in the early 1930s (cf. Ekström von Essen 2003). This political vision influenced Swedish society throughout the postwar period due to the long rule of the social democrat party. Welfare and social care became in this period a social right and a responsibility of the state and its public sector, which among many things implied an expanding engagement in and increased professionalization of social work. For this reason, volunteering for social causes and charity associations decreased as it was considered not only paternalistic and immoral but also outmoded, unscientific, and amateurish.

---

[1] Instead of the term "corporate philanthropic foundation," we will henceforth use the term "corporate foundation" (CF) to be congruent with the other chapters in this edited volume. However, we will restrain our discussion to corporate foundations acting as providers of welfare.

Sweden is still largely influenced by this modernist vision of society with the welfare state and the social democratic civil society regime as its cornerstones. But, since the 1980s, it has been challenged by competing political visions (cf. Reuter et al. 2012) that, among many things, promote welfare provision by actors outside the public welfare system. This (re)hybridization process (Wijkström 2011), which also affected Swedish civil society and nurtured the return of charity associations, has opened up an increased and polemic debate over the future of both the welfare state and civil society in Sweden. Here, between the traditional social contract and new critical political visions is where there currently seem to exist a space where CFs and the political visions related to them can emerge and develop.

13.2.1 Foundations in Sweden

Alluding to Nielsen (1972), foundations can be described as a strange and contested political creature in the Swedish social landscape, and their existence has been questioned. This skeptical stance toward foundations can be related to the popular mass movement mentioned above (cf. Lundström and Svedberg 2003; Hvenmark and Wijkström 2004), according to which open and democratic member-based associations constitute the role model for how interests and services ought to be organized (Hvenmark 2008). Another reason relates to the fact that the state and the public sectors, for well over a century, have dominated the provision of welfare in Sweden (cf. Sivesind 2016). This hegemonic situation has left little or no room for foundations to participate. These two reasons have contributed to characterizations of the Swedish civil society as a social democratic regime, implying that social care and welfare services are more peripheral than in other civil society models (Salamon and Anheier 1996).

Despite earlier estimates, it remains unclear how many foundations exist in Sweden. One of the few and more comprehensive surveys concludes that Sweden, in the early 2000s, had somewhere between 35.000 and 45.000 foundations, of which the large majority (20.000 or 30.000) were small with reference to the capital they managed (Wijkström and Einarsson 2004). The knowledge of this numerous group of smaller foundations is scarce, but the reverse applies for the approximately 15.000 foundations holding more substantial resources and that largely seems to be "/.../ embedded in a social-democratic vision" (Wijkström 2007: 290).

As the existence of foundations depends on economic surplus, it follows the argument that the bigger the foundation, the more likely it has been set up by an actor disposing of larger amounts of accumulated monetary resources (cf. Wijkström 2007). This seems to apply particularly well to a more detailed analysis of the most capital-heavy Swedish foundations, among which some 4.700 can be categorized as being government related as they have been established by public sector actors at national or municipal levels (Wijkström and Einarsson 2004)—an expected finding (ibid.) considering the fact that actors in the Swedish public sector presumably have been able to accumulate substantial resources within the high-tax regime that formed Sweden's welfare system during the latter half of the twentieth century. While about 6.000 of these wealthy foundations could be categorized as either independent or civic related, there were only about 450 that could be related to a corporate context (ibid.). An explanation to the difference in numbers, compared to the survey presented in this chapter, is that in comparison with definitions Wijkström and Einarsson (ibid.: 26ff) elaborate upon, we are applying a much narrower and more specific definition of corporate-related foundations engaged in providing welfare.

13.2.2 Defining Corporate Philanthropic Foundations

Our understanding of CFs relates to a commonly applied criterion that a foundation exists when property or an asset is formally set aside from a donor so that it can be administered separately and permanently with the explicit purpose to serve one or several specific goals defined by the donor (cf. Wijkström 2007). This basic criterion defines foundations in general. Yet, in order to distinguish the type of foundations, we add additional three criteria. First, CFs stem from initiatives and assets related to one or several corporate contexts, which do not have to be Swedish as long as the CF in question has its base and main operations in Sweden. Second, we only include CFs pursuing goals serving a greater good and whose activities serve broader citizen groups rather than narrow stakeholder groups, such as current or former employees of the founding corporation(s). Third, CFs must have operations relating to one or several of the core domains of the Swedish welfare system (education, healthcare, social care). This latter criterion does not imply that we discriminate between CFs that have set up proper operations from those dedicated to raising and distributing funds for a particular cause or organization. In fact, most of the CFs in our survey tend to do both.

13.2.3 The Political Nature of CFs

As the core of our analysis includes an interest for the ideological underpinnings of foundations' existence and participation in society, our perception of the meaning of "political" goes beyond more common understandings, which often refer to institutionalized politics and politicians, public policy, or party politics (Sörbom 2010). That is, foundations pursue a variety of visions and fulfill various roles in society as they engage in a wide range of charitable and philanthropic activities ranging from preservation of traditions and social values, redistribution of private wealth to underprivileged, and provision of public or quasi-public goods that substitute or complement state actions to driving social change and innovations (Anheier and Daly 2007a). All of this tends to relate to government initiatives or party politics but also beyond, since foundations also may provoke discussions in media, influence public opinions, and cause societal conflicts.

Moreover, we argue that the political character of CFs emerges as soon as corporate representatives decide to set aside monetary resources with the intention to create a foundation aimed at dealing with specific social issues or serving certain citizen groups. Hence, the sheer act of establishing a CF is a political act (see Himmelstein [1997] for a similar argument regarding corporate philanthropy more generally). This political act is then transformed into a political character of the established CF as it, with a privately anchored agenda and nontransparent feature toward external control, engages in the larger society by, for example, serving or granting funds to needy people or lobbying for specific issues or social causes (Karl and Katz 1987; Anheier and Toepler 1999). Or put differently, the creation of CFs and the way in which they are composed and how they are perceived in society constitute crucial aspects of their political character since this is what determines whether they will be able to enact a founder's will beyond any type of democratic control, in a given public realm.

It has, furthermore, been argued that the political nature of foundations in general is inevitably associated with an independence from "…market forces, the ballot box and outside stakeholders" (Anheier and Daly 2007b: 4). Put differently, the independence of foundations relates to how legitimate they appear in a given context. This legitimacy is also what determines the political space in which they are allowed to exist and act. Consequently, the ample space foundations tend to be given in many contemporary welfare community suggests that they also enjoy a great amount of legitimacy and a far-reaching independence (cf. Anheier and Leat 2006). Yet this independence can neither be taken for granted nor regarded as complete, since it will differ over time and between contexts due to prevailing societal visions, roles, and expected contributions emanating from an even greater "…dependence of other institutional forms such as the public agency or the private business firm" (Anheier and Daly 2007b: 4).

13.3 Methodology and Empirical Material

13.3.1 Selection of Foundations

Since no records exist regarding Swedish CFs, we have conducted a survey of relevant foundations. For this, we used the registers of the Swedish County Administration Boards where data regarding names, purposes, amount of capital and location of Swedish foundations are available online (http://web05.lans-styrelsen.se/stift). This register can be searched by an entry of freely chosen words, and we applied "corporation," "philanthropy," and "charity," which gave a total of 614 entries. Discussions with the Swedish County Administration Boards validated that our search was correctly executed. A preliminary screening indicated that very few of these entries would meet our three criteria mentioned above. A second and more rigorous review resulted in a list of 34 entries matching our definition and criteria.

We also conducted Google searches applying "Swedish," "business," "corporation," "foundation," "corporate foundation," "philanthropy," and "charity" together with a search of a register over civil society organizations dedicated to fundraising (www.insamlingskontroll.se). Since neither of these measures gave anything further, we have found a total of 34 Swedish CFs, which indicates that this is not only a rare type of foundation but also a rare type of organization in Sweden. None of these CFs were older than 30 years, and most had been founded during the last two decades. This may indicate a connection with the societal and political changes of that era.

13.3.2 Four Corporate Philanthropic Foundations

In order to meet our aim, we adopted a case study approach (cf. Yin 2014). For the selection of case organizations, it was crucial that they disposed of a capital exceeding € 10 million since this ought to imply substantial yearly dividends, fairly extensive operations, and a potential to have a societal impact. We also selected case organizations that differed with respect to operations, background, age, and scope in order to see if the organizational context would affect the way in which social imaginaries were expressed. This led us to select four case organizations out of the 34 CFs found in our survey. Apart from the conducted interviews, we also gathered and analyzed formal documentation, such as annual reports, charters, policies, and historical descriptions, from these foundations' web pages. The following is a brief presentation of the four selected CFs:

Ronald McDonald Children's Foundation in Sweden This foundation aims at making life easier for families with seriously ill and hospitalized children. This is achieved through playrooms at pediatric clinics and so-called Ronald McDonald Houses, allowing families to stay close to a hospital in a homelike environment. The foundation was created in 1990 on the initiative of the first CEO of McDonald's Sweden, who lost a daughter to cystic fibrosis. During his daughter's prolonged hospital stays, the idea of the foundation was initiated. McDonald's Sweden continues to be the largest financier of the foundation.

The H&M Foundation With its 60th anniversary in 2007, the board of the global clothing company H&M decided to set aside 60 million SEK to start the H&M Foundation. A few years later, the foundation had received further endowments of over €100 million from the founding family and majority owner of the H&M company. The foundation aims at achieving social change and improved living conditions for people in Sweden, Romania, USA, India, and Myanmar, and it operates by partnering with local actors on issues related to education, clean water, and equality.

Ideas for Life (Idéer för Livet) In 1987, the CEO of the Swedish insurance company Skandia established Ideas for Life as a response to increased social tensions. By distributing grants and scholarships, this foundation aims at contributing to dignified living conditions and a safer, socially sustainable society by preventing ill health and exclusion among younger generations. It supports local projects, developments of methods to estimate societal costs, and research. While most of its financial resources stem from the original endowment, the founding corporation helps out carrying administrative costs and expenses of the foundation.

The Swedish Postcode Foundation The Swedish Postcode Lottery Foundation, which was founded in 2005 by the Swedish Postcode Lottery, puts the improvement of society and protection of the environment at the center of attention. It supports charitable projects and organizations in both Sweden and elsewhere. Central to its work is the distribution of lottery surplus from the Swedish Postcode Lottery to local and countrywide charitable initiatives and organizations for issues such as antidiscrimination, integration, inclusion, and education.

13.3.3 Interview Questions

For our purposes, we conducted semi-structured interviews with seven key persons in the four case organizations around the following thematic issues: Why did the corporations behind the CFs choose foundation as the organizational form? How can the relationship between the CFs and their founding corporations be described? How do the existence and operations of the CFs relate to the surrounding public welfare system? How and to what extent are the CFs responsible for securing and providing welfare in society? Our analysis of how the interviewees elaborated on these issues will unfold the contours of an emergent social imaginary concerning CFs and their role in the Swedish welfare system.

13.4 Empirical Accounts

13.4.1 A Natural but Still Unexpected Choice of Form

Why the founding corporations had opted for the foundation as the organizational form we cannot tell for sure since the interviewees expressed uncertainty in this respect. Yet, when explicitly asked to speculate, some concluded that this probably had to do with traditions different from the prevailing Swedish civil society tradition. One interviewee from Ronald McDonald House stated that since its cultural linkages to the US and an Anglo-Saxon charity tradition always had organized its activities in the form of foundations, it was probably natural to also do that in Sweden. Another interviewee, with vast experiences from Ideas for Life and its founding company, Skandia, said that a foundation was the obvious choice, since Skandia earlier had formed foundations for other activities. Hence, with the decision to formalize a social engagement on behalf of McDonald, as well as Skandia, the interviewees concluded that the foundation appeared as a default choice.

Answers imply that traditions and habits were the decisions driving the companies to initiate a corporate foundation, wanting to deal with social issues. If Sweden's prevailing civic tradition had influenced these choices, the obvious form would probably had been the membership-based association. But as the initiatives came from the business sphere, traditions or taken-for-granted rationales other than this tradition seem to take effect as civic organizations obviously at odds with the ruling organizational ideals are created.

Despite the interviewee's uncertainty regarding underlying reasons for why their respective organization had been given in the form of a foundation, they were rather clear about advantages of this form. A recurrent argument in this respect was that being organized as a foundation renders the organization and its activities a distinctive character and a clear identity. One manager in Ideas for Life elaborated upon this as she discussed the background of this foundation:

> …the fact that it is a foundation implies a proper identity and that one also has to be loyal to its charters and its mission and role in society.

She expanded upon this distinctiveness by emphasizing the importance of being able to distinguish what the foundation stands for and does, from a commercial logic viewpoint and the operations of the founding corporation. A manager at a local Ronald McDonald House argued along similar lines as she claimed that it must be clear to everyone that the foundation in question is not there to make profits at the same time as its operations need to be controlled by public authorities.

In order to appear trustworthy and legitimate, according to the interviewees, it is essential that their foundations are perceived as noncommercial organizations that act independently from their founding corporation. Moreover, when the interviewees were asked to elaborate on the reasons behind the decisions to establish foundations, it is possible to also start discerning how they perceive the societal role of their respective foundation. As CFs originate in the business sphere, they are also primarily modeled upon corporate traditions. At the same time, this choice clarifies that the foundation is not the same thing as its founding corporation, a separation that seems essential as the interviewees also claim that these foundations need to be associated with something other than the commercial logic of the business sphere. CFs are hereby given a potential role of existing and acting in between the business sphere and the public welfare system.

13.4.2 An Ambiguous Relation Between the Creator and the Created

The interviewees emphasized the importance of establishing and maintaining an institutional and physical distance between the foundation and its founding corporation in order to avoid that the latter could use the foundation for its own marketing and sponsor purposes or for more "general charity activities," as one put it. Several interviewees also described this distance as a sort of protection from being affected by cutbacks if the founding corporations were facing economic or other problems.

A few interviewees also talked about the importance of being independent and autonomous vis-a-vis its founding corporation as a way of guaranteeing efficiency and an ability to be close and faithful to the needs of the foundation's own beneficiaries and stakeholders.

When the interviewees talked about differences between their foundations and the founding corporations, they recurrently referred to each organization's mission, strategy, and inner logic. Upholding these differences was also pronounced in descriptions of everyday relations between these foundations and their founding corporations. Several interviewees pointed out that since their foundations are compelled to follow their own organizational logic and mission to provide welfare, it is very important that their managers and board members communicate the foundation's specific mission and nature to its founding corporation. Maintaining a formal distinction between these foundations and their founding corporations was put forth to distinguish between the corporation's responsibility to make profit and the foundation's responsibility to provide welfare.

Parallel to this, the interviewees also talked about the close and often informal relations with the founding corporation. For example, while the managers and board members in Ideas for Life and the managers in Ronald McDonald House were or had previously been employed in the respective founding corporation, they had also been able to maintain good informal relations with staff and former colleagues in these organizations. These and other examples of informal relations and mixed roles can be understood as creating a certain flexibility but also dependency and potential requests for solidarity with the founding corporation. Obviously, this type of dependency stands in stark contrast to the earlier mentioned importance of being independent of and separate from the founding corporation. This ambiguity becomes even more complex as the interviewees also talked about how important the resources are, coming from the corporation. One board member in Ideas for Life touched upon this in a discussion on how resources tend to be related to dependency and expectations of loyalty. When the interviewees talked about resources coming from the founding corporation, they were also talking about their foundations' potential dependency on their founding corporations.

Moreover, while the foundations can make use of networks, knowledge, finances, goodwill, etc., from the corporations, they can potentially also operate more efficiently and successfully. In this sense, the interviewees were talking about the operations of the founding corporation as an asset per se. A manager in Ideas for Life recalled that Skandia is one of the most important house-owner in Sweden, which gives the corporation both incentives and knowledge to act against social unrest in housing areas. This is an example of how the operations of the corporation can be used as resources available for the foundation, making it a more efficient and credible welfare provider. However, resources go in both directions; when the foundation acts in the same area as the corporation, it can be used as a resource by the corporation. A manager in the H&M Foundation explains that the foundation's engagement in improving work conditions within the clothing industry constitutes a resource for the H&M, as it can benefit commercially from the goodwill and knowledge this renders.

In sum, there exists an ambiguous relation between these CFs and their founding corporations as the interviewees describe how their foundations are being both independent from and dependent on their founding corporations. On the one hand, there is an emphasis on the importance of being independent in order to maintain a clear identity, appear legitimate, and be able to fulfill one's mission. On the other, there is an emphasis on how one may benefit through close personal relations and exchanges of knowledge, goodwill, and resources. These benefits may, after all, also come with expectations of solidarity, loyalty, and dependency.

13.4.3 Supplement to Public Welfare

When elaborating on relations to public welfare, an all-pervading theme was the claim that the interviewees did not want their organizations to compete with, challenge, or replace the public welfare system. This opinion is not unique for individuals engaged in CFs. The reluctance to challenge the welfare state and the public welfare system is in fact recurrent in Sweden and other Nordic countries (von Essen et al. forthcoming). The welfare state tradition and the public welfare system appeared as a necessary condition for how the interviewees defined the societal role of their foundations as providers of welfare. Hence, the missions and purposes they attributed for themselves depended on how they conceived the logics and limits of the public welfare system. According to the interviewees, these foundations are supposed to handle social needs beyond the limits of the public welfare system. By doing this, they expressed a common outlook of society in Sweden, which implies that non-state organizations are legitimate as welfare providers, as long as they act outside the scope of the welfare state (cf. Vamstad and von Essen 2013).

With a point of departure in organizational mission, a manager in a local Ronald McDonald House stated the difference between professional hospitals and their own foundations by stating that "… our focus is on the families and the children, whereas hospitals have their focus on the sick children." The global manager in the H&M Foundation had another approach as she declared that this foundation's role was not to interfere with education or medical care but to meet needs related to people's leisure time. Hence, home and leisure time, which often are beyond the limits of the public welfare system, are perceived by these foundations as legitimate social spaces where they can provide welfare.

Other areas and possibilities where these CFs appear able to operate beyond the limits of the public welfare system relate to states of emergency or sudden and unexpected social challenges. For example, some of the interviewees related to the great influx of refugees that evoked challenges for Swedish society during the fall of 2015. Since the public welfare system could not handle this extraordinary situation, it opened up an arena where some of these foundations and other Swedish civil society organizations were able to contribute by providing shelters, food, and comfort. The manager of the Swedish postcode foundation recalled, for example, how they supported organizations that offered medical aid to refugees without legal documents—a task for which the Swedish public welfare system did not assume responsibility. Thus, sudden and acute social needs emerging from extraordinary situations such as the one described above may imply possibilities for both CFs and other civil society organizations to act as legitimate providers of welfare.

Another way in which the interviewees described how these CFs could assume a role in the welfare area is related to the competence and expertise these organizations dispose of due to close linkages with commercial corporations. For example, both the manager and the board members in Ideas for Life referred to the knowledge and information regarding social issues and social unrest they can access, because of a tight relationship with the founding assurance company Skandia. And along similar lines, one board member recount that Skandia has set aside resources for financing academic research aimed at providing Ideas for Life with data on which the foundation can base its decisions regarding the initiation of projects that will give it a leading position in relation to other actors in the Swedish welfare system. Finally, by having access to resources, Ideas for Life can take the role of an avant-garde and initiate and develop ideas and practices that can be transferred and used by the public welfare system. The board member argued that the foundations' origin from an entrepreneurial environment is crucial for its ability to find and test new practices and roles. Here it is, once again, possible to discern how important it appears to be for these CFs to remain both distanced from their founding corporations in order to maintain a proper identity and appear trustworthy and, at the same time, close to be able to access vital knowledge and resources. Regardless of how complex or difficult this situation maybe, we would like to propose that it is precisely this simultaneous proximity and distance that make these CFs appear legitimate providers of welfare.

Moreover, while the interviewees all agreed that the CFs they represented were not aimed at challenging or replacing the current public welfare system, several expressed a belief that the importance of this particular type of foundations would increase as the Swedish public welfare system would not be able to meet future social needs. Others talked about a new approach among CFs and corporations toward becoming more of welfare providers. Some years ago, some claimed CSR activities and initiated social projects were more linked to business strategies as corporations and their foundations tended to compete with each other over being visible and gaining as much PR as possible. For example, according to the global manager at the H&M Foundation, this approach was now changing so that different actors in the business sector were willing to work more together as they strived to contribute to society.

13.4.4 Who Should Be Responsible for Providing Welfare?

From earlier statements that their CFs were not intended to challenge or replace the current public welfare system, several interviewees stated that it is the politicians who should be responsible for welfare provision in society. This is, for example, how a manager in Ronald McDonald children's foundation put it:

> The foundations should not take the main responsibility [for welfare], but the politicians ought to. This has to be handled at the level of politics.

Yet from how the interviewees talked about the role of politicians and politics in this respect, they did not seem to perceive the issue of how responsibility for welfare is distributed in society, to be a topic with political connotations. Instead, most interviewees seemed to consider welfare to be an issue dependent on efficiency and resources, not political ideologies or discussions on justice and equality. A board member in Ideas for Life stated that although the board explicitly never had discussed how welfare ought to be distributed on the level of society, some members had at times expressed a center, right wing, or a social democrat position in this respect. He continued stating that while this kind of political positions and perspectives largely were left aside, discussions and decisions were instead generally approached with a practical and issue-focused attitude. This seemingly apolitical attitude toward the distribution of responsibility for welfare in society and to approach such topics more in terms of finding the right technical solution or assigning resources for welfare provision to the most efficient actor reflects a broader trend of making society more "caring" and "responsible." Civil society is generally held to be the ideal of such a caring society (e.g., Garrow and Hasenfeld 2014; Grubb 2016), while actors in the business sphere more are expected to behave in a responsible manner toward society (e.g., Shamir 2008). Such a moralization of the business sphere and the depoliticization of civil society organizations are present in the way these interviewees refer to politics, politicians, and responsibility for welfare in society (cf. Sachar 2017).

However, politics, politicians, and public bureaucracy were not put forth as completely neutral or anonymous by the interviewees, as they discussed the main obstacles for these CFs, to be able to act as welfare providers. Even if the interviewees expressed a mission for their CFs beyond the scope of the public welfare system, they were also aware of the fact that this could imply a simultaneous dependency on that system. An example of this is the manager for the Ronald McDonald fund who was troubled by a high rate of cancelled or postponed operations at hospitals which made it almost impossible for them to plan and offer decent stays for families and their sick children. Furthermore, some of the interviewees were critical toward the public debate where private and especially commercial welfare providers regularly got rejected or condemned for not being part of the public welfare system. In this respect, the interviewees argued that professionalism and efficiency for the good of the beneficiaries must be more important than organizational form. Hence, they underscored the importance of what is being done rather than the form or position of the organization's position toward welfare in society (cf. Eliasoph 2011).

Since several interviewees expressed criticism toward commercial interests in the welfare system, it is important to note that the abovementioned critique toward the public welfare system should not necessarily be understood as an argument in favor of profit-seeking welfare providers. What they seemed to promote instead resembles more of a mixed economy of welfare, in which efficient and competent commercial actors are also allowed to participate and take responsibility for the provision of welfare (cf. Evers 1995). In this respect, the interviewees stated that if we are to handle both current and future social needs in society, it is not enough with organizations from the public sector alone. It is, instead, necessary that organizations from all societal sectors are allowed to participate and collaborate.

13.5 Summary and Discussion

From our aim to revisit the political nature of CFs, we have explored an emergent social imagery, concerning the provision of welfare from the outlook of CFs. To do this, Sweden has been deemed to serve as a suitable example due to the historical development of its welfare system and prevailing civil society tradition, which assumingly help clarify the political nature of CFs as they, to some extent, historically have been at odds with both Sweden's welfare system and normative ideals of how to organize civil society activities. A survey of Swedish CFs contributed to this assumption, partly because this type of organization seems rare in Sweden and partly because most of the 34 CFs that were found had been established rather recently and in parallel with the arrival of neoliberalism and its impact on both Sweden's welfare system and civil society tradition.

Further in-depth interviews with managers and board members representing four case organizations demonstrate how the political nature of CFs relates to a dual and ambiguous situation, where they are caught between a concurrent independence and dependence in relation to institutionalized politics, the business sphere, and the public welfare system. This is in line with earlier observations regarding the role of foundations (Anheier and Daly 2007a; Wijkström 2007). These interviewees described the operations of their respective organization in terms of complementing rather than supplementing the public welfare system. At the same time, they also emphasized how important it is for their organizations to remain independent not only vis-a-vis their founding corporation(s) but also in relation to the Swedish welfare state and its public sector. We argue that this somewhat unobtrusive role of being a complement relates to the political nature of the CFs since it corresponds to the political space they are given and in which they appear legitimate and may enjoy a certain amount of independence, allowing them to exist and operate (Anheier and Daly 2007b).

Yet the flip side of this independence involves an interesting duality or ambiguity, which Anheier and Daly (ibid.) touch upon as they assert that the independence of foundations always is contextually contingent and thereby neither total nor eternal, since these organizations are dependent on visions and expectations expressed by politicians or corporate agendas. The interviewees were clear on this point as they stated that in order for the CFs to function properly, they are also dependent on good informal relations with their founding corporation(s) and the resources they can provide. Taken together, this creates a situation in which CFs supposedly only may appear as legitimate welfare providers as long as they are perceived as being independent vis-a-vis a corporate world, on which they also are dependent on in order to function properly. In short, the nexus between CFs, on the one hand, and their founding corporation(s) and the business environment surrounding them, on the other, is characterized by a simultaneous duality and a certain amount of ambiguity.

Even the nexus between CFs and the public welfare system seems to be characterized by a similar duality and ambiguity. In line with the perceived complementing role of CFs, the interviewees unanimously declared that the organizations they represented in no way challenge the welfare state or the public welfare system. Yet as foundations belonging to the Swedish civil society, these CFs can partly be seen as operating independent from larger political decisions concerning welfare, which potentially makes it easier for them to choose how to operate and which may make them more efficient than many actors in the public welfare system. However, to appear legitimate providers of welfare, they seem compelled to occupy a position where they are filling gaps and mending cracks on the fringes of a public welfare system, their raison d'etre rests. Again, a dual and ambiguous situation in which independence and legitimacy only can be maintained through negotiations and cautious acting does not challenge the dominating public welfare system. Along these lines, we also argue that CFs are potentially given an intermediary character as they may help transfer norms, values, ideals, rationalities, and practices between these two institutional domains (cf. Wijkström 2017). By adopting techniques and knowledge from the corporate world, at the same time as they operate in the welfare system, they may contribute to a sort of depoliticization of welfare as ideological positions on justice and political decisions may be turned into matters of optimizing efficiency and common sense. And as CFs engage in social issues and provide welfare to the general public, they may imply a potential to contribute to a moralization of the corporate world as these organizations in a longer run may influence corporations to instill social values into their operations and thereby become more caring and responsible actors in society.

This intermediate position of CFs implies an increased political significance as they imply a political vision concerning the distribution of responsibility for welfare in Swedish society that challenges the prevailing welfare state tradition. As CFs can be viewed as expressions of this political vision, it may not come as a surprise that managers and board members in CFs envisage that the business sphere in the future will become more moral and less profit seeking and that ideologies and politicians will become more and more obsolete in relation to the provision of welfare in society.

Furthermore, we argue that it is not a coincidence that it is the CFs that fulfill this intermediate role. There are, of course, other organizations in civil society trying to combine the efficiency of the business sphere with the moral legitimacy of civil society (e.g., Åberg 2012). However, as corporations are founders of CFs and since the foundation seems to be the default organizational form in the business sphere, it is at odds with the traditional view that they influence the business sphere. They are, at the same time, maybe also freer to act as welfare providers in Swedish society since they are independent civic organizations that also are distinct from corporations. If our assertion is accurate, it is not the limited number of CFs that is crucial; it is rather their role as expressions but also containers of an emergent political vision of welfare in society that render them political significance (compare with, e.g., Himmelstein 1997 and his view of corporate philanthropy). In their operations, they naturalize the idea that welfare is not a political but technical issue and that the business sphere has a responsibility for society (Hilgers 2010).

In conclusion, our main contribution is an improved conceptual understanding regarding the political nature of CFs, a type of organization we know relatively little about. We are here especially thinking of the intermediate position these organizations seem to occupy as they straddle the boundaries of corporate contexts and a public welfare system with the obvious potential they hereby have to influence both these worlds by carrying norms, values, and practices between them. With respect to the future, we hope that these results will encourage scholars interested in corporate, civil society, or welfare state contexts to pose further inquiries regarding CFs and their activities. One question that begs for further scholarly work concerns the legitimacy, political character, and societal role of CFs in different welfare regimes. Along similar lines, it would also be interesting to extend the kind of analysis presented above to CFs in Sweden and elsewhere, whose activities either only involves an engagement for political issues or go beyond the provision of welfare as they engage in politics.

References

Åberg, P. (2012). Managing expectations, demands and myths: Swedish study associations caught between civil society, state and market. *VOLUNTAS: International Journal of Voluntary and Nonprofit Organizations, 24*(3), 537–558.

Anheier, H. K., & Daly, S. (Eds.). (2007a). *The politics of foundations: A comparative analysis*. London: Routledge.

Anheier, H. K., & Daly, S. (2007b). Philanthropic foundations in modern society. In H. Anheier & S. Daly (Eds.), *The politics of foundations: A comparative analysis*. London: Routledge.

Anheier, H. K., & Leat, D. (2006). *Creative philanthropy: Towards a new philanthropy for the 21st century*. London/New York: Routledge.

Anheier, H. K., & Toepler, S. (Eds.). (1999). *Private funds and public purpose: Philanthropic foundations in international perspectives*. New York: Plenum Publishers.

Ekström von Essen, U. (2003). *Folkhemmets kommun: Socialdemokratiska idéer om lokalsamhället 1939–1952*. Stockholm: Stockholm University.

Eliasoph, N. (2011). *Making volunteers. Civic life after welfare's end*. Princeton: Princeton University Press.

Evers, A. (1995). Part of the welfare mix: The third sector as an intermediate area. *VOLUNTAS: International Journal of Voluntary and Nonprofit Organizations, 6*(2), 159–182.

Garrow, E., & Hasenfeld, Y. (2014). Social enterprises as an embodiment of a neoliberal welfare logic. *American Behavioral Scientist, 58*(11), 1475–1493.

Grubb, A. (2016). *"Vi skal bare hjælpe og spise chokoladekiks" – En kvalitativ undersøgelse af unge frivilliges deltagelse i en ikke-medlemsbaseret, digitalt koordineret organiseringsform af frivilligt socialt arbejde*. Aalborg: Aalborg University.

Hartman, L. (Ed.). (2011). *Konkurrensens konsekvenser. Vad händer med svensk välfärd?* Stockholm: SNS Förlag.

Hilgers, M. (2010). The three anthropological approaches to neoliberalism. *International Social Science Journal, 61*(202), 351–364.

Himmelstein, J. L. (1997). *Doing good and looking good: Corporate philanthropy and Business Power*. Bloomington, Ind.: Indiana University Press.

Hvenmark, J. (2008). *Reconsidering membership: A study of individual members' formal affiliation with democratically governed federations*. Stockholm: EFI.

Hvenmark, J. (2013). Business as usual? On managerialization and the adoption of the balanced scorecard in a democratically governed civil society organization. *Administrative Theory & Praxis, 35*(2), 224–248.

Hvenmark, J., & Wijkström, F. (2004). *The popular movement marinade: The dominant civil society framework in Sweden.* SSE/EFI Working paper series, 18. Retrieved from http://swoba.hhs.se/hastba/abs/hastba2004_018.htm

Karl, B., & Katz, S. (1987). Foundations and the ruling class. *Daedalus, 116*(1), 1–40.

Lundström, T., & Svedberg, L. (2003). The voluntary sector in a social democratic welfare state: The case of Sweden. *Journal of Social Policy, 32*(2), 217–238.

Nielsen, W. A. (1972). *The big foundations.* New York: Columbia University Press.

Reuter, M., Wijkström, F., & von Essen, J. (2012). Policy tools or mirrors of politics. Government-voluntary sector compacts in the post-welfare state age. *Nonprofit Policy Forum, 3*(2).

Sachar, I. (2017). *The making of corporate volunteering: A multi-Sited ethnography.* Ghent: Department of Sociology, Ghent University.

Salamon, L. M., & Anheier, H. K. (1996). *The emerging nonprofit sector: An overview.* Manchester: Manchester University Press.

Shamir, R. (2008). The age of responsibilization: On market-embedded morality. *Economy and Society, 37*(1), 1–19.

Sivesind, K. H. (2016). *Mot en ny skandinavisk velferdsmodell? Konsekvenser av ideell, kommersiell og offentlig tjenesteyting for aktivt medborgerskap.* Oslo: Institutt for samfunnsforskning.

Sörbom, A. (2010). It is merely changing: An analysis of the concept of individualization in relation to contemporary political participation. In E. Amnå (Ed.), *New forms of citizen participation: Normative implications.* Baden-Baden: Nomos.

Svedberg, L., & Olsson, L. E. (2010). Civil society and welfare provision in Sweden: Is there such a thing? In A. Zimmer & A. Evers (Eds.), *Third sector organizations facing turbulent environments: Sports, culture and social services in Germany, Italy, U.K, Poland and Sweden.* Baden-Baden: Nomos Verlag.

Trägårdh, L. (2012). Det borgerliga samhällets återkomst. In F. Wijkström (Ed.), *Civilsamhället i samhällskontraktet. En antologi om vad som står på spel.* Stockholm: European Civil Society Press.

Vamstad, J., & von Essen, J. (2013). Charitable giving in a universal welfare state – Charity and social rights in Sweden. *Nonprofit and Voluntary Sector Quarterly, 42*(2), 285–301.

von Essen, J., Frederiksen, M., & Loga, J. (forthcoming). The ambiguities of volunteering. In L. S. Henriksen, K. Strømsnes, & L. Svedberg (Eds.), *Scandinavian civic engagement.* New York: Springer.

Wijkström, F. (2007). Sweden. In H. Anheier & S. Daly (Eds.), *The politics of foundations: A comparative analysis.* London: Routledge.

Wijkström, F. (2011). Charity speak and business talk. The on-going (re)hybridization of civil society. In F. Wijkström & A. Zimmer (Eds.), *Nordic civil society at a cross-roads.* Baden: Nomos.

Wijkström, F. (2017). Nytt svängrum för filantropi och frivillighet. Migrerande idéer och transnationella projektioner. In F. Wijkström, M. Reuter, & A. Emami (Eds.), *Civilsamhället i det transnationella rummet.* Stockholm: European Civil Society Press.

Wijkström, F., & Einarsson, S. (2004). *Foundations in Sweden: Their scope, roles and visions.* Stockholm: EFI.

Yin, R. K. (2014). *Case study research: Design and methods.* London: SAGE.

Web Sources

http://hmfoundation.com. Accessed during the Spring of 2017.
http://www.ideerforlivet.se. Accessed during the Spring of 2017.
http://www.postkodstiftelsen.se/en/about-the-foundation. Accessed during the Spring of 2017.
https://www.ronaldmcdonaldhus.se. Accessed during the Spring of 2017.
www.insamlingskontroll.se. Accessed during the Winter of 2016/2017.

Johan Hvenmark is Associate Professor in Business Administration at the Department of Social Sciences at Ersta Sköndal Bräcke University College, Sweden. His overall research interest focuses on organizational change and strategic leadership in civil society. Currently, he is involved in studies concerning civil society–market–state intersections, changing relations between citizens and civil society organizations, nonprofit management education, and issues of gender and other power relations in civil society.

Johan von Essen is associate professor at the Ersta Sköndal Bräcke University College, Stockholm, Sweden, and affiliated with the Department of Theology at Uppsala University. His main field of empirical research is the perceived meaning of volunteering and the intersection of religion and volunteering. Besides empirical research, he has done philosophical work on the moral plurality in civil society.

Chapter 14
Nonprofit Organizations' Views on Corporate Foundations

Sterre Swen, Lonneke Roza, Lucas Meijs, and Alexander Maas

Abstract The aim of this chapter is to provide a deeper understanding of how nonprofit organizations view their collaborations with corporate foundations. The views of nonprofit organizations presented in this chapter explain nonprofit organizations' current practices in engaging in these collaborations, including the associated (social) benefits and challenges. The exploratory study was based on 23 semi-structured interviews with nonprofit employees, corporate foundations, and experts in the field conducted between October 2016 and March 2017. The results indicate that employees of nonprofits use three different views for corporate foundations. They consider corporate foundations as (1) moral agents of their founding firms, in which case the foundations hold resources that the nonprofits need in order to do their job as experts in addressing social issues; (2) they regard corporate foundations as instrumental agents of companies, where collaborations should create a win-win situation for the founding firm of the foundation as well as for the nonprofit organization; and (3) nonprofits see corporate foundations as change agents of their parent companies, in which corporate foundations actively work together with nonprofits to tackle social issues. The results further imply that it is difficult to describe one typical corporate foundation (as with the chapter of Bethmann and von Schnurbein), and working with them as nonprofits requires a flexible view on what a corporate foundation may entail, their focus, and their goals and should adapt their practices accordingly.

Keywords Nonprofit organizations · Corporate foundations · Nonprofit business collaboration · Qualitative research

---

S. Swen (✉) · L. Roza · L. Meijs
Rotterdam School of Management (RSM), Erasmus University Rotterdam, Rotterdam, The Netherlands
e-mail: lroza@rsm.nl; lmeys@rsm.nl

A. Maas
University for Humanistics, Utrecht, The Netherlands
e-mail: amaas@rsm.nl

14.1 Introduction

It seems indisputable that companies are nowadays, one way or another, involved in corporate philanthropy (Gautier and Pache 2015; Liket and Simaens 2015). Corporate philanthropy is the voluntary act of giving money, time, or in-kind goods by a for-profit company, without any direct commercial benefit expected, to one or more organizations whose core purpose is to serve the community's welfare (Madden et al. 2006). This distinguishes philanthropy from sponsorship as sponsorship evolves around the principle of something being provided in return for the given support (Gautier and Pache 2015). Godfrey (2005) even argues that "the non-reciprocity condition [is] the acid test of philanthropic activity" (p. 778). This condition is contested and challenged, however, by the rise of strategic corporate philanthropy (Porter and Kramer 2002). Porter and Kramer (2002) advocate that companies should "do good" while improving their competitive position. They argue that "the acid test of good corporate philanthropy is whether the desired social change is so beneficial to the company that the organization would pursue the change even if no one ever knew about it" (p. 12). In their opinion, the benefits for companies to engage in philanthropic activities should, therefore, be considerable.

Companies can display the extent of their philanthropic commitments by organizing them in different ways. A particular person (e.g., an employee, the founder or the CEO) or a department within the company can be made responsible for philanthropic activities. In this case, strategic corporate philanthropy (see Porter and Kramer 2002) would most arguably prevail everything that the company does contribute to the mission of this organization. This is in particular the case in listed companies, where creating value for shareholders is the dominant logic. At the same time, companies increasingly formalize and institutionalize their charitable giving by setting up corporate foundations (Alvarez-Gonzalez et al. 2012; Bethmann and von Schnurbein 2015; Jordan and Hartley 2014; Varcoe and Sloane 2003). A corporate foundation is a nonprofit entity, in which a company's resources are allocated for the public benefit (Mindlin 2012) and where an ongoing relationship exists between the foundation and its founding firm (Clarke et al. 2008). By definition, corporate foundations are separate legal entities (Alvarez-Gonzalez et al. 2012).

The mission of these foundations is focused on the public benefit, so theoretically, we would expect that the dominant logic here would be beneficial to society. Though if we look at the reasons why companies set up such a foundation, it is arguable whether the community is the primary, let alone only, focus. Companies set up corporate foundations for societal-orientated reasons indeed, such as to separate charitable activities from the commercial activities of the firm (Varcoe and Sloane 2003; Werbel and Carter 2002); to demonstrate a long-term, serious commitment to philanthropy; to provide structure and focus (Jordan and Hartley 2014; Varcoe and Sloane 2003); and to ensure more constant levels of giving (Bethmann and von Schnurbein 2015; Brown et al. 2006; Clarke et al. 2008; Haskell 2013; Petrovits 2006; Varcoe and Sloane 2003). At the same time, it is found that companies set up corporate foundations to strengthen their image or PR (Bethmann and von Schnurbein 2015; Clarke et al. 2008; Marquardt 2001; Minciullo and Pedrini 2011; Strachwitz 1994; Toepler 1996; Varcoe and Sloane 2003; Webb 1994; Westhues and Einwiller 2006), to achieve higher levels of employee engagement (Bethmann and von Schnurbein 2015; Minciullo and Pedrini 2011), to limit the number of internal and external requests (Bethmann and von Schnurbein 2015; Clarke et al. 2008), to serve as antennas for societal and stakeholders' expectations (Westhues and Einwiller 2006), and to realize tax benefits (Jordan and Hartley 2014).

So even though corporate foundations are focused on the public benefit and are separate legal entities on paper, they often serve one or more functions to their founding firms and are, therefore, often explicitly tied to them, for example, through their name (e.g., the Philips Foundation, ING Nederland fonds or the Vodafone Foundation) or appointed board members (Alvarez-Gonzalez et al. 2012). Many corporate foundations are in fact highly dependent on their founding firms, as these firms often are their main source of income (Jordan and Hartley 2014). This makes corporate foundations complex, as they have to adhere to the expectations of the companies that established them while focusing on their own social mission at the same time (Mindlin 2012). This results in a large number of stakeholders who they have to take into account while carrying out their activities.

These different motivations, the adherence to multiple stakeholders, against the background of the dominant presence and visibility of their founding firms, raise the question of how people make sense of corporate foundations. It is particularly interesting to study those relatively new in working with corporate foundations in collaborative arrangements, such as nonprofit organizations. This is especially apparent in the Netherlands, where corporate foundations are on the rise the past decade and are increasingly sought after by nonprofit organizations to collaborate. An understanding of how Dutch nonprofit organizations make sense of these foundations can explain their current practices of engaging in these collaborations.

Corporate foundations are relatively new and unknown partners for nonprofit organizations in the philanthropic sector in the context of this research (the Netherlands). It appears that corporate foundations do not behave or act as traditional grant-making foundations or as governmental institutions that grant subsidies to nonprofit organizations. It is here where this study aims to unravel how nonprofit organizations view these organizations and how they set up collaborations with them.

Therefore, we investigate the following research question: How do nonprofit organizations' employees view their collaborations with corporate foundations? Thereby, this study fills the gap in the literature about corporate foundations as a relatively new phenomenon through understanding how key stakeholders make sense of their collaborations with these actors. The purpose of this chapter is to provide insights into views that nonprofit employees use to make sense of the situation around corporate foundations, to clarify their potential future with corporate foundations, and to build a basis for collaborating with them. For this purpose, we have set up an exploratory research design, in which we conducted 23 interviews with representatives from 13 nonprofit organizations (i.e., public benefit organizations or ANBI organizations in Dutch) located in the Netherlands, corporate foundations, and experts in the field to construct the views and develop a typology of corporate foundations. By doing so, we demonstrate how the view that is chosen by nonprofit employees is consequential for everyday practice, such as how the collaboration gets started, evolves, and produces benefits for both parties.

In the following sections, we briefly explain our methodology and will thereafter share the results. In the discussion, we reflect on how our findings contribute to a better understanding of nonprofit employees' views regarding corporate foundations, and we include a future research agenda.

14.2 Methodology

To address our research question, we conducted an exploratory research using qualitative data. Qualitative research is considered to be most appropriate for this study, as the research question seeks to provide an in-depth understanding into the yet relatively unknown phenomenon (Cooper and Schindler 2014; Ritchie et al. 2013) of perceptions and reflections of nonprofit organizations in their collaborations with corporate foundations. This study focuses on the meaning of such collaborations from interpreting the stories of the respondents (i.e., nonprofit organizations' employees) rather than looking for correlations between variables in these collaborations or investigating the frequency of such collaborations (Cooper and Schindler 2014).

To answer the research question, we conducted 23 semi-structured interviews in 13 nonprofit organizations between October 2016 and March 2017. During the interviews, we used questions to provide direction while also leaving enough room and flexibility for probing questions (Cooper and Schindler 2014). For selecting our respondents, we followed a purposive non-probability sampling method, in which we carefully selected the respondents based on their experience and knowledge about corporate foundations. Additionally, we used maximum variation sampling (Vitcu et al. 2007; Coyne 1997; Palinkas et al. 2015). Respondents from different types of nonprofit organizations have been selected to participate in this study to gain a broad enough understanding of perceptions, attitudes, and views. This variation has been realized by selecting nonprofit organizations that differ on three aspects: (1) their size, (2) the type of cause they support, and (3) whether they have experience in collaborating with corporate foundations.

Representatives from 13 nonprofit organizations have participated in this study. One employee per nonprofit has been interviewed, except for one nonprofit, in which case three employees have shared their views. Five nonprofit organizations have been interviewed twice. Eight respondents were female and seven were male. The respondents work as (senior) project or program coordinator, head of fundraising, partnership or relationship manager, or marketing/communications manager. Six have worked considerably longer in the private sector than in the nonprofit sector, while seven worked considerably longer in the nonprofit sector, of which two have no experience at all in the private sector. Two respondents have worked a comparable amount of years both in the private as well as in the nonprofit sector.

Out of our 28 interviews, six were conducted with corporate foundations to gain a better understanding of their organizations and perspective related to nonprofit organizations. The interviews have been conducted and transcribed by the leading author of this chapter, which limits the possibility for transcribing errors (Easton et al. 2000). We used a two-step coding process (Kenny and Fourie 2015), from (1) "initial" or "open coding" to (2) "refocused coding." This has led to the identification of the three cognitive frames discussed below. Cognitive frames are used to structure people's thoughts and explain their behavior and actions (Weick 1995). Names of respondents, nonprofit organizations, corporate foundations, and companies have been made anonymous during the transcribing process to protect the privacy of the interview respondents. We refer to our respondents from nonprofit organizations as NP 1, NP 2, and so forth and respondents from corporate foundations as CF 1, CF 2, and so forth.

14.3 Results

Coding and analyzing the interviews resulted in the formulation of three types of views used by nonprofit employees about corporate foundations. The first one assumes that companies have a mere moral obligation to offer part of their resources for tackling social issues, which they can do through setting up a corporate foundation that supports nonprofits. The second view considers corporate foundations as being instrumental agents for the companies who founded them, because these foundations create benefits for their founding firms. In the third view, nonprofit employees see corporate foundations as social change agents and consider them as active partners in addressing social issues. These three views indicate various roles for corporate foundations as collaboration partners for nonprofits.

Although nonprofit employees rarely question corporate foundations' expectations for their giving, they do question the time and energy required by collaborating with corporate foundations that might manifest themselves in longer working hours or increased job demands. The views determine how much time and efforts nonprofit employees are willing to invest in engaging in collaborations with corporate foundations.

14.3.1 View 1: Corporate Foundations Are Moral Partners of Companies

In this view, nonprofit employees perceive corporate foundations as holding resources that they need so that they, as key experts in the field to address social issues, can focus on solving these issues. Corporate foundations seen through this view are mere resource providers. They consider the collaborations as moral and perhaps even altruistic. It is simply part of the social responsibility of companies to give back, and the most proper way to do so is to set up a separate foundation that supports nonprofits. As NP 3 explains:

> It [supporting nonprofits] is not a favour, because you [nonprofits] are of personal interest of the CEO or because you fit with the marketing goals [of the company], but because this is simply how grant-making works, how doing good by companies is done.

In the first view, nonprofits assume to spend the smallest amount of organizational resources on setting up the relationship compared with the two other views. For example, NP 3:

> I think that having these corporate foundations is a big advantage for nonprofit organizations, because they are here to donate money; not to ask for anything in return and because their goals are clearly defined. That makes it much easier and more time efficient for nonprofit organizations.

NP 2 further illustrates:

> The [name corporate foundation] for example, is just a grant-making foundation; so you can just apply for a grant; let us say, I need half a million and they will say yes or no.

Some nonprofit employees explained that they prefer to collaborate with corporate foundations rather than with companies, because the goals of these foundations are often focused on providing resources. NP 7:

> If I consider my contacts, I would not want to say that I work much more with companies than with corporate foundations, simply because a company has very different goals compared to our organization. So that makes it much harder to receive support, while the goal of a corporate foundation is usually focused on giving money to societal initiatives; so, that makes it easier to talk with them. I would rather talk with ten corporate foundations than with hundred companies.

The type of resources that nonprofits request from corporate foundations in this view is mostly focused on financial donations, albeit some value other resources as well. NP 9:

> So, organizations can support us in several ways. Giving us money? Yes please, that is easiest. Then, we can see where it is needed the most at that moment, but all other forms of support are for us just as valuable.

In contrast, NP 3 explains:

> Money is not everything. In the case of [name company], it brings us much more that these super smart guys and girls are walking around here than if [name company] had given us money.

However, NP 7 illustrates the need of money above anything else:

> In-kind support. Honestly, we are often not in need of that. These people should have [knowledge] what we need at that moment. That does not happen very often honestly.

Corporate foundations often require nonprofit organizations to make a request for resources through specific templates. The collaboration often does not evolve any further after the resources have been provided, as it concerns only a short-term engagement. NP 13:

> A foundation wants to receive an application on paper, according to their format. It has to align with their goal of course; and if it aligns and meets their criteria then oftentimes they provide the money, partly or in full, and then that is where it ends.

Some nonprofits that use this moral view abandoned their efforts to initiate collaborations with corporate foundations due to disappointing results from previous efforts. Here, the collaboration *simply led to too little results [...]* (NP 1). Rather, it seems that this nonprofit has become more reactive in their collaborations with as little time and effort from their side as NP 1 explains:

> There are some corporate foundations that come to [name nonprofit] though… This is the ideal match when a company approaches us and says: we support you for a certain amount of money every year. But we like to keep these things to ourselves because everyone is looking for these matches.

This demonstrates that nonprofits are not always transparent about their partnerships. Their continuous need for support creates a situation, in which they keep external stakeholders, including other nonprofits and donors, in the dark about the resources they received. At the same time, despite the nontransparency of nonprofits themselves, they are looking for more transparency from corporate foundations, for instance, by means of a list of corporate foundations and their focus areas, so that they can find suitable foundations more easily. Again, it is a constant balance of investing organizational resources to get the resources from corporate foundations and secure them.

Another reason why collaborations between nonprofits and corporate foundations may lead to disappointing experiences in this view is that some foundations have very specific demands in terms of the projects they wish to support. NP 1:

> They often have a very clear image of what they want to support. Then, the question becomes: do we also want to support it?

Not only the corporate foundation is looking for a specific fit with their mission, also nonprofit organizations are critical towards potential collaborations and are looking for a fit from their side as well. It seems that some are very conscious of the potential of mission drift. NP 11:

> The more collaborations we have, the better for [name nonprofit]. The more money we can generate to do what we want to do, but it should fit with their goals [of a corporate foundation] and it should also fit with what we do so you should not engage in collaborations just for the sake of engaging in collaborations.

However, others seem more sensitive for mission drift as for them the wishes of corporate foundations increasingly direct their programs. NP 4:

> Then you get a couple of conditions: it should be primary education, something with girls, a sustainable model, which will be self-supporting at some point in time. A couple of conditions and then we actually wrote a program for that with a partner we already knew in that field. Conditions of such a foundation are often directing for us, and that is happening more and more.

14.3.2 View 2: Corporate Foundations Are Instrumental Partners of Companies

The second view that nonprofit employees use while making sense of corporate foundations is considering these actors as instrumental agents of the company. There is a mutual resource exchange between the two organizations. Here, nonprofit employees are convinced that collaborating with a corporate foundation should create a win-win situation for the nonprofit as well as for the founding firm of the foundation. For instance, NP 2:

> Of course, they don't do this out of pure philanthropy. They do this because of deliberate self-interest, and that's why I feel it is a sustainable collaboration. They basically have two important reasons of doing this: they want their employees to feel passionate about this. So, they will remain interested in working for [name company], so employee engagement and pride... Second, by collaborating with us [...], they learn quite a lot about the situation on the ground [...], a situation which they themselves would never experience without us.

This is also illustrated by the following quote by NP 5:

> What I see is that if we don't clearly define what there is to gain for the company, what they want to get out of it, then we sign a contract for 3 years and then it ends after these 3 years, because then you don't have enough to offer to each other. Then, we [the nonprofit] are dependent on a philanthropic donation and they can feel good about the number of children they have helped, but then there is no urgency to keep doing this, while [name company] can just see that if they work together with us [the nonprofit] in terms of knowledge and efforts, then they will get market insights that they can actually use.

Several nonprofit employees actually mentioned that they prefer collaborations with corporate foundations that create clear benefits for their founding firms, instead of merely receiving resources from the foundation. In their perception, the collaboration is more sustainable if the company sees a clear benefit for them as well. As explained by NP 5:

> It is most valuable when it concerns a collaboration that is in line with our mission and vision, and through which we really feel like we are going to get something out of the collaboration and them as well. If it is a pure financial donation, of course, that makes us very happy, but if that does not have any impact on the company except for them saying: "How nice of us to do that," then it is just not sustainable.

In this view, nonprofits are even investing more resources in order to convince the corporate foundation to start collaborating with them. NP 1:

> Companies are just commercially focused. As a nonprofit you also have to start acting commercially. You have to start building a relationship, because you want something from them [the corporate foundation]. You have to show them [the corporate foundation] that the company gets something out of it.

It was indicated by nonprofit employees that the type of partnership with corporate foundations and the involvement of these foundations depend on the intention of the founding firm with the foundation. NP 8:

> Some [corporate] foundations are managed in a rather professional manner and request key performance indicators every 6 months, while other corporate foundations are just the "toy"

of the owner, so to say, who, every once in a while, wants to get the feeling that the money is well spent with a couple of nice photos and a movie.

Some nonprofits see corporate foundations as being closely connected to their founding companies and, therefore, consider corporate foundations as a stepping-stone toward more corporate resources from the company. Corporate foundations on the other hand often see themselves positioned at a certain distance from their founding firms and prefer to refrain from influencing corporate policies and practices, as this quote from NP 13 illustrates:

> We tried to engage them [name company] in our work at [name nonprofit] in several ways [via the corporate foundation], because it could benefit both our brands. But, that is just not the way the corporate foundation works. They are just very low profile.

This is also indicated by the following quote, NP 7:

> We hoped that we could also start doing things with the company [name company]. So far, they have really refrained from that. They keep that very much separated. The board of the foundation wants as little entanglement as possible and especially wants to prevent that the company will start using the foundation as some sort of PR instrument.

One nonprofit employee did indicate, however, that their partnership with a corporate foundation has led to the possibility of exploring collaborations with the founding firm of that foundation. NP 13:

> The person who is connected to [name company] CSR has always also been connected to the foundation; so, you are building a relationship with that person who happens to also have connections within the company. Partly because of that, we will be talking soon to discuss what we can do within the value chain. So, if you do not have the opening through the foundation, then maybe the connection to the company is more difficult. But, because you have been working together for such a long time and know what you can expect from each other and how you can support each other, at some point in time doors may open and more may be possible.

14.3.3 View 3: Corporate Foundations Are Strategic Social Change Partners of Companies

The third view is based on the perception that corporate foundations are strategic social change agents of the company. Here, they are seen as part of the solution, as active and engaged partners for nonprofits in tackling social issues. As NP 2 explains:

> We [name nonprofit] receive really nice donations from them [name corporate foundation], but they [name corporate foundation] say: "Don't come to us for the money. If you want money go to [name corporate foundation]. But if you need expertise, we do have relevant experts for your organization and if you take that seriously then we are a very committed partner".

It is here that — according to nonprofit employees — the two partners share the ownership of the social issue, particular problem, or project. Here, each of the actors contributes the resources available to solve this social issue.

This does not necessarily mean that the corporate foundation is always (primarily) funding the project but can also leverage other corporate resources when that is needed for particular projects to solve social issues. For instance, corporate foundations can leverage employees of the founding firm that have the knowledge, skills, and expertise to help solve the particular issue. This is also the reason why one nonprofit prefers to work with a corporate foundation rather than directly with companies. NP 5 illustrates:

> If you work with a CSR department, I think they will say: "You have to talk to them [people within the company]", but that they won't consider it from a foundation's perspective like, "You need an integrated solution, you need a designer, an expert and a data analyst", and in case of the [name corporate foundation] that is really their added value: they know the company very well and really bring the parties together and set it up in a very thorough way.

It seems that nonprofits that view corporate foundations like this are more interested in:

> Fewer, bigger, better [partnerships]. We can collaborate with many parties, but we favour to take up a few that are really big and can make lots of impact. This means that we need to be very critical with whom to collaborate. (NP 5)

As soon as there is a partnership established in this view, nonprofit organizations feel that there becomes potential for deeper and more long-term collaboration between the two actors. Here, mutual understanding is key in evolving the collaboration, as NP 9 describes:

> Because it concerns long-term collaborations [with corporate foundations], intensive collaborations and you get more insights in the goals [of the corporate foundation], it becomes much easier to see whether a [corporate] foundation fits with your organization and how you can expand the collaboration together.

Initiating collaborations with corporate foundations based on this view can take up lots of time and organizational resources from nonprofits:

> […] as it takes a considerable amount of time to really get to know each other. Here, it helps to go on a trip together, see the local circumstances where we work together and also get to know each other's partners, colleagues and each other's way of working. (NP 5)

In addition, this approach requires patience and flexibility on both ends, as NP 2 explains:

> What we really need to get used to is that we don't speak each other's language. If we say: "there needs to be a report on this project", you will get a thorough report, as we always want to have it written down in detail. It takes collaboration to find out that [name corporate foundation] does not want that report at all. They just want to receive one piece of paper with what we are currently doing; an executive summary for the Board.

However, it seems that as the collaboration develops, it generally produces even greater benefits.

> […] generally it comes with substantial contributions, and collaborations are much deeper. (NP 9)

14.4 Discussion

Corporate foundations are seen as contemporary actors in the field of philanthropy. In academia, little is known about these vehicles. For the philanthropic sector itself, corporate foundations are perceived as "the new kid on the block." It is important for both scholars and practitioners to delve into how important stakeholders of corporate foundations, here nonprofit employees, view these organizations. This is particularly relevant as particular views on who they are and what they do guide individual perceptions, inferences, and actions. Here, understanding the view also explains certain actions of nonprofit employees. This study aims to fill that gap in our understanding by devoting attention to nonprofit employees' views of corporate foundations, thereby allowing them to voice their interpretations of the meaning of collaborating with this relative unknown actor in the field of philanthropy.

Nonprofit employees enact or produce their own environment by setting up collaborative arrangements between their organization and corporate foundations and by considering corporate foundations as resource providers or partners in tackling social issues. Subsequently, these nonprofit employees receive stimuli based on their actions, such as creating organizational legitimacy, searching for needed resources, and ultimately establishing social change.

For this purpose, nonprofit employees use three different views to look at corporate foundations. First, we found that they view corporate foundations as moral actors of companies. In this case, nonprofits expect companies to do the right thing by providing resources through a corporate foundation to nonprofit organizations that address social issues. This is very much in line with a corporate philanthropic discourse, in which companies are powerful and wealthy agents that have moral and social obligations toward tackling issues in society (Shaw and Post 1993).

Second, nonprofits view corporate foundations as instrumental agents for companies. This is in line with the literature on strategic corporate philanthropy (Porter and Kramer 2002) and the prevalent literature in management and business studies arguing that corporate philanthropy should have a business case and should provide benefits for the company in question (Liket and Simaens 2015).

The third view is based on the perception that corporate foundations are the social change partners of their founding firms. Here, they are seen as part of the solution, as "partners in crime" for nonprofits to tackle social issues. They can do this by making meaningful connections between nonprofit employees who are in need of support and employees from the founding firm with relevant knowledge, skills, and expertise. Corporate foundations are also expected to act as boundary spanners (Herlin and Pedersen 2013) between civil society and the private sector. They can leverage corporate resources for civil society while at the same time lobby for different standards and practices in the private sector, starting with their founding firm.

What is absent in nonprofit employees' discourse, however, is a critical reflection of corporate foundations' role in philanthropy or of corporate power that allowed setting up corporate foundations in the first place. This might be the case due to the fact that the social environment in which the nonprofit organization acts influences their view. Stakeholder pressures (e.g., from governments and grant-making foundations; see also Roza et al. 2017) to engage in collaborations with corporate foundations might influence the positive notions of nonprofit employees toward these collaborative arrangements. In addition, quotes included earlier in this chapter illustrated the position of nonprofits as resource seekers and corporate foundations as resource providers. Nonprofits may therefore feel "forced" to speak positively about corporate foundations, since they need something from them, which may unconsciously foster a positive association with them in general.

It is interesting to learn that these views are not mutually exclusive and the chosen view depends on several factors. Indeed, multiple nonprofit employees indicated during the interviews that it is difficult to describe a "typical" corporate foundation. NP 2:

> So all these foundations, [names corporate foundations], they are differently organized, they have different goals, from expertise to fundraisers to cash-donations, and they all have their charm.

Differences are perceived in terms of (1) their objectives or mission, (2) the reason why they were founded, (3) which corporate resources are leveraged by them, (4) their degree of professionalism, and (5) the closeness of the foundation to their founding firm. This may explain why nonprofit employees sometimes apply multiple views in describing their relationships with corporate foundations.

14.5 Limitations and Future Research Suggestions

As with every study, this study has its limitations. This study provides a reflection of collaborations between nonprofit organizations and corporate foundations in the Netherlands. These collaborations are established through personal contact between individuals, and experiences about such collaborations are, therefore, expected to be highly personal and situation specific. We have carefully selected 13 nonprofit organizations in the Netherlands to include in this study, but the generalizability of our study is low. A different sample may as well have yielded an even richer picture of nonprofits' views on corporate foundations, as it concerns a phenomenon that is difficult to grasp and still relatively unknown.

In addition, we only managed to conduct one interview with a nonprofit organization that consciously refrains from collaborations with corporate foundations. Such nonprofit organizations are expected to draw on different views in their decision-making process. Including several of such actors in the study would have provided a more critical reflection of corporate foundations from the perspective of nonprofits.

Moreover, we interviewed most of our respondents at only one point in time. To really understand views and how that influences attitudes and behavior, a sensemaking approach could be helpful to go into the underlying dynamic process to comprehend reality in order to anticipate and act effectively (Klein et al. 2006). It might be more effective to approach this topic with a longitudinal research to capture the sensemaking process in a richer way and to be able to notify changes during the process over time.

Future research could compare corporate foundations with other types of foundations from the perspective of nonprofit employees. This would generate other questions as well. Which type of foundation do these nonprofit employees consider to be most valuable to engage in collaborations with, and which aspects determine this? Do nonprofits even distinguish among different types of foundations? Answers to these questions could provide more insights into the views on corporate foundations.

More attention might also be devoted in future research to identifying differences between corporate foundations, as this will be of influence to their engagements with nonprofit organizations. Results of this study have shown that it is difficult to describe one "typical" corporate foundation due to the differences that exist among them. The general term "corporate foundation" may, therefore, not be sufficient to fully understand this type of organization.

In addition, more implicitly mentioned in this research, the role of decision-makers or leaders from corporate foundations seem to play a pivotal role. However, in line with calls on researching the microfoundations of corporate social responsibility (see, e.g., Aguinis and Glavas 2012), little do we know on the role of leadership in corporate foundations on their decisions regarding with whom to collaborate and why. Also, what happens with the (current) collaborative arrangements with nonprofits if leadership of corporate foundations changes? Similarly, we could also question what the role of nonprofit leadership is in collaborating with corporate foundations. What are the characteristics of leadership that makes the initiation and collaborations successful? And what are the definitions of a successful collaboration?

References

Aguinis, H., & Glavas, A. (2012). What we know and don't know about corporate social responsibility: A review and research agenda. *Journal of Management, 38*(4), 932–968.
Alvarez-Gonzalez, L. I., Martin-Cavanna, J., & Rey-Garcia, M. (2012). Assessing and advancing foundation transparency: Corporate foundations as a case study. *The Foundation Review, 4*(3), 77–89.
Bethmann, S., & von Schnurbein, G. (2015). *Effective governance of corporate foundations* (No. 8). University of Basel, Basel, Switzerland.
Brown, W. O., Helland, E., & Smith, J. K. (2006). Corporate philanthropic practices. *Journal of Corporate Finance, 12*(5), 855–877.
Clarke, P., Magalhães, I. d. O., Di Tella, A., Faure, E., Hizette, D., Piette, I., & Salole, G. (2008). *Foundations in the European Union: Facts and figures*. Brussels: European Union.
Cooper, D. R., & Schindler, P. S. (2014). *Business research methods. Business research methods* (12th ed.). New York: McGraw-Hill.

Coyne, I. T. (1997). Sampling in qualitative research. Purposeful and theoretical sampling; merging or clear boundaries? *Journal of Advanced Nursing, 26*(3), 623–630.

Easton, K. L., McComish, J. F., & Greenberg, R. (2000). Avoiding common pitfalls in qualitative data collection and transcription. *Qualitative Health Research, 10*(5), 703–707.

Gautier, A., & Pache, A. C. (2015). Research on corporate philanthropy: A review and assessment. *Journal of Business Ethics, 126*(3), 343–369.

Godfrey, P. C. (2005). The relationship between corporate philanthropy and shareholder wealth: A risk management perspective. *The Academy of Management Review, 30*(4), 777–798.

Haskell, J. D. (2013). Keeping your corporate foundation compliant. *Financial Executive, 29*(9), 76–80.

Herlin, H., & Pedersen, J. T. (2013). Corporate foundations, catalysts of NGO-business partnerships? *The Journal of Corporate Citizenship, 50*, 58–90.

Jordan, A., & Hartley, V. (2014). *Corporate foundations – A global perspective*. London: Corporate Citizenship.

Kenny, M., & Fourie, R. (2015). Contrasting classic, Straussian, and constructivist grounded theory: Methodological and philosophical conflicts. *The Qualitative Report, 20*(8), 1270–1289.

Klein, G., Moon, B., & Hoffman, R. R. (2006). Making sense of sensemaking: Alternative perspectives. *IEEE Intelligent Systems, 21*(4), 70–73.

Liket, K., & Simaens, A. (2015). Battling the devolution in the research on corporate philanthropy. *Journal of Business Ethics, 126*(2), 285–308.

Madden, K., Scaife, W., & Crissman, K. (2006). How and why small to medium size enterprises (SMEs) engage with their communities: An Australian study. *International Journal of Nonprofit and Voluntary Sector Marketing, 11*(1), 49–60.

Marquardt, J. (2001). *Corporate Foundation als PR-Instrument. Rahmenbedingungen – Erfolgswirkungen – Management*. Wiesbaden: Gabler.

Minciullo, M., & Pedrini, M. (2011). Italian corporate foundations and the challenge of multiple stakeholder interests. *Nonprofit Management & Leadership, 22*(2), 173–197.

Mindlin, S. E. (2012). A study of governance practices in corporate foundations. *Revista de Administração, 47*(3), 461–472.

Palinkas, L. A., Horwitz, S. M., Green, C. A., Wisdom, J. P., Duan, N., & Hoagwood, K. (2015). Purposeful sampling for qualitative data collection and analysis in mixed method implementation research. *Administration and Policy in Mental Health and Mental Health Services Research, 42*(5), 533–544.

Petrovits, C. M. (2006). Corporate-sponsored foundations and earnings management. *Journal of Accounting and Economics, 41*(3), 335–362.

Porter, M. E., & Kramer, M. R. (2002). The competitive advantage of corporate philanthropy. *Harvard Business Review, 80*(12), 56–68.

Ritchie, J., Lewis, J., Nicholls, C. M., & Ormston, R. (2013). *Qualitative research practice – A guide for social science students and researcher*. London: Sage.

Roza, L., Shachar, I., Meijs, L. C. P. M., & Hustinx, L. (2017). The nonprofit case for corporate volunteering: A multi-level perspective. *The Service Industries Journal, 37*(11–12), 746–765.

Shaw, B., & Post, F. R. (1993). A moral basis for corporate philanthropy. *Journal of Business Ethics, 12*(10), 745–751.

Strachwitz, R. (1994). *Stiftungen: nutzen, führen und errichten; ein Handbuch*. Frankfurt: Campus Verlag.

Toepler, S. (1996). *Das gemeinnützige Stiftungswesen in der modernen demokratischen Gesellschaft: Ansätze zu einer ökonomischen Betrachtungsweise*. München: Maecenata Verlag.

Varcoe, L., & Sloane, N. (2003). *Corporate foundations – Building a sustainable foundation for corporate giving*. London: Business in the Community.

Vitcu, A., Lungu, E., Vitcu, L., & Marcu, A. (2007). Multi-stage maximum variation sampling in health promotion programs' evaluation. *Journal of Preventive Medicine, 15*, 5–18.

Webb, N. J. (1994). Tax and government policy implications for corporate foundation giving. *Nonprofit and Voluntary Sector Quarterly, 23*(1), 41–67.

Weick, K. E. (1995). Sensemaking in organizations (Vol. 3). Sage.
Werbel, J. D., & Carter, S. M. (2002). The CEO's influence on corporate foundation giving. *Journal of Business Ethics, 40*(1), 47–60.
Westhues, M., & Einwiller, S. (2006). Corporate foundations: Their role for corporate social responsibility. *Corporate Reputation Review, 9*(2), 144–153.

Sterre Swen graduated in 2017 from the Erasmus University Rotterdam in International Management/CEMS. The content of this chapter formed the basis for her master thesis on corporate foundations. She currently works as a trainee at Friesland Campina and has a personal interest in corporate social responsibility and sustainability.

Dr. Lonneke Roza is Adjunct Assistant Professor at Rotterdam School of Management (RSM), Erasmus University Rotterdam. Her research focuses on (microfoundations of) corporate philanthropy/corporate citizenship. Her work is published in Journals such as the Journal of Business Ethics, Nonprofit and Voluntary Sector Quarterly, and Voluntas.

Lucas Meijs is Professor of Strategic Philanthropy and Volunteering at Rotterdam School of Management (RSM), Erasmus University Rotterdam. His current research focuses on strategic philanthropy, volunteer/nonprofit management, corporate community involvement, and involved learning. He served two terms as first non-American coeditor in chief of Nonprofit and Voluntary Sector Quarterly and was a member of the Raad voor Maatschappelijke Ontwikkeling — the official policy advisory body for the Dutch government and parliament.

Alexander Maas is Associate Professor of Organizational Change and Social Integration at Rotterdam School of Management (RSM) of Erasmus University Rotterdam and professor in Humanizing and Change of Care at the University for Humanistics in Utrecht (the Netherlands). His research and practice interests include organization and change theory, social constructionism, storytelling, and changes and innovations in the life and care of older people. He has published and (co-)edited a dozen books (in Dutch) and articles, in English and Dutch journals in the fields of Organization Studies and Change Studies.

Chapter 15
Discussion and Conclusion

Lonneke Roza, Steffen Bethmann, Lucas Meijs, and Georg von Schnurbein

Abstract In this concluding chapter, we start by discussing how the chapters on management and governance inform the literature on governance, corporate giving, and foundations. Second, we summarize the overlapping themes in the regional and country chapters, including the presence and strength of a tradition in (corporate) foundations or (corporate) giving, which institutional framework is present, how (theoretically) autonomous corporate foundations are able to act within that particular context, what their main focus is, and how corporate foundations are funded. Finally, we discuss how different stakeholders, such as employees and beneficiaries, might have different perspectives on corporate foundations. We end this final chapter with a short overall discussion and a conclusion in which we start to shape a potential research agenda based on the key findings and discussions in this book.

Keywords Conclusion · Management · Governance · Comparative study · Stakeholder

The *Handbook on Corporate Foundations* provides an in-depth exploration of various aspects of an oftentimes overlooked vehicle that facilitates corporate philanthropy: corporate foundations. We divided the volume in three parts. First, the volume addresses managerial and governance challenges of corporate foundations due to their unique relationship with a founding firm, often the single donor. Here, authors describe and analyze unique attributes of the relationship between the corporate foundation and the founding firm and how that results in governance challenges. In addition, we add two unique governance situations: one where the corporate foundation is the owner of the company and one where there is a

---

L. Roza (✉) · L. Meijs
Rotterdam School of Management (RSM), Erasmus University Rotterdam, Rotterdam, The Netherlands
e-mail: lroza@rsm.nl; lmeys@rsm.nl

S. Bethmann · G. von Schnurbein
Center for Philanthropy Studies (CEPS), University of Basel, Basel, Switzerland
e-mail: georg.vonschnurbein@unibas.ch

collective corporate foundation in which multiple (small to medium sized and large) companies jointly practice philanthropy.

Second, we explored the positioning of corporate foundations in philanthropy in various countries and regions. The authors of these chapters describe in detail the institutional context in which corporate foundations operate and how corporate foundations function within this particular institutional context. For instance, they describe the historical, cultural, and legal framework and the main focus areas of corporate foundations.

The third part of this book is aimed at stakeholders of corporate foundations. Here, authors have addressed several key stakeholders' perspectives, involvement, and/or how they are influenced by corporate foundations. We include a civil society perspective, employee engagement in corporate foundations, how beneficiaries might be influenced by corporate giving, and how nonprofit partners make sense of corporate foundations.

In this concluding chapter, we start by discussing how the chapters on management and governance inform the literature on governance, corporate giving, and foundations. Second, we summarize the overlapping themes in the regional and country chapters, including the presence and strength of a tradition in (corporate) foundations or (corporate) giving, which institutional framework is present, how (theoretically) autonomous corporate foundations are able to act within that particular context, what their main focus is, and how corporate foundations are funded. Finally, we discuss how different stakeholders, such as employees and beneficiaries, might have different perspectives on corporate foundations. We end this final chapter with a short overall discussion and a conclusion in which we start to shape a potential research agenda based on the key findings and discussions in this book.

15.1 Section 1: Management and Governance of Corporate Foundations

The foundation literature generally assumes that a foundation's ability to create social impact and social innovation rests to a large extent on their independence from external control from the donor(s) and/or the government (Anheier and Leat 2006; Fleishman 2007; Frumkin 2006; Kania et al. 2014). At the same time, (strategic) corporate philanthropy literature oftentimes describes corporate philanthropy as a means to corporate interests, either on the relative short-term (e.g., reputational and branding motives) or medium to long-term investments in society. For instance, corporate giving is an instrument to create legitimacy for companies, create a favorable competitive context, and in the long term build resilient societies which are needed to thrive as a business (Porter and Kramer 2002). These seemingly contradictory viewpoints—or at least friction between different approaches to the same phenomenon—in both research and practice perfectly exemplify the challenging managerial environment of corporate foundations. Here, corporate foundations are expected to act like the boundary spanner (see Herlin and Pedersen 2013) who are able to leverage key elements from one domain to another, at the appropriate time for the appropriate stakeholder. As such, the presence of a (collective) founding company (companies), albeit dominant or at a distance, and the (traditional) philanthropic institutional framework in which corporate foundations are active result in various governance, managerial, and operational challenges. The four chapters on management and governance in this volume revealed the complexity of effectively leading a corporate foundation.

The section starts with a broad chapter (Chap. 2) that focuses on the challenges experienced by those who govern corporate foundations. Based on three key theoretical perspectives (agency theory, resource dependency theory, and institutional theory) and insights drawn from interviews and informal conversations with leaders and decision-makers from more than a dozen corporate foundations in the US and the Netherlands, the chapter builds a theoretical framework in which the most common governance conditions and dynamics are identified. The framework defines three key challenges based on 11 correlated tensions in hybrid organizations: (1) Why do corporate foundations exist and to what end? (2) Who really governs a corporate foundation and with what orientation? (3) To whom are corporate foundations accountable and for what? The chapter demonstrates that corporate foundations are subject to multiple and divergent logics posing tensions and challenges. Dynamics experienced vary by the type of corporation and are not always considered as problematic, relative to the way they are experienced as problematic by other types of hybrids (e.g., social entrepreneurs). This seems to be caused by the ongoing relationship with the company.

In the subsequent chapter (Chap. 3), the relationship between the related company and the foundation is further examined. Based on the closeness of the foundation mission with the core business of the corporation and the relative degree of independence of the foundation, Bethmann and von Schnurbein developed a typology of corporate foundations that enhances our understanding of the complex relationship between the corporate foundation and parent company. Departing from the assumption that independence and autonomy are key strengths of foundations, restraining these features would leave a corporate foundation with a limited potential for social impact. And as corporate foundations are in themselves set up as independent institutions for public benefit, working toward a high social impact should be the legitimate main focus of the foundation. However, Bethmann and von Schnurbein argue that none of the identified types is necessarily better than the other. Their success depends on the context in which they operate. However, strong pull and push factors lead to a closer alignment of the foundations with their parent company. By means of several mini-cases and a survey among 35 corporate foundations in Europe, it becomes clear that if you have seen one corporate foundation, you have seen them all (see also Ostrower 2006).

Bothello, Gauthier, and Pache (Chap. 4) describe another interesting governance structure that could be seen as a corporate foundation which they label as a shareholder foundation. A shareholder foundation exercises both voting rights and ownership over a for-profit enterprise, and in many instances, they invest the profit both back into the company, as well as society. In their chapter, the authors demonstrate the question whether the choice for this particular governance structure is based on a specific context of a foundation, in line with the ideas of institutional thinking (e.g., DiMaggio and Powell 1983; Pache and Santos 2013; Powell and DiMaggio 2012). They show that corporate foundation leaders are not only recipients but also producers of the "rules of the game" that affect the legitimacy of their organizations. Thus, a social constructionist point of view applies to corporate foundations, the same for not-for-profit and for-profit organizations: Is the institutional context and the corporate foundations are in a constant process of shaping each other?

Maas (Chap. 10) describes how decision-makers in the make-or-buy decision of corporate giving should first make a strategic decision on whether the activities of the corporate foundation are peripheral or integral. Focusing on two rationales derived from resource dependence and agency theory—the amount of available resources and the need for efficiency—the case description shows the strategic decision of companies to pair up in a collective structure, albeit a collective corporate foundation.

15.2 Section 2: Corporate Foundations and the Institutional Environment

Although valid, reliable, and comparable data on corporate foundations in various regions and countries appears to be limited, to say the least, the descriptive regional chapters show that the role of corporate foundations varies due to the institutional environment in which they operate. The chapters in this book offer a first exploratory insight in how the institutional context might influence corporate foundations' functioning (see how the institutional context shapes individual giving behavior; Wiepking and Handy 2016). Table 15.1 provides an overview of the similarities and differences among the institutional context in the countries and regions covered in this book.

15.2.1 History and Tradition

The history and tradition in corporate philanthropy vary significantly among the regions that are studied in this volume. While the US has a long-standing tradition of fostering foundations, with endowed charities dating back to the late eighteenth century, other traditions in countries such as China and Russia are shaped more recently. Indeed, it is only after the millennium China's philanthropic sector is booming and private, and entrepreneurial forms of philanthropy are "disruptive" to long-standing government-controlled philanthropic organizations. Here, corporations and entrepreneurs are the key drivers of this robust growth and dramatic change. In Russia, the rise of corporate philanthropy and the more recent

Table 15.1 Similarities and differences among the institutional context throughout world regions

Country/region	CF tradition	CF institutional framework	CF autonomy	CF main focus	CF Funding
USA	Long-standing, dating back to the late eighteenth century	Rather strict legal framework for CFs on federal and state levels	Fairly autonomous, within strict (tax) legislations	Heterogeneous	Endowments by single source (mostly parent corporation)
China	Young, emerging (since millennium)	Strict legal framework (state level) for CFs	Fairly strictly state supervised, acting in accordance to government agendas	Issues mostly in line with state policy, though focus on cultural projects is growing	Endowments by single source (mostly parent corporation)
Latin America	Young, emerging (since mid-1980s)	Mostly loose legal framework for CFs with regional differences	Autonomous; (local) government both as funder and partner	Heterogeneous	Annual contributions, endowments, and other resources
Europe	Emerging since mid-twentieth century	Rather loose: Few countries set legal boundaries for CFs to have distinct activities from core business	Autonomous	Heterogeneous	Annual contributions, endowments, and other resources
Russia	Slowly emerging since a few decades	Poor institutional framework for CFs, limiting perspectives of CF development	Unknown, although (local) government seems to be partner of CFs	Heterogeneous	Annual contributions (no endowments). Fully reliant on related company

development of establishing corporate foundations were driven by the emerging presence of multinationals in Russia. Not only did these organizations take along their Western views of the role of businesses in society, these companies were also pressured by various Russian stakeholders to behave socially responsible and to contribute to the Russian society.

In Latin America, the tradition in corporate philanthropy has been rising since the 1960s. Large, local, family-controlled business groups started modern corporate philanthropy initiatives, most of which had close connections with American firms and foundations. Although by the roots corporate giving still departs from the ideas of church or state paternalism, this development was due to a combined growth in competition among NGOs for funding and evolving pressure from society on for-profit organizations to behave responsibly. This flourishing of corporate foundations in the region coincided with a period of intense engagement and investment in philanthropic infrastructures by a bevy of foreign donors.

In Europe, as in Latin America, corporate foundations go back several decades in the twentieth century, although a broad distinction into its appearance and growth could be made in accordance with the political context. As with the rise of corporate philanthropy and corporate foundations in other regions, the emergence of this is most likely the result of a combination of realization of the role of businesses in society and societal stakeholder influences. In addition, as a consequence of the economic recession in 2008/2009, many European governments cut down their public funding in areas such as arts and culture. Private initiatives such as corporate foundations became more needed and important partners for topics where the state couldn't invest effectively or sufficiently (Gautier and de Nervaux 2015).

15.2.2 Legal and Fiscal Arrangements

Although there are country-specific rules and regulations, in every country and region in our volume, corporate foundations are positioned in the broader institutional framework of the nonprofit sector instead of the business sector, due to their legal entity and their public benefit mission. In most countries, these rules and regulations are fairly recent, such as the 1969 Tax Reform Act in the USA, and even more recent in China where the government launched the first Charity Law in 2016. This law aims to expand a space in civil society for more people to act by lowering the threshold for nonprofit registration and fundraising. In addition, the diverse cultural and fiscal tradition of the European member states and the fact that there is no harmonization of foundation law in Europe contribute to substantial differences in the definition and interpretation of corporate foundations (EFC 2011), leading to a wide era of different fiscal and legal laws. For instance, in Switzerland and Germany, corporate foundations are not treated differently than classical independent foundations. In many other countries, the legal framework is designed to limit company (mis)use and to make sure the donations given to corporate foundations are worth the tax exempt. In the United Kingdom, attempts by the corporation to influence foundation's decision-making for corporate benefits are punished by the retraction of the tax-exempt status.

At the same time, it also appears that in some regions, strict regulatory regimes in fact might hinder the development of corporate foundations. For instance, in Russia, corporate foundations' regulatory and advocacy possibilities are limited. Self-regulation in this sector is mainly informal and voluntary. There are in these countries no nongovernmental councils or umbrella organizations particularly for corporate foundations that would advocate or provide and introduce specific rules of formal and obligatory nature. Most councils or umbrella organizations are in fact grant-making foundations. In some cases, these organizations have subgroups of corporate foundations.

In addition, the legal and fiscal framework for corporate philanthropy in the Latin American region is often rather unfavorable in comparison to countries like the Netherlands, USA, Germany, or Switzerland. In general, the policy context for nonprofit and philanthropic activity is characterized by complexity, and its enforcement is often marked by hostility (Appe and Layton 2016). Tax law, which is the most common manner to regulate and incentivize philanthropy, is quite inconsistent across countries, with many nations offering no incentives, and those who do narrowly select the beneficiaries of private generosity (Layton 2010).

15.2.3 Autonomy

The level of autonomy of corporate foundations to act as a private actor varies across regions. In the USA, Latin America, and Europe, corporate foundations can operate fairly autonomously from government. Indeed, within the imposed legal boundaries in each country (or state), corporate foundations in these countries and regions have the liberty to autonomously choose direction and interventions. An important restriction, however, in the more liberal regions and countries is that corporate foundations in most instances cannot make donations or execute interventions that promote or enhance self-dealing of the company. This is a critical prohibition for corporate foundations, as boards and volunteers are often composed of corporate staff members.

Russian corporate foundations are likely to avoid contradictory or complex projects, such as palliative care and support to marginal groups of adults, as these are sensitive topics for both government and the related company of the foundation. In this sense, corporate foundations are in more restrictive conditions than private or grant-seeking foundations as they face restricted autonomy on their own operations. Chinese corporate foundations are also heavily constrained by an authoritative Chinese political environment and a highly compliant culture. As in the Russian case, Chinese corporate foundations are rarely engaged in controversial social or political issues and tend to follow or choose projects, interventions, and activities that comply with government's political agenda.

15.2.4 Main Focus Areas

The main focus areas of corporate foundations are heavily influenced by the associated company and/or the government in the different countries and regions. In Russia, the focus of a significant share of corporate foundations seems to lie on supporting specific target groups in society. They do so either by providing direct financial grant support or by implementing programs to these socially vulnerable groups, such as health-care, educational, or sports programs. As with most countries in Europe and Latin America, the activities of US-based corporate foundations are fairly heterogeneous, funding and conducting a vast array of different types of interventions, such as projects for the underprivileged, arts projects, health-related programs, special events, infrastructure, and research projects (Guthrie 2010). However, while grants vary in focus, business interests of the parent corporations are never forgotten. From a strategic perspective, US corporate foundations tend to give locally and to fairly uncontroversial causes, therewith aiming to create goodwill from the community and a more loyal customer base.

In China, there is much more compliance with the government, and corporate foundations seem to favor missions that meet the pressing needs of Chinese society or advance the government's agenda. However, there has been a recent widening in CF activities from purely political, moral, and strategic priorities to personal enrichment and plural "imaginations" of the public good, expressing and preserving traditional Chinese values and cultures. Nevertheless, the priority remains mostly focused on education and other immediate need areas.

15.2.5 Funding and Distribution of Resources

In this last paragraph, we highlight the differences among the chosen funding and distribution of resources. US corporate foundations do not receive contributions from many different sources but generally receive all of their funds—mostly endowments—from a few or single source, the parent corporation. In contrary to the US, corporate foundations in Latin America, Europe, and Russia rely mostly on annual corporate contributions. For instance, most of the corporate foundations in Europe are funded on a one- to three-year basis through investment income on assets given by the company, regular donations by the company, an endowment linked to the company, money donated by the company's employees or customers, and donations of in-kind gifts. In Russia, the revenue structure of corporate foundations is a combination of contributions from the founders, fundraising activities, and endowments. In China, corporate foundations are party endowed. Corporate foundations are considered to be non-public foundations. To establish such a foundation, the law requires that the original funds of non-public foundations should be not less than 317,460 USD (or RMB two million); and they must retain those funds in their current account.

The chosen distribution models also differ. In the USA, corporate foundations are mostly grant-making vehicles, while in Europe and in Russia, it is a mix of operating and grant-making. And in China, corporate foundations are mostly operating nonprofits. It differs in Latin America; where in Mexico corporate foundations have adopted a US model of grant-making, Brazilian CFs tend to organize themselves as operating nonprofits.

15.3 Section 3: Stakeholders of Corporate Foundations

Corporate foundations do not operate in an isolated system. They are part of an ecosystem with multiple stakeholders. Stakeholder theory takes the principle of who or what really counts for an organization as its core. In the case of corporate foundations determining who key stakeholders are, it is not very straightforward. With their social mission, it is inevitably the nonprofit organizations and the beneficiaries, but we cannot leave the company and their employees out of this equation as they are the most important sources of resource availability to most corporate foundations, in addition to the control they oftentimes have (see Chap. 1). To determine who indeed really counts, it is important to take three attributes into account: power (the extent to which the actor can impose its will in a relationship), legitimacy (socially accepted and expected structures or behaviors), and urgency (time sensitivity or criticality of the stakeholder's claims) (Mitchell et al. 1997). In Sect. 1 of this book, we already looked implicitly at the company as a stakeholder of corporate foundations. In Sect. 3 of this book, we deliberately took the perspective of four important other stakeholders: (1) employees from the associated company, (2) nonprofit organizations, (3) the beneficiaries of corporate foundations, and (4) the society.

The growing trend of measuring impact of corporate foundation's activities is the focus of Vermeulen and Maas (Chap. 11). Through a single case study, albeit not exactly a corporate foundation, the authors are bridging the research gap concerning the social impact of corporate citizenship programs for beneficiaries (see also Samuel et al. 2016). Although the present level of knowledge of the effect of corporate citizenship programs on beneficiaries prevents generalization of research results at this point, Vermeulen and Maas show that initiatives within corporate citizenship programs, regardless of the question if they are executed inside or outside a foundation, can be valuable not only for employees but also for society.

Haski-Leventhal (Chap. 12) zooms in further on corporate foundations as the corporation's agents for promoting volunteer opportunities. By actively encouraging employees to volunteer, whether employer-led or employee-led, the corporate foundation could change culture, awareness, and even exposure to the work of the corporate volunteers. And the knife cuts both ways. Next to a moral motivation, whereby corporate foundations focus on having their volunteers just being good corporate citizens that do the right thing and actively contributing to society, a more instrumental motivation is to better engage corporate employees with the corporation, attracting and spotting new talent and yielding HRM benefits, such as commitment and performance. The author identifies some recent trends in corporate volunteering, including the rise of skill-based volunteering and the increasing strategic focus of these programs. This means that corporate foundations are shifting away from a single-day volunteering per year toward a more ongoing and meaningful way of volunteering, including a more global focus and an increasing tenure to measure social impact of the voluntary activities.

Stakeholders form the point of departure of von Hvenmark and von Essen (Chap. 13). Based on empirical research in a Swedish context, this chapter explores the political nature of corporate foundations. The political nature of corporate foundations relates to a dual and ambiguous situation where they are caught between a concurrent independence and dependence in relation to both institutionalized politics, the business sphere, and the public welfare system. Corporate foundations supposedly only may appear as legitimate welfare providers as long as they are perceived as being independent vis-a-vis a corporate world on which they also are dependent in order to function properly. In short, the nexus between CPFs on one hand and their founding corporation(s) and the business environment surrounding them on the other is characterized by a simultaneous duality and a certain amount of ambiguity. By adopting techniques and knowledge from the corporate world, at the same time as they operate in the welfare system, they may contribute to a sort of depoliticization of welfare as ideological positions on justice and political decisions that may be turned into matters of optimizing efficiency and common sense. And as CPFs engage in social issues and provide welfare to the general public, they may imply a potential to contribute to a moralization of the corporate world as these organizations in a longer run may influence corporations to instill social values into their operations and thereby become more caring and responsible actors in society.

The aim of Swen, Roza, Meijs, and Maas (Chap. 14) is to provide a deeper understanding of the sensible process for nonprofit organizations while working with corporate foundations. This is particularly relevant as nonprofits are increasingly involved in collaborations with these foundations, and their process explains their current practices. Employees of nonprofits use three different cognitive frames for corporate foundations. They consider corporate foundations as (1) moral agents of their founding firms, in which case the foundations hold resources that the nonprofits need, in order to do their job as experts in addressing social issues; (2) they regard corporate foundations as instrumental agents of companies, where collaborations should create a win-win situation for the founding firm of the foundation as well as for the nonprofit organization; and (3) nonprofits see corporate foundations as change agents of their parent companies, in which corporate foundations actively work together with nonprofits to tackle social issues. The results further imply that it is difficult to describe one typical corporate foundation (as with the chapter of Bethmann and von Schnurbein), and working with them as nonprofits requires a flexible view on what a corporate foundation may entail, their focus, and their goals and should adapt their practices accordingly.

15.4 Discussion

Based on all chapters in this volume, a few central themes for discussion emerge. First, the chapters in this book clearly outline that corporate foundations are a global phenomenon with various institutional contexts in which they resonate. The relationship between the corporate foundation and its institutional context is reciprocal, as illustrated in many chapters in this book. Indeed, organizations can influence their specific institutional context, for instance, when they collectively lobby for legal and fiscal arrangement, lobby against any formal framework, or influence the position of a corporate foundation within a system.

The case described by Maas offers example of how corporate foundations could successfully influence their institutional environment, as a way of influencing the institutional context, be it only by improving the organization's power position within their dependency network and thereby improving both, their access possibilities to vital resources (Pfeffer and Salancik 1978) and being able to better manage and influence the external environment (Pfeffer 1972). Bothello et al. (Chap. 4) argue that boards and management of corporate foundations can handle competing objectives, by acquiescing to or taking advantage of regulatory constraints in their institutional environment. In the myriad of competing institutional push and pull factors, managers can just use the domestic institutional arrangements to shape their response to constraints. And even more, they can set regulatory precedents by strategically applying appeals and lobby activities, therewith changing the regulatory landscape that favors the creation of (new forms of) foundations.

Similarly, stakeholder perceptions of corporate foundations may also be influenced by the institutional framework and how and when corporate foundations were established in those regions. Indeed, the chapter on nonprofit benefits of corporate foundations is clearly influenced by the norms and philanthropic traditions in the Netherlands and might therefore be different in another context.

In many other instances, the institutional context influences corporate foundation's decision-making. A French corporate foundation, e.g., is restricted by foundation law not to allow any commercial interests for the related company, based on its activities or services. This outside-in perspective suggests that complying to institutional rules affirms legitimacy of the foundation. And legitimacy is deemed an important part of institutional success and progress (DiMaggio and Powell 1983; Pache and Santos 2013; Suchman 1995). It is therefore expected that in this institutional context, leadership decision-making might differ from those contexts in which this frame is not set. For instance, it might influence how distant (or close) the corporate foundation is toward its related company—albeit the founder of the company that started the foundation (i.e., the shareholder foundation).

The chapters show an interesting diversity in the institutional environments in which corporate foundations are being active. From a civic perspective, institutional arrangements seem to be more explicit and deeper embedded in local customs for philanthropy than institutional arrangements for companies. Or to put it differently, the institutionalized arrangements for companies seem to be more globalized and harmonized than those for foundations. For instance, in the European Union, there is formalized internal market for commercial activities but not for philanthropy. As such, cross border giving—even within the European Union—is still complicated (see, e.g., Buijze 2017).

Second, corporate foundation acts as a boundary-spanning organization for challenges that may occur. In addition to what we found in the chapters specifically covering stakeholder perspectives, Gehringer and von Schnurbein (Chap. 5) suggest that "corporate foundations have the potential to build new linkages and connections between the civil society and the business world" (see also Herlin and Pedersen

2013). These new linkages or this boundary spanner function is twofold. For one, corporate foundations are able to leverage corporate resources to civil society and therefore contribute to the social good. Second, corporate foundations could also bring civil society interests into the main corporation. For instance, Chap. 12 of Haski-Leventhal, employee engagement in corporate foundations shows that corporate volunteering is an effective stimulus to start volunteering. Here, their behavior in one domain (working environment) is being duplicated into another domain (private sphere), which refers to a multiple domain perspective (see also Rodell 2013). This multiple domain perspective helps to explore underlying linked mechanisms between two domains, based on spillover effects. Spillover refers to the effect of one domain on the other, creating similarities in affect (such as mood or satisfaction), values, skills, and behaviors (Edwards and Rothbard 2000). Not only does this apply for spillover from the work environment to the private realm as in Chap. 12, but it could also occur vice versa. Here, employees' experiences through corporate foundations could well trigger employees to take societal issues, developments, or perspectives into account when returning to work, thereby bringing social awareness into the organization (see also transformative learning theory [Mezirow 1997] or experimental learning theory [Roza and Meijs 2014]). As a result, employees have different conversations with their colleagues, think of different solutions to organizational issues, are more satisfied with their jobs, and could ultimately act as so-called social entrepreneurs, i.e., aligning societal needs with business (commercial) solutions (for a classification of potential ways to engage employees, see Mirvis and Googins 2018).

Third, even though the legal form sets corporate foundations apart from companies, it remains questionable if corporate foundations are really seen as a separate legal entity by their stakeholders, such as corporate management (Chap. 2), beneficiaries (Chap. 11), employees (Chap. 12), and charitable organizations (Chap. 13). The question arises whether it really makes a difference for end-beneficiaries (or impact) if the interventions are supported by corporate foundations or a company. And even though the nonprofit respondents were talking about their partnerships with corporate foundations in particular, the three frames that evolved from the research are very much in line with previous research on the motivation of companies to be engaged in corporate philanthropy (Garriga and Melé 2004; Gautier and Pache 2015).

Nonetheless, being a corporate foundation rather than an in-house department could well influence the partnership selection, thematic selection of social issues, and other decisions made on corporate philanthropy. For instance, in the chapter of Maas (Chap. 10), it becomes apparent that little strategic corporate philanthropy has taken place in the collective corporate foundation, and decision-making on who to support and what to grant is more in line with an overall view on the support needed in the local community rather than on what is strategic to a single company.

Fourth, in many individual chapters, it became evident—sometimes very explicit and in other instances more implicit—that the role of people that have the most power over the foundation at a certain time cannot be underestimated (see Chaps. 2, 3, 4, and 5). Changes in the leadership of the company and board of corporate foundations often have a direct effect on the strategic direction of the foundation.

Due to the common situation that the CEO of the company is often the chair of the board of directors, the foundation depends to a strong degree on the personal likes and dislikes of the CEO. As most employees of the foundation remain on the payroll of the company, this power position is particularly strong. Key to understand the behavior of corporate foundations is to better understand the personal motivation and aims for the foundation, by the company CEO.

15.5 Conclusion and a Research Road Map

This book offers novel insights in an oftentimes overlooked organization in corporate philanthropy: foundations. The editors and authors of this book see that this is a missed opportunity, especially given:

1. The potential of corporate foundations to leverage corporate resources for the public good, in a potentially different way than internal departments of companies do.
2. The emergence of corporate foundations around the world and the prominence these foundations are increasingly viewed by the philanthropic sector.
3. The unique positioning of corporate foundations in a social issue ecosystem as a boundary spanner or linking pin, with unique challenges to this particular vehicle in comparison to private or public foundations, nonprofit organizations, and social enterprises and companies.
4. The need for broader (public) understanding of these corporate foundations to be better able to judge if they are actually serving public benefits or are in fact more focused on the interest of the parent company.
5. The ongoing debate about the different roles of non-state actors in providing welfare services and pushing for social innovations.

This book provides initial insights that help the reader understand corporate foundations better, how they relate to their institutional contexts, what unique governance structures they may take, and what challenges these bring for parent companies, governments, societies, and NPOs, notwithstanding the contributions of the authors that have focused on specific stakeholders that are influenced by and influence corporate foundations' functioning.

Although the book provided preliminary insights into where, when, and how institutional contexts can influence and are influenced by corporate foundations, we are far from grasping the full institutional complexity in which corporate foundations thrive. We recognize that in the business literature, corporate foundations are mostly seen as an extension of the company and consequently interpreted in that institutional environment. As they are (also) operating the philanthropic institutional environment, future research should include those perspectives in our understanding of the functioning of corporate foundation. Although we covered some elements briefly in this book (e.g., legal frameworks), research is required on the influence and role of normative-cognitive elements, such as national culture (Scott 2013) and various philanthropic traditions (Wiepking and Handy 2016).

Furthermore, on this macro-level, research on the role of corporate foundations for systemic change might be explored, and when and how corporate foundations can influence systemic change in society. We have found no examples where corporate foundations have had a major influence on systemic changes. However, with their growing number and trend to professionalize, we might see a stronger role of corporate foundations in general.

We observe a trend that corporate foundations increasingly understand themselves as special foundations and discuss their own challenges. One sign of this is that on the European level, corporate foundations have started to organize themselves, holding annual meetings and increasing their networking with other umbrella organizations in global philanthropy. Also in Latin America, corporate foundations are increasingly organized. Following this trend, we can presume that corporate foundations will become more visible in the third sector and the society as a whole. That in turn will raise questions of legitimacy again. An interesting question will be how traditional third sector organizations will embrace or distance themselves from the growing new kids on the block. We already see some nonprofits rejecting to collaborate with corporate foundations that receive their funds from companies from controversial industries such as tobacco or oil exploitation.

What we briefly touched upon in this book, in the chapter of Bethmann and von Schnurbein, is the alignment of the corporate foundation with the business, i.e., the parent company or the dominant donor. It is interesting to further explore to what extent and how corporate foundations can strategically align to the business without either conflicting with, e.g., their regulatory environment, their social impact, and the legitimacy of philanthropy. This strategic alignment may very well be beneficial to the core business as Chap. 3 suggests, in aspects such as corporate culture, values, or even external business interests, although the popular opinion of the business world is nonalignment may be a good (or even the better) option. For instance, from a societal perspective, certainly not every alignment is socially desirable. If we, again, think of a tobacco company, it seems difficult for its foundation to organize activities aimed directly at increasing tobacco sales. It is at least questionable if this may result in favorable societal outcomes.

Finding alignment between the company and the foundation may also result in increasing the resources that are available to the corporate foundation as the goals—albeit on the long run—are similar. In this case, the company may see long-term value and is willing to do more investments. This line of research will be important if and when alignment is beneficial and to whom. As touched upon in several chapters in this volume, hybridity in corporate foundations is inherent and not a chosen mechanism that can be easily changed. Especially in terms of governance and strategic alignment, there is more research needed to explain how competing goal orientations can be managed through structures and processes within the organization.

A third path of research is to see what influences the direction and functioning of corporate foundations, next to institutional forces. For instance, the motivation for companies to engage in corporate philanthropy may shape the direction of the corporate foundation. Also, as briefly suggested in Chap. 5, the type of company might influence the direction and functioning of a corporate foundation. Indeed, family businesses have very distinct motives and see their role very different than shareholder companies do, and we see in practice that this also influences the direction and functioning of corporate foundations. More generally, research on corporate philanthropy, nonprofit business partnerships, and corporate social responsibility should more often take the perspective of corporate foundations, given their unique positioning. This unique positioning may open up new opportunities, but also might restrict possibilities to contribute to the public good.

A fourth research opportunity is more focused on the organizational features of the corporate foundations, as vehicle for corporate philanthropy. Maas starts her chapter by sketching the development of the "how" of corporate philanthropy from an individual company agent, to a department, to a foundation, and maybe even more distant in a community foundation or through intermediaries. In this book, we did not compare these separate vehicles of corporate philanthropy although it is not difficult to hypothesize that the business interest is more dominant in the internal department than in the corporate foundation or that the voice of the beneficiaries is heard better through the board of the corporate foundation or the community foundation than by the stakeholder dialogue instruments of the internal department. If these hypotheses hold true, is left up to further research. Likewise, the "how" of philanthropy can matter from the social impact perspective as corporate foundations, especially when they are based upon an endowment, theoretically to safeguard the foundation against potential changes in the parent company, such as changes in leadership, mergers, and acquisitions or takeovers. The latter can be even more important when it is done by a foreign company. Case analysis of these situations would be very welcome.

A fifth interesting avenue for research might be to apply the developed knowledge on corporate foundations to other organizational forms, e.g., governmental agencies, small and medium enterprises (SMEs), associations that run large shopping malls, family foundations or celebrity foundations, and so forth, that might have similar challenges on balancing the interest of the single visible donor versus the social impact.

All and all, this volume is a research handbook that opens up the black box of corporate foundations. We looked at various constellations in the universe of nonprofit organizations and more specifically in the galaxy of charitable foundations. By doing so, we have furthered our understanding of these very specific types of foundations that are rapidly gaining territory in the philanthropic domain. And lastly, we paved the way for future research on this interesting phenomenon.

References

Anheier, H. K., & Leat, D. (2006). *Creative philanthropy: Toward a new philanthropy for the twenty-first century*. New York: Routledge.

Appe, S.M., & Layton, M.D. (2016, June). Government and the nonprofit sector in Latin America. In *Nonprofit Policy Forum* (Vol. 7, No. 2, pp. 117–135). De Gruyter.

Buijze, R. (2017). *Philanthropy for the arts in the era of globalisation: International tax barriers for charitable giving.* Erasmus University Rotterdam, Rotterdam, The Netherlands.

DiMaggio, P., & Powell, W. W. (1983). The iron cage revisited: Collective rationality and institutional isomorphism in organizational fields. *American Sociological Review, 48*(2), 147–160.

Edwards, J. R., & Rothbard, N. P. (2000). Mechanisms linking work and family: Clarifying the relationship between work and family constructs. *Academy of Management Review, 25*(1), 178–199.

EFC. (2011). Comparative highlights of foundation laws–The operating environment of foundations in Europe. [pdf] Brussels: European Foundation Center. Available at: http://efc.issuelab.org/resource/comparative_highlights_of_foundation_laws_the_operating_environment_for_foundations_in_europe_2015. Accessed 22 May 2017.

Fleishman, J. L. (2007). *The foundation: A great American secret; how private wealth is changing the world.* New York: Public Affairs.

Frumkin, P. (2006). Accountability and legitimacy in American foundation philanthropy. In *The legitimacy of philanthropic foundations: United States and European perspectives* (pp. 99–122). New York: Russel Sage Foundation.

Garriga, E., & Melé, D. (2004). Corporate social responsibility theories: Mapping the territory. *Journal of Business Ethics, 53*(1–2), 51–71.

Gautier, A., & de Nervaux, L. (2015). La France qui donne. *Etat de la recherche sur le don en France [The France that gives. The state of research on donation in France] Chaire philanthropie de l'ESSEC*, Observatoire de la Fondation de France December.

Gautier, A., & Pache, A. C. (2015). Research on corporate philanthropy: A review and assessment. *Journal of Business Ethics, 126*(3), 343–369.

Guthrie, D. (2010). Corporate philanthropy in the United States: What causes do corporations back. In *Politics and partnerships: The role of voluntary associations in America's political past and present* (pp. 183–204). Chicago: University of Chicago Press.

Herlin, H., & Pedersen, J. T. (2013). Corporate foundations: Catalysts of NGO-business partnerships? *The Journal of Corporate Citizenship, 50,* 58.

Kania, J., KraMer, M., & Russell, P. (2014). Strategic philanthropy for a complex world. *Stanford Social Innovation Review, 12*(3), 26–33. Retrieved September 1, 2015.

Layton, M. D. (2010). Philanthropy in Latin America. In *International encyclopedia of civil society* (pp. 1201–1209). New York: Springer.

Mezirow, J. (1997). Transformative learning: Theory to practice. *New Directions for Adult and Continuing Education, 1997*(74), 5–12.

Mirvis, P., & Googins, B. (2018). Engaging employees as social innovators. *California Management Review, 60,* 0008125618779062.

Mitchell, R. K., Agle, B. R., & Wood, D. J. (1997). Toward a theory of stakeholder identification and salience: Defining the principle of who and what really counts. *Academy of Management Review, 22*(4), 853–886.

Ostrower, F. (2006). Foundation approaches to effectiveness: A typology. *Nonprofit and Voluntary Sector Quarterly, 35*(3), 510–516.

Pache, A. C., & Santos, F. (2013). Inside the hybrid organization: Selective coupling as a response to competing institutional logics. *Academy of Management Journal, 56*(4), 972–1001.

Pfeffer, J. (1972). Merger as a response to organizational interdependence. *Administrative Science Quarterly, 17,* 382–394.

Pfeffer, J., & Salancik, G. R. (1978). The external control of organizations: A resource dependence perspective. Harper and Row, New York, United States.

Porter, M. E., & Kramer, M. R. (2002). The competitive advantage of corporate philanthropy. *Harvard Business Review, 80*(12), 56–68.

Powell, W. W., & DiMaggio, P. J. (Eds.). (2012). *The new institutionalism in organizational analysis.* University of Chicago Press, Chicago, Illionois, United States.

Rodell, J. B. (2013). Finding meaning through volunteering: Why do employees volunteer and what does it mean for their jobs? *Academy of Management Journal, 56*(5), 1274–1294.

Roza, L., & Meijs, L. C. P. M. (2014). Involved learning. In L. Bridges Karr, L. Meijs, & J. Metz (Eds.), *Volunteering and youth services: Essential readings on volunteering and volunteer management for social work, social policy and urban management* (pp. 139–157). Amsterdam: SWP.

Samuel, O., Roza, L., & Meijs, L. (2016). Exploring partnerships from the perspective of HSO beneficiaries: The case of corporate volunteering. *Human Service Organizations: Management, Leadership & Governance, 40*(3), 220–237.

Scott, W. R. (2013). *Institutions and organizations: Ideas, interests, and identities*. Thousand Oaks: Sage Publications.

Suchman, M. C. (1995). Managing legitimacy: Strategic and institutional approaches. *Academy of Management Review, 20*(3), 571–610.

Wiepking, P., & Handy, F. (Eds.). (2016). *The Palgrave handbook of global philanthropy*. New York: Springer.

Lonneke Roza is an adjunct assistant professor at Rotterdam School of Management, Erasmus University. Her research focuses on (microfoundations of) corporate philanthropy/corporate citizenship. Her work is published in among others Journal of Business Ethics, Nonprofit and Voluntary Sector Quarterly, and Voluntas.

Steffen Bethmann (PhD, University of Heidelberg) is a research fellow of the Center for Philanthropy Studies of the University of Basel. He is also an organizational consultant and associated researcher of the Centro de Filantropía y Inversiones Sociales of the University Adolfo Ibañez in Santiago, Chile. His area of expertise lay especially in strategies and governance of foundations as well as in the field of social innovation.

Lucas Meijs is professor of Strategic Philanthropy and Volunteering at Rotterdam School of Management (RSM), Erasmus University, Rotterdam (Netherlands). His current research focuses on strategic philanthropy, volunteer/nonprofit management, corporate community involvement, and involved learning. He served two terms as first non-American co-editor in chief of Nonprofit and Voluntary Action Quarterly and was a member of the Raad voor Maatschappelijke Ontwikkeling—the official policy advisory body for the Dutch government and parliament.

Georg von Schnurbein is associate professor for foundation management at the Faculty of Business and Economics and founding director of the Center for Philanthropy Studies (CEPS) at the University of Basel. He serves in several functions in boards in the field of international research on philanthropy and has coauthored the latest edition of the Swiss Foundation Code and published in several impact journals such as Nonprofit and Voluntary Sector Quarterly and European Management Journal. His research interest is on nonprofit governance, financial health of nonprofits, and impact measurement.

Correction to: Handbook on Corporate Foundations: Corporate and Civil Society Perspectives

Lonneke Roza, Steffen Bethmann, Lucas Meijs, and Georg von Schnurbein

Correction to:
L. Roza et al. (eds.), *Handbook on Corporate Foundations*, Nonprofit and Civil Society Studies, https://doi.org/10.1007/978-3-030-25759-0

The book was inadvertently published with an incorrect title "Handbook on Corporate Foundation". This has now been updated as "Handbook on Corporate Foundations".

The updated online version of the book can be found at
https://doi.org/10.1007/978-3-030-25759-0

Printed by Printforce, the Netherlands